Genocide

Genocide:
A History

William D. Rubinstein

Harlow, England • London • New York • Boston • San Francisco • Toronto
Sydney • Tokyo • Singapore • Hong Kong • Seoul • Taipei • New Delhi
Cape Town • Madrid • Mexico City • Amsterdam • Munich • Paris • Milan

PEARSON EDUCATION LIMITED

Edinburgh Gate
Harlow CM20 2JE
Tel: +44 (0)1279 623623
Fax: +44 (0)1279 431059
Website: www.pearsoned.co.uk

First edition published in Great Britain in 2004

© Pearson Education Limited 2004

The right of William D. Rubinstein to be identified as author
of this work has been asserted by him in accordance
with the Copyright, Designs and Patents Act 1988.

ISBN 0 582 50601 8

British Library Cataloguing in Publication Data
A CIP catalogue record for this book can be obtained from the British Library

Library of Congress Cataloging in Publication Data
A CIP catalog record for this book can be obtained from the Library of Congress

10 9 8 7 6 5 4 3 2 1

Set by 3 in 9.5 pt Melior
Typeset by Fakenham Photosetting Ltd, Fakenham, Norfolk, NR21 8NN
Printed in China
EPC/01

The Publishers' policy is to use paper manufactured from sustainable forests.

To the Memory
of
Raphael Lemkin
(1900–59)

Acknowledgements

A number of persons commented on various parts of this work. Among them are Dr Judy Berman, Professor Albert Lindemann, Dr Philip Mendes, Barbara Rogers, Dr. Hannah Starman and Keith Windschuttle. I am most grateful to them for their helpful advice; everything here is my responsibility. I am also most grateful to Heather McCallum, my editor, for her encouragement and wisdom.

Contents

CHAPTER 1

Genocide in history

Mass murder is probably as old as the human race, but only in the twentieth century has it become so significant a part of the world scene as to become an issue of world-wide importance or, indeed, to have been given a name. (The term 'genocide' was coined by Raphael Lemkin only in 1944.) This work is an account of mass killings throughout history which have been termed 'genocide', and an attempt to understand when and why they have occurred.

Perhaps the most difficult single task confronting the historian of this subject is to define the term 'genocide' in a universally acceptable way. Despite numerous attempts during the past 30 or 40 years, there is no universally agreed definition of the term and there is never likely to be one.[1] On the contrary, definitional differences at the most basic level have led to some of the most fiercely contested and ill-tempered debates in scholarly circles of recent decades, debates which have only become sharper as more and more academics and activists have joined in.

The archetypal example of genocide in modern times, on any conceivable definition, was, of course, the Nazi Holocaust of European Jewry before and, most directly and murderously, during the Second World War. Explicitly or implicitly, all debate over the meaning of 'genocide' proceeds from the Holocaust as the central, core example. Much of the fierceness of debate over the use of the term 'genocide' revolves around the question of whether or not the *Holocaust* was unique. To emphatic proponents of the view that it was, it constituted the only genuine attempt in recorded history literally to exterminate an entire people, an

effort in which millions were killed in modern history's clearest example
of a dedicated, purposeful death machine, and which failed in its objective only because Nazi Germany lost the war.[2] To those who dissent, often
passionately, from this view, the Holocaust was not only not unique, but
was not a particularly extreme example of genocide, at least in terms of
the numbers of its victims: according to the proponents of this view,
Hitler killed far fewer European Jews than the number of Indians of North
and South America who died in the century or so after European discovery in 1492, while other genocides and democides might have been just
as bloody.[3] The debate which has emerged on this question has become
anything but 'academic', with such charges as those of antisemitism and
the distortion of evidence being made by the fiercer proponents on either
side. Moreover, given the growing importance of genocide, and the punishment of convicted war criminals, in contemporary international law
and even in the active foreign policy goals of many nations and international bodies, an accepted definition of genocide has become a serious
and major consideration in international affairs.

How does one reasonably define 'genocide'? This is the most difficult
question of all – a surprisingly difficult and vexatious question indeed –
to which there is no easy or readily acceptable answer. Probably the best
place to start is with a 'common sense' definition of the sort which most
well-informed persons might give if asked. Genocide might then be
defined as the deliberate killing of most or all members of a collective
group for the mere fact of being members of that group. Genocide is normally carried out against an ethnic or religious minority, and entails the
deliberate killing of such groups of non-combatants as women, children
and the elderly, who are normally seen as protected by international law
or common moral custom.

This is, one might suggest, a clear and straightforward definition
which, to the well-informed 'man or woman in the street', seems surely
to embrace what is commonly meant by 'genocide'. Yet to virtually every
word in this definition scholars and historians have taken exception,
often furious exception. Even so seemingly basic a requirement as that
the victims of a genocide must be killed for an example of genocide to
have taken place has been queried repeatedly by historians, who have
viewed as genocidal the forced removal of large numbers of children
from a minority ethnic group in order to raise them as members of the

dominant group. (Memories of the forced removal of large numbers of half-caste Australian Aborigines to be raised as Europeans, which occurred on a widespread basis between the 1920s and the 1960s, became, in the 1990s, a dominant political issue in Australia.) Indeed, under the United Nations Convention on Genocide, officially adopted in 1948 (extracts reprinted in the Appendix to this book) *most* 'acts' which are construed as genocide in international law do *not* entail the actual killing of a group, but comprise such categories as 'forcibly transferring children of the group to another group' and 'imposing measures intended to prevent births within the group'. Similarly, the element of deliberate intention to kill large numbers of a group would seemingly, on our 'common sense' definition, be an absolutely necessary requirement for genocide to have occurred, yet recent historians sympathetic to the plight of the American Indians at the hands of European settlers from 1492 onwards have repeatedly noted that while up to 95 per cent of Indians living in the Americas perished (according to those historians) over the century or so after the coming of the white man, most of this diminution in population occurred through such factors as the importation of virulent diseases previously unknown in the Americas, the destruction of settled life-styles, enslavement, and the psychological effects of conquest rather than through overt murders and slaughters, although plenty of these took place. According to these historians, however, a relatively sudden population decline of 95 per cent constitutes 'genocide', regardless of its origins, especially as entire tribes certainly disappeared. Some of these scholars have become involved in angry exchanges with those who argue (as many do) that the Jewish Holocaust was a unique example of genocide; given the vastly larger number of Indians who (according to them) perished after 1492, the Jewish Holocaust was not only not unique, but was not an especially large-scale example of genocide, as horrifying and evil as it obviously was.

The central example of the Holocaust demonstrates that it is, classically, an ethnic or religious minority which is slaughtered in a genocide. Yet probably *most* victims of deliberate mass murder by totalitarian regimes in the twentieth century were not members of an ethnic minority but those perceived as belonging to an allegedly dangerous political or social class group or those defined, by their killers, as belonging to such a group. Most of the millions who perished at the hands of Stalin, Mao

Tse-tung, Pol Pot and the other Communist dictators died because the party's leaders believed they belonged to a dangerous or subversive social class or political grouping; they perished, in other words, on ideological rather than ethnic or religious grounds (although Stalin certainly killed ethnic minorities on a mass scale, as did other Communist dictatorships). How to define or characterise such ideologically based mass killings has long been something of a difficulty for historians of genocide: unlike an ethnic category such as the Jews of Nazi-occupied Europe, for whom a fairly precise number in the at-risk group could be given, the number of, say, Stalin's enemies or groups perceived as dangerous or subversive to the Soviet regime could not be stated with precision, waxing and waning with the witch-hunting psychopathology of Stalin and his inner circle almost whimsically. To accommodate them in the catalogue of deliberate mass murders of a collective group, the political scientist R.J. Rummel has coined the term 'democide' to describe the mass killing of collective groups of persons apart from ethnic minorities. The term has also come to include mass killings on a smaller scale than the attempted slaughter of an entire group, for instance those who perished in the population transfers which accompanied the birth of independent India and Pakistan in 1947, or the mass killings in Indonesia in the 1960s. It is also sometimes used to describe such events as the bombings of civilians in Germany and Japan by the Allies during the Second World War, although to many any linkage of Allied bombing raids to 'genocide', however the term be modified, is a distortion of history.

Many other questions about the concept of genocide and its historical occurrence remain in dispute or unanswered. There is, for instance, an obvious sense in which genocides must be organised and carried out by a government or instrumentality (such as the Nazi SS) which was a direct arm of government. Certainly the genocides carried out by the totalitarian regimes of the twentieth century were all organised and directed by a government. But it may also be the case that genocides can be carried out by rebel armies, as some of the mass killings of the Taiping Rebellion in mid-nineteenth century China appear to have been; by irregular military forces under what might be termed 'warlords', as, perhaps, in former Yugoslavia in the 1990s; by loosely organised, perhaps spontaneous (but armed) gangs of 'ordinary' persons, not necessarily directed by a government body at all, as occurred in the intercommunal violence between

Hindus and Muslims during the division of British India in 1947 and during the Rwanda genocide of 1994; by bands of religious fanatics, as was the case with Thuggee in India; or, on some definitions, in the context of long-standing customary folk mores, as with infanticide carried out on a wide scale in many hunter-gatherer societies. All of this shows the looseness of the term genocide and the difficulties in defining it precisely or limiting it to certain historical situations and to no others. Similarly, there is arguably a widespread sense that genocides can take place chiefly, if not almost always, in the unusual and abnormal conditions of a major war, such as the Second World War. Yet many genocides and democides – Stalin's Purges of the 1930s and the Pol Pot massacres, to name only two – certainly occurred in peacetime, against internal 'enemies'. Wars, even very major wars, are, historically, not necessarily linked with genocide. No genocide took place during the American Civil War, for instance, although perhaps 600,000 soldiers perished on both sides, while Napoleon conquered virtually all of Europe arguably without deliberately killing a single noncombatant civilian, and certainly never engaged in the systematic slaughter of any collective group. 'Genocide does not equate with war,' one historian who has closely studied war and genocide in the twentieth century has concluded.[4]

While many of the most infamous examples of genocide and democide were carried out by totalitarian dictators such as Hitler and Stalin, not all totalitarian dictators engaged in genocide: Mussolini certainly did not, at least in Italy (as opposed to Abyssinia) before about 1943. Lenin was no innocent in his treatment of perceived enemies of the Bolshevik regime, but compared with Stalin his rule was almost angelic. Some leaders of genocide and their henchmen were sadistic psychopaths who might well have been clinically insane, but Adolf Eichmann's bureaucratic blandness has become notorious, through Hannah Arendt's famous description, as the epitome of the 'banality of evil'. Tamerlane, the medieval Mongol warlord whose trademark was the pyramids of skulls, numbering tens of thousands, that he made from the corpses of his murdered victims, was a highly cultivated man who enjoyed having works of history read to him as he ate. The remarks on history made by Hitler himself, in *Mein Kampf* and his *Table Talk* monologues, often exhibit very considerable talent, although of an entirely autodidactical kind.

Most typologies of genocide focus on the varieties of mass murder, with no direct attempt to employ chronological divisions as a central defining matrix. For instance – to cite one of many such schemas of genocide – Chalk and Jonassohn see four different types of genocide which they classify 'according to their motive': 1. 'to eliminate a real or potential threat'; 2. 'to spread terror among real or potential victims'; 3. 'to acquire economic wealth'; and 4. 'to implement a belief, a theory, or an ideology'.[5] Plainly, such typologies are very useful and greatly enlarge our understanding of the motivations for genocide, although, in the twentieth century, virtually all genocides surely come under the fourth of their headings.

This work, however, attempts to classify genocides quite differently, according to the historical epoch in which they occurred: each specific genocide, it is argued here, was highly specific to the era in which it occurred and ought not to be seen, except in a very general way, as affecting or determining genocides in other of the eras of this schema. The historical typology of genocides which is argued for in this book is as follows:

1. Genocides in Pre-Literate Societies;
2. Genocides in the Age of Empires and Religions, c.500 BC–1492;
3. Colonial Genocides, 1492–1914;
4. Genocides in the Age of Totalitarianism, 1914–79;
5. Contemporary 'Ethnic Cleansing' and Genocides, 1945–date.

A number of features of this schema should be mentioned from the outset. Genocides in pre-literate and other pre-modern and non-Western societies are given much more attention in this book than in many other works on genocide. Commonly, indeed, genocides in the pre-literate and non-Western world are simply ignored in accounts of genocide and mass murder, thus giving the impression – often, it seems, deliberately intended – that only modern Western man is capable of genocide, which is often seen as a component of 'modern' society.[6] The view argued in this book is that such an interpretation is emphatically wrong: mass murders occurred – so far as the archaeological and anthropological record permits us to reach a conclusion – in nearly all societies with, indeed, a near-certainty that much higher levels of mass killing existed in pre-literate societies than in 'modern' ones, as well as a range of other unimaginably horrifying, repellent and barbaric practices. This was perfectly obvious to Western observers who encountered pre-literate societies first-hand at any time between the period of the Voyages of Discovery and, perhaps, the Second World War, but has been obfuscated in a fairly consistent manner during the past 40 or 50 years, in part (arguably) because of our all-too-well internalised knowledge of the barbaric and murderous record of the modern European world, and in part because of what might fairly be termed 'political correctness' (in this case, an extension of the time-honoured 'Myth of the Noble Savage', so often a component of the post-Renaissance Western consciousness) which judges the enormities committed by non-Western peoples systematically more lightly than those committed by the modern West. In this work, it should be noted, the incredibly violent, savage and cruel beliefs and practices of most pre-literate societies are, if anything, not described at sufficient length or in frank detail: many volumes could be written on this subject, as, in fact, they were in ages past.

A second feature of this typology is that it sections off those genocides and democides which occurred in what is termed the 'age of totalitarianism', the period seen here as extending from the outbreak of the First World War in 1914 to the end of the Pol Pot regime in Cambodia in 1979. The 'Age of Totalitarianism' included nearly all of the infamous examples of genocide in modern history, headed by the Jewish Holocaust, but also comprising the mass murders and purges of the Communist world, other mass killings carried out by Nazi Germany and its allies, and also the Armenian genocide of 1915. All these slaughters, it is argued here, had a common origin, the collapse of the elite structure and normal modes of government of much of central, eastern and southern Europe as a result of the First World War, without which surely neither Communism nor Fascism would have existed except in the minds of unknown agitators and crackpots. The horrors of the 'Age of Totalitarianism' were, most certainly, not a universal product of this era: the English-speaking democracies were notably immune from virtually any hint of anti-democratic ideologies achieving power or influence, and their steadfastness eventually saw both Fascism and Communism disappear from the earth: a resolution and dedication for which they, and their leaders and peoples, cannot be thanked or praised too highly.

It is also argued in this book that the contemporary world has *not* seen an 'age of genocide'. Contrary to popular belief, recent genocides have not been common and have occurred only rarely and unpredictably, even in Third World countries with endemic poverty, tribal and ethnic divisions, and no democratic traditions of any kind. The best-known alleged examples of contemporary genocide and 'ethnic cleansing', for instance, in former Yugoslavia and in Rwanda, were not part of a general pattern at all. Unlike Yugoslavia, the Soviet Union split into separate, independent states with no violence of any kind apart from that in the Caucasus region; dozens of Third World states have achieved independence without genocide resulting.

It follows from what has been said that it is largely if not wholly wrong for the observer to carry the experience of genocide from one of the eras posited in our typology into another. It seems highly unlikely, for instance, that anything remotely like the Jewish Holocaust could happen again in the contemporary world, certainly not as a product of an ideologically driven regime and its deliberately murderous policies. Needless to say, however, mass murders of an unimaginably horrifying kind can readily happen, as the world knows too well since September 11, 2001. But these must be distinguished from slaughters occurring in the past, which provide no guide to their understanding. Yet, as always, for Western civilisation and its values to prevail – as it should – its enemies must be crushed whenever they cannot be contained or co-opted. It seems perfectly justified to draw this lesson, at least, from the tragic history of the world.

These are among the fundamental considerations which any history of genocide must address. One important aim of this book, then, is to examine accounts of mass murders down the ages and ascertain whether it is reasonable to say that genocide occurred. This is not a straightforward procedure, and almost everywhere there are loose ends, especially in weighing the evidence which exists of the extent of mass killings, particularly from the distant past. It will be seen that many monstrously savage purported examples of genocide or democide are included here which are not normally encountered in histories of genocide, many of which discuss only the bloody events of the twentieth century.[7] It will also be seen that a good deal of attention is paid in this work to setting out the facts as accurately as possible, with many close examinations of the statistics of genocide and, indeed, whether the reports of mass slaughter as they have come down to us are even credible. To some, remembering Stalin's famous adage that the death of one man is a tragedy while the death of millions is a statistic, this might seem as if this work is somewhat callous regarding the infinite human tragedy represented by the suffering of each and every victim. To this, the author can only reply that he writes as an historian whose main task is to set out 'what actually happened', and why, as accurately as possible. No normal human being can possibly write a history of genocide without breaking down unless that author psychologically distances himself or herself from the infinite tragedy of each and every victim, while the allusive and indirect is arguably more effective in conveying these infinities of tragedy than numbing the reader with gratuitous horror after horror.

Notes and references

1   On the definition of 'genocide', see Frank Chalk and Kurt Jonassohn, eds., *The History and Sociology of Genocide: Analysis and Case Studies* (New Haven, Conn., 1990), pp.3–43; Isidor Wallimann and Michael N. Dobkowski, eds., *Genocide and the Modern Age* (Syracuse, N.Y., 2000); Helen Fein, 'Genocide: A Sociological Perspective', *Current Sociology*, Vol.38 (1990); Jennifer Balint and Israel W. Charny, 'Definitions of Genocide' in Israel W. Charny, *Encyclopedia of Genocide* (Santa Barbara, Cal., 1999), Vol.I, pp.3–15; Alan S. Rosenbaum, ed., *Is the Holocaust Unique?* (second edition, Boulder, Col., 2001); and Scott Straus, 'Contested Meanings and Conflicting Imperatives: A Conceptual Analysis of Genocide', *Journal of Genocide Research*, Vol.3(3), 2001, pp.349–75. Straus's article is probably the most comprehensive analysis of the ways in which the term has been used.

2   Proponents of this view seemingly include Steven T. Katz, Yehuda Bauer and Deborah Lipstadt, among others.

3   See, for example, David E. Stannard, 'Uniqueness of Denial: The Politics of Genocide Scholarship', in Rosenbaum, ed., *Is the Holocaust Unique?*

4   Paul Bartrop, 'The Relationship Between War and Genocide in the Twentieth Century: A Consideration', *Journal of Genocide Research*, Vol.4 (4), 2002, p.531.

5   Chalk and Jonassohn, *History of Genocide*, p.29.

6   That the Holocaust was a distinctive product of 'modernity' was argued most famously by Zygmunt Bauman in *Modernity and the Holocaust* (Ithaca, N.Y., 1989). While the Nazi Holocaust might have been a product of 'modernity'

(and without parallel in previous epochs), the democratic (and for that matter, Soviet) forces which wiped Nazism off the earth were similarly a product of 'modernity'. Bauman and those who agree with him ignore this fact.

7 Chalk and Jonassohn, *History and Sociology of Genocide*, is a notable exception to this narrow coverage, as will be Steven T. Katz's three-volume *Holocaust in Historical Context* when it is completed.

CHAPTER 2

Genocide in pre-modern societies

Genocide in pre-literate societies

One of the most pervasive and powerful images in Western society during the past 250 years has been 'the myth of the noble savage', the pervasive notion which apparently began with the eighteenth-century *philosophe* Jean-Jacques Rousseau, that 'primitive', pre-literate societies were idyllic, and that all the corruptions and evils of mankind emerged from settled civilisation, especially from modern urban societies. Rousseau himself was apparently responding to Thomas Hobbes' famous view that 'life in a state of nature' was, in his celebrated phrase, 'brutal, nasty and short'. Rousseau's opinion of pre-literate societies became commonplace and, even if not accepted as literally true, has come to pervade the depiction of 'primitive' societies in art, music, the cinema and other popular depictions. To modern sociologists such as Claude Lévi-Strauss and Margaret Mead, in Roger Sandall's phrase, 'primitive culture is not inferior to modern civilization – only different'.[1] In the field of genocide studies, too, there is a pervasive notion that genocides are a modern phenomenon, the Jewish Holocaust, occurring in mid-twentieth century Europe, being, of course, its archetype. Indeed, one of the best-known sociological critiques of the Holocaust, enunciated by the Polish-born British scholar Zygmunt Bauman, holds that it was a typical artefact of 'modernity', employing scientific conveyor-belt tactics to carry out the implications of modern, 'scientific' racism.[2] The theme of genocide being a twentieth-century phenomenon and an artefact of our age has been echoed over and over again in contemporary studies of the subject. Only in a limited sense, however, does this appear to be true. The genocides and democides of the 1914–79 period were certainly more extreme and murderous than anything known in the Western world for centuries, if ever, but – it will be argued in this work – these killings represented a chronologically delimited period with no parallels in the Western world for generations before or since. On the contrary, it appears clear that the 'civilising process' over many centuries has resulted in an almost constant reduction in the incidence of brutal warfare and massacres, which were much more a typical product of pre-literate societies than of later ones. This constant reduction in the incidence of mass slaughter, even in historical situations which are, to us, notorious for their barbarism, will become clear from this chapter, in which genocides and democides from pre-literate societies to the early modern world will be examined.

One of the few works to deal in an objective way with the destructiveness of many pre-literate societies is Lawrence H. Keeley's important *War Before Civilization: The Myth of the Peaceful Savage* (Oxford, 1996). Keeley, an anthropologist at the University of Illinois, notes that the percentage of the male population mobilised for combat in many pre-literate tribes where there are reasonably accurate statistics was characteristically much higher – not lower – than in all but a handful of modern industrialised societies engaged in war. Among a range of pre-literate peoples from the Zulus to the Tahitians, between 33 and 45 per cent of adult males were mobilised for combat in wartime.[3] Among modern armies engaged in serious combat, only France in the First World War, where about 42 per cent of adult males were mobilised, rivalled or exceeded the figures for many pre-literate societies. Remarkably, neither Nazi Germany (33 per cent) nor the Soviet Union (23 per cent) mobilised as high a percentage of its male population for combat as was the case among the most warlike pre-literate tribes.[4] Casualties in battle were also far higher than in modern wars, with casualties ranging up to 87–100 per cent killed among the losing side in conflicts where estimates can be made of the number of casualties. At one battle lost in 1857 among the Mohave-Yumas, 49.6 per cent of combatants were killed; in a great Aztec battle fought in 1478, 87.1 per cent of 24,000 combatants were killed, while 100 per cent of combatants were killed during the Blackfoot Indian raid which annihilated the Assiniboins in 1849.[5] These figures compare with the fact that only 4.0 per cent of 65,000 Confederate soldiers engaged at the Battle of Gettysburg in 1863 died. Even at the Battle of the Somme in 1916, the deadliest and costliest engagement in British military history, only 13.5 per cent of the 156,000 British soldiers present at the battle were killed.[6] In pre-literate societies, battles between warring tribes were 'typically preceded and accompanied by considerable taunting and exchanging of insults', although the fact that combat is strictly limited by the primitive nature of the weaponry employed 'gives to primitive battles their ritualized allure'.[7] 'Small raids or ambushes' were the most common means by which one pre-literate tribe attacked another.

> One common raiding technique (favoured by groups as diverse as the Bering Straits Eskimos and the Mae Enga of New Guinea) consisted of quietly surrounding enemy houses just before dawn and killing the occupants by thrusting spears through the flimsy walls, shooting arrows through doorways and smoke holes, or firing as the victims emerged after the structure has been set on fire.[8]

Massacres – 'whose purpose [was] to annihilate an enemy social unit' – have also been frequently noted, although in pre-literate societies much of the evidence for massacres (and what would now widely be termed 'genocide') has to be inferred from archaeological and other sources. The goal of one tribe in northern Canada, the Kuchin,

> was to surround and annihilate an encampment of their traditional enemies, the Mackenzie Eskimo, leaving only one male alive. The male, called 'The Survivor', was spared only so he could spread word of the deed.[9]

Although some anthropologists have argued that full-scale slaughters only occurred after contact with Europeans, Keeley points out that there is ample archaeological evidence for full-scale massacres prior to the coming of Europeans. At Crow Creek, South Dakota, for instance, 'archaeologists found a mass grave containing the remains of more than 500 men, women, and children who had been slaughtered, scalped, and mutilated during an attack on their village a century and a half before Columbus's arrival (c. A.D. 1325)'.[10] Evidence of similar massacres have been found in prehistoric burial sites throughout North America and, indeed, in prehistoric France from 2000 BC.[11] Murderous inter-tribal warfare has also been recorded among Australia's Aborigines by early European settlers. Normally, such tribal conflict occurred as a result of the abduction of women of one tribe by raiders from another, although long-standing tribal vendettas and other causes were also common.[12] As Windschuttle notes,

> *Internecine combat and the injury and death wreaked on other tribes was one of the favourite topics of native story tellers. The orthodox opinion that, before the British arrived, the Aborigines enjoyed an arcadian existence that was 'inoffensive, innocent, and happy' is belied by the pleasure they took in describing the pain and suffering they regularly inflicted on their tribal enemies.*[13]

Windschuttle also cites the 1831 diary entry of one settler who befriended a local Tasmanian Aborigine, who told him that

> *the Brayhelukequonne natives spear plenty of his and neighbouring tribes, that they stop behind trees and when they see a native go by himself they go and spear him. When the natives relate those exploits they do it by singing it, accompanying the same with different gestures corresponding with the circumstances of the story – the manner of fighting, the blows given, where inflicted and how . . .* [14]

Anthropologists have also echoed such views of the warlike proclivities of pre-literate peoples. Steven A. LeBlanc's comprehensive study of *Prehistoric Warfare in the American Southwest*, surveying conflict in pre-Columbian tribal societies in what is now Arizona, New Mexico, and southern Colorado over several millennia, summarises the situation by noting that 'the conclusion drawn from the data is that, instead of being almost nonexistent, warfare in the prehistoric Southwest was a driving force behind much cultural behaviour'.[15] According to that scholar, climatic-impelled changes in resources available to the local tribes has been the chief driving force behind aggression and warfare, which (not surprisingly) increased markedly when competition for scarce resources became fierce, either because of population growth or a diminution in resources.[16] In no sense were these pre-literate peoples more pacific or idyllic than modern Western cultures, despite superficial appearances.

This view has recently been reiterated by LeBlanc, a Harvard anthropologist, and Katherine E. Register, in their important book *Constant Battles: The Myth of the Peaceful, Noble Savage* (New York, 2003). Echoing Keeley, they see pre-literate societies not as peaceful and idyllic, but as places of constant warfare and death. They relate, for instance, the experiences of 'a party of European gold seekers' in the 1930s who entered an unknown area in the New Guinea highlands. 'The prospectors soon realized that they had entered a dangerous, brutal world of constant warfare.'[17] 'Warfare [was] endemic, with formal battles, ambushes, and even occasional massacres going on almost continuously.'[18] Research has found that

> *New Guinean men see their warfare as very dangerous and frequently experience nightmares about being isolated from their compatriots and bludgeoned to death ... And it is deadly: 25 per cent of the men and about 5 per cent of the women die from warfare. About 30 per cent of all independent highland social groups become extinct each century because they are defeated. These groups are either massacred or killed or the survivors ... take refuge with ... distant relatives.*[19]

Since the nineteenth century, anthropologists have tended to view an evolutionary scale of human cultures based largely in economic relationships and the modes of organising and exploiting economic resources. At the most 'primitive' level (a term which is, of course, judgemental and possibly tendentious) are nomadic hunter-gatherer peoples such as the Australian Aborigines and South African Bushmen, with peoples (like many American Indian tribes) economically organised around both hunting and primitive pastoral/domesticated animal agriculture representing the next 'highest' level, and so on 'up' to civilisations with cities, written cultures and law codes.[20] Each of these levels demonstrates its own fairly similar attitudes towards such matters as warfare, slaughter, killings and the sanctity of human life in the modern Western sense. As a general rule, no society anywhere prior to the ancient Hebrews or Greeks or at a level of development 'lower' than these peoples *ever* demonstrated or held any notion of human rights or the sanctity of human life in the modern Western sense.[21] As a general rule, too, the more 'primitive' the society, the less in the way of any proto-concern for 'human rights' in the modern, Western sense exists, and the greater the willingness to sacrifice or slaughter for the sake of group survival. The main reason for this lack of concern for abstract rights, and the (often shocking and disturbing) willingness to kill for the sake of group survival is economic: hunter-gatherer peoples cannot store food and exist permanently on the margins of starvation and systematic extermination, while more 'advanced' peoples can acquire a food surplus only with difficulty and (usually) in fierce competition with other tribes at the same level. There is, however, a moral and ethical dimension to this question and to these practices: 'primitive' peoples have, inevitably, failed to evolve a religiously based ethical system associated in the West with the Judeo-Christian religions and with the Classical philosophical systems which see the abstract protection of human lives and human rights as a primary goal.[22]

These points would have been self-evident to any Western observer of 'primitive' societies writing before the Second World War, but with the post-colonialist era's anti-Western notions of 'political correctness', virtually hegemonic since about 1960, have been systematically obfuscated; indeed, of course, the range of slaughters and massacres in the 'civilised' Western world since 1914, above all the Jewish Holocaust, has made most commentators far less willing to advance this conclusion in its old, strong form, an unwillingness enhanced by the overtones of racism sure to be alleged about any such characterisation. Nonetheless, the virtual absence of any Western-style concern for abstract human rights is a true and accurate observation about 'primitive' societies. Australian Aboriginal society may serve as an exemplar of the complete lack, in hunter-gatherer cultures, of *any* abstract notion of human rights in the modern Western sense. Because of the consistent scarcity of food, and the inability of the Aborigines to develop the cultivation of food plants or the domestication of livestock, an absolute premium was placed, in Aboriginal society, on keeping the numbers of mouths to feed as low as possible consistent with the continuing existence of the tribe. As a result, deliberate infanticide was widespread. Nineteenth-century European observers of Aboriginal life in South Australia and Victoria reported that about 30 per cent of Aboriginal infants were killed at birth.[23] Deformed children were 'always killed at birth', as were 'one or both of twins', and illegitimate children.[24] The 'usual reason given' for killing was that another baby was 'still being suckled by the mother' – in other words, because of the scarcity of food.[25] The practice of the cannibalism of a murdered baby was apparently common among Australian Aborigines. Some observers 'report the neonate being roasted and fed to an older child who is weak or sickly'.[26]

> In the Wotjobaluk tribe infants were killed in the old times, no difference being made between boys and girls. If a couple had a child, either boy or girl, say ten years old, and a baby was then born to them, it might be killed and cooked for its elder brother or sister to eat, in order to make him or her strong by feeding on the muscle of the infant. The mother killed the infant by striking its head against the shoulder of its elder brother or sister.[27]

If the Aboriginal population of Australia was 300,000 in 1788, and if the Aboriginal birth rate was 4 per cent per annum, and if only about 20 per cent of infants were killed, this suggests that about 2,500 infants were killed every year prior to European settlement, or 250,000 per century. In the estimated 40,000 years of Aboriginal habitation of Australia prior to 1788, it therefore follows that *100 million* [*sic*] infants were deliberately murdered in Australian tribal society. This statistic takes no account of other horrors such as tribal wars, often apparently ending in massacre. It would appear that Aborigines exterminated a race of native Pygmies who once lived in Australia.[28] As elsewhere throughout the world, women could be killed for almost no reason at all.[29]

Conditions very similar to those in Aboriginal Australian society were found in many other pre-literate cultures. In Eskimo society – normally viewed in the West as benign – 'infanticide, invalidicide, senilicide, and suicide are privileged acts: socially approved homicide'.[30] As in Australian Aboriginal society, 'in the event of birth of twins, one infant is almost invariably disposed of'.[31] Moreover, 'if one twin is a girl and the other is a boy, the girl is disposed of'.[32] Cannibalism has been well-documented around the world, from Fiji to the Amazon Basin to the Congo to Maori New Zealand. Despite efforts by recent post-colonialist writers to deny that cannibalism ever existed in any culture, the repeated and numerous reports by trustworthy and independent observers on many continents leave not the slightest doubt that it was, on the contrary, extremely widespread.[33] It is also a striking fact that several of the societies in which cannibalism was ubiquitous, such as Fiji, Polynesia and

Maori New Zealand, only shortly afterwards became known for their gentleness and idyllic life-style. In the twentieth century, for instance, the image of Polynesians in the West has largely been taken from works like *South Pacific*, and is overwhelmingly one of the idyllic life-style of a tropical paradise. Slightly earlier, however, it often more closely resembled the life-style found in hell. Writing of the Marquesas, a French island colony in the South Pacific, the anthropologist A.P. Rice had this to say:

> *It was considered a great triumph among the Marquesans to eat the body of a dead man. They treated their captives with great cruelty. They broke their legs to prevent them from attempting to escape before being eaten, but kept them alive so that they could brood over their impending fate.*
>
> *Their arms were broken so that they could not retaliate in any way against their maltreatment. The Marquesans threw them on the ground and leaped on their chests so that their ribs were broken and pierced their lungs, so that they could not even voice their protests against the cruelty to which they were submitted. Rough poles were thrust up through the natural orifices of their bodies and slowly turned in their intestines. Finally, when the hour had come for them to be prepared for the feast, they were spitted on long poles that entered between their legs and emerged from their mouths, and dragged thus at the stern of the war canoes to the place where the feast was to be held.*
>
> *With this tribe, as with many others, the bodies of women were in great demand. Very often a man who was condemned to be killed and eaten could be visited by his relatives, always naked and painted black. There are records of cases where the relatives have volunteered to be killed and eaten in their stead, but it is probable that the bodies of these self-sacrificing individuals merely constituted an additional course when the time came.*[34]

Cannibalism was particularly rife in central Africa. Sidney Langford Hinde, a captain in the Congo Free State Force, in a book published in 1897, recalled that

> *A young Basongo chief came to our Commandant while at dinner in his tent and asked for the loan of his knife, which, without thinking,*

the Commandant gave him. He immediately disappeared behind the tent and cut the throat of a little slave-girl belonging to him, and was in the act of cooking her when one of our soldiers saw him. This cannibal was immediately put in irons, but almost immediately after his liberation he was brought in by some of our soldiers who said he was eating children in and about our cantonment. He had a bag slung around his neck which, on examining it, we found contained an arm and a leg of a young child.[35]

Some of the practices of central African cannibals, which continued well into the nineteenth century, simply defy belief, especially their delightful habit of selling captives to be butchered for meat while they were still alive. Two extracts from contemporary accounts will surely suffice. On the Mobangi, tribes 'kept and fattened slaves for butchery as we do cattle and poultry', following raids organised for the deliberate purpose of capturing men and women to be killed and eaten.

They divided up their human booty and kept them, tied up and starving, until they were fortunate enough to catch some more and so make up a cargo worth taking to the Mobangi. When times were bad, these poor starving wretches might often be seen tied up, just kept alive with the minimum of food. A party would be made up and two or three canoes would be filled with these human cattle. They would paddle down the Lulongo, cross the main river when the wind was not blowing, make up the Mobangi and sell their freight in some of the town for ivory. The purchasers would then feed up their starvelings until they were fat enough for the market, then butcher them and sell the meat in small joints. What was left over, if there was much on the market, would be dried on a rack over the fire, or spitted, and the end of the spit stuck in the ground by a slow fire, until it could be kept for weeks and sold at leisure.

Sometimes a section of the people would club together to buy a large piece of the body wholesale, to be retailed out again; or a family man would buy a whole leg to divide up between his wives, children and slaves. Dear little bright-eyed boys and girls grew up accustomed to these scenes from day to day. They ate their own morsels from time to time, in the haphazard way that they have, and carried the rest of their portion in their hands, on a skewer or in a leaf, lest anyone should steal and eat it. To this awful depth have these children of the Heavenly Father fallen! This is no worked-up picture, it is the daily life of thousands of people at the present time in Darkest Africa.[36]

On one of the Congo tributaries, Herbert Ward found the following in a slave market:

A visit to one of these slave-depots revealed a condition of savagery and suffering beyond all ordinary powers of description. It was no uncommon experience to witness upwards of a hundred captives, of both sexes and all ages, including infants in their mothers' arms, lying in groups; masses of utterly forlorn humanity, with eyes downcast in a stony stare, with bodies attenuated by starvation, and with skin of that dull grey hue which among coloured races is always indicative of physical disorder. The captives were exposed for sale with the sinister fate in view of being killed and eaten.

Proportionately, a greater number of men than women fall victims to cannibalism, the reason being that women who are still young are esteemed as being of greater value by reason of their utility in growing and cooking food.

Probably the most inhuman practice of all is to be met with among the tribes who deliberately hawk the victim piecemeal whilst still alive. Incredible as it may appear, captives are led from place to place in order that individuals may have the opportunity of indicating by external marks on the body, the portion they desire to acquire. The distinguishing marks are generally made by means of coloured clay or strips of grass tied in a peculiar fashion. The astounding stoicism of the victims, who thus witness the bargaining for their limbs piecemeal, is only equalled by the callousness with which they walk forward to meet their fate.[37]

What accounts for the extraordinary change in both the actual social mores and values of pre-literate societies and in Western perceptions of them? One answer was provided by the Australian anthropologist Roger Sandall, who pointed out that 99 per cent of anthropological expeditions and surveys have been carried out after these societies were colonised by Europeans and 'defanged', their worst and most horrifying customs and practices already suppressed by Western administrators and missionaries.[38] As well, the ubiquitous 'Myth of the Noble Savage', and more recent

Western guilt over colonialism, have also accounted for much of this distortion of what pre-literate societies actually were like, as does the wish to avoid anything which smacks of racism, even when this means distorting the actual and often appalling facts of life in many pre-literate societies.

The sheer horror and ubiquity of death throughout virtually all pre-literate societies can be found in many other aspects of their cultures as well, for instance in their legal systems. In most pre-literate societies, the prevalent notion of 'justice' was entirely different from that in the modern West. There was, characteristically, little or no distinction between 'public' and 'private' offences, and most penal sanctions existed to punish wrong-doing against tribal mores, not against individual persons or their rights.

> *Some, indeed, of the public offences are hardly even of the nature of crimes: when a woman or child is killed in Australia [among Aborigines] because she or he has seen the sacred* tchuringa *(or bull-roarer), or an old or sick person is killed as being unable to travel, or an unwanted girl-child or one of a pair of twins or a man who is brutal or for other reasons unpopular, it is difficult to equate any of such cases with the punishment of a crime.*[39]

The rise of more advanced societies, characterised by more sophisticated modes of feeding a larger population, more sophisticated governmental structures and religious ideologies, had a number of important effects on the proclivity of societies to genocide and mass murder. On the one hand, the ability of armies to wage war and to kill grew enormously, and the history of warfare from ancient times became the history of more and more advanced and sophisticated weaponry and modes of attack (and defence), with milestones ranging from the development of the catapult, stirrups for horses, and gunpowder to the highly developed military establishment of modern states.[40] The ability of societies to kill and slaughter thus invariably increased over time. On the other hand, while advanced societies seldom lost the urge to conquer, they often lost the urge to kill, and substituted a variety of modes of enslavement and of the incorporation of newly conquered groups and nations for outright murder. This tendency to subordinate rather than to kill was probably augmented by the rise of the higher religious and more sophisticated

group philosophies, which regularly gave subjugated peoples the opportunity to convert (although often as slaves) rather than be killed. Western
European civilisation, with its origins in the Judeo-Christian religion and
the culture of the ancient world, its virtually unique development (after
the Renaissance) of secular and liberal modes of ethics and social organisation, and its equally unique ability to develop and harness advanced
technology, began as well to develop a concept of inalienable human
rights in the abstract and in law which was, arguably, found nowhere
else, even in the often relatively benign and humane atmosphere of the
Islamic world. According to some recent Muslim scholars in the West,
even now Islam simply lacks a concept of abstract human rights similar
to that found in the secular West.[41]

As well, one point worth keeping in mind concerning the growing
willingness of more advanced societies to refrain from actual killing is
that until modern times few mass slaughters were likely to be more
destructive than natural disasters, especially plagues, which could wipe
out a major portion of any society in a short period of time. Regardless of
how horrifying and murderous any man-made killing spree was, until
modern times it was likely to be exceeded in its deadliness, and in the
dread and fear in which it was held, by natural disasters and plagues. It
might be argued that the diminution in the incidence and virulence of
plagues from the eighteenth century onwards made the killings accompanying wars and other forms of mass murder stand out as particularly
dreadful, whereas earlier in human history they were merely one among
many thousand natural shocks to which flesh was heir.

Pre-literate societies, even those organised in a relatively advanced
way, were renowned for their studied cruelty, and great tribal or national
leaders in such societies chiefly rose on the back of mountains of corpses.
Shaka Zulu (reigned 1817–28), of the South African Zulu kingdom,
reigned in a manner which is even now celebrated for its comprehensive
destruction.

> One element in Shaka's destruction was to create a vast artificial desert
> around his domain ... 'to make the destruction complete, organized
> bands of Zulu murderers regularly patrolled the waste, hunting for any
> stray men and running them down like wild pig.' ... Flynn reported that
> a belt of more than 25 miles around Natal was uninhabited except for a

*few living skeletons who stayed alive by eating roots ... An area 200
miles to the north of the centre of the state, 300 miles to the west, and
500 miles was ravaged and depopulated ... Shaka had anticipated the
Nazis.*[42]

According to one contemporary report, in 1826 Shaka and an army of
50,000 literally destroyed the Ndwandwe, a rival tribe. This report stated
that the Ndwandwe numbered at least 40,000: 'they were all put to
death'. Shaka destroyed 'nearly every human being of the tribe, man,
woman, and child'.[43] When asked by a European traveller why he had
exterminated the whole tribe, including women and children, Shaka's
reply was that 'they can propagate and bring children, who may become
my enemies'.[44] Himmler gave a similar reason (among others) for exterminating all the Jews in Nazi-occupied Europe.

The statistics of Shaka's alleged slaughters raise another series of
important questions about pre-modern genocides and mass killings
which will have to be addressed over and over again. Are they accurate?
How did this Western observer know that '40,000' Ndwandwe (twice
the number of British troops killed at the Battle of the Somme) were
killed? Were there not distinct limitations to the number of casualties
which might be accepted as accurate in pre-twentieth-century slaughters
– limitations of weaponry, and modes of killing, of the willingness and
indeed the energy of the killers to engage in continuing slaughter, of the
ability of some of the potential victims to escape? As civilisation
advanced by stages, was it not the case, too, that moral and ethical considerations played a larger role, and that, for instance, conversion to the
religion of the conquerors or enslavement became the rule rather than
outright mass murder? These are among the central and crucial questions which must be kept in mind in considering the issues surrounding the alleged genocides carried out by a range of peoples prior to
modern times.

The Amalekites and the Carthaginians

Modern and perhaps early modern examples of genocide and mass
murder can, within certain limits, be verified, and the numbers of their
victims estimated with some accuracy. The testimonies of Western
observers of pre-literate societies, if verified as independent and

impartial, about horrifyingly murderous practices in their societies, can also be accepted as accurate, while always bearing in mind the sources of bias and distortion which might be present. In the case of alleged massacres and genocides in pre-modern history which were described as such at the time and which have been accepted as such by the mainstream ever since, much less certainty is possible, and the difficulties confronting the historian of this subject soon become plain. Two of the best-known and most famous of alleged ancient genocides might serve to illustrate these difficulties, the slaughter of the Amalekites by the Hebrews and the eradication of Carthage by the Romans.

The Amalekites were a nomadic people who wandered between what is now southern Israel and the land of the Canaanites, probably in modern Syria.[45] They were the first enemies encountered by the Israelites after crossing the Red Sea, attacking the Jews at Rephidim. Joshua succeeded in killing many but not all Amalekites – he missed their king Amalek – and at the end of the war Moses was prompted by the Lord to write a document proclaiming 'The Lord will be at war against Amalek throughout the ages'. The Amalekites were thenceforth regarded as an eternal foe of the Israelites, their extermination being seen as a national mission. According to Chapter 30 of the First Book of Samuel, David fought and defeated the Amalekites so heavily that only 400 escaped. Amalekite influence was finally destroyed, but only after hundreds of years of fighting. 'Amalek' is still used by religious Jews to refer to an incorrigible enemy of the Jewish people such as Hitler.

It is difficult to know what to make of these accounts. The Amalekites comprised a group of nomadic tribes, and therefore were presumably small in number, yet it took the Hebrews many centuries to conquer them, despite being commanded to do so by the Lord. The treatment of the Amalekites by the Israelites is sometimes cited as an early example of genocide, although it seems more notable for the failure of the Hebrews to carry out what they were specifically ordered to do by the Divinity. The Lord's injunction of perpetual hostility to the Amalekites has struck many Christians and secularists as an example of immorality rather than of Divine justice, and this unpleasant story has not been widely publicised in recent times. Paradoxically, although the intention to commit genocide was there, the will to carry it out was lacking, which may indeed be the story's intended message.

From the viewpoint of the historian, the story of the Amalekites raises many problems. It is simply impossible to know whether the Bible presents an accurate account or not, or how many Amalekites were either killed or survived. It is thus categorically different from accounts of more recent mass murders or genocides, which are based upon credible and verifiable evidence of various kinds.

Perhaps an even more famous example of alleged genocide in the ancient world was the destruction of Carthage in 146 BC by Scipio Aemilianus, at the climax of the Third Punic War of 149–146 BC. In the previous century, Carthage, in what is now Tunisia in North Africa, initiated a remarkable war of conquest throughout the Mediterranean under its great leader Hannibal (246–c.183 BC), whose army crossed the Alps riding elephants.[46] After a terrific struggle, the Romans defeated Hannibal in 201 BC. Over the next 50 years, however, Carthage steadily rose again, especially in economic terms. In 150 BC, Carthage attacked Rome's ally Masinissa of the Massyli in Numedia, flaming fears among conservative Romans of a Carthaginian revival. At this point, the Roman Senate moved decisively to a position of bitter hostility to Carthage, symbolised by Cato's celebrated injunction *Delenda est Carthago* ('Carthage must be destroyed'), a message he constantly repeated. Carthage was feared by many Romans as its only possible successful rival for domination of the Mediterranean. In 146 BC Carthage was totally destroyed. It seems likely that perhaps 150,000 out of 200,000 Carthaginians were massacred by the Romans: proverbially, the Romans covered the ruins of Carthage with salt to prevent anything from ever growing. Recent historians have, however, emphasised that the 50,000 Carthaginians who surrendered were not killed but were sold as slaves.[47] As Steven Katz has noted, 'when the Romans had a clear choice of killing or not killing the population of Carthage, after its final defeat, they chose *not* to kill the great majority of those captured'.[48]

As with the example of the Amalekites, it is difficult for the historian today to know quite what to make of the defeat of Carthage. Ancient estimates of the population of Carthage at 700,000 are almost certainly exaggerated, and it is similarly impossible to know precisely how many people perished, or survived, in Carthage. The apparently thorough destruction of Carthage shocked the Romans, a people even then not unused to slaughter and bloody conquest. Perhaps curiously, in both the case of the Amalekites and the Carthaginians, it was the extent of their destruction which shocked, stood out, became proverbial – and was not carried out to the letter. The history of the ancient world is indeed (at least according to written narratives which survive) one of virtually unremitting and barbaric violence, yet, within the more advanced societies of the ancient world something approaching humanitarian values may have been in the process of formation, however embryonically. Plainly, the religious beliefs of the ancient Hebrews, as well as some of the philosophical doctrines of the Greco-Roman world, contained the seeds of world-views which would eschew mass killing as, in most circumstances, intrinsically wrong.

The Barbarians: Attila the Hun, Genghis Khan, Tamerlane

The period of the Roman Empire's decline and the Middle Ages in Europe became renowned for seeing the destruction and depredation wrought by a number of conquerors from central Asia whose names are still synonymous with barbaric slaughter on a grand scale. Enormous casualty figures caused by deliberate mass killings, the mass murder of the entire populations of towns and regions, and entire provinces laid waste are commonly said to be the legacy of these conquerors.

The earliest of these destructive conquerors was Attila the Hun (c.406–53) who reigned as king of the Huns from 433 until his death.[49] Remarkably little is known of the Huns, who appear to have been a Turkic people from central Asia, although that is unclear.[50] They are often said to be the ancestors of today's Hungarians, although even this is unproven. The Huns conquered a weakened and declining Roman empire by means of an army of mounted archers, and were regarded as the most destructive and murderous of all the barbarian tribes which laid waste to Rome, the 'scourge of God', as they were widely know. Attila, a short, squat man, developed field armies as well as mounted cavalry, and, even by the standards of the barbarian destroyers of Rome, was renowned for his murderous cruelty. At Naissus (441–2) in the Danubian region, Attila killed so many inhabitants that several years later the river banks were still covered with human bones. In 449 Attila invaded the Rhineland with an army estimated at the time at 300,000–700,000 (a doubtless much-exaggerated figure). He conquered, sacked and burned numerous cities, including Cologne and Rheims – 20,000 Burgundians were allegedly massacred in 447 – before finally being defeated by the Roman general Aetius, 'the last of the Romans', at the Battle of Châlons in 451. This battle, according to contemporary sources, produced 200,000–300,000 dead. It is quite possible that the Huns simply exhausted the number of available horses – still their chief means of battle transport – which were, in any case, more appropriate to the Steppes than to a more settled region.[51] While Attila's destructiveness remains legendary, it was arguably exaggerated by contemporaries who believed that, as Christians, they were witnessing the end of the world. Indeed, the western Roman Empire was already in terminal decline and 'fell' only 23 years after Attila's death. As well, after Attila's death the Huns virtually disappear from history, a point noted by many historians.[52] Nevertheless, even today, so many centuries and so many destructive conquerors later, 'Attila the Hun' is still an interchangeable term for a murderous barbarian.

Over 700 years after Attila came the Mongols, another mighty conquering people from the Asian Steppes, whose empire was among the largest ever known and who, like the Huns, became infamous for mass murder in pursuit of conquest.[53] The founder of the Mongol empire was the celebrated Genghis Khan (c.1167–1227), born to a minor but royal Mongol tribal leader and named Temujin at birth. ('Genghis Khan' was the title bestowed on him after 1206: its literal meaning is variously translated as 'Emperor of all Emperors', 'Oceanic Ruler', 'Invincible Ruler' and the like.) From 1189 Temujin became leader of the Kyat people and then proceeded to conquer more territory than arguably any single person in history, ruling an empire which extended from Korea and Manchuria to the Black Sea. In 1217 Peking fell; Genghis Khan was militarily undefeated throughout his career. The mobile Mongol field army became known in the West as a 'horde', because it was assumed to be vastly large, but in reality it never numbered more than 240,000 men and was generally about half that in size.[54] It conquered by superb organisation, discipline and tactical mobility said never to have been matched by any other ground army. Genghis Khan's conquests spared no one: 60,000 were alleged to have been killed by the Mongols at Na-Chung in China, and no fewer than 700,000 in 1221 at Merv in Khurasan (Persia).

Such figures are very difficult to believe, but it seems clear that Genghis Khan slaughtered in great number whenever this was necessary.

His successor as leader of the Mongols 150 years later, however, probably made Genghis Khan appear a humanitarian. This was Timur (1336–1405), known to history at Tamerlane (also known as Tamberlaine or Timerlane), that is, Timur the Lame, who was probably a descendant of Genghis Khan and a non-orthodox Muslim. His conquests became bywords for mass murder.[55] Leading able military units of 10,000 men, he arguably carried out bloodier mass murders than anyone in Eurasian history before the modern age. His speciality was building pyramids of the skulls of his victims, slaughtered in truly appalling numbers. At Isfahan (Persia) in 1387, Tamerlane's army massacred the entire population and built a pyramid of 70,000 severed heads. At Baghdad (1401) Tamerlane exceeded even this with a pyramid of 90,000 heads. Near Delhi, India in 1398–9, Tamerlane slaughtered 100,000 captive Indian soldiers. In Assyria (1393–4) – Tamerlane got around – he killed all the Christians he could find, including everyone in the Kurdish Christian city of Tikrit, thus virtually destroying Christianity in Mesopotamia. Impartially, however, Tamerlane also slaughtered Shi'ite Muslims, Jews and heathens. In 1405, he began organising for the conquest of China, but died *en route* at Otrar, near Samarkand. Remarkably, he was universally regarded as a cultured and intelligent man, fluent in several languages, who liked works of history read to him while he ate.

The death tolls presented in this section obviously raise many questions of evidence and accuracy: it is, clearly, impossible to know if they are true, and it is very likely that they are exaggerations, perhaps wild ones. Given the modes of killing available at the time, generally hand-to-hand individual killing, the burning alive of mass groups, mass starvation and so on, it is difficult to believe that conveyor-belt death tolls of such astronomical dimensions could actually have occurred. Nevertheless, rulers such as Attila and Tamerlane became infamous for their gross brutality and numbers of victims, even in an age when life was cheap. There is, however, another side to the coin: most other rulers, in contrast, were far less brutal, seeking stability and prosperity, and moved, perhaps, by the moral teachings of their religions.

Religious conflict and persecution in Europe, 1096–1648

For over 500 years between the start of the First Crusade in 1096 and the end of the Thirty Years War in 1648 (if not, indeed, for even longer) Europe experienced continuing and bloody religious conflict which has often been considered genocidal or democidal. In this section, a number of the most important alleged examples of genocide or democide occasioned by Europe's religious conflicts will be examined – the persecution of Jews by the Crusaders, the brutal suppression of the Cathars (Albigensians), the Inquisition and its horrors, the anti-witchcraft hysteria, and the effects of the Thirty Years War between Catholics and Protestants in Germany. This is not an exhaustive list, but it comprises most of the best-known cases of alleged religious genocide or democide. Europe's record during this long period was certainly an unenviable one, but, as always, our aim is to establish whether the terrible massacres and persecutions which occurred can properly or accurately be termed genocidal.

Eight Crusades, attempts by Christian European warriors to reconquer the Holy Land from the Muslims, took place between 1096 and about 1271. While their aim was seemingly the displacement of Muslims by Christians in Palestine, they unleashed a tidal wave of violent anti-semitism in Europe. In the course of travelling through Europe towards Palestine in 1096, they launched numerous murderous attacks at Jewish communities in Europe, especially in the Rhineland, where massacres of Jews occurred in such towns as Mainz in Germany and Speyer in northern France, Prague, and elsewhere. In Palestine itself Jews were massacred when Jerusalem was captured in 1099.[56] Antisemitic pogroms also took place in the Second Crusade (1147–9) and in the Third (1189–92), especially the infamous massacre at York, England, in 1190, as well as in later Crusades. The summer of 1096, when the first antisemitic attacks on Jews by Crusaders began, is often seen as a central turning point (for the worse) in Christian-Jewish relations in medieval Europe.[57] Nevertheless, the antisemitism engendered by the Crusades differed from that found in modern 'racial' antisemitism, above all in Nazi-occupied Europe, in that Jews were almost always given a choice between baptism as Christians and being killed: unsurprisingly, many saved their lives by the former course.[58] Jews were also consistently protected by local noblemen and bishops, who regarded and often feared the Crusaders as an uncontrollable and dangerous mob.[59] Indeed – and contrary to popular belief – Jews were, as a rule, consistently protected from massacre in medieval Europe throughout most of its history: they were – it should not be forgotten – the only non-Christians legally permitted to live in medieval Christian Europe, albeit under demeaning conditions. Katz has noted what he terms the 'positive paradox' that although Christianity 'possessed the power . . . to destroy that segment of the Jewish people it dominated, it chose not to do so'.[60] There were several reasons for this: while the economy was primitive and 'usury' forbidden to Christians, governments needed the financial expertise and resources of the Jews; Jewish survival was regarded as a proof of Christianity, since their conversion would herald the Second Coming and would be delayed until then; unlike the followers of Islam, the Jews, who did not make converts and minded their own business, presented no threat to either Christianity or to the established European order.[61] As a result, the scale of Jewish murders during the Crusades was surprisingly small.

Katz estimates the total percentage of European Jews murdered in all the Crusades at 1–2 per cent or less.[62] Léon Poliakov, in his magisterial series of books on the history of antisemitism, estimated the total number of Jewish victims of the Crusades at 'several thousand at least'.[63] (It is, of course, difficult to estimate the number of Jews living at that time in western and central Europe, but the total probably amounted to several hundred thousand or more.) Nevertheless, individual and local massacres of an appalling kind certainly occurred. For instance, at Mainz 900 Jews were murdered. 'It was pitiful to see the great and many heaps of bodies that were carried out of the city of Mainz on carts,' one contemporary source reported.[64] The wave of antisemitism inspired by the Crusades was also responsible for many of the stocks-in-trade of later antisemitism, such as the 'Blood Libel' (the belief that, at Passover, Jews kidnap and kill Christian children, particularly boys, to use their blood in baking *matzoh*) and (during the Black Death period) the notion that Jews spread plagues and 'poisoned the wells'. The rise of a Christian bourgeoisie at this time also impacted negatively on Europe's Jews: the expulsion of Jews from various European countries, most famously from England in 1290, has been associated by many historians with the rise of a local, gentile middle class who made the economic skills and resources of the Jews unnecessary to local rulers, and who resented the financial privileges the Jews had enjoyed.[65] It seems clear that the massacres of Jews unleashed during the Crusades were not genocidal in the commonly understood sense of the term, however appalling the fate of Jews in individual towns was.

For evidence of what would now probably be regarded as genocide in medieval Europe one must, however, turn from the persecution of Jews to the persecution of a sect of gentiles. The Albigensian Crusades and the resultant massacre of the Cathars of southern France, carried out in stages between about 1202 and 1229, was certainly one of the bloodiest slaughters of medieval Europe deliberately directed against one small group: in its determination literally to wipe out the Cathars, it certainly bore many (but not all) of the hallmarks of a modern genocide.[66] Catharism was one of several heresies which flourished in southern France (and elsewhere in Europe) at the end of the twelfth century, a 'dualist' belief, derived from age-old Manichaen doctrine, which regarded Satan as co-equal and co-eternal with God, and the material world as evil through and through. Despite or because of these beliefs, it was a doctrine which was opposed to all forms of killing of human and animal life, and required forgiveness of all who persecuted it: as René Weis notes, a startlingly modern set of beliefs, grotesquely out of place in the barbaric world of medieval Europe.[67] Perhaps more dangerously from the viewpoint of the Church, it established a separate system of religious leadership based around a separate group of religious leaders, the 'Prefects', and a separate ritual and catechism. It believed in reincarnation (under certain circumstances), and rejected many key Christian doctrines.

Rather surprisingly, Catharism spread rapidly in what is now southern France and northern Spain, then independent or semi-independent realms; it was centred, in particular, at Albi near Toulouse. It was officially denounced as a terrible heresy by the Pope in 1179. Catharism also made the crucial error of becoming popular at a time when the medieval papacy was at the point of making its most extreme claims regarding both its religious and secular powers – these reached their zenith under Pope Innocent III, who reigned from 1198 until 1216 – and also at the time when the French monarchy was determined to consolidate its governing powers throughout France's later, more familiar boundaries. Their joint interests in suppressing Catharism came together in the early thirteenth century under Innocent III and the French King Philip II Augustus. In 1216 Innocent proclaimed a crusade against the Cathars, the attack being led chiefly by barons of northern France and the half-English Simon de Montfort (ironically, the father of the better-known man of this name who is regarded as the progenitor of England's Parliament). De Montfort and his troops captured the Cathar lands during brutal campaigns in 1208–13 when the Cathars were ruthlessly slaughtered. Probably the most notorious slaughter occurred at Béziers, where French and Papal forces massacred the entire town. A medieval chronicler concluded: 'I do not believe that such an enormous and savage massacre ever took place before, even in the time of the Saracens.'[68] An estimated 15,000 persons – small by modern standards, enormous, given the technological capabilities for mass killing at the time, in medieval Europe – were killed. The papal legate, the Abbot of Cîteaux, advised the French forces to 'kill them all. God will recognize his own.'[69] In the second stage of the crusade against the Cathars, which lasted from 1213 to 1226, similar massacres occurred in town after town. At Marmande, in 1219, according to a contemporary, 'no one was left alive, man or woman, young or old'.[70] De Montfort was killed in a siege in 1222; his successors carried on until the Cathars were annihilated or rejoined the orthodox Church, an option which some historians such as Steven T. Katz claim was widespread and general, and distinguishes the anti-Cathar crusade from later genocides.[71] Catharism survived in isolated pockets in the Pyrenees for another century, but was persecuted by the Church until it finally disappeared. The crusade against the Cathars has been seen as paving the way for the Inquisition. Had it occurred in the twentieth century it would almost certainly be termed a genocide by most observers.

The Inquisition, the Catholic Church's war on heretics of various kinds, was another infamous example of what many have claimed to be a kind of genocide. The Inquisition is often seen as growing directly out of the crusade against the Cathars, and especially out of the efforts of Dominic de Gusmán (1170–1221), the founder of the Dominican order, who was canonised as St Dominic in 1234.[72] Dominic founded an order of itinerant monks who were trained to combat heresies of the Albigensian kind, and became an adviser to Simon de Montfort. In 1233 one of Dominic's associates became Pope as Gregory IX, and empowered the Dominican order to create a permanent tribunal which was originally directed against heretical priests but gradually evolved into a general police force against all heretics.[73] Its ambit became ever wider, its methods more ghastly and extreme. 'Confessions' were often extracted under torture, in a manner foreshadowing the Gestapo and NKVD 700 years later. Groups of armed Inquisitors went on circuit throughout Catholic European towns in order to root out local 'heretics'. While rules remained in force prohibiting most forms of torture, these were often disregarded. The Inquisitors climaxed their visits by burning 'heretics' and others at the stake, the *auto de fés* which became a symbol of the most degenerate form of Catholic Medievalism. In Spain, of course, the Inquisition reached its most horrifying extremes, most infamously under Tomás de Torquemada, the first Spanish Grand Inquisitor, whose reign of terror lasted from 1483 to 1498, the years when Spain was unified and the Jews expelled. Jewish 'conversos' (converts to Christianity who still in many cases regarded themselves as Jews) were particularly targeted, with 2,000 burned or killed in other ways and 15,000 subjected to lesser punishments.[74] Much 'converso' property was confiscated, which many have seen as the real aim of the Inquisition. Although unconverted Jews were not originally subjected to the Inquisition, in 1492 they were given the choice of converting or emigrating, with Spain's Muslims given the same choice in stages between 1502 and 1525. Most Muslims chose to convert, and remained in Spain where they were known as 'Moriscos', like the Jews only superficially converted.[75]

With the Jews and Muslims, Catholic 'heretics' of various kinds became subject to the terrors of the Inquisition, following a procedure of mutual mass denunciation and accusation similar to that employed centuries later in the Stalin Purges. At Toledo in 1486, 2,400 persons denounced one another for 'heresy' or some other offence, often business rivals or neighbours settling scores.[76] In Castile during the 1480s, upward of 1,500 persons were burned at the stake as a result of false denunciations.[77] *Auto de fés* were generally carried out on public holidays, and became notable public spectacles held before huge throngs. Many victims were strangled before the burnings began, but others suffered the full horrors of burning at the stake. The Inquisition spread out to encompass any and all perceived enemies of the Church – witches, Protestants,

Freemasons, Rosicrucians, religious dissenters such as the Bohemian religious reformer Jan Hus, who was burned alive at Constance in 1415, ordinary 'blasphemers' and sexual immoralists. The Inquisition was less severe in regions of Catholic Europe which had their own legal codes that precluded judicial proceedings carried out by religious bodies. For this reason, the Inquisition never operated in England, subject to common law rather than to Roman law, where trial by jury was always supreme.[78]

Nothing in the whole history of the Catholic church did more than the Inquisition to damn it in the eyes of rational, enlightened thinkers, or to give it the reputation for medieval barbarism it held in many quarters until recently. The Inquisition was only formally abolished in the early nineteenth century. Yet it also seems clear that the number of victims of the Inquisition can easily be exaggerated. Juan Antonio Llorente (1756–1823), a fierce enemy of the Inquisition, whose *Critical History of the Inquisition* of 1817–19 remains the most famous early work attacking everything connected with it, estimated the number of executions carried out during the whole of the period that the Spanish Inquisition existed, from 1483 until its abolition by Napoleon, at 31,912, with 291,450 'condemned to serve penances'.[79] The last person executed (by being burned at the stake) in the Spanish Inquisition was a woman 'for having made a pact with the devil' in November 1781.[80] Most recent historians regard even this figure as far too high, with Kamen estimating the number of executions carried out by the Spanish Inquisition at only 1,394 in the entire period between 1484 and 1820.[81] Only 11 persons were executed by the Inquisition, according to this historian, between 1504 and 1820.[82] About 12,000 persons were punished by the Inquisition in other ways.[83] It seems clear that the death toll wrought by the Inquisition can be wildly exaggerated, and that it simply cannot be compared to the death figures of twentieth-century secular totalitarian regimes, for whom a total of only 1,400 deaths, or even 32,000, would constitute laughable leniency.

Yet another of the best-known offshoots of the Inquisition was the persecution of witches, which began in 1484 with a Papal Bull affirming the reality of witchcraft chiefly consisting of women allegedly in league with the devil – and the duty of the Church to root it out.[84] As Baigent and Leigh wryly note, previously the Church had officially denied most vehemently that witchcraft existed, so that 'in the past it had been heresy to believe in witchcraft. Now, at a single stroke, it became heresy to disbelieve.'[85] The key text in the persecution of witches was *Malleus Maleficarum* ('The Hammer of Witches', that is, the hammer to be used against witches), which was written by Heinrich Kramer and Johann Spranger, two Dominican priests from German-speaking Europe, who produced the 500-page work in 1486. Demonstrating every conceivable Freudian neurosis and psychosis, the work recommended an all-out war against the menace of witches, especially women witches, who were said to be creatures and allies of Satan. The attack on witches in early modern Europe was virtually unique among all instances of deliberate persecution of a group in that it was directed primarily at women: normally, women were spared the worst horrors of any outbreak of mass murder, which was aimed first and foremost at men of military age. Perhaps not until the Jewish Holocaust was there an example of deliberate mass murder in which there were more female than male victims. Attempts by recent historians at linking the persecutions of women in the anti-witchcraft hysteria of the early modern period, for instance to anxiety at the spread of syphilis, or to a reassertion of orthodox religious authority at the expense of surviving folk beliefs such as witchcraft, have become commonplace in recent decades, especially with the rise of feminist history.[86] Yet none is wholly convincing, for none can really explain why the persecution of witches occurred then, rather than earlier (in a more 'primitive' European society) or later (in a Europe whose traditional social and economic structure was certainly more generally disrupted). In the end, one can only recount the facts and place them in a wider context.

Witch trials became the main vehicle for identifying and sentencing witches. They closely resembled the previous persecutions of the Inquisition in engendering scare campaigns with ever-widening circles of accusers and accused.[87] The witch trials occurred later than other types of persecutions examined here, chiefly between about 1580 and 1650. Between 1587 and 1593 the Archbishop-Elector of Trèves burned 368 witches. In 1585, two German villages were victimised to the extent that only one woman was left alive in each.[88] More than 600 witches were burned by the Prince-Bishop of Bamburg between 1623 and 1633, more than 900 by the Prince-Bishop of Wurzburg in the early 1600s.[89] Many were men, among them 19 priests killed by the Prince-Bishop of Wurzburg. The total number of witches executed at this time is unknown and subject to wide dispute: 50,000–100,000 is the figure preferred by Katz, but over a period of many generations.[90]

Self-evidently, even the worst misogynist on earth could not kill literally all women or the human race would come to an end. Women from powerful or wealthy backgrounds, as well as most nuns and other conventionally respectable women, were nearly always protected. In all likelihood witchhunters turned on 'witches', especially women witches, because they had already established an infrastructure of persecution and needed victims, and 'witches', almost invariably from the fringes of society, were the most vulnerable and readily available; the witchhunters unquestionably also drew on an already-present wellspring of widespread belief in and, presumably, hostility to witches. Significantly, too, the persecution of witches spread to the Protestant world: indeed, probably the most famous of all witch-hunts occurred in Salem, Massachusetts, New England in 1692. Puritan New England at this time was apparently in a state of near-crisis, with liberal winds introduced by the consequences of the 'Glorious Revolution' of 1688 felt simultaneously with an economic crisis. As a result, historians believe that a group of poor Puritans tried to avenge themselves against wealthier ones by bringing charges of witchcraft against them, assisted by a threatened theological elite. About 174 men and women were arrested and 22 executed.[91] Witch trials and executions also took place in Presbyterian Scotland and in seventeenth-century England, where Matthew Hopkins (d.1647) was appointed 'Witchfinder-General' and was responsible for the hanging of several hundred women in East Anglia and Lancashire before himself being hanged as a sorcerer.

Probably the witchhunts occurred in large measure because structures of traditional authority were being undermined, especially by rival religious movements, or were breaking down, but stating this, to reiterate, explains little about the movement's ultimate causes. As well, the witchhunts occurred at a time when the Renaissance and the growth of scientific knowledge made it possible for men to believe that they could understand and challenge the forces of the unknown, in contrast to the medieval period, when they were to be passively accepted, or the later Enlightenment, when superstition became despised. It is clear, too, that, however horrifying, the witchhunts were not an instance of genocide in the commonly understood sense, although the peaking of the number of victims in particular times and places produced what might fairly be termed massacres aimed at a specific type of victim.

The last murderous frenzy in Europe whose origins lay in religious conflict probably occurred in Germany in the Thirty Years War of 1618–48, fought – very roughly – between Protestant and Catholic Europe. The losses suffered in Germany during these wars is often estimated at astonishing levels: one estimate is that 7.5 million perished in the German areas of Europe in this conflict, with the population of Bohemia allegedly declining from 4 million to 750,000.[92] Once more, it is almost impossible to know whether these figures are accurate, and much allowance must be made for the near-certainty of exaggeration in statistics of this range in the early modern era. But even if vaguely accurate, the Thirty Years War was certainly among the most destructive wars ever fought in European history, one in which religion served as the basis of slaughter on a grand scale. Many died from pillaging carried out by the invading armies, others from famine and disease occasioned by the war. According to John Gagliardo, 'the extraordinary misery caused by this conflict almost from the outset had no real parallel in earlier European history', and included 'ordinary and extraordinary cruelties of the imaginative maiming, torture and death regularly visited on some human beings by others in the name of religion . . .'.[93] In particular, the losses of life and property among the peasantry were 'staggering', and were reported as such in innumerable eye-witness accounts.[94] One million soldiers served in the armies of the Thirty Years War at one time or another.[95] The Treaty of Westphalia in 1648 left the German-speaking areas of central Europe in a political and economic limbo from which they did not recover for centuries.[96] The Thirty Years War also coincided with deep internal conflict throughout almost all of Europe (including, for instance, the English Civil War of 1642–9), often based loosely in religious causes, which was the main hallmark of what some historians have seen as a 'general European crisis' of the period. The destructiveness of the Thirty Years War was thus something of an exception to the long-term decline in the barbarism of both society and of warfare, caused perhaps by a range of factors including the patchwork of small, weak states in central Europe and new modes of killing by mass armies, as well as religious hostility. For whatever reason, however, the mid-seventeenth century also saw the end of mass slaughters occasioned by religious conflict, although such events as the Revocation of the Edict of Nantes in 1685, as a result of which 50,000 Huguenot (French Protestant) families fled abroad as refugees, while thousands were slaughtered, continued for some time. The eighteenth century was, however, renownedly a time of cynicism over religion, when few or none of the many European conflicts of the period any longer had an overt religious basis.

One other terrible slaughter which occurred during the period of the Thirty Years War does deserve special mention, the slaughter of Jews (and others) by the Ukrainian Cossack leader Bogdan Chmielnicki (1593–1657). In 1648, at the close of the war, he led an uprising of Cossacks and Ukrainians aimed at the Polish landowning class and Catholic clergy but, above all, at Jews. Prior to Hitler, Chmielnicki was regarded by Jews as their most deadly foe in modern times. Most accounts claim that Chmielnicki destroyed 744 Jewish communities in Poland and the Ukraine, killing vast numbers. Unlike Hitler, however, Jews who accepted baptism were often spared.[97] Traditionally, the number of Jews who perished at Chmielnicki's hands has been estimated at 100,000 to 500,000, a very large percentage of the number of Jews alive in Europe at the time, who are believed by demographers to have totalled no more than about 1 million. Chmielnicki's death machine appears, on the traditional reading, to have approached that of the Nazis in its murderous intensity. Recent historical research (by Jewish historians) has, however, radically scaled down the death toll. It now appears that about 30,000–37,500 Jews were killed in the Chmielnicki slaughter, out of a total Jewish population in the immediate area of perhaps 150,000.[98] A higher figure, perhaps 100,000 Jews killed out of a total population of 450,000, is preferred by some historians, but the evidence for a much lower death toll seems more plausible.[99] Needless to say, Chmielnicki and his hordes operated without the twentieth-century assembly line killing methods available to the Nazis, and still, evidently, viewed Jews as primarily a religious group who could be saved through conversion rather than an irredeemably evil racial group. As well, the scale of these massacres appears tragically unremarkable in the context of the Thirty Years War.

Conclusion

It would appear from all this that the civilising process has continuously worked to limit mass slaughters in all but the most extreme cases. Even in most historical situations infamous for their barbarity such as the Inquisition, the number of victims was relatively small, certainly smaller in comparative terms than either the dimensions of violence and killing in pre-literate societies or during the Age of Totalitarianism from 1914 until 1979. As always in pre-modern times, it is extremely difficult to provide accurate quantitative figures for the levels of killings, but all the evidence suggests that, engendered by the monotheistic religions which instilled some sense of the worth of the individual (side-by-side with religious fanaticism and fundamentalism), and of Western humanism, the most virulent outbreaks of slaughter became progressively rarer.

Notes and references

1 Roger Sandall, *The Culture Cult: Designer Tribalism and Other Essays* (Boulder, Col., 2001), p.viii.

2 Zygmunt Bauman, *Modernity and the Holocaust* (Ithaca, N.Y., 1989).

3 Keeley, *op.cit.*, p.34.

4 *Ibid.*

5 *Ibid.*, Appendix 4.1, p.194.

6 *Ibid.*

7 *Ibid.*, p.60.

8 *Ibid.*, p.65.

9 *Ibid.*, pp.67–8.

10 *Ibid.*, p.68.

11 *Ibid.*, p.69.

12 Keith Windschuttle, *The Fabrication of Aboriginal History: Volume One, Van Diemen's Land, 1803–1847* (Sydney, 2002), pp.108–9, 369–70, 381–2.

13 *Ibid.*, p.109. Windschuttle is specifically referring to Tasmania.

14 Cited in *ibid.*, p.109, from the Diary of George Augustus Robinson.

15 Steven A. LeBlanc, *Prehistoric Warfare in the American Southwest* (Salt Lake City, 1999), p.307.

16 *Ibid.*, pp.309ff.

17 LeBlanc and Register, *op.cit.*, p.150.

18 *Ibid.*

19 *Ibid.*, p.151.

20 An excellent summary of the anthropological literature, one with a clear relevance to this work, is A.S. Diamond, *Primitive Law Past and Present* (London, 1971), esp. pp.157, 327.

21 The ancient Hebrews obviously brought forth a religious-judicial system in which 'Thou Shalt Not Kill' was a central moral component, and, through the Noachian (or Noahide) Laws (binding upon all peoples) first attempted to formulate a universal moral code. The Greek philosophers such as Aristotle separately originated a universal philosophical system of moral laws for all mankind.

22 It is also doubtful if pre-literate societies have any notion of individual legal guilt or innocence in the modern Western sense. As Sir Henry Maine noted long ago, 'the penal law of ancient communities is not the law of Crimes, it is the law of Wrongs, or, to use the English technical word, of Torts'.

23 Gillian Cowlishaw, 'Infanticide in Aboriginal Australia', *Oceania*, XLVIII, No.4 (1978), p.263. Cowlishaw (*ibid.*) also states that other reports suggested a lower rate but then notes 'a more meaningful idea of the frequency of the practice comes from reports that a woman would raise two [of] three infants', reports which were very widespread.

24 *Ibid.*, pp.263–4.

25 *Ibid.*, pp.264–5.

26 *Ibid.*, p.265.

27 A.W. Howitt, *The Native Tribes of South-East Australia* (London, 1904), p.751. This is one such anecdote of many similar ones of infanticide and cannibalism (pp.748–56) related by Howitt.

28 Keith Windschuttle, 'The Extinction of the Australian Pygmies', *Quadrant* (Sydney, Australia), June 2002.

29 *Idem, Fabrication*, pp.379–80.

30 E. Adamson Hoebel, *The Law of Primitive Man: A Study in Comparative Legal Dynamics* (Cambridge, Mass., 1964), p.74.

31 *Ibid.*, p.75.

32 *Ibid.*

33 The best account probably remains Garry Hogg, *Cannibalism and Human Sacrifice* (London, 1958). See also Christy G. Turner II and Jacqueline A. Turner, *Man Corn: Cannibalism and Violence in the Prehistoric American Southwest* (Salt Lake City, 1999) for a detailed archaeological account of cannibalism among Indian tribes in the American south-west and Mexico. For the contrary view, that cannibalism never actually existed anywhere, see Francis Barker, Peter Hulme and Margaret Iversen, eds., *Cannibalism and the Colonial World* (Cambridge, 1998). Hogg's book is apparently unknown to the authors of this work, who do not cite it in an extensive bibliography.

34 A.P. Rice, article in *The American Antiquarian* xxxii (1910), cited in Hogg, *Cannibalism*, p.163.

35 Sidney Langford Hinde, *The Fall of the Congo Arabs* (London, 1897), cited in *ibid.*, p.103.

36 Rev. W. Holman Bentley, *Pioneering on the Congo* (London, 1900), cited in *ibid.*, p.105.

37 Herbert Ward, *A Voice from the Congo* (London, 1910), cited in *ibid.*, p.108.

38 Sandall, *op.cit.*, p.64.

39 Diamond, *op.cit.*, p.192.

40 On which see John Keegan, *A History of Warfare* (London, 1993).

41 See the remarks of Iman Zaid Shakir, 'spiritual adviser to Muslim students at Yale University', reported in the *Chronicle of Higher Education*, 14 March 2003.

42 Eugene Victor Walter, *Terror and Resistance: A Study of Political Violence* (Oxford, 1969), pp.138–9, reported in Chalk and Jonassohn, *History and Society of Genocide*, p.225.

43 Walter, *ibid.*, cited in Chalk and Jonassohn, p.227.

44 *Ibid.*

45 See 'Amalekites', in *Encyclopedia Judaica* (Jerusalem, 1971), volume 2, pp.787–91; John H. Hayes and J. Maxwell Miller, *Israelite and Judaean History* (London, 1977), pp.326–39.

46 B.R. Warmington, *Carthage* (London, 1960); Gilbert Charles Picard and Colette Picard, *The Life and Death of Carthage* (London, 1968); 'Carthage', in Frank Chalk and Kurt Jonassohn, *History and Sociology of Genocide* (New Haven, Conn., 1990), pp.74–93.

47 Steven T. Katz, *The Holocaust in Historical Context, Volume I, The Holocaust and Mass Death Before the Modern Age* (Oxford, 1994), p.92, n.107; Chalk and Jonassohn, *ibid.*

48 Katz, *ibid.*

49 E.A. Thompson, *A History of Attila and the Huns* (Oxford, 1948); J. Otto Maenchen-Helfen, *The World of the Huns: Studies in their History and Culture* (Berkeley, Cal., 1973); Katz, *Historical Context*, pp.92–3.

50 Maenchen-Helfen, *ibid.*, pp.358–493. Most, it seems, spoke 'a Turkish language' (*ibid.*, p.441).

51 John Keegan, *op.cit.*, pp.186–8.

52 Maenchen-Helfen, *op.cit.*, pp.165–8.

53 Peter Brent, *The Mongol Empire: Genghis Khan – His Triumph and Legacy* (London, 1976) is an excellent history. See also the extracts from J.J. Saunders, *The History of the Mongol Conquests* (London, 1971), in Chalk and Jonassohn, *Genocide*, pp.94–113; and R.P. Lister, *Genghis Khan* (New York, 2000).

54 R. Ernest Dupuy and Trevor N. Dupuy, *The Collins Encyclopedia of Military History* (London, 1993), p.367.

55 Hilda Hookham, *Tamburlaine the Conqueror* (London, 1962); Katz, *Holocaust*, pp.93–6.

56 Léon Poliakov, *The History of Anti-Semitism, Volume One: From the Time of Christ to the Court Jews* (London, 1956), pp.41–100, 203–9; Steven T. Katz, *Historical Context*, pp.317–400.

57 Poliakov, *op.cit.*, pp.41–6.

58 *Ibid.*

59 *Ibid.*, p.45.

60 Katz, *op.cit.*, p.317.

61 *Ibid.*, pp.318–19.

62 *Ibid.*, p.335. Katz (*ibid.*, n.86) takes to task such historians as Arno Mayer who drew parallels between the Crusades and the Nazi Holocaust.

63 Poliakov, *op.cit.*, p.45.

64 Cited in *ibid.*, p.52.

65 W.D. Rubinstein, *A History of the Jews in the English-Speaking World: Great Britain* (London, 1996), p.40. Jews in England had previously been denied admission to any guild (*ibid.*).

66 See René Weis, *The Yellow Cross: The Story of the Last Cathars* (London, 2000); Joseph P. Strayer, *The Albigensian Crusades* (New York, 1971); 'The Albigensian Crusades and the Knights of the Temple', in Chalk and Jonassohn, pp.114–38; 'The Albigensian Crusade: Motives and Realities' in Stephen T. Katz, *Historical Context* (Oxford, 1994), pp.530–7; and Michael Baigent and Richard Leigh, *The Inquisition* (London, 1999), pp.4–18.

67 Weis, *ibid.*, pp.xxv-xxvi.

68 Cited in Katz, *op.cit.*, p.533.

69 Cited in Baigent and Leigh, *op.cit.*, p.12.

70 Cited in Katz, *op.cit.*: the number of victims were said to be 5,000.

71 *Ibid.*, pp.534–7.

72 Michael Baigent and Richard Leigh, *The Inquisition* (London, 1999), pp.14–19. This is a vivid and harrowing account, but its relentless anti-Catholicism detracts from its balance. See also Henry Kamen, *The Spanish Inquisition* (London, 1965); Stanley G. Payne, *Spanish Catholicism: An Historical Overview* (Madison, Wis., 1984), pp.32–281 and Juan Antonio Llorente, *A Critical History of the Inquisition of Spain* (originally Paris, 1817–18; English edition, London, 1823; reprinted Williamstown, Mass., 1967).

73 Baigent and Leigh, *op.cit.*, pp.20–1.

74 Payne, *op.cit.*, p.35.

75 *Ibid.*

76 *Ibid.*

77 Baigent and Leigh, *op.cit.*, p.69.

78 *Ibid.*, p.41.

79 Llorente, *Critical History*, p.583.

80 *Ibid.*, p.582.

81 Kamen, *op.cit.*, p.285.

82 *Ibid.*

83 *Ibid.*

84 Baigent and Leigh, *op.cit.*, p.104.

85 *Ibid.*, p.106. On the crusade against witches, see also Katz, *op.cit.*, pp.401–507; Jeffrey B. Russell, *Witchcraft in the Middle Ages* (Ithaca, N.Y., 1972); and Chalk and Jonassohn, *op.cit.*, pp.152–72.

86 Katz, *op.cit.*, pp.433–507, provides hundreds of footnote references to recent works on this topic.

87 Baigent and Leigh, *op.cit.*, pp.118–20.

88 *Ibid.*, p.110.

89 *Ibid.*

90 Katz, *op.cit.*, p.502.

91 See Katz, *ibid.*, pp.426–32, for a full bibliography. Most were middle-aged women, but some were men. Some other sources say that 19 were killed. The Salem Witch Trials were stopped in 1693 by the new governor of Massachusetts, William Phipps.

92 R.J. Rummel, *Death by Government* (New Brunswick, N.J., 1994), p.54.

93 John G. Gagliardo, *Germany Under the Old Regime, 1600–1790* (London, 1991), p.70.

94 *Ibid.*, p.71.

95 *Ibid.*, p.77.

96 Hajo Holborn, *A History of Modern Germany: The Reformation* (London, 1965), pp.371–4.

97 Katz, *op.cit.*, pp.162–5.

98 *Ibid.*, p.164.

99 *Ibid.*

CHAPTER 3

• • • • • • • • • • • • • • • •

Genocide in the Colonial Age, 1492–1914

The discovery of America by Columbus in 1492 initiated a long period in which white Europeans first came into contact with and then conquered many indigenous peoples, often, in the temperate world, settling in their lands in great numbers. The European impact upon the peoples of the non-European world was certainly tremendous and, in the recent past, is often seen as the source of genocides and democides of historical dimensions. The depopulations which occurred among the Indians of North and South America, the Australian Aborigines, and among many peoples of the Pacific region, have often been cited, in recent years, as some of the most catastrophic in history. As well, African slavery and the slave trade are often also cited as a prime example of a democide in which literally millions perished. During the past 40 years, in fact, a post-colonial genre of enumerating the crimes of European man in the colonial world has arisen, whose exponents are often deeply resentful of claims that only events such as the Jewish Holocaust constituted 'genocide'.[1] These concerns are certainly legitimate, and there is little doubt that depopulation of the indigenous population on an enormous scale probably occurred in the Americas and Australia. There is also no doubt that the slave trade and the institutions of slavery cost millions of lives. Yet it is not necessarily the whole story, for 'genocide', on any common sense definition, implies deliberate intent, and it is far from certain that the intention of the colonists was often – or, perhaps, ever – 'genocide' in this sense. Moreover, the very definition of the 'colonial age' as comprising only European colonisation of the non-European world is itself partisan, excluding, for example, colonialising ventures by Muslims, Chinese, Hindus or indigenous African, Latin American or Australian kingdoms and tribes whose results may have been just as 'genocidal' as those of Europeans, as well as murderous intra-ethnic attacks and slaughters in what is now termed the 'Third World'.

This chapter thus considers and examines some of the best-known examples of alleged genocides in the Age of Colonialism. Several large-scale, continent-wide genocides are discussed here: the treatment of the Indians of North and South America, of the Australian Aborigines, and the course of the African slave trade and slavery. As well, a number of smaller-scale, and in some cases little-known, but no less interesting and possibly no less murderous examples of genocide and democide during the nineteenth century, chiefly in the Third World, are also examined: Thuggee and its suppression in India, the Irish Potato Famine of 1846–51, the Taiping Rebellion in China in 1850–64, Paraguay and the War of the Triple Alliance of 1864–70, the Congo Free State during King Leopold II's personal rule from 1885–1908, and the suppression of the Hereros in German South-West Africa from 1904–07.

The Indians of North America

As with so many other alleged examples of genocide, the most basic question concerning the American Indians is just how many there were when Europeans first came to the New World, and how many perished as a consequence of European settlement. This question must be addressed before examining the even more relevant question of how they perished, especially whether as a result of deliberate genocide. The question of Indian numbers before European settlement is much more than an arcane debate about historical demography: as has often been noted by recent partisans of American Indian life, conservative historians, those who do not necessarily regard the fate of the Indians at the hands of the Europeans as a genocidal catastrophe, have seen Indian numbers as relatively low prior to the coming of the Europeans, and hence their undoubted decline in population as less than a near-total slaughter. Recent partisans of the American Indian, who are likely to view their fate as a genocide possibly exceeding in its comprehensiveness that visited by the Nazis on European Jews, have seen Indian numbers in America prior to the Europeans as much higher than have previous historians, and their decline in numbers as consequently greater.

In North America – Latin American Indian numbers and the question of genocide will be discussed below – the traditional figure, common in the nineteenth century and then into the second half of the twentieth century, was that about 1 million Indians were living on the continent in 1492. Estimates made in the nineteenth century were often even lower: for instance a comprehensive study of the Indian wars in the Far West placed the number of Native Americans in the boundaries of what became the United States at between 500,000 and 1 million.[2] The two best-known early twentieth-century estimates, by Alfred Kroeber (1939) and James Mooney (1928) were, respectively, 900,000 and 1,153,000, for the whole Indian population of North America, including Canada and Alaska. Until the 1960s, all other estimates of reputable scholars were in this range.[3] A somewhat higher figure, of 1,213,000–2,639,000, was that suggested by the authoritative multi-volume *Handbook of North American Indians*, published by the Smithsonian Institution in the 1970s.[4] Since the 1960s, however, vastly higher estimates have become common, especially the figure of 9,800,000–12,250,000 proposed by Henry Dobyns in 1966, an estimate he revised upward in 1983 still further to 18 million.[5] Dobyns' estimates were based simply on taking the nadir low figures for Indian population, reached in the United States and Canada around 1900, and multiplying arbitrarily by 20 to 25.[6] Although Dobyns' methodology and conclusions have been widely questioned, most experts today apparently place the figure in the range of 4–5 million.[7]

That there was a very considerable decrease in North American Indian numbers following the coming of the Europeans is not seriously questioned – the only issue is by how much Indian numbers declined.[8] The most accurate way of approaching this question is to examine each Indian tribe separately, to ascertain the level of population decline, making an appropriate allowance for tribes which disappeared entirely, or merged with other tribes. This was actually done in a truly remarkable but virtually unknown work first published in English in 1934, Ludwik Krzywicki's *Primitive Society and its Vital Statistics* (London, 1934).[9]

Krzywicki's work contains *all* population estimates, going back to the first contact with Europeans, of all North American Indian tribes for which such population estimates exist. At the time of first contact with Europeans, the 505 Indian tribes for which population estimates existed comprised 186 tribes numbering fewer than 500; 125 numbering 500–1,000; 120 with 1,000–2,500 persons; 44 with 2,500–5,000; 21 numbering 5,000–10,000; and 7 with over 10,000 inhabitants. In addition, there were 19 confederacies of tribes with fewer than 5,000 people, 7 with 5,000–10,000 and 7 numbering over 10,000.[10] A high total estimate, based on the likely median numbers of persons in each tribe, is that there were about 1,336,000 North American Indians at the time each tribe was first described by white explorers, with the Dakota (or Sioux) and Sik sika (Blackfoot) being the largest tribes/confederacies, numbering in the order of 50,000–60,000 persons each. This figure may well not take into account the disappearance or amalgamation of some tribes before their numbers were estimated by explorers, or their decrease through disease or other causes. On the other hand, it must clearly be noted that this figure also includes Mexican Indians in the North American total: the total for the United States and Canada is probably in the region of 1.1 million. There is simply no convincing evidence, from contemporary sources, of significantly higher figures. The 'nadir' population figures in the early part of the twentieth century, after several centuries of depopulation, was about 351,000, suggesting that the population of North American Indians had declined by about two-thirds since European contact.[11]

It would thus appear from this evidence that the early low figures of Mooney and Kroeber are likely to be accurate. Some recent scholars object to this conclusion, arguing that considerable demographic decline had occurred before European contact, chiefly through raging epidemics of diseases introduced into North America by the Europeans by inter-tribal contact.[12] One estimate, by Douglas Ubelaker in 1976, taking this and other factors into account, placed the total North American Indian population at the time of first European population at 2,172,000.[13] This would suggest a decline to the 'nadir' level in the early twentieth century of about 84 per cent. These are the likely parameters of the debate over the demographic decline of North American Indians.

The next fundamental question is what accounted for this drastic decrease in North American Indian numbers. There now seems no doubt that most of this decline was caused by the effects of diseases introduced by the Europeans.[14] So virulent were these pathogens that, according to some historians, they wreaked demographic havoc, especially in Latin America, ahead of actual conquest, spreading from the earliest European explorers.[15] These diseases – especially cholera, smallpox, scarlet fever, typhoid and syphilis – not only destroyed, but reoccurred again and again in periodic epidemics and plagues.[16] Before the coming of the Europeans, American Indians were, it seems, remarkably healthy, with average life expectancies at approximately the same as in contemporary Europe.[17] Apart from the isolation of North America from the Old World, their longevity might have been due to the weeding-out process when humans first came, via the frozen Alaska-Siberian land bridge, to the New World, which eliminated the unfit, and to the lack of domesticated animals, apparently a potent source of recurrently virulent microorganisms.[18] After European settlement, virulent contagious diseases returned again and again to individual tribes, often bringing mortality rates of 50–75 per cent. For instance, the Omaja Indians were decimated by epidemics of smallpox, cholera and measles six times between 1801 and 1889, reducing the tribe's population from over 3,000 to about 1,100.[19]

But virulent diseases were not, of course, the whole story. Other major elements in the Indian population included intertribal warfare, warfare with the whites, the forced relocation of tribes, alcoholism, the destruction of food supplies, especially buffalo numbers, the profoundly negative psychological effects of the destruction of traditional ways of life, and demographic decline brought about by the structure of the tribe. Finally there is deliberate murder, the blatantly criminal and even genocidal acts of the Europeans against the North American Indians.

Intertribal warfare among the North American Indians accounted for a continuing source of population reduction and confounds the image of the peaceful 'noble savage'. 'The history of every one of these peoples [among the North American Indians] is a series of almost incessant struggles with neighboring tribes,' Krzywicki has observed.[20] The Iroquois confederacy, for instance, although it numbered (according to that writer) no more than 10,000 persons, went to war with tribes up to 900 miles away. In his view they 'exterminated' the Erie and 'ravaged' the Illinois.[21] By incorporating the remnants of these tribes into their own, they diluted their own identity even while making good their own enormous losses.[22] In 1643 the Neutral Nation (an Iroquoian confederacy) sent an army of 2,000 warriors to strike at the 'Nation of Fire' with whom they were 'always at war', attacking a village with 900 warriors. After capturing it, they 'killed many on the spot and took 800 captives – men, women, and children; after having buried 70 of the best warriors, they put out the eyes and girdled [sic] the mouths of all the old men'.'[23] An escalation in both the scale and intensity of violence certainly followed the coming of the Europeans, who introduced guns, horses and alcohol, and whose conquests forced some native tribes to move into areas where they were compelled to fight other tribes. Nevertheless, such massacres occurred long before the Europeans came. According to Lawrence H. Keeley, 'archaeology yields evidence of prehistoric massacres more severe than any recounted in ethnography [i.e., after the coming of the Europeans]'.[24] At Crow Creek, South Dakota, as noted, archaeologists found a mass grave of 'more than 500 men, women, and children who had been slaughtered, scalped, and mutilated during an attack on their village a century and a half before Columbus's arrival (ca. A.D. 1325).'[25]

Indeed, it was the Indians' reputation for fearsome violence which, rightly or wrongly, accounted for much white hostility towards them, even among highly intelligent observers who wished them no harm. For instance, John Adams wrote to Thomas Jefferson in 1812 about the 'Time when Indian Murders, Scalpings, Depredations, and Conflagrations were as frequent on the Eastern and Northern Frontier of Massachusetts as they are now in Indiana, and spread as much terror,' although by 1812 the few remaining Massachusetts Indians were regarded fondly.[26] According to Keeley, as a percentage of total population killed *per annum*, war deaths among North American Indians in intertribal fighting far exceeded those in twentieth-century Europe.[27] Wars between American Indian tribes were characterised by often relatively low levels of casualties in individual battles, but also by very frequent and frequently renewed battles, meaning that the overall levels of casualties over time were extraordinarily high.[28]

Alcoholism and the destruction of native ecological environments – for instance of buffalo herds – also accounted for a major component of the demographic decline among North American Indians. As is well known, the number of buffalo in North America declined catastrophically from an estimated 60 million before European settlement to only 1 million in 1875, and then to less than 1,000 in 1895 (in 1983 buffalo numbers were estimated at 50,000).[29] The introduction of alcohol and environmental destruction were the direct result of European settlement and it is, of course, the negative effects of the coming of the white man which is pointed to as genocidal. As a general rule, Europeans in North America simply took the lands of the Indians, justifying their acts on the grounds that the Indians were heathens and savages who failed to cultivate the land or trigger the bounty provided by nature, in a manner equivalent to that of the newcomers; white settlement of America was also justified as the country's 'manifest destiny'.[30] Provision was often made for payment of some kind to the Indians, and for the setting aside of some distant lands for Indian reservations, but the enforced transfers of Indians to these reservations were compulsory – in fact, an egregious example of 'ethnic cleansing' – while the Americans simply whittled down, again and again, the size of the land set aside for Indian reservations, such that today Indians legally occupy less than 3 per cent of the area of the United States.[31] The Indian saga, put in this way, seems an unanswerable case of what might be termed genocide and of ethnic cleansing on a vast scale, and was arguably one of the greatest examples of theft and expropriation in history. Nevertheless, it is a fact that no one proposes giving North America back to the Indians, while today the population of the United States and Canada is over 310 million, probably more than one hundred times greater than in 1492. After generations of demographic decline, the Indian population of North America is again rapidly increasing, and now probably numbers around 4 million, twice as many as before the coming of the Europeans.

Within this pattern of gross and often appalling injustice visited by the white man upon the Indians, a central question remains, in this study of genocide, of how many Indians died directly at the hands of the white man. The best available answer is only a small percentage of those who died through other causes. An 1894 estimate by the US Bureau of the Census claimed that 'about 30,000 Indians' were killed by white men 'since 1775'.[32] This estimate seems extremely low, and even the Census Bureau was careful to note that the actual number killed was probably much higher, since Indians 'carry their killed and wounded off and secrete them' after battle. 'Fifty per cent additional would be a safe estimate to the numbers given', or about 45,000 dead.[33] Adding in an estimated 8,500 Indians killed in 'individual conflicts' during the period, Thornton provides an overall estimate of about 53,500 Indians killed by whites between 1775 and 1894, although that historian believes that a vastly higher number were killed prior to 1775 or in (as he puts it) 'intertribal wars resulting from European involvement in tribal relations'.[34] It should also be noted that, according to the 1894 US Census report, 19,000 white persons were killed by Indians in wars, in addition to another 5,000 'killed in individual affairs with Indians'.[35] Taking the figure of 53,500 Indians killed from 1775 to 1894 as accurate, however, Steven T. Katz has called attention to the fact that this represents only 3.7 per cent of his estimate of the overall Indian population decline in the same period.[36] Even in California, which became the scene of many horrifying massacres of Indians, only 8.64 per cent of the decline in Indian numbers – according to Katz – was due to 'military casualties'.[37] According to Katz and many other historians, this is simply not comparable to the Jewish Holocaust of the Second World War, in which certainly over one-half of all Jews in Nazi-occupied Europe were intentionally murdered by the Nazis. Pro-Indian historians have, of course, taken great exception to Katz's view, seeing his figures as grossly underestimating the actual number of casualties and making no allowance for the intention of virtually all white Americans to be rid of the Indians by any means necessary.[38]

Grotesquely awful and appalling deliberate massacres of Indians by whites can certainly be cited literally *ad nauseam*. The Pequots, a Massachusetts tribe, were deliberately exterminated in the seventeenth century, as were many other tribes: by the time of the American Revolution there were virtually no Indians left in New England.[39] In the mid-nineteenth century many California and Oregon tribes were deliberately murdered in genocidal fashion, the killers publicly gloating at their killings.[40] The last great Western 'battle', at Wounded Knee, South Dakota, in December 1890, saw the massacre of 146 Sioux men, women and children.[41] Many dozens of other appalling, gratuitous massacres occurred, some of which would not have seemed anomalous in Nazi-occupied Europe. As well, down the generations many well-placed and intelligent Americans openly wished for the total extermination of the Indians. 'The only good Indian is a dead Indian,' General William Tecumseh Sherman's legendary remark, was echoed by many others.

Ward Churchill, for instance, cites a newspaper editorial written a few days after Wounded Knee by (of all people) L. Frank Baum, later renowned as the author of the children's classic *The Wizard of Oz*, who claimed that 'the best safety of the frontier settlements will be secured by the total annihilation of the few remaining Indians. Why not annihilation? Their glory has fled, their spirit broken ... better that they should die than live the miserable wretches that they are.'[42]

There is, nonetheless, another side to the story. However wretched American policy towards the Indians was before the twentieth century, it never actually encompassed genocide, and attempts, however half-hearted and unrealistic they were, to find a *modus vivendi* with the Indians always constituted a part of official American policy. In general the American pattern which emerged was very similar to that which was in place in other areas of European settlement. Most of the extreme nastiness and genocidal brutality was carried out by local individuals, groups, or regular troops on the frontier virtually beyond the control of the national centre, while the central government, increasingly influenced and lobbied by liberals and reformers, would have preferred to pursue a more conciliatory set of policies. Much of this reformist and humanitarian impetus came from metropolitan elites, typically composed (in the United States) of Evangelical Protestants and secular liberals. On the frontier itself, there were also some proponents of humanitarianism, especially local missionaries. Although the policy of the enforced removal of Indians to reservations came to symbolise Indian-white relations, most famously the exodus to Oklahoma in the 1830s of the 'Five Civilised Tribes' – the so-called 'Trail of Tears' – this policy was enacted in order to preserve Indian existence in some form, not, paradoxically, to destroy it.[43] The horrifying massacres of the Indians which occurred, by and large, took place because the most barbaric frontiersmen and local militias were, as noted, outside the control of the central government. As Lawrence Keeley has put it:

> *Precisely this weakness of state control over frontier 'militias' made massacres of native people more common by such agents than by the 'regular' forces of the State. Indeed, the most notorious massacres of North American Indians ... during the European conquest were all inflicted by local militias.*[44]

In the United States itself, the most characteristic attitudes towards the Indians were those of men such as Supreme Court Chief Justice John Marshall, who, in a landmark decision in 1831, recognised the Cherokee Nation as a 'domestic dependent nation' which retained internal sovereignty, and President Ulysses S. Grant, who initiated a 'peace policy' towards the Indians in 1869.[45] From the mid-nineteenth century, the American policy towards the Indians was hallmarked by an attempt to bring about Indian 'assimilation'. This policy deliberately attempted to eliminate 'all vestiges of their traditional *tribal* consciousness and classical forms of life', but did not entail either the physical destruction of the Indians or the elimination of an Indian consciousness.[46] Thereafter, until the 1950s, the position of the American Indian occupied a limbo land. White Americans with some Indian ancestry frequently boasted of their forebears, in complete contrast to the shameful taboos which surrounded any hint of black ancestry: American Indians were never strictly segregated in the same manner as were blacks, and not regarded as automatic 'second-class citizens'.[47] During the first half of the twentieth century, American Indians were stereotyped in hundreds of B-Grade Hollywood westerns. Although almost always depicted at first as mindless savages, movies came more and more to depict 'good Indians', while the true 'bad guy' was almost invariably a white man. The negative stereotype of Indians began to change in the 1950s, and vanished, with the growth of the civil rights movement, in the 1960s.[48] It seems inconceivable that this derogatory imagery will ever return: indeed, nowadays it is the Western pioneers who are iconoclastically demonised.

In summary, the treatment of Indians by the United States comprised one of the darker stains on the country's record, but it seems a distortion of the facts to view this treatment as genocidal in the sense normally understood by this term. The great majority of Indians who died did so through the introduction of diseases and other causes ancillary to deliberate killing. If mass deaths caused by the inadvertent introduction of virulent diseases is 'genocide' then the Genoese traders, or returning Crusaders, who introduced the 'Black Death' into Europe in 1348 (which killed perhaps one-third of Europe's total population) were guilty of carrying out one of the greatest 'genocides' in history, and obviously they were not.[49] It is much more accurate to view what would now be termed 'ethnic cleansing' as clearly an underlying intention of America's white settlers, but even this was almost always accompanied, among America's policy-makers and opinion-leaders at any rate, by attempts at rough justice for the Indians aimed at assimilation and peaceable settlement. These attempts were generally half-hearted, condescending and inept, but they formed a major component of official policy.

The Indians of Latin America

The demographic history of the Indians of Latin America is both similar to, but also very different from, that of the Indians of North America. In Latin America, a catastrophic and rapid decline in Indian numbers certainly occurred within a brief period of time after the first European settlement. But, unlike North America, relatively few European settlers came, at least compared to the United States and Canada, and these were less often 'pioneering' owner-occupying farmers and individual traders as was the case in North America. The influence and aims of the Catholic Church, and the leadership of the local Hispanic or Portuguese governing elite, was also much greater than were their equivalents in North America. Nevertheless, the demographic decline of the Indians in both cases was fairly similar.

Latin America was also distinguished from the North in containing two now-renowned Indian civilisations, those of the Aztecs in Mexico and the Incas in Peru and Bolivia, which had all the characteristics of cultures we term civilisations in the Old World, including large cities, trading routes, written communication and elaborate social structures. Nothing like them existed in North America at the time, with the possible exception of the Navaho peoples of America's south-west. Like so much else among the 'noble savages', there is an abiding tendency to downplay the faults of these peoples and exaggerate the harmony and idyllic qualities found in Latin America before the Europeans conquered it. For instance, while for many years the existence of a feudal-type social structure, or even of social classes, among the Aztecs and other Mexican peoples, was strongly denied, it is now generally recognised that there were dominant groups and strata in the same sense as other societies.[50] Notoriously, Aztec society in its religious aspects was centred around human sacrifice. About 2,000 persons were sacrificed each year at Tenochitalàn (now Mexico City), the Aztecs' capital city, with another

8,000–18,000 sacrificed each year in other Mexican cities.[51] (These figures, harrowing enough, must be multiplied up for each year they represented the approximate total of human sacrifices: at 15,000 sacrifices a year, 150,000 would die in a decade, 1.5 million in a century.) As Fiedel put it:

> *To celebrate the dedication of the renovated Great Temple [of Tenochitalàn] in 1487, sacrifices went on for 4 straight days. A steady stream of prisoners, probably numbering about 14,000, was led up to the pyramid's summit. There, four priests grabbed each victim's arms and legs, bent his body backwards over a stone, and a fifth priest slit the victim's chest open with a flint knife and pulled out the heart, which was burnt as an offering to the gods.*[52]

At the dedication of the pyramid of Tenochitalàn in 1487, executioners 'despatched' four lines of prisoners, each reportedly stretching for two miles. Although the figure of 14,000 victims on that occasion is widely accepted, one cardiovascular surgeon, Francis Robiscek, believes that an 'experienced surgeon' could work much faster, and has placed the likely death toll at 78,000.[53]

War captives were the most common sacrifices, but slaves and children were also killed.

> *The highlight of some ceremonies was the sacrifice of a privileged young man or woman who had been pampered for a year as the impersonator of a god or goddess. These sacrificial victims were flayed, and their putrid skins were worn for 20 days by priests or penitents, in imitation of the god of spring, Xipe Totec.*[54]

The royal court at Tenochitalàn was a remarkable place, which included a zoo (where the animals were fed on the remains of the sacrificial victims), a 'skull rack' (*tzoupantli*) where 60,000 skulls of sacrificial victims were displayed, and 'apartments for human freaks'.[55]

As well, the Aztecs were constantly at war with neighbouring peoples, employing an army of 100,000 men. One of their main aims was to obtain captives who could be sacrificed to the gods.[56] According to Shelburne Cook, a combination of human sacrifices and warfare increased mortality in Mexico by 20 per cent and was an important factor in limiting population growth which was at the point of far exceeding the food capacity of the local environment. One anthropologist, Marvin Harris, has suggested that the sacrifices were a pretext for cannibalism, in order to augment the meagre supply of animal proteins in Mexico.[57] Most of the flesh of the victims was apparently consumed by the high-status castes of nobles, warriors and priests. The Aztec practice of cannibalism had apparently been taken over from their predecessors the Toltecs.[58] This was the civilisation the Spanish found in Mexico. According to the archaeologist Richard E.W. Adams, writing in 1991, 'The Aztec state had become a mad world of bloody terrorism based on the cynical, psychopathic policies of the high imperial rulers. Coronation ceremonies of the later kings were accompanied by the offering of fantastic quantities of human victims to the gods. These victims were purchased slaves from Aztec society itself, and the collected captives from the constant campaigns of the Aztec armies.'[59] The other great empire in Latin America, the Inca realms which extended from Ecuador to central Chile, in contrast had few cities, with even Cuzco, the capital, being occupied only by the royal court. It lacked most of the bloodthirsty features of the Aztec realms, but human sacrifices were also periodically performed. Selected boys and girls, about 10 years old, were taken from their provinces to Cuzco for a special ceremony and then despatched to the various provinces, where they were sacrificed.[60]

As in North America, the population of Latin America at the time of the arrival of the Europeans has been the subject of great controversy. It is clear that the population of what is known as Ibero-America in 1492 was vastly greater than the population of North America, but even its approximate size remains in doubt and much debated. As well, estimating the population of Latin America is subject to even wider ranges of variation than the population of North America. In general – but not invariably – earlier estimates tended to be considerably lower than more recent ones. The lowest serious estimate was that of Kroeber, made in 1939, which put the population of Latin America from Mexico to Tierra del Fuego in 1500 at 7.5 million, of whom 4.2 million lived in the Aztec realms and 3.0 million in the Inca Empire.[61] Scholarly estimates made during the next 20 years tended to be higher, but not vastly higher. In 1952, Rivet, for instance, produced a revised estimate for the whole Western Hemisphere of 15.5 million.[62] From the 1960s, and as with North America, much higher estimates for Latin America became the rule:

Dobyns, writing in 1966, produced an estimate of 80.2 million–100.3 million for Latin America on the eve of European settlement, of whom 30 million–37.5 million were to be found in Mexico and the same number in the Inca realms.[63] All these figures, however, are keenly contested and subject to wide margins of error: there are evident pitfalls in very high estimates. An example of the extraordinary variations to which population estimates in pre-Columbian Latin America are subject is that of Hispanola, the island in the Caribbean on which Haiti and the Dominican Republic are located. Estimates of Hispanola's population in 1492 made by specialist historians range from 60,000 to 7,975,000, an extraordinary variation of 13,000 per cent.[64]

Over the two centuries or so after European conquest, most authorities are in agreement that Latin America suffered a decline in its indigenous population of considerable proportions, with some experts placing the level of population decline at levels virtually without equal in history. Moderate demographers, who see Latin America's population as relatively low before 1492, have seen an indigenous population decline of about one-quarter in the period between 1492 and 1650. Angel Rosenblat, a respected Venezuelan demographer, writing in 1954, viewed Latin America's population as declining from about 13.3 million to 10 million in this period.[65] More recent historians, however, such as Dobyns, see the population decline as of truly catastrophic dimensions, a decrease from 90 million or so in 1492 to only 4.5 million in the mid-seventeenth century, a decline of 95 per cent.[66] As Steven T. Katz (who apparently accepts the accuracy of these figures) notes, this level of population decline was greater than that experienced by European Jewry during the Holocaust.[67] These figures are, however, highly controversial, being based on inferences from Spanish taxation records of the indigenous adult male population. These show a decline, but, it seems, not of such an enormous order. For instance, the indigenous population of Peru fell from an estimated 1,264,530 in 1570 to only 589,033 in 1620. Nevertheless, that there was a catastrophic decline in population throughout indigenous Latin America seems not in real doubt.

The question, clearly, is why. As among North American Indians, the major reason was the virulence of epidemic diseases introduced by the Europeans, a factor noted by most contemporary observers.[68] As in North America, virulent epidemics of diseases such as smallpox came and wreaked havoc, and then reoccurred in equally virulent form at regular intervals. Epidemics 'of virtual continental extent' occurred in Spanish Latin America seven times during the sixteenth century. Isolated for millennia from the Old World, Latin America's Indians were especially vulnerable to these outbreaks.[69] Apart from epidemic disease, most of the other factors so evident among North America's Indians were also present in Latin America, especially the loss of the will to survive, the ecological effects of European settlement on indigenous societies, and widespread enslavement and peonage.[70]

From the viewpoint of this work, the most pertinent question is that of how many died as a result of deliberate killings, that is, genocide in the strict sense. That deliberate murder was at the heart of Latin American Indian depopulation was a contention voiced very early indeed, by the Dominican friar Bartolomé de Las Casas (1474–1566), who became known as the 'Protector of the Indians'. According to Las Casas, the Spanish killed sadistically and wantonly on a grand scale. In his words, two Spaniards

> met two twelve-year-old Indian boys one day, each carrying a parrot; they
> took the two and just for pleasure beheaded the boys. Another tyrant,
> angry at an Indian chief because he did not do what he ordered, hanged
> twelve of his vassals, and another eighteen, all in one house . . .[71]

Thousands also died, according to Las Casas, as a result of exhaustion caused by the exploitation of Indian labour on plantations and in mines. Other contemporary writers throughout Latin America made the same point.[72] This view of deliberate Indian depopulation became known as the 'Black Legend'.[73] It was attacked almost immediately by other contemporary observers, who pointed to disease and the negative psychological effects of societal change as the main culprits.[74] The best conclusion which the historian can reach about these claims is that while some deliberate mass slaughters took place, disease and societal change probably accounted for the bulk of Indian deaths in Latin America. Claims have been made, for instance, that 'the Spaniards systematically slaughtered an estimated 350,000 captives' among the Aztecs of Tenochitalàn when it was captured by Herman Cortés in 1521.[75] As the expedition mounted by Cortés started with only 508 soldiers and 110 sailors, such a claim seems incredible, and most serious accounts of the fall of Tenochitalàn blame smallpox carried by the newcomers' black slaves, rather than deliberate slaughter, for ravaging the Aztecs: the fall of Tenochitalàn 'was as much a triumph for Spanish disease as for Spanish arms', as J.H. Elliott put it.[76] It was certainly the case, however, that smaller-scale slaughters took place. At the Cholula Massacre of 1519, Cortés and his invaders may well have killed 6,000 Aztec warriors in battle.[77] Cortés also had the support, in his war of conquest against the Aztec ruling elite, of many local helot peoples. His 'conquest was as much a revolt by a subjugated population against its overlords as an externally imposed solution', according to J.H. Elliott.[78]

The conquest of Latin America by the Spanish and Portuguese led to the injustices of the *encomienda* ('assignment') system, the assignment of Indians to compulsory labour, a close approximation to slavery.[79] The psychological effects of this system, and the exploitation of labour it produced, is widely blamed for many Indian deaths. Yet even this differed from other forms of slavery, for the Spaniards given land grants had specific responsibilities towards the Indians, who were regarded as 'deposited' on them. Almost immediately, the Catholic Church became probably the most visible single institution in Latin America, its divine mission to convert the heathen Indians to Christianity, which it did over the next few generations.[80] The Spanish also immediately ended the enormities which were part of Aztec and other Indian societies: the human sacrifices, cannibalism, constant tribal warfare and the like.[81] Although during the Inquisition the Catholic Church at its most rigorous was opposed to overt slaughter or genocide, the Indians (like so many others) often embraced the saints and ceremonials of Catholicism as akin to elements of their previous belief-system.[82] By 1600, 31 bishoprics had been established in Spanish America.[83] A Catholic parish system, with numerous priests, quickly emerged. By 1570, there were 85 Catholic priests ministering to the Indians in the Mexican valleys, while by 1800 there were over 8,000 priests in Mexico City, an extraordinary number.[84] A number of priests, most famously Las Casas, became well-known supporters and champions of native rights (within the context of the Counter-reformation Catholic Church), and are among our most important sources of information about their plight. In short, the more extreme claims which have been made about the genocidal effect of the Spanish and Portuguese conquerors of Latin America are certainly exaggerated: as in North America, virulent diseases brought by the Europeans killed far more Indians than did the settlers themselves.[85] Spanish and Portuguese settlement in the Americas almost certainly resulted in a sharp decline in the number of Indians in Latin America, but this was not caused by a deliberate policy of extermination in any obvious or straightforward sense.

Australia's Aborigines

The fate of Australia's Aboriginal population following Britain's colonisation of this remote continent which began in January 1788 offers some close parallels to the situation of the American Indians, although there were also significant differences. Australia is the only continent whose indigenous inhabitants never advanced beyond the hunter-gatherer stage: they built no settlements or cities and failed to domesticate livestock or cultivate plants for food, certainly not on any scale. As a result, the size of their tribes was not large and their overall population was small, although how small has become a matter of recent controversy. As in the New World, however, there seems no doubt that their numbers declined precipitously after European settlement. In the case of the Tasmanian Aborigines, all full-blooded natives disappeared by 1888 (although mixed-blood Tasmanian Aborigines still survive). Aboriginal numbers in south-eastern Australia, where significant numbers of Europeans settled, in particular declined precipitously. Most historians believe that substantial numbers of Aborigines were murdered by Europeans, often in conditions which could be described as massacres. As with the case of America's Indians, the total number of Aborigines probably reached its nadir in the early part of the twentieth century, and has since begun an upward climb. Until the Second World War there was a general belief that full-blooded Aborigines were destined to disappear. During the past few decades, as Australia's Aboriginal question has moved to the centre of domestic political discussion in that country, a separate political debate involving questions of possible genocide has arisen over the so-called 'Stolen Generation', the fact that from the late nineteenth century until the 1960s, many mixed-raced children, those with Aboriginal mothers and European fathers, were forcibly taken from the mother to be raised in settlements with white families. Despite the remoteness of

Australia, therefore, the issues raised by European treatment of Aborigines are both important and wide-ranging.[86]

As always, the first point which any discussion of this topic must examine is the overall population of Australia's Aborigines prior to European settlement and the dimension of its subsequent decline.[87] This is not particularly easy, since no Aborigines were literate and many, perhaps most, lived in remote areas unsettled by Europeans for decades. Until the 1920s, it was widely assumed that the number of Australian Aborigines in 1788 did not exceed about 150,000 persons. In 1930 the eminent anthropologist A.D. Radcliffe-Brown recalculated this figure at 251,000, or 'quite possibly, or even probably, over 300,000'.[88] This figure, of about 300,000 Aborigines in 1788, was widely accepted for many years. More recently, a wide divergency of opinion about this question has developed. In 1970, F. Lancaster Jones argued that Radcliffe-Brown's figure was too high, and a total of perhaps 215,000 mainland Aborigines were alive in 1788.[89] Lancaster Jones based his calculation upon average tribal sizes known from anthropological studies. More recently, the well-known economic historian Noel Butlin argued the opposite proposition, that the number of Aborigines alive in 1788 was much higher, totalling around 250,000 in New South Wales and Victoria alone (or even more) and conceivably 750,000 for the whole continent.[90] It is, of course, extremely difficult for a non-expert to judge these theories, but it seems plain enough that Butlin's view takes no account whatever of the anthropology of hunter-gatherer tribes and their size.[91] In fact, as nomadic hunter-gatherers in a continent with a lower protein content than any other, Australia's Aborigines invariably lived in very small tribal units, much smaller than, say, the typical tribes of North America's Indians, let alone the urban-based settlements found in Mexico and perhaps among the Incas. Krzywicki's study contains comprehensive statistics on the Australian Aboriginal tribes known to him, drawn from the original reports of the earliest settlers: of the 123 tribes on which he provides information, 70 contained fewer than 500 persons, 37 from 500 to 1,000 persons, 12 from 1,000 to 2,500, and only 4 more than 2,500 persons.[92] The average size of an Aboriginal tribe was 550. The 4 tribes numbering 2,500 or more were really, in his view, aggregates of several tribes, the largest of which contained perhaps 7,000 persons when first seen by Europeans in 1845.[93] Australian Aboriginal tribes were thus categorically smaller than those found among the North American Indians. Krzywicki's view was confirmed in the much more extensive research of Norman B. Tindale, writing in 1940, who identified 571 mainland tribes, with an average size of only 435.[94]

Pre-1788 Australia contained no permanently inhabited towns (or even permanent buildings of any kind, apart from the most primitive), or any form of agriculture based on what might be termed farming.[95] For the size of Australia's Aboriginal population in 1788 to have been vastly greater than the range of 215,000–300,000 commonly suggested before Butlin, either the average size of the tribes must have been enormously greater than that found even by the first European observers, or there must have been literally hundreds of tribes, especially in south-eastern Australia, which simply vanished within a few decades of European settlement. There is no evidence for either proposition. There is no evidence that the average size of tribes was more than marginally greater in south-eastern Australia than anywhere else (including areas of Australia not visited by Europeans for many decades).[96] While the number of tribes certainly declined, chiefly through the introduction of virulent diseases by the Europeans, as soon as the 'First Fleet' arrived, there is no evidence that hundreds of tribes vanished before their existence could be noted. Because the Aborigines were invariably hunter-gatherers, their geographical distribution was quite different from that of European settlers, who hugged the verdant coastal areas and almost wholly eschewed the 'outback' or remote districts: of Australia's 571 tribes identified by Tindale, no fewer than 440 lived in the remote areas of Queensland, Western Australia and the Northern Territory, the last parts of Australia to be settled by whites.[97] These were areas beyond the reach of whites, their diseases and depredations, until relatively late. As well, no internal mechanisms of governance existed among Australia's Aborigines for very large-scale tribal units: small-scale kinship 'networks' were always all-important.

For all of these reasons, it seems clear enough that Butlin's very high figures for Australia's pre-1788 Aboriginal population are unlikely to be accurate.[98] On the contrary, it appears difficult to question Lancaster Jones's downward revision of the estimated Aboriginal population in 1788 from 300,000 to perhaps 215,000, bearing in mind, of course, that the last word has yet to be said, and that compelling evidence is slim.

There is, however, little doubt that European settlement resulted, almost immediately, in a substantial, perhaps catastrophic, decline in Aboriginal numbers, especially in south-eastern Australia where settlement occurred first. Working from initial estimates and later Census figures, Lancaster Jones believed that Aboriginal numbers declined from 251,000 in 1788 (Radcliffe-Brown's estimate) to only 66,950 in 1901, a figure derived from the Australian census of that year.[99] Aboriginal numbers in Victoria dropped from 11,500 to only 521 and in Western Australia from an estimated 52,000 to 5,261. Butlin sees a catastrophic decline as occurring almost immediately following white settlement, with Aboriginal numbers in Victoria and New South Wales dropping almost incredibly from (in his view) 250,000 in 1788 to only 145,000 in 1800, then to the order of 70,000–90,000 in 1830, and to only 10,000–15,000 in 1850.[100]

As with America's Indians, there is no doubt that the main culprit was the introduction of virulent contagious diseases: even Butlin concedes that 'smallpox and venereal disease' were primarily responsible for the sharp decline.[101] A smallpox epidemic which first became evident in 1789, a year after the landing of the 'First Fleet', was especially devastating.[102] Population stability was achieved within 20 years, when a second virulent outbreak of smallpox struck in 1829–31.[103] Many of the factors which brought about the decline in the indigenous population in the Americas were also present in Australia, including the psychological effects of colonisation, alcoholism, venereal disease (apparently a very important factor) and a change in resource uses, especially the cultivation of land for livestock (particularly sheep) and grain, which impacted on the use of land by the Aborigines.[104] Nevertheless, there were also very significant differences between Australia and North America. European settlement in Australia was much smaller in numbers than in America. There was little or nothing resembling the American pioneers who constantly moved west to virgin territory, ejecting the Indians as they went: white settlement in Australia was limited to the coasts, with Australia's vast inland areas virtually uninhabitable by whites.[105]

To reiterate, it seems clear that there was a sharp decline in Aboriginal numbers, especially in south-eastern Australia, caused primarily by introduced virulent diseases and by the usual highly negative indirect effects which accompanied white settlement in the New World, but in the context of the very uneven pattern of European settlement in Australia. Although this seems clear enough, strikingly the past few decades have seen very considerable attention devoted by historians to the alleged direct and deliberate killing of Aborigines on the Australian frontier by whites, killings which continued into the early twentieth century.[106] Apart from a general pattern of killing, many historians have also examined the disappearance of the indigenous peoples of Tasmania, sometimes cited as one of the only truly complete examples of genocide known in the modern world, since not a single pure-blooded Tasmanian Aborigine survived after 1888. Many historians believe that a significant number of Aborigines were killed by whites, especially in frontier encounters. The most generally accepted figure of such killings is 20,000, the total suggested by Professor Henry Reynolds of the University of Tasmania, who has written widely on this subject.[107] (As well, about 2,000 whites and Asians were murdered by Aborigines.) In Western Australia alone, according to the historian Ian Clark, 107 massacre sites exist, mainly dating from the 1840s: at each site between one and 20–40 Aborigines were killed.[108] Clark estimates that in all about 500 Aborigines were murdered in Western Australia, chiefly in the 1840s.[109] Many of these killings were reprisals for the murder of white settlers or soldiers by Aborigines. Very typically, at Pinjera, Western Australia, in 1834, between 10 and 30 or more Aborigines were shot dead by a party of British troops, in retaliation for the killing of a soldier. Many other similar incidents of this type were apparently recorded, often carried out with what appeared to be a denial of the humanity of the Aborigines.

If these are accurate accounts of what occurred, these killings were criminal and barbaric, but were they genocide in any common sense meaning of the term? Here there is much more reason for doubt. Settlers who killed Aborigines operated in an atmosphere of near-complete autonomy. In the early days, many were former convicts. By and large, they killed not merely without the support of their central government, but in direct opposition to it. On mainland Australia, the only likely exception to this was in central Queensland, where the elimination of Aborigines (after strong Aborigine resistance to white settlement), often by massacres, was carried out with the cooperation of the Native Police and other official forces.[110] Elsewhere, however, the governments, both the British colonial administrators and (less strenuously) local governments, tried to protect the Aborigines from at least the grosser forms of murderous elimination – certainly in a more determined way than did the American authorities *vis-à-vis* the Indians. The leader of the First Fleet, Arthur Phillip, was instructed to ensure that Britons lived in 'amity and kindness' with the Aborigines. For several decades, Aborigines were in general left entirely alone, unless they molested British settlers (in which case they were dealt with harshly), with no attempt made, until 1836, to apply British law to Aboriginal society.[111] For their part in the Myall Creek massacre of Aborigines of 1836, seven Europeans were hanged. As local Australian colonial parliaments emerged from the 1840s, a mixed record developed, a sense both that Aborigines were outside Western law and could when necessary be subject to harsher punishments, but that the Protection of Aborigines would be a deliberate aim of policy, for instance in forbidding the sale of liquor.[112] As elsewhere in the Western world, there emerged a steady stream of pro-Aboriginal white Christians, liberals, crusading editors, radical activists and metropolitan bureaucrats keen to ensure justice, who constantly campaigned on behalf of Aborigines and against their mistreatment.[113]

Only in the 1960s (particularly as a result of an amendment to the Constitution which gave the more liberal Federal government the right to overrule state laws dealing with Aborigines) were the Aborigines made absolutely equal in law, although the gap in income and living standards between whites and blacks remains very wide. While Aboriginal numbers fell sharply, as has been discussed, the precise level of decline remains unclear, and most of the decrease – perhaps virtually all – was caused by introduced virulent diseases and the psychological and environmental consequences for indigenous peoples which almost everywhere accompanied European settlement. Except in certain areas of the frontier – such as parts of Queensland – Australia's record in protecting its indigenous peoples seems clearly better than was the case in the United States. In vast areas of northern and western Australia, Aborigines continued (and continue) to live as their ancestors did. With limited exceptions, then, the notion of the deliberate 'genocide' of Australia's Aborigines seems misconceived and inaccurate.

Indeed, some historians have now begun to question whether the scale of deliberate white killing of Aborigines was anything like that suggested by Reynolds and other pro-Aboriginal historians. For instance, Keith Windschuttle, a Sydney historian, received international publicity when, after painstaking research, he questioned such claims as those made about an alleged 'massacre' at Hobart in 1804. There, a settler and his wife were surrounded and threatened by more than 200 Aborigines with spears. British soldiers, coming to the rescue, 'shot, at most, three people'.[114] At a government inquiry in 1830, however, a former convict testified that in 1804 he thought 'forty to fifty' blacks had been killed, even though he acknowledged he had not been at the scene at the time. Most recent historians have accepted as fact that 'up to fifty' Aborigines were killed.[115] An apparently even more egregious example is that of the alleged massacre at Forest River in Western Australia in 1926, one of the last great massacres of blacks by whites, and the subject of a state royal commission. At least 11 natives, it concluded, were killed by two policemen.[116] By the 1970s this figure had grown to '100 dead', based purely on oral histories taken from elderly Aborigines.[117] In 1999 a Western Australian journalist, Rod Moran, after extensive research, published *Massacre Myth*, in which he proved, apparently beyond reasonable doubt, that no killings whatsoever had taken place.[118]

Some claims by recent white liberal historians might be seen, in fact, as seriously misleading. In *Our Original Aggression*, Noel Butlin stated that 'although the origins of the main killer, smallpox, are obscure, it is possible and, in 1789, likely that infection of the aborigines was a deliberate exterminating act'.[119] There is absolutely no evidence for such a contention except for a report from Watkin Tench, present on the 'First Fleet', that, last among the five possible ways in which smallpox arrived in Sydney, was that 'our surgeons had brought out variolous matter in bottles'.[120] Butlin drew this conclusion from nothing more than the fact that Sir Jeffrey Amherst had, in 1763, attempted to use smallpox-injected blankets against the Indians during Pontiac's Rebellion. 'Smallpox could then have been loosed deliberately as a first and possibly the most important shot in the white campaign to capture black resources,' Butlin noted elsewhere.[121] When widely criticised (Governor Phillip had always enjoyed a reputation as sympathetic to the Aborigines), Butlin responded that hospitalised convicts might have stolen some of the 'variolous matter' and infected the Aborigines – ignoring the convicts' complete lack of medical knowledge, and the fact that savage punishment (quite probably including execution) awaited anyone apprehended.[122] 'I have not, in my book, proposed that it was deliberate,' Butlin wrote a year after *Our Original Aggression* appeared and controversy swirled around it. 'I did not imply deliberate policy. If it occurred deliberately, transmission might have been the work of some embittered or deranged individuals.'[123] Moreover, since Butlin wrote, several things have become clear. First, what he suggested about the transmission of smallpox to Aborigines by 'variolous' matter on the First Fleet is almost certainly impossible: it has been established that the smallpox virus cannot remain virulent for more than three weeks in the tropical heat encountered by the First Fleet, which had sailed many months before.[124] Second, it seems more likely than not that the smallpox was transmitted by traders from Macassar (a town in the south of Sulawesi, an island in what is now Indonesia), and spread from Northern Australia to migratory Aborigines.[125]

The event in Australian history which has most often been labelled genocide in the strict and narrow sense occurred in Tasmania, the island colony (later an Australian state) 150 miles off the south-east coast of the mainland. While little is known of them, the Tasmanian Aborigines were apparently ethnically unrelated to those of the mainland: like them, however, they were hunter-gatherers, living on the rather abundant marsupials, birds and shellfish of the island.[126] With the coming of the British in 1803, life became grim for the Tasmanian natives. Sealers and whalers decimated a traditional source of food, their crews often in open conflict with the local inhabitants.[127] Other native animals, especially kangaroos, were killed for food in large numbers.[128] The usual story of virulent diseases, including venereal infections, quickly followed. It is widely claimed as well that Tasmanian natives were deliberately killed in significant numbers, often for sport.[129] One alleged reason for this murderous record is that Tasmania had been settled as a penal colony *par excellence*, most of its inhabitants being hardened criminals, often vicious, who could not easily be supervised. The natives fought back, actually killing more whites than the other way round, at least according to inquest records.[130]

The British authorities were, as always, sympathetic to the natives and deplored violence against them. A continuing 'Black War' broke out in the 1820s, followed by attempts by white 'roving parties' to capture the natives dead or alive. This 'Black War' has been described by Henry Reynolds as a 'fierce guerrilla warfare'.[131] In 1830, appalled by continuing native attacks on white settlers, the Governor, George Arthur, established a 'Black Line' of 2,000 soldiers and others who were to march through the eastern part of the island to round up the remaining natives. Of only limited success, this nevertheless ended black hostility against the whites. Changing tactics, a 'Conciliator', George Augustus Robinson, was appointed, to persuade all surviving natives to come out of the bush and live under the authority of the British. Most were moved to Flinders Island, off the Tasmanian coast, where they continued their steep demographic decline. By 1888 at the latest, all full-blooded Tasmanian Aborigines had died out.

The Tasmanian Aboriginal population had always been very small. Although Tasmania is the same size as the Republic of Ireland or Sri Lanka, the latest estimates suggest that there were only 4,000–7,500 Aborigines in the whole island when the British arrived.[132] (Given the relatively protein-rich environment of pre-European Tasmania compared with the mainland, this is also striking evidence that pre-1788 mainland numbers – *contra* Butlin – were probably low.) By 1824, the beginning of the 'Black War', they numbered only about 1,500, and then declined catastrophically to only about 350 in 1831.[133] Much of this decrease must have been caused by killings by soldiers or settlers, or from exhaustion caused by the 'Black War'. Yet, grim as this picture is, whether it constituted genocide has been questioned even by a strongly pro-Aboriginal historian such as Henry Reynolds. While George Arthur 'was determined to defeat the Aborigines and secure the permanent expropriation of their land ... there is little evidence to suggest that he wanted to reach beyond that objective and destroy the Tasmanian race in whole or in part ... [H]e had been specifically warned against such action by his superiors in London and carrying it out would serve no particular purpose.'[134] The end of the Tasmanian Aborigines appears to have been caused by a variety of factors, especially their very small (and hence especially vulnerable) initial size and the virulence of introduced diseases. Wanton killings by settlers and soldiers were of course also a factor, but almost certainly not a crucial one and the colonial government plainly did not have a deliberate policy of genocide as an aim.

Butlin's works of the early 1980s appeared at the beginning of a long period when white 'dispossession' and 'genocide' against the Aborigines moved to centre-stage as the primary concern of a wide range of intellectuals, activists and academics. The centrality of white mistreatment of the Aborigines has caused a fundamental re-evaluation of the thrust of Australian history. Previously, post-1788 Australian history was depicted as unusually placid, a record of the step-by-step triumph of a highly successful Western society committed to equality, democracy and tolerance. 'Old left' historians of Australia, such as the famous Manning Clark, generally viewed the main theme of Australian history as the growth of a democratic settler-society in place of British-imposed order based on a pseudo-aristocracy and the transportation of convicts. The treatment of the Aborigines was, to them, a minor side-issue. During the past 30 years, and heavily influenced by post-modernism, post-colonialism and feminism, white Australia's alleged dispossession of the Aborigines has, in contrast, become so central to recent historiographical narratives of Australian history that dissent, especially among academic historians, has been almost non-existent. The centrality of the mistreatment of the Aborigines by whites is certainly far more evident in Australia than, say, the dispossession of the Indians is to American history.

One could offer a number of explanations for this striking phenomenon. Until the 1960s Australia regarded itself as a wholly British outpost, and debate about Australia's past and future was made in terms of Australia's British origins. The steady diminution of Britain's links with Australia has led to an Australian identity crisis in which the nature of these links has been increasingly questioned by the intellectual left. The discrediting of Marxist modes of analysis has led the intellectual left to look for new ways of undermining the legitimacy of established society, with their critiques now voiced in ethnic and gender terms rather than in terms of class and economic 'exploitation'.[135] Then, too, there is the specific nature of Australia's Aboriginal population, which is highly visible only in very remote rural areas with small white populations, these areas being of interest only to reactionary mining companies and large-scale ranching barons. Most recent pro-Aboriginal activism has revolved around the securing of Aboriginal 'land rights', especially the *Mabo vs. Queensland* High Court judgment of 1992, which held that traditional 'native title' to outback land must be recognised by the courts. While the majority of Aborigines live in Australia's big cities, they are only a tiny, and virtually unnoticed, part of the urban population. Thus, the securing of 'land rights' can in no way affect the income, status or authority of urban white liberals (but, on the contrary, by setting a new political agenda may well enhance their authority), and is, plainly, an easy cause to support, a reform movement which can have no adverse effects for oneself. It is, in fact, very similar to the attitude of northern white liberal support for black civil rights in America in the 1950s and 1960s, a 'movement for justice' 1,500 miles away. (But one which, most notably, usually came to a halt when it involved social change in northern cities.)

For all these reasons, the years since about 1970 have seen the growth of a veritable industry highlighting the suffering of Australia's Aborigines. Dubbed the 'black armband' view of history by Professor Geoffrey Blainey, it has, for many, almost completely reversed the common understanding of post-1788 Australian history from one stressing the development of a benign and tolerant society to one with genocide and dispossession at its core. Claims of genocide and comparisons with the Nazi Holocaust have become a stock-in-trade of the writings of many recent liberal commentators and historians of Australia. Thus Philip Knightley, author of *Australia: A Biography of a Nation* (2000), wrote that

> *It remains one of the mysteries of history that Australia was able to get away with a racist policy that included segregation and dispossession and bordered on slavery and genocide, practices unknown in the civilised world in the first half of the twentieth century until Nazi Germany turned on the Jews in the 1930s.*[136]

In similar vein, Tony Barta, a Melbourne historian, asked why Australian historians have failed to confront the appropriation of a continent 'by an invading people and the dispossession, with ruthless destructiveness, of another'.[137] Barta was among the first historians consciously to compare white treatment of Aborigines with Nazi treatment of the Jews. He realised the obvious objection to such a comparison, that the Nazis deliberately murdered millions of Jews with the intention of eradicating them from Europe, while white settlers in Australia did no such thing to the Aborigines. Nevertheless, according to him, Australians have never been confronted by the idea 'that the society in which they live is founded on genocide', and that there is a 'relationship of genocide with the Aborigines which cannot [*sic*] be understood only in terms of a clear intention to wipe them out'.[138] The National Museum of Australia in Canberra, which opened in 2001, 'commemorated the genocide thesis in the very design of the building itself', being shaped 'as a lightning bolt striking the land', in conscious imitation of the Jewish Museum in Berlin, 'signifying that the Aborigines suffered the equivalent of the Holocaust'.[139]

Most of these trends came together in the debate which emerged in the 1990s over the so-called 'stolen generation' of Aboriginal children, which deeply divided Australian society. In 1994 the Australian government announced that an official inquiry would be held into the fact that, between about 1910 and 1970, many part-Aborigine children had been taken from their mothers, often without consent, and raised with white families or in dedicated mission stations and schools. This inquiry, headed by Sir Ronald Wilson, a former High Court judge, and Mark Dodson, a member of the Human Rights Commission, took evidence from hundreds of witnesses and in 1997 tabled a report, *Bringing Them Home*, which detailed the fact that probably about 10 per cent of Aboriginal children (all part-Aborigines, probably 20,000–25,000 in all) had been separated from their mothers in this way. The report recommended a formal apology and monetary compensation.[140] More relevantly for the purposes of this work, it branded the 'stolen generation' (as the removed Aborigines became known) as an example of 'genocide'. Since no 'stolen' child was killed, such a claim may seem startling, even preposterous, to many ordinary people (as indeed it struck many Australians). The claim of 'genocide' emerges from the United Nations Genocide Convention, adopted in December 1948, which Australia ratified the following year. Under Article II of this convention, 'forcibly transferring children of [a] group to another group' is deemed to be an act of genocide.

There is no doubt that hundreds of half-Aboriginal children were forcibly removed from their mothers, often in harrowing circumstances, in a manner which would universally be regarded today as constituting kidnapping.[141] (Nevertheless, one should bear in mind that probably hundreds of children are legally taken from their mothers every day in the democratic world, often following a custody battle, without any claims of 'genocide' being made.) These children were taken because the authorities at the time believed their life-chances would be materially improved if they were raised as Europeans, rather than as illiterate hunter-gatherers among a race who were, in a frequently heard view at the time, doomed to die out. Most reports of the treatment of these children in schools and mission stations are almost wholly negative, being viewed as hallmarked by hostility and violence.[142]

There is thus no dissent from the view that kidnapping half-Aboriginal children is seen today as wholly unacceptable. The question here, however, is whether the 'stolen generation' constitutes an example of genocide in any plausible sense, notwithstanding the terms of the United Nations Convention. It seems self-evident to me that it was not an example of genocide in any sense whatever, although the reasons for this have seemingly been missed by the very commentators on this question. In the first place, those 'stolen' were not Aborigines, but children with a European father and an Aboriginal mother: in other words, they were just as much Europeans as Aborigines. Why, then, should the European part of their heritage be entirely disregarded? Full-blooded Aborigines were, in fact, left entirely alone. There was thus no intent to destroy the Aboriginal community in Australia, but to raise part-Europeans in European society. Second, it is not generally known that the policy of the large-scale removal of children was common at the time throughout the democratic world, especially among impoverished and single mothers. The 1910 United States Census found that among nearly 25 per cent of white single mothers and more than 30 per cent of African-American single mothers aged under 35, their children were living in foster care: of these about 20 per cent were living in institutions.[143] Italian- and Irish-born mothers were much more likely to have 'missing' children.[144] The article detailing this does not discuss whether the fostering of such children was always voluntary, except to say that unwed mothers 'probably were more pressed than others to place children in substitute care'.[145] Fostering was often attacked by child-welfare advocates at the time.[146] Its aim was to improve the life-chances of these children by removing them from mothers deemed, rightly or wrongly, to be unfit to raise them. This may well be totally unacceptable today, but no one at the time or since ever described the practice as 'genocide'.

There is, finally, the use of the term 'genocide' to describe a policy, however wrong-headed, in which no one was killed and whose aim was to enhance the life-chances of those affected. Even among harsh critics of this policy, few are entirely happy with a usage of the term which seems to fly in the face of common sense. So, indeed, there should be profound dissatisfaction with the use of the term 'genocide' in this way. Suppose that Nazi policy towards Europe's Jews had consisted precisely of what white Australia did to the 'stolen generation' of Aborigines? Suppose that, instead of mass murder, Nazi policy consisted of forcibly removing half-Jewish children, those with an 'Aryan' father, from their Jewish mothers, and raising them in German schools and Lutheran missions as Germans, leaving all other Jews entirely alone? Would anyone in his senses regard this as 'genocide', let alone the greatest crime in modern history? The answer is obviously 'no', and is evidence of how common sense has largely ceased to be a factor in recent debates about this topic.

Slavery and the slave trade

For centuries, millions of human beings lived out their lives as slaves: in order to procure these slaves, millions more died in the process of being captured, kidnapped and transported or died prematurely while in bondage. Slavery existed in most societies prior to the modern era, including Greece, Rome, India and China, but most critiques of slavery have focused on the enslavement of Africans by European Christians to be transported and employed in North and South America and, to a lesser extent, on the enslavement of many peoples, including white Europeans, in the Muslim world, especially in north Africa.[147] That slavery was a grotesquely barbaric and inhuman institution no one doubts: the question here is whether it can be described as genocide. Recent essays by historians of genocide have tended to focus on both the racism and the wanton destruction of life in the institution of slavery, but have also carefully contrasted slavery with (most notably) the Jewish Holocaust.[148] This is just as it should be, since the aim of both the enslavement process and the institution of slavery was, by definition, to keep a significant slave population alive as workers, while the aims of the Nazis during the Holocaust was, by definition, to kill all of Europe's Jews. In fact, if slavery was a form of 'genocide', in the commonly accepted meaning of this term, then it was a very peculiar kind of genocide, since its aim was to keep a great many of its victims alive. Conceptually, one is on firmer ground in viewing slavery as a prime example of what is often termed 'democide', mass killing, since unquestionably very great numbers of persons died as a result of slavery, although, again, these deaths were incidental to (but some would say an intrinsic part of) the very institution of slavery.

Western slavery, as it was organised by Europeans and practised against Africans between the early sixteenth century and the mid-nineteenth century, actually consisted of three unrelated components, each of which had its own dynamics and casualty figures. The first was the capture and enslavement of Africans; this was followed by the 'Middle Passage', the shipment of Africans to the New World (or, occasionally, elsewhere); finally, there was the world of slavery itself in the western hemisphere, especially plantation slavery in which most blacks found themselves and were forced to live and work.[149] The opinion most often voiced by contemporary anti-slavery advocates was that the most murderous phase of the three was the first, the capture and enslavement of blacks and their transportation to coastal slave ports and 'factories', there to be shipped to America, and that most of the murderous destruction (often genocidal in the narrowest and most direct sense of the term), although organised by Europeans, was carried out by local black African tribes against other Africans. Sir Thomas Fowell Buxton (1786–1845), one of the greatest and most influential of British Abolitionists, believed, based on eye-witness accounts, that more Africans were killed by the slave capturers than were actually exported to America: more than half died in the process of capture.[150] Nearly all this bloodshed was carried out by local African tribes: Europeans seldom moved far from the coastal trading ports and were always too limited in number to capture any considerable number of Africans. The 'royal middlemen', the tribal rulers of coastal Africa, enriched themselves (with the full blessing of the European slave traders) by enslaving their fellow Africans. As Oliver Ransford put it, citing an (unnamed) contemporary source,

Every year, the instant the season was favourable, the whole of Guinea became involved in the fighting [for slaves]. 'Scarcely are the rains over . . . ere the noise of battle and the din of warfare is heard at a distance with all its attendant horrors; mothers snatching at their children, with a few necessary articles, flee for their lives; towns after being pillaged of as much cattle as the banditti require are immediately set on fire; columns of smoke ascend to the heavens; and the cries of those who are being butchered may be more easily conceived than expressed.' The slave trade, as a contemporary chronicler of Africa comments, had ensured that *'the whole or greater part of that immense continent is a field of warfare and desolation; a wilderness in which the inhabitants are wolves to each other'.*[151]

'The world has known many petty tyrants, but few so pretentious, barbarous and avaricious as the caboceers [African 'middlemen' slave traders] of the Niger delta. They were utterly without scruple. Whenever the slavers' ships appeared off the coast they would send a fleet of war canoes out on the "grand pillage", and when they returned with captives, drove hard bargains for them with white customers.'[152] The King of Wydah (on the Gold Coast) was said to earn 'near twenty thousand pounds' in a few years.[153] In one raid, 4,500 persons were allegedly killed 'on the spot', with earlier eye-witnesses reporting (very implausibly) that 10,000 or even 60,000 natives were killed in 'grand pillages' by local kings.[154] As well as the slaughters occasioned by the process of capture, vast numbers of slaves also died on the march to the coast from inland districts, often 500 or even 1,000 miles away. The suffering of these wretched people, men, women and children, in these forced marches was unbelievable: according to Buxton, mortality often reached 30 per cent in ten days of travel.[155] High rates of slave mortality were also known when they were in 'detention' on the slave coast, awaiting the arrival of the slave ships.[156]

Because they were largely carried out by blacks against other blacks (although they were organised by white Europeans) comparatively little has been written about this aspect of enslavement compared with the infamous 'middle passage', the voyage to America. With slaves packed like sardines into tiny, primitive vessels, high mortality rates were only to be expected as the norm. The usual estimate is that about 15 per cent of slaves died during the voyage. This appears to have fairly firm statistical backing. Eltis' comprehensive study of transatlantic slave migration between 1500 and 1760 (of course some slaves were transported after 1760) found that 4,380,000 Africans left that continent for North or South America, of whom 3,770,000 arrived, 86.1 per cent.[157] Thus, it would seem that 610,000 African slaves died *en route* to America in the first 260 years of slavery in the western hemisphere, about 2,346 per annum. Most readers will probably regard this as an unexpectedly (very) low number, especially as many would have died, in common with the crew of the ship, in ocean storms or of disease. But it was, after all, the purpose of any slave ship to bring her human cargo safely to America, or the voyage would be unprofitable. Most slaves transported to America were males, just over 60 per cent.[158] Despite these considerations, the inhuman horrors of the 'Middle Passage' should not in any way be minimised. 'No words can describe the horrors of the scene, or the sufferings of the Negroes,' a naval officer wrote to Buxton about conditions on board a slave ship. 'It is not in the power of human imagination to picture to itself a situation more dreadful or more disgusting.'[159] 'The shrieks of the slaves, especially women, on awakening in the morning, expecting to find themselves in their own country, but realising that they were in chains on a slave ship, bound for an unknown destination, were a memorable feature of the transatlantic voyage.'[160]

Once in the New World, Africans faced a world of slavery, that is, of ceaseless toil without pay, without freedom of movement, without citizenship rights or education, and without the legal structure of marriage, inheritance or a normal life. Rates of mortality were very high, especially in the West Indies, where the death rate was calamitous. 'In the British and French West Indies, in Dutch Guyana, and in Brazil, the death rate of slaves was so high, and the birth rate so low, that these territories could not sustain their population levels without large and continuous importations of Africans,' Fogel and Engerman concluded.[161] They believe that the 'rate of natural decrease' varied from 2 to 5 per cent per annum, in part because of the low number of women. Many died 'in seasoning', an initial period following importation, when 'planters made a deliberate attempt to break the slaves' spirits and loosen their links with Africa'.[162] In the United States, however, the slave population grew considerably and constantly, although the importation of slaves to America from Africa was prohibited in 1807. The number of slaves in the United States rose from 697,624 in 1790 to 1,538,022 in 1820, to 3,204,313 in 1850 and to 3,953,760 in 1860, just before the outbreak of the Civil War.

Putting all this together into some kind of credible demographic picture is difficult, given the paucity of truly exact information. If 50 per cent of enslaved blacks were killed before they left Africa, and if, say, 6 million were successfully transported to America over the whole period 1500–1870, this would suggest that 6 million blacks died before even embarking for America, albeit over a 370-year period (or 16,216 per annum over the whole period).[163] To this figure, however, must be added perhaps 900,000 who died on the 'Middle Passage', and at least several million who died prematurely in slavery in America, especially in the West Indies and also, in all likelihood, in Latin America.[164] The death toll from slavery in the western hemisphere over the 370-year period of its existence must thus be reckoned at 10 million or so, bearing carefully in mind that this figure contains so many estimates which may be wildly mistaken that it might well be inaccurate by orders of magnitude. And bearing carefully in mind that American slavery was organised by white Europeans, purely in order to secure economic gain, it is also nonetheless true that of these 10 million estimated dead blacks, possibly 6 million were killed by other blacks in African tribal wars and raiding parties aimed at securing slaves for transport to America. Although this death toll of 10 million occurred over a 370-year period (27,027 per annum over the entire period), it is obviously one of the very greatest demographic catastrophes definitely known to history before the twentieth century.

American slavery also sparked one of the greatest and most successful reform movements in history, led by just those elements which, in the English-speaking world, have almost always been responsible for ameliorating the condition of indigenous and oppressed peoples: Evangelical Christians and secular liberals. In 1772, Granville Sharp obtained the famous judgment from Lord Mansfield that slavery could not legally exist in Great Britain, and that any slave who touched British soil automatically became free (this freeing the estimated 20,000 slaves living in Britain). From 1787 onwards came the British Abolitionist movement, led by the Evangelical William Wilberforce (1759–1833), which managed to secure the end of the British (and American) slave trade in 1807. The emancipation of slaves in the Empire, chiefly in the West Indies, came (with compensation to the slave owners) in 1834, thanks to such activists as Sir Thomas Fowell Buxton. It has frequently been observed that the British parliament countenanced the abolition of slavery only when it became unprofitable, and had been overtaken by newer manufacturing industries.[165] The abolition of slavery in the British Empire was intended to be accompanied by the widespread return of former slaves to Africa, with Sierra Leone being organised for this purpose.

In the United States, of course, the end of slavery had to wait for nearly another 30 years, the rise of the American Abolitionist movement, the secession of the Southern states in 1860–61, and a Civil War in which over 600,000 men were killed. American Abolitionism had Protestant Evangelicalism and secular radicalism at its heart, especially the former, and the rhetoric of the anti-slavery cause was almost always redolent of Evangelical millenarianism. 'If God wills ... that all the wealth piled by the bondman's 250 years of unrequited toil shall be sunk, and every drop of blood drawn with the lash shall be paid by another drawn with the sword, so we must still say, as it was said three thousand years ago, "The judgments of the Lord are true and righteous altogether"'; the English language's greatest orator thus summarised and defended the Abolitionist cause shortly before slavery's end. That slavery was also grossly inconsistent with the very foundations of both American liberalism and, most emphatically, American capitalism, with its assumption of free and voluntary labour, was also self-evident and lost on few. For Victorian Christian morality, too, the fact that slave families could be broken up and individual family members, including children, literally 'sold down the river' at the whim of the slave-owner, made it not merely an intolerable abomination but one whose eradication was worth fighting for and dying for. Slavery lingered on in parts of Catholic Latin America where there was a large black population, being finally abolished in Cuba only in 1886 and in Brazil only in 1888.

The slave trade to the New World was, however, only a part of a larger picture. In addition to the slave trade and the institution of slavery masterminded by Europeans, there was the slave trade and the institution of slavery directed from the Muslim world. Slavery in the Muslim world lasted far longer than did slavery in the Christian world: it is reputedly not extinct even now.[166] It would appear that during the centuries in which slavery existed in the Christian world, about one-quarter of the total number of captured African slaves were transported to the Muslim world.[167] Under Islamic law, no Muslim is (theoretically) allowed to enslave another Muslim, and all slaves transported to the Muslim world from Africa were pagans.[168] They were subject to all the sources of mortality experienced by slaves intended for the western hemisphere, although catastrophically high rates of mortality on forced marches and transports across the desert replaced the horrors of the 'Middle Passage'. It would thus seem that about 1.5 million African blacks were shipped from the interior of Africa to the Muslim world during the centuries when slavery existed in the Americas, with (presumably) at least an equal number perishing in the process of being captured or transported. This figure frankly sounds very low, and could easily have been far higher; whatever the actual figure, it must be *added* to the estimates of slaves captured or transported to the New World.

Muslim slave-traders did not, however, content themselves with 'pagans', but also captured *Christians* as slaves in large numbers, especially on the dreaded Barbary Coast (Morocco, Algeria, Tunisia, Libya) of North Africa. According to one recent historian, 'between 1530 and 1780 there were almost certainly and quite possibly a million and a quarter white, European Christians enslaved by the Muslims of the Barbary Coast'.[169] Between 1530 and 1730, extraordinarily, 'nearly as many Europeans were taken forcibly to Barbary and worked as slaves as were West Africans hauled off to labour on plantations in the Americas'.[170] The possibility of enslavement became dreaded throughout the Christian world, and continued until Western navies became strong enough to challenge this Islamic barbarity; indeed, the possibility of enslavement only ceased with the colonisation of Algeria by France in 1830. Death rates among Christian Barbary slaves were apparently extra-ordinarily high, about 24–25 per cent per year.[171] Some Western Christian slaves were successfully ransomed or escaped, but many quickly died of disease or starvation, or remained in bondage for years. Just before the end of Barbary slavery, some *Americans* were captured and enslaved; the United States fought a little-known war with Tripoli [now Libya] in 1804–05 over the enslavement and holding for ransom of its citizens. The well-known 'Millions for defence – not one cent for tribute' became a popular slogan at the time. In 1815, an American squadron of eight ships killed the last great Barbary corsair leader, Raïs Hamidon, whereupon the Bey [king] of Tripoli was compelled to return all American captives.[172] This hopefully did not come too late for one young American seen by Captain (later Admiral Sir) William Dillon, a British officer, who visited Algiers in 1812:

During my leisure hours I had visited the grounds where the Christian slaves were set to work. It was a painful sight to behold those poor fellows under the lash of a Moor, watching all their actions and inflicting a cut with his whip if he noticed anyone idle. Several spoke to me, but I could not give them any hopes. While listening to their misfortunes, a fine fellow came and caught hold of the skirt of my coat ... He was an American, a lad about 17, most beautifully limbed ... However, painful as it was to refuse the supplications of this Adonis, his being a subject of the United States, I explained to him, prevented my interference in his behalf, and I hurried away from the spot, regretting that I had been near it.[173]

Although many accounts of Islamic slavery stressed that it was often relatively more benign than Negro slavery in the New World, it was subject to hazards unknown in the West. As late as the early twentieth century, eunuchs (castrated males) still presided over the harems of the sultans and other local rulers. The death rate following castration was extraordinarily high. Some British observers said that 199 out of 200 selected for castration died in the process. One well-informed British consul of the 1880s, A.B. Wylde, reported that each eunuch represented 'at the very least, 200 Soudanese done to death ... say there are 500 eunuchs in Cairo today: 100,000 Soudanese had to die to produce these eunuchs'.[174] Arab and Muslim slave trading and raiding for slaves in east Africa, orchestrated from Zanzibar, continued long after it had ended in the Christian West. Indeed, remarkably, it apparently continues today throughout the Islamic world.[175] Sudan and Mauritania are among the worst offenders, although slavery still survives, or survived until very recently, in Saudi Arabia and the Gulf States.[176] Unlike the Christian West, there was little or nothing whatever in the way of an Islamic reform movement aimed at the abolition of slavery: anti-slavery reforms invariably came from Western 'imperialism', especially the colonial governments and Christian missionaries. Western governments invariably abolished slavery, often quite effectively, whenever they colonised an Islamic area (such as the 'Barbary Coast'), or put extreme pressure on Islamic governments to abolish slavery, as the British did in Egypt when they conquered it after the 1870s.[177] Slavery would presumably not, even today, have been abolished in the Islamic world had it not been for

Western imperialism and the West's influence. In recent years these facts have been successfully obfuscated – who, today, even knows of the slaves of the 'Barbary Coast'? – and pointing them out invites charges of 'Orientalism' and 'racism'; nonetheless, the Islamic slave trade continued long after it had ended in the Christian West.[178]

A number of smaller-scale instances of alleged genocide, all occurring during the century before 1914, deserve to be considered separately.

The Thugs of India and their suppression, 1809–40

For centuries, a religious sect existed in India to rob and murder hapless strangers. This was the Thugs or Thuggees, who lasted for at least 500 years before they were suppressed by the British authorities between about 1809 and 1840. They are reliably estimated to have murdered at least 40,000 persons each year (some reports say 50,000). A very conservative estimate is that the Thugs murdered 1 million people between 1740 and 1840, although it seems likelier to one writer on the subject that 'probably nearer three million than one' were killed.[179] Thuggee apparently began no later than the thirteenth century, and they were already numerous in north India and the Bengal area by around 1600.[180] Over this long time-period, it is, indeed, quite possible that Thuggee claimed literally tens of millions of victims. Thugs were devotees of the goddess Bhowani or Kali, the 'Black Mother', the Hindu goddess of death and destruction. For hundreds of years gangs of Thugs (the word is derived from the Sanskrit *sthag*, to conceal, and is pronounced 'tug'; the plural or descriptive term, 'thuggee', is pronounced 'tuggee'), usually numbering between 20 and 50 men, but on occasion numbering up to several hundred, roamed the roads of India looking for victims for Kali. The normal Thuggee mode of operation was to pretend to be merchants or soldiers, but travelling without weapons in order to disarm suspicion. Most Thuggees made a point of seeming to be courteous and mild looking, and gradually won the confidence of their victims, in particular in learning whether travellers were likely to be quickly missed by relatives. Thuggees sometimes travelled long distances with their intended victims before striking: there was one case known to the British authorities where a gang travelled with a family of 11 persons for 20 days before murdering the whole party without being detected; another gang accompanied 60 persons for 160 miles before they found a suitable occasion to murder the whole party.[181]

Once the Thuggee gang succeeded in gaining the confidence of an individual or party – generally this occurred in the evening when everyone sat together talking and smoking – a signal would finally be given by the gang leader. Two of the gang would grab the hands and feet of the victim, while the third, the leader, manipulated the *ruhmal*, the strangling handkerchief, quickly murdering their victim without bloodshed. Thuggees proverbially showed no moral qualms whatever about murdering wholly innocent men, regarding their acts as a religious sacrifice to Kali. Many compared killing a man to stalking and killing a deer or water buffalo.[182] Bodies were buried in graves dug by the *kussee*, the sacred pick-axe.[183]

By the early nineteenth century, hundreds of Thuggee gangs roamed the Indian countryside, organised in elaborate corps with various ranks, the *bhurtotes*, the actual stranglers, being the highest, to be achieved only after promotion through the lower ranks of scouts, buriers of the dead and holders of limbs. Thuggee practice forbade the murder of women or children, although towards the end of its existence, women were often murdered so there would be no witnesses, while child survivors of murdered parties were often recruited into the Thuggee gangs.[184] Indigenous Indians were alone targeted by the Thugs: no European was ever known to have been killed by Thuggee.[185] Some especially proficient Thuggee killers became well-known. The best-known of all was Buhram, also known as Buhram Jemedar or Behram, the 'King of the Thugs', from Oudh, who murdered 931 victims over a 40-year period before he was hanged by the British around 1830. Buhram still figures in popular accounts of 'record-breakers' as the world's greatest-ever individual murderer (that is, as opposed to bomb-droppers or mass murderers in wartime); indeed, his record makes that of 'Jack the Ripper', who became world-famous for brutally killing five prostitutes in London's East End in 1888, look like that of an amateur who raids the church poor box.[186] Other leading Thuggees known to the British when they suppressed the movement included Ramzam, who murdered 604 persons, and Futty Khan, whose record of 508 victims in just 21 years made him seem a worthy rival to Buhram.[187] On average, it was assumed that a typical Thug murdered eight persons a month, when victims were available.[188] It was also estimated that, just before suppression, 10,000 persons were murdered every year by Thuggees in the region of central India between the Nerbudda and Sutlef rivers.[189]

By the early nineteenth century, while the Hindu religious element in Thuggee was still strong, many believed that it had degenerated into a system of highway robbery *per se*, with Thugs protected by local rulers and receiving a percentage of the booty stolen from the hapless victims. Although Thuggee was, theoretically, a purely Hindu religious cult, it was also clear that many Thugs were local Indian Muslims, despite the fact that the 'worship' of Kali would presumably be regarded as sacrilegious by Islam. From about 1826 until the 1840s, the British launched a great campaign, led by Lord William Bentinck (1774–1839), the Governor-General, and Colonel (later Sir) William Sleeman (1788–1856), to suppress Thuggee, which the British succeeded in doing by about 1850, with the approval of virtually all Indians. About 1,400 Thugs were hanged or transported for life between 1826 and 1835.[190] By the end of 1841, over 3,806 Thugs had been arrested and tried.[191] By the 1850s it appears that Thuggee was virtually extinct.

Thuggee was only one of many enormities in pre-colonial India effectively suppressed by the British. Dacoity (gangs of non-religious armed robbers and murderers who plagued India at this time) was also suppressed. Like the Thugs, they planned their raids with meticulous care, employing disguises and bribing local officials if caught.[192] Sleeman was also instrumental in suppressing Dacoity by 1850. The British also suppressed human sacrifices, infanticide, suttee (widow burning) and other barbaric local practices. One wonders what today's 'post-colonialists', automatically critical of Western 'Orientalism' and imperialism, think of this. Perhaps, indeed, in their view the Thugs should be resurrected and welcomed back as practitioners of an authentic custom among an indigenous people with whom the imperialists had no right to interfere.

Little today is remembered of Thuggee. While the term 'thug' has of course passed into the English language, probably not one person in a thousand who uses the term to describe a drug-addicted urban mugger knows the origin of the term. Despite its luridness, no work has appeared on Thuggee in English in 35 years, and the best-known popular depiction of Thuggee probably remains the classic film *Gunga Din*. This famous 1939 Hollywood classic contains the memorable portrayal of a Thug leader by the virtually unknown actor Eduardo Giannelli, one of the unforgettable depictions of villainy in screen history.[193] Few histories of modern India written in the past quarter-century even mention Thuggee, let alone those written from a 'post-colonial' viewpoint: it is precisely the sort of appalling practice, wholly the product of 'noble' indigenous peoples and whose suppression was wholly the work of Europeans, which today's 'post-colonialists' would prefer to ignore.

Was Thuggee genocide? Not, of course, in the commonly accepted sense, since no group was targeted for extermination. Thuggee was, however, certainly an example of mass murder on a grand scale, mass murder which was at least countenanced by the pre-colonial local authorities and which was ostensibly based in religious practice. Thuggee may well have claimed more victims than all the wars of the nineteenth century combined.

The Irish Potato Famine, 1845–51

The Irish Potato Famine was almost certainly the greatest demographic catastrophe to strike Europe between the Thirty Years War and the First World War. The currently accepted view by scholars is that 1,082,000 more people died in the Famine than would have been the case in normal times.[194] In addition, no fewer than 2.1 million Irishmen emigrated between 1845 and 1855 – 1.5 million to the United States, 340,000 to Canada, 200,000–300,000 to other parts of Britain, several thousand to Australia and elsewhere – thus creating an enormous Irish Diaspora, with profound political and cultural consequences for these societies.[195] As a result, chiefly of the Famine, Ireland was one of the few places in the Western world whose population declined in the late nineteenth century: after increasing from 6,802,000 in 1821 to 8,175,000 in 1841 (and to perhaps 8.5 million at the beginning of the Famine in 1845), it declined by 1.6 million by 1851, when the census revealed a population of only 6,552,000, and then, through steady emigration caused by the lack of opportunities at home and by chain migration, fell to 5,799,000 in 1861 and to only 4,459,000 in 1901, barely 55 per cent of its population in 1841.[196]

The cause of the Irish Potato Famine is seemingly as clear as anything can be. In September 1845 Ireland was suddenly struck by a particularly virulent epidemic of potato blight caused by the fungus *phytophthora infestans*, which also ravished potato crops elsewhere in Europe. Its source is unknown: it may have been brought in guano (bird droppings used as fertiliser) from South America, or via an infection from potatoes imported from the United States.[197] Despite the appointment by the British government of a distinguished scientific committee headed by Dr Lyon Playfair, no one knew how to combat the fungus, which destroyed much of the Irish crop for several years in a row. While Ireland produced other foodstuffs, especially oats, most of the large, already impoverished rural population of small tenant farmers and agricultural labourers fed on potatoes as a staple of life, and quickly perished of starvation or diseases caused by malnutrition.

Nothing like this was seen, or was to be seen, in the English-speaking world in modern times, and apart from its enormous and tragic human costs, the Famine was a seminal event in Irish history, doing much to increase hostility to the Union with Great Britain which had been instituted in 1801. Nevertheless, its sole relevance to this work lies in claims that it constituted an act of 'genocide' by the British authorities. Plainly, since the Famine was caused by a happenstance fungal epidemic rather than by deliberate action, such a claim must seem as far-fetched as it would be to label the deaths caused by a catastrophic earthquake or volcano as 'genocide'. Nevertheless, since the 1860s it has repeatedly been made. In an influential work published in 1861, *The Last Conquest of Ireland (Perhaps)*, the revolutionary Irish nationalist John Mitchel (1815–75) claimed savagely that 'The Almighty, indeed, sent the potato blight, but the English created the Famine', and that the British government could, if it had wished, saved many more lives, inaction which Mitchel attributed to deliberate malignity.[198] Mitchel's charge was one of the earliest accusations of what might now be termed deliberate genocide ever made about a modern state. Despite what one recent Irish historian has stated to be its 'evident distortions of fact and suppression of evidence that did not fit his thesis', Mitchel and his work began a recurrent theme in discussions of the Irish Famine, to be echoed from time to time by Irish nationalists and British radicals.[199]

In the twentieth century, Cecil Woodham-Smith, in his well-known popular account of the Famine, *The Great Hunger: Ireland 1845–49*, severely indicted British government policy: reviewing this work in the

New Statesman, gadfly historian A.J.P. Taylor stated that 'all Ireland was a Belsen', and that 'The English governing classes ran true to form. They had killed two million Irish people.'[200] Rather surprisingly given this description, Taylor does not argue that the British government consisted of Himmlers and Eichmanns. 'Russell, Wood, and Trevelyan [British government ministers of the time] were highly conscientious men ... [who] were gripped by the most horrible, and perhaps the most universal of human maladies: the belief that principles and doctrines are more important than lives. They imagined that rules, invented by economists, were as "natural" as the potato blight.'[201] Taylor's reference here was to the prevalent belief in laissez-faire economics, based in 'economic law' as the best solution to the plight of the Irish, a belief that had also triumphed emphatically in 1846 with the repeal of the Corn Laws and the general enactment of free trade by the British government. In the late twentieth century, a strand of Irish nationalist activism and post-colonialist historiography has re-emphasised the allegedly genocidal aspects of the Irish Famine. A New York-based Irish Famine/Genocide Committee exists. In the 1980s, most remarkably, the New York State Legislature passed a law making it mandatory to teach, in colleges and universities in New York state, that the Irish Famine was a deliberate act of British genocide, as grotesque an example of interference with academic freedom, based purely in political pressuring, as can be imagined.[202] The alleged origins of the British response to the Famine in anti-Irish racism have been stressed by some recent historians.[203]

Britain's response to the Famine went through a number of phases. When the Famine first struck in the autumn of 1845, a Tory government headed by Sir Robert Peel was in office in London and, of course, had responsibility for Ireland. There is general agreement that its response to the crisis was reasonably good. It purchased large amounts of Indian corn (maize) from America (a grain apparently detested by many Irishmen), initiated public works schemes, and held inquiries into the causes of the potato blight. Peel's Tory government, however, fell in July 1846 following his repeal of the Corn Laws, unpopular with most of his own party, and was succeeded by a Whig-Liberal government, headed by Lord John Russell, which held office until February 1852. It was much more committed, in a doctrinaire sense, to laissez-faire and individual initiatives than was Peel's government, and its progressive mid-Victorian liberalism, although fully committed to religious freedom, did contain an element of anti-Catholicism, its leaders viewing the Catholic church as the fountain-head of backwardness and superstition.[204]

There is general agreement, even among modern historians, that the Russell government failed to do all it might have done to alleviate Irish suffering between 1846 and 1851. Its reliance on workhouses, on voluntary aid by religious groups like the Quakers, its refusal to extend eligibility for substantial relief to anyone owning more than one-quarter acre of land, its failure to restrict the *export* of grain *from* Ireland by the few successful farmers, and above all its niggardliness in spending during a dire emergency, have all been widely criticised.[205] The contrast drawn by the economic historian Joel Mokyr, between British government expenditure on the Famine – £10.5 million – and the cost of the ill-fated Crimean War, which began a few years later – £69.3 million – has become widely known.[206] On the other hand, the efforts of the British government should not be automatically dismissed. In July 1847 a total of 3,030,712 persons, an incredible number, were being fed under the Soup Kitchen Act. [207] The requirement that no 'outdoor relief' (that is, outside a workhouse, as was forbidden at the time) could be given, was almost uniquely waived during the Famine. With the best will in the world, it took from one to three months for grain to arrive in Ireland from America.[208] Free trade and laissez-faire were seen by most British intellectuals as panaceas of a kind, especially given the extraordinary struggle, capped by success in 1846, to repeal the Corn Laws. Ireland was regarded, even by many Irishmen, as hopelessly overcrowded, given its failure to industrialise and its primitive one-crop agricultural base, and many viewed emigration, to America and the Empire, as inevitable.[209]

None of this, however, can deny the extraordinary scenes of horror and suffering which the Famine brought. In scenes reminiscent of Dachau and Belsen a century later, one eyewitness in west Cork in December 1846 'entered some of the hovels' of those dying of starvation.

In the first, six famished and ghastly skeletons, to all appearances dead, were huddled in a corner on some filthy straw ... I approached with horror, and found by a low moaning that they were still alive ... in a few minutes I was surrounded by at least 200 such phantoms, such frightful spectres as no words can describe, either from famine or fever. Their demonic yells are still ringing in my ears, and their horrible images are fixed upon my brain.[210]

While starvation was apparently the major cause of death in the least industrialised areas of western Ireland, dysentery and other diseases probably killed far more people overall, including those in workhouses: while a government in the 1840s could indeed alleviate starvation, it could do almost nothing about cholera or typhoid.[211] Expectations and stereotypes of Irish Catholic backwardness almost certainly also had an effect on the extent of relief: had those caught in the Famine been British Protestants, it is at least arguable that more might have been done.[212] On the other hand, there *was* no Famine in the rest of Britain, even though the 'hungry forties' are often seen as the nadir of poverty created by the British Industrial Revolution: most factory workers and miners in Britain living in appalling conditions were mainly Protestants, as were those affected by the Highland Clearances. The Irish Famine cannot in truth be described as an example of genocide, but nor, in truth, was it nineteenth-century Britain's finest hour.

The Taiping Rebellion, 1850–64

Arguably the most murderous military action fought in modern times before the twentieth century was the Taiping Rebellion, the insurrection and civil war which raged in central China between about 1850 and 1864. Nearly all accounts of the Taiping Rebellion state that 20 million people were killed as a result.[213] By way of contrast, there were an esti-mated 8,021,000 military battle deaths by all combatants in the First World War, in addition to an estimated 6,643,000 civilian deaths (of which 2 million occurred in Russia and 2,150,000 in Turkey).[214] Even low-keyed historians, not prone to hyperbole, concede that, as Jack Gray puts it, Taiping was

> *the longest, fiercest, and most destructive war of the nineteenth-century world. A million insurgents were under arms. An area as great as that of France and Germany combined was devastated and much of it depopulated. No quarter was given, and none asked for; a hundred thousand Taipings died in Nanjing rather than surrender. Almost none survived.*[215]

The course of the Taiping Rebellion, although thoroughly bizarre, has been well-documented by historians. Its underlying causes, however, remain in considerable dispute.[216] Taiping was led by Hong Xinquan (1813–64; generally known before the recent reform of Chinese transliterations as Hung Hsiu-ch'iian), a member of the Hakka minority, ethnic Chinese who were known for their high literacy rate and hard work, but who were seen as recent migrants and disliked by the majority.[217] Hung, like many other bright youths, sat for and four times failed the examination to join the Mandarin civil service, an examination with a pass rate of only 1 per cent. On the journey to Canton to take the examination yet again he read a pamphlet by a Chinese follower of Christianity, and, following a nervous breakdown induced by his repeated failures, in 1844 became converted to a variant of Christianity in which (after hearing voices in a vision) he became convinced that he was the younger brother of Jesus Christ.[218] Hung began to convert members of his family and other Hakka to his new religion, which combined an extreme form of puritanical Calvinism with an authoritarian structure, and by the end of 1850 there were at least 10,000 'God-worshippers' and perhaps as many as 30,000, who were increasingly organised into an army having as its goal nothing less than the overthrow of the Manchu (or Qing) dynasty, which had ruled China since 1644. Hung declared himself to be the emperor of a dynasty or kingdom known as Taiping Tianguo ('Heavenly Kingdom of Transcendent Peace'), by which his rebellion is known. It was intended to be a theocracy, combining pseudo-Christian and Confucian elements, and had certain proto-socialist elements as well as fierce hostility to drug addiction and other antisocial behaviour then rampant in China.

During the early 1850s Taiping enjoyed remarkable success, capturing a swath of major cities including Wuhan, Jinjiang and Nanjing. It appeared that by about 1853 Taiping could easily capture Beijing and install itself as the new dynasty, but a combination of poor tactics, bad luck and a revivified Qing government eventually stopped them after much bloodshed. The Qing forces were crucially aided by Western, particularly British soldiers, such as Captain Charles 'Chinese' Gordon and the American mercenary Frederick T. Ward, who headed the so-called 'Ever-victorious army'. It was during the latter phases of the rebellion that the extraordinary slaughters of this civil war occurred, generally slaughters initiated by the Qing armies against Taiping and their supporters, who resisted with religiously derived fanaticism. Eventually the Qing forces were victorious, with Hung dying in July 1864, either through suicide or disease.[219]

Taiping was only the most far-reaching of many rebellions and instances of civil strife in China during the nineteenth century. Most historians agree that the corrupt and inefficient Qing dynasty, unable to cope with the challenge presented by the Western world and the threat of Western imperialism, brought this situation upon itself. Why Taiping should have so nearly succeeded remains disputed. Many have remarked on the diverse nature of the support it enjoyed, as well as its rigorous puritanism. It appealed to many diverse marginal elements in Chinese society, ranging from failed examinees to river pirates who lost their 'livelihood' after British military intervention.[220] In the latter phases of Taiping, one of its major leaders, Hong Rengan, sought to introduce a policy of thorough-going westernised reform somewhat similar to that successfully introduced in Japan a decade later.[221] Had he succeeded, the entire course of modern Chinese history might have been different and lacking in the murderous turmoil which distinguished it until very recently. The affinity of Taiping (despite many differences) to both the Chinese Nationalists and to the Chinese Communists has frequently been noted by historians.

This work has often been critical of apparently exaggerated casualty statistics offered for many genocides and democides, and the casualty figures of the Taiping rebellion appear, if anything, to be even more dubiously hyperbolic than most. The proposition that a civil war insurrection in a remote area of China, fought with primitive weapons between two ethnically identical armies, in a venue where the intended victims could often flee, might have been responsible for more than twice as many deaths as resulted from all the military operations in the First World War seems, frankly, absurd. Some experts have, indeed, warned against exaggerating the numbers of Taiping casualties. Writing in 1973 about the recapture of Nanking (Nanjing) from the Taipings in 1864, Jen Yu-Wen stated that 'According to Tseng Kuo-fan's memorial, over 100,000 rebels were killed'. But this, he further states, 'would have been impossible. Reliable accounts put the total population before the fall, about half soldiers, at 30,000 or less and subtracting those who died in fighting ... [or] escaped ... the number of "rebels" actually killed by the Hsiang Army must have been less than 10,000.'[222] Other casualty figures suggested by this expert also appear very much lower: 10,000 dead in Fukien, the same number in the Kiangsi border region.[223] One might assume, too, that many horrifying depictions of this extraordinary carnage would be common from the numerous Western missionaries, merchants and soldiers in China at the time. In fact, such depictions from Western sources are *not* common.[224]

One might, therefore, dismiss accounts of the Taiping death-toll as yet another exaggeration, with even less in the way of credible supporting evidence, than most alleged massacres outside the modern West. Yet a careful consideration of all the evidence does seem to suggest that a slaughter of epochal dimensions occurred at the end of the Taiping rebellion, and that reasonably good quantitative and qualitative evidence exists to confirm this conclusion. Most of this has been compiled by the historian Ping-ti Ho, in his *Studies on the Population of China, 1368–1953* (Cambridge, Mass., 1959). Ho compared the census figures in eleven localities and prefectures in Anhwei, Chekiang and Kiangsu provinces, the most heavily affected areas of China, before and after Taiping, and found a decline in population from 8,939,000 to 2,887,000, a decrease of 6,052,000 or 68 per cent.[225] In one of the hardest-hit areas, Kuang-teh county, total population declined from 310,999 in 1855 to only 5,078 in 1865, a loss of 98 per cent.[226] Chin-t'an county, 50 miles southeast of Nanjing, saw its population decline from 700,000 to 33,000 by 1864.[227] Some provinces of the lower Yangtse region had larger populations in 1850 than in 1953.[228] Much of this huge loss appears to have been caused by starvation and disease, but deliberate slaughter on a grand scale was certainly commonplace. In Kiangsi province, the Hsui river was coloured red for 100 li (about 30 miles), and navigation was blocked by corpses.[229] According to Frederic Wakeman Jr, 'Travellers passing through the once populous Yangtze provinces could go for days without seeing more than rotting corpses, smoking villages, pariah dogs. Ningpo became a "city of the dead", with no trace of its half million inhabitants, save for the canals, "filled with dead bodies and stagnant filth".'[230]

How many actually died in the Taiping Rebellion remains unclear, but the number must be very large indeed. Probably 10 million dead is a reasonable estimate: 15 million is probably more likely, even if 20 million may be an exaggeration. Arguably nothing like a slaughter of this magnitude was seen again before the Second World War. 'Although we have had an Auschwitz in modern times, it would really seem as though the Germans were only beginning to reach the degree of massacre that the Taipings came to regard as normal, and even if the Jews had been able to retaliate on the same scale, Central Europe would still have scarcely been as desolated as was a large part of China during the Taiping rebellion,' T.H. Hollingsworth has written.[231] The ultimate cause of this catastrophe – religious fanaticism, the systematic breakdown of China's traditional ruling structure, rural overpopulation, the direct or indirect consequences of the West's impact on China – are debatable, and probably reflect as well the happenstance response to the rise of a charismatic religious leader in an empire internally weakened, although strong enough to defeat and eradicate this challenge to its authority.[232]

Paraguay and the War of the Triple Alliance, 1864–70

One of the strangest but most interesting examples of something very akin to genocide in the nineteenth century took place in Paraguay, the remote inland state in South America, between 1864 and 1870. Paraguay's previous history was extraordinarily peculiar. Paraguay was developed during the seventeenth century as a missionary colony of the Jesuit order, who ruled the Christianised Indian population as a virtual slave society. Overseen by Jesuit priests, parties of Indians were marched 'to the sound of music, and in procession to the fields, with a saint borne high aloft' to work the various fields, returning in the same way, a 'perpetual Sunday school' in the words of one Scottish visitor.[233] The state continued to bear the mark of its Jesuit-dominated past after the Jesuits were expelled by the Spanish in 1768. Paraguay achieved its independence in 1811, and from 1814 until his death in 1840 was ruled by Dr José Rodriguez de Francia (1766–1840), a creole lawyer, who proclaimed himself 'supreme dictator' of Paraguay ('*el supremo*', apparently the first man to be known by this title). In a manner somewhat resembling Pol Pot in Cambodia 150 years later, Francia attempted to exclude all foreign influences of any kind from Paraguay, making it entirely economically self-sufficient. No relations with any foreign power existed during most of his reign. Increasingly paranoid, he killed or tortured on a grand scale.[234] He was succeeded as dictator by Carlos Antonio Lopez (1790–1862), who relaxed Francia's rule somewhat but enriched himself and his family whenever possible. Both Francia and Lopez were of partially Indian descent and spoke fluent Gurani, the native language; they were probably supported by the Indian majority, who apparently approved of their campaigns against local Spanish aristocrats and Paraguay's neighbouring states. Lopez was succeeded as president by his son Francisco Solano Lopez (1827–70), a theatrical, murderous megalomaniac of the familiar Latin American kind. Napoleonic in his ambitions, Solano Lopez wished to declare himself emperor of Paraguay, in imitation as well of neighbouring Brazil, which at the time was a monarchy.

Solano Lopez now became embroiled in a festering dispute with his larger neighbours, Brazil, Argentina and Uruguay, intervening in Uruguayan internal politics in a way which provoked conflict. In 1864 he declared war on Brazil, entering Argentinian territory in an effort to attack Brazilian bases. The three neighbouring states responded by forming, in 1865, the Pact of the Triple Alliance, whose armies attacked Paraguay and destroyed the Paraguayan army. Instead of a short war, however, Paraguayan resistance continued in suicidal fashion for the next four years, Solano Lopez leading his armies in six major battles in which no quarter was given. Slaughter followed upon slaughter. Solano Lopez routinely executed anyone suspected of cowardice or lack of zeal. Disease and starvation became rampant throughout Paraguay. It appears that in the latter phases of the war, the Triple Alliance was carrying out a deliberate war of annihilation against the Paraguayan population.[235]

At the end of the War of the Triple Alliance, the condition of Paraguay 'almost beggar[ed] description'.[236] It is quite possible that no war fought in modern times, even on the Eastern Front in the Second World War, was quite so destructive. The normal estimate is that of a Paraguayan population of somewhere between 450,000 and 900,000, only 221,000 survived the war, of whom *only 28,000 were adult males*.[237] Women aged 15 or over outnumbered men by (according to the source) four to one or seven to one. About 35,000 Paraguayan soldiers were killed, and at least 415,000 from the direct effects of the war, disease and hunger.[238] These figures are, of course, not necessarily precise and subject to revision, but it appears certain that a slaughter of historical dimensions occurred in this remote

South American state.[239] Amazingly, two generations later Paraguay fought yet another bloody conflict with its neighbours, against Bolivia and *de facto* against Chile, the Chaco war of 1932–5, over the disputed, possibly oil-rich Chaco desert area, in which Paraguay acquitted itself well, gaining the greater part of the Chaco area.[240]

King Leopold and the Congo Free State, 1885–1908

What in recent years has become one of the best-known and most widely discussed instances of nineteenth-century colonial genocide occurred in the Congo Free State (later known successively as the Belgian Congo, Zaire and the Democratic Republic of the Congo) between 1885 and 1908. At the time, this enormous area of nearly 1 million square miles, virtually unknown and unexplored by Europeans until the third quarter of the nineteenth century, was the personal property of King Leopold II (reigned 1865–1909) of Belgium, who ran it as a personal fiefdom, largely for profit. (Leopold referred to himself as the 'proprietor' of the Congo, and 'willed' it in 1890 to the Belgian people after his death.) Such an arrangement had no parallel in European colonialism: all other colonies were administered, at least in theory, by the government of the European colonial power, and were therefore subject, at least theoretically, to public oversight and review of some kind. King Leopold II was not a tyrant or megalomaniac, but actually already had a reputation as an anti-slavery reformer and presided, at home, over a relatively democratic, progressive nation, one whose neutrality was guaranteed by treaty and had no conscription until 1913.[241] Leopold regarded himself as a 'royal businessman' and was a skilled financial manipulator. The Belgian bourgeoisie showed little interest in colonising the Congo: Leopold appears to have been its driving force, possibly in order to rival Belgium's neighbour the Netherlands, which owned the Dutch East Indies and other colonies. He was also motivated by the philanthropic ends of ending slavery and spreading Christianity, but his chief aim was to make money for himself.[242] As early as 1871, it was Leopold who sent H.M. Stanley to 'find' the missionary David Livingstone. The Congress of Berlin of 1884–5 confirmed Leopold's personal rule of the Congo, which was then confirmed by the Belgian Parliament, and which formally began in August 1885.

Under Leopold's reign, the Belgian army gradually extended Belgian rule throughout the Congo, ousting the Islamic slave traders and merchants who had previously controlled the foreign trade of the area.[243] Leopold's administration of the Congo was headed by the *Force Publique*, a largely Belgian administrative cadre, chiefly consisting of men of lower middle-class origin, with many Italians and others. It also gradually built up an African army, numbering over 19,000 by 1898, one of the largest in Africa.[244] It was this native army, controlled by Leopold's cadre, which carried out the enforcement of what some have seen as the genocidal aspects of Belgian rule. The European administrative apparatus in the Congo was remarkably small, numbering only 1,428 men in 1908.[245] There were, additionally, only another 2,500 or so Europeans – missionaries, nuns, merchants, doctors, teachers and the like – in the Congo, even in 1910.[246]

The charges of genocide which have been made about King Leopold and the Congo arose out of his peculiar methods of economically exploiting and 'developing' this vast country.[247] Under Leopold's direct rule, the Congo was divided into a series of areas of economic concession, somewhat like the chartered companies of the seventeenth century, which were, in effect, joint partnerships between Leopold and friendly private trusts. In addition, a vast area of the central Congo was reserved for Leopold as a private Crown Domain.[248] The development of a private native economy, or of independent foreign companies working in the area, was strictly forbidden. After a briefly profitable venture into the barbaric ivory trade, Leopold made the exploitation and export of rubber (which, rather oddly, is derived from plants grown in the tropics) the mainstay of the Congolese economy. With the vast expansion of bicycle use in the 1890s and of motor cars in the 1900s, demand for rubber soared, and the value of Congolese rubber exports grew from 459,000 Belgian francs in 1889 to 47.3 million by 1903.[249] Vast armies of native labourers, virtually slaves, were coerced by the Belgian authorities in the Congo into obtaining rubber for export. Each concession company had districts under its control, which were 'taxed' for quotas of rubber and other products. Pay was as low as possible, and the *Force Publique* ensured the quota was met by force and bloodshed. Vast areas of the Congo were apparently turned into virtual slave labour camps or gulags to obtain rubber for Leopold's coffers.

Rumours quickly reached Europe of something truly scandalous in the Congo Free State, whose economic and political structures were radically different from the other African colonies. Leopold's activities became internationally notorious, however, with the crusading work of E.D. Morel (1873–1924), a clerk of radical inclination working in the offices of Elder, Dempster, a major Liverpool shipping firm. Morel had known of previous charges of outrageous practices in the Congo but discovered, from the books of his company, that the natives were being paid virtually nothing, that vast quantities of firearms were being imported secretly into the Congo, and that huge profits were being made at enormous human cost.[250] Working almost single-handedly, he launched what became an extraordinarily well-publicised campaign against the 'Congo atrocities', writing innumerable articles and books such as *King Leopold's Rule in Africa* (1904) and *Red Rubber* (1907) which became internationally known. He also enlisted the support of Sir Roger Casement (1864–1916), a British consular official, to investigate the Congo firsthand; Casement's *Report* (1903) had an international impact. (Casement, a dedicated radical of similar ilk to Morel, was controversially hanged for treason in 1916 for allegedly conspiring with Germany to foment revolution in Ireland.) In 1908 Leopold was forced, through international pressure, to give up control of the Congo and totally reform its administration.

Recent historians, especially Adam Hochschild, have made truly extraordinary claims about the catastrophic nature of Leopold's rule in the Congo. According to a variety of expert opinion noted by Hochschild, between 1880 and 1910 the population of the Congo declined by half, from 20 million to 10 million.[251] If accurate, this obviously represents one of the greatest examples of population decline in modern history. Hochschild is clear, however, that 'outright murder was not the major cause of death in Leopold's Congo, although it was most clearly documented'.[252] Hochschild cites such examples as a 'state officer, Simon Roi', who in 1899, not realising that a missionary was present, 'bragged about the killing squads under his command'. The missionary believed that Roi and his soldiers killed (or mutilated) 6,000 people in six months, with many children killed 'with the butt of their guns'.[253] In his 1904 work on the Congo, Morel himself presented a 'Table showing roughly depopulation where data are available [*sic*]', which enumerated such alleged events as 'Mongrella concession – Many thousands killed since 1897 in rubber wars undertaken with assent and cooperation of authorities'.[254] Outright murders, according to Hochschild, were less important than 'starvation, exhaustion, and exposure' as thousands fled their villages to avoid forced labour, disease, especially an epidemic of sleeping sickness, and an allegedly plummeting birth rate as men were forced to labour on the rubber plantations.[255]

A demographic catastrophe of historic proportions might have occurred in the Congo Free State as Hochschild and others believe but there are also good grounds for considerable doubt about the scale involved, even while readily admitting the horrors of Leopold's appalling regime. That *some* population decline occurred was conceded by the Belgians, as well as local missionaries, who attributed most of it to a sleeping sickness epidemic of extraordinary virulence which killed 500,000 Congolese in 1901 alone.[256] That a catastrophic sleeping sickness epidemic did occur in the Congo between 1895 and 1906 is well-documented in medical sources.[257] Spread by tsetse flies and long present in the Congo basin, the incidence of sleeping sickness escalated greatly as Belgian trading stations spread.[258] Because drugs were unavailable (that the disease was spread by the tsetse fly was not yet fully understood) the Belgians 'treated' the disease by isolating infected villages into special hospitals, where thousands died. In 1903 Leopoldville, the capital, 'was reportedly left with less than 100 natives' because of the epidemic.[259] Leopold actually attempted to fight the epidemic by inviting a team from the Liverpool School of Tropical Medicine to study the disease first-hand. The epidemic subsided only in 1912.[260] It can, of course, be argued, as Hochschild does, that epidemics like sleeping sickness 'almost always take a drastically higher and more rapid toll among the malnourished and the traumatized', and epidemics were certainly responsible for most of the deaths of indigenous peoples in the New World and Australia.[261] Nevertheless, this epidemic was apparently greatly augmented by the fact that Belgium's trading stations exposed many more natives to this epidemic than previously.

More basically, it appears almost certain that the population figures given by Hochschild are inaccurate. There is, of course, no way of ascertaining the population of the Congo before the twentieth century, and estimates like 20 million are purely guesses. Most of the interior of the

Congo was literally unexplored if not inaccessible. For many years until 1908 *Whitaker's Almanac*, the standard reference work, stated that the population of the Congo 'probably did not exceed eight million'. In that year, for no apparent reason, and long after Leopold's depredations began, it suddenly revised its population estimate upward to '15 to 20 million'. The first Congolese census was held in 1921 (not 1924 as Hochschild, p.238, states), and revealed a population of 6,481,000. This then increased to 8.8 million in 1930 and to 10.4 million in 1942, a generation after Leopold's enormities had ceased. It seems perfectly clear from this that the Congo's population was never anything like 20 million under Leopold, and that any reduction in population was of a much more limited number.

As well, European missionaries on the spot seldom blamed the Belgians for any population losses, often attributing destruction and decline to such factors as pillaging by tribes in revolt.[262] Most long-term missionaries saw the Congolese natives as greatly benefiting from the coming of the Belgians, who ended slave trading, vastly improved the rights of women (previously virtually slaves), and introduced Western medicine, education, sanitation , and new trades.[263] Some recent scholars have also viewed components of the evidence used against Leopold's regime as distorted. 'The sight of abandoned villages was a depressing spectacle to an inexperienced European, who assumed that the villagers had fled in terror, not realizing that they might have left to pursue shifting cultivation,' Gann and Duignan have claimed.[264] Belgium was, in the view of some, a 'soft target', surprisingly unpopular in Britain and elsewhere until it was invaded by Germany in 1914. Protestant missionaries, resenting Catholic domination, formed another source of possible exaggeration.[265] Producing an accurate account sheet from all this is difficult. On balance, it is possible that, say, 1.0–1.5 million persons died in the Congo under Leopold's rule, reducing the net population by 1 million or so. Most died of disease, which may well have been augmented by the appalling features of Belgium's rule. It seems, however, almost impossible to believe, on the evidence available, that 10 million people died in the Congo Free State, while any fair judgement must also take into account the positive features of Belgian rule, such as the ending of slavery and endemic tribal warfare, and the introduction of Western medicine and education.

The Hereros of South-West Africa, 1904–7

The most recent of the genocides and democides examined in this section was the slaughter of the Herero people of German South-West Africa (now Namibia) between 1904 and 1907. Although one of the most remote instances of mass killing in this section, and one probably involving the smallest loss of life, it has attracted considerable attention from scholars of 'genocide studies', especially as it seems to presage some of the more infamous slaughters of the twentieth century.[266] The Hereros were one of three or four indigenous peoples in German South-West Africa, a remote corner of the continent mainly consisting of the Kalahari desert, but with potential for cattle farming and for German naval bases. The other peoples there were the Berg Damara and the Ovambos – like the Hereros Bantu-speakers – and the Nama, better known in the West as 'Hottentots'. All were nomadic hunter-gatherers like the Australian Aborigines, although the Hereros were nomadic cattle herdsmen; their earlier notion of communal ownership of the land had evolved into a kind of feudalism with influential tribal chiefs, the most influential of whom was Supreme Chief Samuel Maharero.[267] Germany, engaged in grabbing the 'crumbs' of the Third World left to it by the older imperial powers, annexed the area in 1883–5, usually by offering conciliatory terms of protection to the local tribes.[268] Initially it attracted few German settlers (remarkably, its 'Imperial Commissioner' in 1888 was Dr Heinrich Goering, father of Hermann), although early in the twentieth century a considerable expansion took place, as German farmers arrived and railways were built. The indigenous peoples were increasingly forced to live in reservations, and German imperial rule proved consistently harsher than most other imperial regimes.[269] In early 1904, Maharero sparked a Herero uprising against the Germans, specifically sparing women, children, the English, Boers and missionaries: they were joined by the Nama people late in the same year. Nearly 150 Germans (and a few others) were killed during this uprising, generally in isolated farmhouses. The corpses of German men were often castrated and mutilated in other ways.[270]

This was the trigger for German retaliation on so massive a scale that it is often labelled genocidal. The German government sent General Lothar von Trotha to South-West Africa. He was a career soldier who had 'resort[ed] to ruthless methods in suppressing popular uprisings in

[German] East Africa ... as well as the Boxer Rebellion in China in 1900–01'.[271] Von Trotha claimed that 'I know enough tribes in Africa. They all have the same mentality insofar as they yield only to force. It was and remains my policy to apply this force by unmitigated terrorism and even cruelty. I shall destroy the rebellious tribes by shedding rivers of blood and money. Only thus will it be possible to sow the seeds of something new that will endure.'[272] This he proceeded to do with consistent and relentless brutality, killing many Hereros and Nama outright, and driving thousands more into the desert to die. Atrocities were apparently commonplace. Women were raped and bayoneted; women were burned alive, while men were 'slowly strangled with fencing wire and left hanging in rows like crows'; and were killed by bayoneting.[273] The war involved 17,000 German soldiers (of whom 2,000 were killed), lasted four years, and cost the equivalent of £20 million, about £1 billion in today's money.[274] At the end of the war the Hereros, and to a lesser extent the Nama, were decimated as peoples. It was widely estimated that the Hereros numbered between 60,000 and 100,000 before the war (with 80,000 the usual figure), with the Namas estimated at 20,000. In 1911 only 15,130 Hereros remained alive, a decrease of over 80 per cent, as well as 9,781 Nama, a decline of over 50 per cent.[275] In addition 'one third of the Berg Damara, who had not joined in the uprising, were killed because the German troops were unable to tell them from the Herero'.[276] As well, vast tracts of native lands were confiscated.

Von Trotha's blood-chilling messages and pronouncements are strongly reminiscent of those issued by Nazi SS officers during the Jewish Holocaust 40 years later. 'Within the German boundaries, every Herero, whether found armed or unarmed, with or without cattle, will be shot. I shall not accept any more women and children. I shall drive them back to their people – otherwise I shall order shots to be fired at them.' This proclamation, issued in October 1904, was signed 'The Great General of the Mighty Kaiser, von Trotha'.[277] Nothing like this, it is fair to say, was ever known in British or French imperialism, certainly after the mid-nineteenth century. As a general rule, von Trotha had the consistent support of the Kaiser and the German 'Establishment'. In the Reichstag, the natives were often referred to as 'baboons', and one settler's petition stated that 'any white man who has lived among natives finds it impossible to regard them as human beings at all in any European sense'.[278]

There was at first a distinct absence of the kind of humanitarian protest movement which was certain to arise in Britain over colonial atrocities. On the other hand, it also must be noted that such a protest movement, from long-serving German officials in South-West Africa, missionaries, and domestic liberal opinion did eventually arise, which forced the German Chancellor, Prince von Bulow, to moderate von Trotha's policies.[279] The destruction of the Hereros does seem, by any standard, to constitute genocide, and – unlike many other examples discussed in this chapter – to unite the colonial period with the Age of Totalitarianism, a bridge to the genocide of the Armenians (carried out by the Turks with some German assistance) a decade later, and then to the horrors of the Nazi regime. In particular, the deliberate use of the state's military power to decimate a civilian population pointed the way ahead.

Conclusion

A number of conclusions and common patterns are evident from a careful analysis of all these appalling events. Most importantly, the impact of European man in the New World, Australia and Africa was, at least initially, catastrophic from a demographic point of view, with sharp declines in population occurring almost everywhere. Nevertheless, it seems equally clear that these population declines were seldom deliberate, and, in America and Australia, were most often the result of the introduction of virulent diseases. The conquest of the New World and Australia by Europeans also engendered movements of humanitarian reform, stemming from Christians and secular radicals, aimed at ameliorating the condition of the indigenous peoples or the abolition of slavery. Such humanitarian movements did not exist in other cultures, for instance in the Muslim world.

As the studies of smaller-scale democides show, too, many of the appalling slaughters which occurred during the nineteenth century were undertaken by Third World peoples against one another, the activities of King Leopold's regime in the Congo Free State (although almost certainly often exaggerated in its extent) and of the German colonialists against the Hereros being the main exceptions. In the case of Thuggee (and of other heinous practices and enormities not considered in detail here) the effects of the European presence was manifestly ameliorative, as were the long-term effects of the introduction of Western medicine, education and legal and customary practices, and the inclusion of these places in the modern global economic system.

Did 'genocide' in its commonly accepted sense, implying the deliberate mass murder of a race or class, occur in any of the milieus or events examined here? Some aspects of the treatment by American Western pioneers and of America's governments towards the Indians of the United States might well be so described, bearing in mind that their removal westwards, rather than the physical destruction of these tribes, was at least officially the aim of America towards its Indians, while the activities of the German military authorities towards the Hereros of German South-West Africa would certainly be termed genocidal by most observers.[280] Apart from these, however, only with difficulty can even the appalling loss of populations described here be considered as genuinely genocidal, while many of the worst massacres were instituted by Third World peoples against other peoples of the Third World.

Notes and references

1   See, for example, David E. Stannard, 'Uniqueness as Denial: The Politics of Genocide Scholarship', in Alan S. Rosenbaum, *Is the Holocaust Unique?* (Westview, Conn., 2001), and Ward Churchill, *A Little Matter of Genocide: Holocaust and Denial in the Americas, 1492 to the Present* (San Francisco, 1997).

2   J.P. Dunn Jr., *Massacres of the Mountains: A History of Indian Wars of the Far West, 1815–1875* (New York, 1886, reprinted New York, 1958), p.11, citing Henry R. Schoolcraft, *Historical and Statistical Information Respecting the History, Condition and Prospects of the Indian Tribes of the United States* (Philadelphia, 1851–5). This estimate is a sophisticated one, based on the number of hunter-gatherers and maize-growers likely to occupy an acre of land.

3   See the discussion in Russell Thornton, *American Indian Holocaust and Survival: A Population History Since 1492* (Norman, Oklahoma, 1982), pp.25–33. Other discussions of this question include Bruce G. Trigger and William R. Swagerty, 'Entertaining Strangers: North America in the Sixteenth Century', in Bruce G. Trigger and Wilcomb E. Washburn, eds., *The Cambridge History of the Native Peoples of the Americas: Volume I, North America – Part I* (Cambridge, 1996), pp.362–9; Noble David Cook, *Born to Die: Disease and New World Conquest, 1492–1650* (Cambridge, 1998); David

E. Stannard, *American Holocaust: The Conquest of the New World* (Oxford, 1992); and Ward Churchill, *op.cit.*, esp. pp.131–7. See also Alfred W. Crosby Jr., *The Columbian Exchange: Biological and Cultural Consequences of 1492* (Westport, Conn., 1972); and 'Indians of the United States in the Nineteenth Century' in Frank Chalk and Kurt Jonassohn, *The History and Sociology of Genocide* (New Haven, Conn., 1990), pp.195–203.

4 Trigger and Swagerty, *op. cit.*, p.363.

5 Thornton, *op.cit.*, p.26.

6 *Ibid.*, pp.30–1.

7 *Ibid.*, pp.26–32. For an impressive critique of these and other recent high estimates of Indian population figures, see David Henige, *Numbers From Nowhere: The American Indian Population Debate* (Norman, Oklahoma, 1998). Henige's work demonstrates the almost wholly arbitrary nature of many recent population estimates, and the apparent refusal of many scholars who have proposed these figures to engage in rational debate with their critics.

8 Although, as Thornton astutely notes (*op.cit.*, p.36) there is no reason to suppose that North American Indian numbers were at their all-time peak in 1492, and then declined. The evidence, especially from the 'mound builder' cultures around the Mississippi valley, is that Indian numbers may well have been higher several centuries earlier, and declined, for unknown reasons, up to 1492 and beyond.

9 Krzywicki (1859–1941) was a leading Polish philosopher and social scientist. Described as 'undoubtedly the greatest Marxist thinker in Polish history', he was injured in an air raid during the Nazi invasion of Poland in 1939 and died of a resultant heart attack in 1941.

10 Krzywicki, *op.cit.*, p.71 and Appendix II, pp.318–543, where comprehensive tribal population data is presented.

11 The 'nadir' figures are given in Thornton, p.31.

12 *Ibid.*, p.28.

13 *Ibid.*, pp.28–9.

14 Thornton, *op.cit.*, pp.44–7; Cook, *op.cit.*, *passim*.

15 *Ibid.*, pp.1–14.

16 Thornton, *op.cit.*, pp.44–7. Syphilis is often said to have been brought to Europe from the New World, but it appears that this is incorrect (*Ibid.*, p.45).

17 *Ibid.*, p.39.

18 *Ibid.*, p.37–41.

19 *Ibid.*, p.92–4. Precise figures between 1702 and 1910 (broadly similar to Thornton's) are given in Krzywicki, *op.cit.*, pp.463–4.

· 20 Krzywicki, *op.cit.*, pp.101–2.

21 *Ibid.*, p.102. On this topic see Jeffrey P. Blick, 'The Iroquois Practice of Genocidal Warfare (1534–1787)', *Journal of Genocide Research*, Vol.3, No.3 (November 2001).

22 Krzywicki, *ibid.*

23 *Ibid.*, p.103, citing the narrative *Jesuit Relations.*

24 Lawrence H. Keeley, *War Before Civilization: The Myth of the Peaceful Savage* (Oxford, 1996), p.68.

25 *Ibid.*

26 Cited in Brian W. Dippie, *The Vanishing American: White Attitudes and U.S. Indian Policy* (Lawrence, Kansas, 1982), p.4.

27 Keeley, *op.cit.*, pp.88–94.

28 *Ibid.*

29 Thornton, *op.cit.*, p.52.

30 For extreme perceptions of the view of the European settlers in North America as little different in their logic of conquest from the Nazis, see Churchill, *op.cit.*, especially pp.129–288, and 'The Dispossession of the Apache', in Mark Cocker, *Rivers of Blood, Rivers of Gold* (London, 1999), pp.187–268. The most famous work on the theme of Indian dispossession remains Dee Brown, *Bury My Heart at Wounded Knee: An Indian History of the American West* (New York, 1970).

31 Churchill, *ibid.*; Klaus Franz, *Indian Reservations in the United States: Territory, Sovereignty, and Socioeconomic Change* (Chicago, 1999).

32 Cited in Thornton, *op.cit.*, p.48.

33 *Ibid.*

34 *Ibid.*, p.49.

35 *Ibid.*, p.48.

36 Steven T. Katz, 'The Uniqueness of the Holocaust: The Historical Dimension', in Alan S. Rosenbaum, ed., *Is the Holocaust Unique?* (second edition, Boulder, Col., 2001), p.51.

37 *Ibid.*

38 See, for instance, Churchill, *op.cit.*, and David E. Stannard's 'Uniqueness as Denial: The Politics of Genocide Scholarship', in Rosenbaum, ed., *op. cit.*, esp. pp.256–9. One of the most important and often intemperate components of the contemporary debate on the Holocaust concerns claims, by such

historians as Katz, that the Jewish Holocaust was 'uniquely unique', a claim which is bitterly contested by other historians, especially those like Churchill and Stannard who are concerned with the decline in America's Indian population.

39 Churchill, *op.cit.*, pp.169–88.

40 *Ibid.*, p.220.

41 Paul M. Robertson, 'Wounded Knee Massacre, 1890', in Frederick E. Hoxie, ed., *Encyclopedia of North American Indians* (Boston, 1996), pp.694–7.

42 *Ibid.*, pp.244–5.

43 Katz, *op.cit.*, pp.50–7.

44 Keeley, *op.cit.*, p.88.

45 Michael D. Green, 'The Expansion of European Colonization to the Mississippi Valley, 1780–1880', in Trigger and Washburn, eds., *op. cit.*, pp.525–7; Katz, *op. cit.*, p.53.

46 Katz, *op.cit.*, pp.53–4. This policy towards the Indians was little different from the policy of 'Americanising' millions of children of European immigrants. See also Henry E. Fritz, *The Movement for Indian Assimilation, 1860–1890* (Philadelphia, 1963); and Frederick E. Hoxie, 'The Curious Story of Reformers and the American Indians', in *idem*, ed., *Indians in American History: An Introduction* (Arlington Heights, Ill., 1988), pp.205–28.

47 For instance, American Vice-President Charles Curtis (1860–1936; Vice-President 1929–33) frequently boasted of his part-Indian ancestry; it is inconceivable that he would have done so about a Negro ancestor, or been nominated or elected if he had known Negro ancestry. As is well-known, until 1945 there was a strict ban on employing black players in Major League baseball, America's national sport: as a result, the black community developed parallel 'Negro Leagues'. In contrast, American Indians were always allowed to play for the 'Major Leagues'. The Cleveland Indians club is named for an Indian player, and Albert 'Chief' Bender (most Indian players were known as 'chief'), a star pitcher of the 1903–17 era, of Chippewa descent, was elected to the Baseball Hall of Fame, baseball's highest honour, in 1954.

48 W. Richard West Jr and Kevin Gover, 'The Struggle for Indian Civil Rights', in Hoxie, ed., pp.275–93.

49 Pro-Indian historians point out, however, that some virulent epidemics were deliberately introduced by whites, via contaminated blankets and other items, in order to spread killing diseases among the Indians (see, for instance, Churchill, *op.cit.*, pp.151–7), for example during the French and Indian War in 1763. There is a good deal of dispute about some of these

cases. For example, the Blackfoot Indian Smallpox Epidemic of 1837–8 (noted by Churchill) was apparently caused by Blackfoot demands for purchased blankets, even though they were explicitly warned by local agents that they were contaminated. (George Childs Kohn, ed., *Encyclopedia of Plague and Pestilence* (New York, 2001), p.28.)

50 Miguel León-Portilla, 'Mesoamerica Before 1519', in Leslie Bethell, ed., *The Cambridge History of Latin America, Volume I: Colonial Latin America* (Cambridge, 1984), pp.14–24; Stuart J. Fiedel, *Prehistory of the Americas* (Cambridge, 1987), pp.301–8.

51 Fiedel, *op.cit.*, p.306.

52 *Ibid.* According to the contemporary monk Fray Diego Duran, 'I am not exaggerating; there were days in which 2,000, 3,000, 5,000 or 8,000 men were sacrificed. Their flesh was eaten and a banquet prepared with it after the hearts had been offered to the devil.' (Cited in David Korn, Mark Radice and Charlie Haws, *Cannibal: The History of the People-Eaters* (London, 2001), p.50.

53 Marvin Harris, *Good to Eat: Riddles of Food and Culture* (London, 1986), pp.106, 27.

54 Fiedel, *op.cit.*, p.306.

55 *Ibid.*, pp.302–4.

56 *Ibid.*, pp.305–6.

57 Cited in *ibid.*, pp.306–7.

58 *Ibid.*

59 Cited in Korn *et al.*, *op.cit.*, p.53.

60 Fiedel, *op.cit.*, p.337.

61 Cited in Thornton, *op.cit.*, pp.24. Thornton's work (pp.23–5) contains comprehensive lists of population estimates. Some scholars writing before Kroeber produced much higher figures: for instance Rivet (1924) estimated the population of the western hemisphere (including North America) in 1492 as 40–50 million.

62 Thornton, *op.cit.*, p.23.

63 *Ibid.*, p.24.

64 *Ibid.*, p.16. There is a table of recent estimates in Noble David Cook, *Born to Die: Disease and New World Conquest, 1492–1650* (Cambridge, 1998), p.23. Estimates of 7–8 million seem very difficult to credit. The combined population of Haiti and the Dominican Republic around 1940, after a century or more of Western control of communicable disease, is estimated at only 4.8 million. By 2001, the combined population of the two countries had risen to 15,546,000. This enormous increase was due entirely to the fact that the natural rate of increase in the populations of the two countries was about 1.8 *per annum,* wholly a product of a sharp decline in the death rate, especially infant mortality, due to modern medical techniques.

65 Nicholas Sánchez-Albornoz, *The Population of Latin America: A History* (Berkeley, Cal., 1974), p.39.

66 *Ibid.*

67 Steven T. Katz, *The Holocaust in Historical Context: Volume I, The Holocaust and Mass Death Before the Modern Age* (Oxford, 1994), p.91. This is an extraordinary admission by Katz, whose magisterial work was written to demonstrate the demographic uniqueness of the Jewish Holocaust.

68 Sánchez-Albornoz, *op.cit.*, pp.60–3.

69 *Ibid.*

70 *Ibid.*, pp.54–60; *idem,* 'The Population of Colonial Spanish America', in Bethell, *op.cit.*, Volume II, pp.3–14; Cook, *op.cit.*

71 Cited in Cook, *op.cit.*, p.2. Las Casas, however, thought that the triumph of Christianity justified the Spanish conquest. For a critique of Las Casas, see Henige, *op.cit.*, pp.67–8, 168–73.

72 Cook, *op.cit.*, pp.5–6. See also 'The Conquest of Mexico', in Cocker, *Rivers of Blood,* pp.27–112.

73 Sánchez-Albornoz, *op.cit.*, p.51. The 'Black Legend' was often popularised in Protestant Europe by anti-Catholic writers.

74 Cook, *op.cit.*, p.7. Sánchez-Albornoz, *op.cit.*, pp.53–4.

75 Ward Churchill, 'Genocide of Native Populations in Mexico, Central America, and the Caribbean Basin', in the article 'Native Americans, Genocide of', in Israel W. Charny, *Encyclopedia of Genocide, Volume II* (Santa Barbara, Cal., 1999), p.432.

76 J.H. Elliott, 'The Spanish Conquest and Settlement of America', in Bethell, *Cambridge History, Volume I,* p.182. Many of the claims made by Ward Churchill in this series of articles in the Charny *Encyclopedia* present dubious, hyperbolic claims as established fact.

77 Michael C. Meyer and William L. Sherman, *The Course of Mexican History* (Oxford, 1983), p.109.

78 Elliott, *op.cit.*, p.183.

79 On which see, for example, 'Encomienda and Corregimiento', in Charles Gibson, *The Aztecs Under Spanish Rule: A History of the Valley of Mexico, 1519–1810* (Stanford, Cal., 1964), pp.58–97.

80 See Josep M. Barnadas, 'The Catholic Church in Colonial Spanish America' and Eduardo Hoornaert, 'The Catholic Church in Colonial Brazil', in Bethell, *Cambridge History, Volume I,* pp.511–40 and 541–56.

81 Gibson, *op.cit.,* p.100.

82 *Ibid.,* p.100. It has been suggested that the ceremony of the Eucharist, in which Christians 'eat' and 'drink' the 'body and blood of Christ', was reminiscent of Aztec ceremonies of human sacrifice: Eli Sagan, *Cannibalism: Human Aggression and Cultural Form* (New York, 1974), p.66.

83 Barnadas, *op.cit.,* p.518.

84 Gibson, *op.cit.,* pp.112–14.

85 Another major contrast to the situation in North America is that, unlike the settlement of the American West, the number of Spanish and Portuguese settlers was relatively small for many decades. The total Spanish population of the Americas in the 1575–99 period was only about 150,000, while there were only about 30,000 Portuguese in Brazil at this time. (Sánchez-Albornoz, *op.cit.,* p.69.)

86 This author lived in Australia between 1976 and 1995, and has followed events there closely since then. For this reason, this section, which is representative of trends in many societies, is somewhat longer and more detailed than one might expect.

87 While there were brief visits to parts of Australia's coast by Portuguese and other travellers and by Captain James Cook in 1770, it might be noted that Australia was effectively unclaimed and certainly uninhabited by Europeans until January 1788. At that time, the 'First Fleet', sent from England with about 700 convicts and several hundred sailors, arrived in Botany Bay, New South Wales (now Sydney). New South Wales (Sydney and its hinterland) was settled by British émigrés and convicts by 1840, Victoria (Melbourne and its hinterland) between 1835 and 1870, and the other four Australian colonies (later states) by the 1880s. By 1890, Melbourne, which had a white population of zero in 1835, had a total population of over 500,000 and one of the most advanced infrastructures in the world.

88 Cited in F. Lancaster Jones, *The Structure and Growth of Australia's Aboriginal Population* (Canberra, 1970), p.2.

89 *Ibid., op.cit.,* p.3.

90 N.G. Butlin, *Our Original Aggression: Aboriginal Populations of Southeastern Australia, 1788–1850* (London, 1983), pp.146–7, 175–6. For many years Butlin and Lancaster Jones held research professorships at the Australian National University in Canberra, their offices perhaps 50 feet apart; this fact did not, however, engender an identity of view!

91 Butlin, as noted, was the *doyen* of Australian economic historians. His work on Aborigines largely consists of 'demographic modelling' of factors such as food supplies, disease, infanticide, abortion, etc., on overall Aboriginal population trends, all extremely hypothetical. His work contains literally not one comment on the size of individual Aboriginal tribes.

92 Krzywicki, *op.cit.*, p.63.

93 *Ibid.*, and pp.316–17.

94 Cited in Lancaster Jones, *op.cit.*, pp.2–3.

95 Primitive hut 'villages', capable of housing up to 1,000 people were, however, occasionally observed in northern New South Wales and elsewhere by early travellers. As well, there were apparently 'eel canals' in Victoria used for a primitive form of fishing (Butlin, p.164). Nevertheless, 'in most parts of the continent . . . the only cloak or rug at night was a tiny elongated fire': Geoffrey Blainey, *Triumph of the Nomads* (Sydney, 1983), p.193.

96 The average size of tribes found by Tindale was 655 in New South Wales and 426 in Victoria, compared with a national average of 435. Butlin relies to an extent on the research of Harry Lourandos, an anthropologist who suggested that harvesting and land management by Aborigines, especially in south-east Australia, changed and intensified, especially through fish farming, drainage and the building of 'villages' of a kind. See 'Palaeopolitics: Resource Intensification in Aboriginal Australia and Papua New Guinea', in Tim Ingold *et al.*, eds., *Hunters and Gatherers: History, Evolution and Social Change* (Oxford, 1988). But the population figures he provides (pp.153–4) – of between '800 and 1,000 people' at one gathering and 2,000–3,000 at an inter-tribal eel festival – simply do not suggest an overall population of the scale claimed by Butlin.

97 Lancaster Jones, *op.cit.*, p.2.

98 Having had no apparent previous interest in this area, in the latter part of his career Butlin became, in print at any rate, a pro-Aboriginal activist, as the title of his work, *Our Original Aggression,* indicates. It is taken from a December 1838 despatch by Lord John Russell, the British Cabinet minister, to Sir George Gipps, a colonial governor in Australia, that 'it is impossible that the [British] Government should forget that the original aggression [against the Aborigines] was ours'.

99 Lancaster Jones, *op.cit.*, Table 1, p.4.

100 Butlin, *op.cit.*, p.147. Butlin sees a brief recovery in numbers to about 155,000 between 1810 and the 1820s (*ibid.*).

101 *Ibid.*, p.175.

102 *Ibid.*, pp.64–5. Many of Butlin's conclusions in this discussion are based on smallpox epidemics elsewhere, e.g. India, and may or may not be relevant to Australia.

103 *Ibid.*, p.70.

104 *Ibid.*, pp.63–119.

105 Thus, with the exception of a brief period in Tasmania's settlement, there were no forced removals of Aboriginal tribes to areas beyond white settlement, as there often were in North America.

106 Probably the most vivid popular account of these alleged massacres is Bruce Elder, *Blood On the Wattle: Massacres and Maltreatment of Aboriginal Australians Since 1788* (Sydney, 2002), although it totally fails to mention recent criticism of the accepted facts of these alleged massacres by Moran (see below, note 118), Windschuttle and others.

107 Henry Reynolds, *The Other Side of the Frontier: Aboriginal Resistance to the European Invasion of Australia* (Melbourne, 1982), pp.121–5. Reynolds' estimate has been severely criticised as a gross exaggeration by Keith Windschuttle (see below). A similar estimate of 20,000 killed was reached by Richard Broome, in M. McKernan and M. Browne, eds., *Australia: Two Centuries of War and Peace* (Canberra, 1998), pp.91–120. According to Philip Knightley, in his *Australia: A Biography of a Nation* (London, 2000), 'experts' believe that '50,000 [killings] would not be an exaggeration. It could be as high as 100,000.' Not a shred of evidence exists to support this view.

108 Ian Clark, *Scars in the Landscape* (1995), cited in Robert Manne, *In Denial: The Stolen Generation and the Right,* Australian Quarterly Essay, Melbourne (2001), p.99.

109 *Ibid.*

110 Henry Reynolds, *An Indelible Stain? The Question of Genocide in Australia's History* (Ringwood, Vic., 2001), pp.119–37. While Reynolds is probably the best-known exponent of the view that a significant number of Aborigines were murdered by whites, this book, specifically on the question of genocide, is extremely balanced.

111 Peter Bayne, 'The Legal Status of Aborigines', in James Jupp, ed., *The Australian People: An Encyclopedia of the Nation, Its People and Their Origins* (Cambridge, 2001), p.116.

112 *Ibid.*, p.119.

113 The best account of them is Henry Reynolds, *This Whispering in Our Hearts* (Sydney, 1998).

114 Keith Windschuttle, 'The Fabrication of Aboriginal History', *New Criterion,*

Vol.20, No.1 (September 2001). See also his three-part account in *Quadrant* (a leading Australian neo-conservative intellectual monthly), 'The Myth of Frontier Massacre in Australian History', October–December 2000. In addition, he is publishing a three-volume account of *The Fabrication of Aboriginal History,* based on extraordinarily wide original research, the first volume of which, on Van Diemen's Land [Tasmania] 1803–1847 (Sydney, 2002) has appeared. Windschuttle's important research represents everything that the critical historian should be doing. Many of his writings are posted on his website 'The Sydney Line' (Sydneyline.com). Windschuttle believes, and makes a compelling case for the view, that not more than about 118 Aborigines were actually killed by Europeans in Tasmania in the period from 1804–34 when they were allegedly exterminated. See Windschuttle, *Fabrication of Aboriginal History, Volume One, Van Diemen's Land, 1803–1847* (Sydney, 2002), pp.387–97.

115 Windschuttle, *ibid.*

116 *Ibid.*

117 *Ibid.*

118 Rod Moran, *Massacre Myth: An Investigation into the Alleged Mass Murder of Aborigines at Forest River, 1926* (Bassendale, W.A., 1999), cited in Windschuttle, *ibid.* The 'evidence' of a massacre was apparently fabricated *in toto* by the head of a local mission.

119 Butlin, *op.cit.*, p.175.

120 Cited in *ibid.*, p.20. Tench also adds 'but to infer that it was introduced from this cause were a supposition so wild as to be unworthy of consideration'. The smallpox 'variolous' was brought on the 'First Fleet' to inoculate its members if smallpox appeared (Judy Campbell, *Invisible Invaders: Smallpox and Other Diseases in Aboriginal Australia, 1780–1880* (Melbourne, 2002), p.62).

121 N.G. Butlin, *Close Encounters of the Worst Kind: Modelling Aboriginal Depopulation and Resource Competition, 1788–1850* (Canberra, 1982), p.27, cited in Reynolds, *An Indelible Stain?*, p.40.

122 Cited in Reynolds, *op.cit.*, p.41.

123 N.G. Butlin, *Massacres and Aboriginal Smallpox: The 1789 and 1829 Epidemics* (Canberra, 1984), p.20.

124 Campbell, *op.cit.*, p.62.

125 *Ibid.*, pp.66–82. This is only the tip of the iceberg of possible misleading accounts often widely accepted as fact about the alleged killing of Aborigines by whites. Although a widely respected and highly intelligent historian, Henry Reynolds has also been accused by conservative critics of reaching dubious conclusions. Keith Windschuttle, his most cogent critic, in mid-2000 'began a project to investigate the evidence behind Aboriginal killings'. One of the first works he looked up was an obscure university monograph which Reynolds produced in 1978, *Race Relations in North Queensland,* which the author later cited as the source of his claim that '10,000 Aborigines were killed by whites' in Queensland. The 1978 work exists only in typescript form in a few libraries. 'To my surprise, I found that it is not about Aboriginal deaths at all. It is a tally of the number of whites killed by Aborigines. Nowhere does it mention 10,000 Aboriginal dead. It produces evidence that Aborigines may have killed between 800 and 850 Europeans from 1850 to 1900. The only mention it makes of Aboriginal deaths is in one sole footnote where the author says that while it is impossible to do anything but guess at the number of natives killed, their death rate "may have been" ten times more than that of the Europeans. In other words, as well as being a false citation of evidence, this document meant that the overall historical consensus about Aboriginal deaths had a gaping hole in its empirical foundation.' When Windschuttle presented his findings at a conference, he became the victim of a campaign comparing him to David Irving. 'Most commentary was outraged that I had dared to question the orthodox position' (Windschuttle, *Fabrication*). This campaign has accelerated since the publication of his book.

126 James Morris, 'The Final Solution, Down Under', in Chalk and Jonassohn, *History and Sociology of Genocide,* pp.204–22; Mark Cocker, 'The British in Tasmania', in *Rivers of Blood,* pp.115–86. They did not use boomerangs, unlike mainland Aborigines.

127 Cocker, *op.cit.,* pp.134–5.

128 *Ibid.,* p.136.

129 Morris, *op.cit.,* p.212.

130 Cocker, *op.cit.,* p.143.

131 Reynolds, *An Indelible Stain?,* p.78.

132 Shayne Breen, 'Tasmanian Aborigines', in Jupp, *Australian People,* p.112. According to Windschuttle, however, the number of Tasmanian Aborigines at the time of the first European settlement was no higher than 2,000 (Windschuttle, *Fabrication, Vol. One,* p.371). Windschuttle makes a compelling case (pp.364–72) for this view.

133 Reynolds, *op.cit.,* p.71.

134 *Ibid.,* p.78.

135 Something of the same evolution is probably at the core of the profound change which has come over the attitude of Australian Christian activists towards the Aborigines. Prior to the 1950s, few would have doubted that

the conversion of 'heathens' to Christianity, and the establishment of mission stations and Christian schools, represented the carrying out of God's will. Loss of belief in the absolute truth of traditional Christianity, and its replacement by a vague, 'politically correct' universalistic belief in the ultimate legitimacy of all faiths has been primarily responsible for a negative reassessment of almost all Christian activities among the Aborigines, whose belief-system is no longer viewed as primitive heathenism.

136 Philip Knightley, *op.cit.*, p.107. Knightley is an expatriate journalist resident in Britain.

137 Tony Barta, 'After the Holocaust: Consciousness of Genocide in Australia', *Australian Journal of Politics and History,* Vol.31, no.1 (1984), p.154.

138 *Ibid.*, p.156. Many other similar comments can be adduced. Paul Bartrop, for instance, claims that 'Australia in the 1930s was possessed of an administrative culture that in reality practised genocide' ('The Holocaust, the Aborigines, and the Bureaucracy of Destruction: An Australian Dimension', *Journal of Genocide Research,* Vol.3, No.1, March 2001, p.83). Although I admire Bartrop as a historian, this statement in my view is very dubious: his evidence consists of comparing Australian policy towards the 'stolen generation' children with the fact that 'three days after the outbreak of war in September 1939, the Australian government announced that no more refugee immigration from ... Germany ... would be permitted' (p.81). This claim (oddly, in view of the fact that he has written several works on the topic) utterly ignores the fact that in the late 1930s Australia agreed to admit 15,000 refugees from Germany, the first time any refugees had been admitted to Australia as a matter of policy, that Australia declared war against Nazi Germany as soon as Britain did, that the 'bureaucrats' responsible for immigration and Aboriginal policy had nothing to do with one another, and, above all, that the genocide of the Jews did not begin until the invasion of the Soviet Union, nearly two years later, and was unknowable beforehand to anyone in Australia.

139 Keith Windschuttle, 'Doctored Evidence and Invented Incidents in Aboriginal Historiography', unpublished conference paper, 2001, p.1.

140 Probably the best study of *Bringing Them Home* from a pro-Aboriginal stance is Robert Manne, *In Denial: The Stolen Generation and the Right* (Australian Quarterly Essay, Issue I, 2001). Manne, a prominent Melbourne academic and journalist, was formerly a leader of Australia's intellectual conservatives but since the 1980s has moved sharply to the left. An excellent and very cogent writer, his other essays on this and related issues can be found in *The Way We Live Now: The Controversies of the Nineties* (Melbourne, 1998), and *The Barren Years: John Howard and Australian*

Political Culture (Melbourne, 2001). On this issue see also Reynolds, *An Indelible Stain?*, pp.155–79; and (on Western Australia) Quentin Beresford and Paul Omaji, *Our State of Mind: Racial Planning and the Stolen Generations* (Fremantle, W.A., 1998).

141 Manne, *In Denial,* pp.6–24, gives four typical examples.

142 See, for instance, Beresford and Omaji, *op.cit., passim.* In today's Australia, 'Aboriginal children . . . are thirteen times more likely to be removed from their homes and placed in care than other children', according to a report by the Australian Institute of Health and Welfare in December 2002. They were also 'nearly eight times more likely to be involved in proven cases of abuse, neglect or harm than other children' (Farah Farouque, 'Carers Warn of a New Stolen Generation', Melbourne *Age,* 9 December 2000, as from the newspaper's website, theage.com).

143 Carolyn M. Moehling, 'Broken Homes: the "Missing" Children of the 1910 Census', *Journal of Interdisciplinary History,* Vol.XXXIII, No.2 (Autumn 2002). The percentage of the children of unmarried mothers living in foster care thus appears probably higher than the percentage of 'stolen' half-Aborigines.

144 *Ibid.,* p.227.

145 *Ibid.,* p.209.

146 *Ibid.,* p.230.

147 The use of slave labourers by modern totalitarian regimes, especially their employment during the Second World War by the Nazis and Japanese, is a separate matter which will not be considered here.

148 Seymour Drescher, 'The Atlantic Slave Trade and the Holocaust: A Comparative Analysis', in Alan S. Rosenbaum, ed., *Is the Holocaust Unique?* (Boulder, Col., 2001), pp.97–118; *idem.,* 'Slavery As Genocide', in Israel W. Charny, ed., *Encyclopedia of Genocide* (Santa Barbara, Cal., 1999), Vol.II, pp.517–18.

149 The literature on this topic is so extensive that it is simply impossible to summarise here. A good recent work, with an extensive bibliography, is David Eltis, *The Rise of African Slavery in the Americas* (Cambridge, 2000). On North American slavery, see such classics as Kenneth M. Stamp, *The Peculiar Institution: Slavery in the Ante-Bellum South* (New York, 1956); Eugene D. Genovese, *Roll, Jordan, Roll: The World the Slaves Made* (New York, 1974); and the controversial work on the profitability of slavery by Robert W. Fogel and Stanley L. Engerman, *Time On the Cross: The Economics of American Negro Slavery* (New York, 1977).

150 Thomas Fowell Buxton, *The African Slave Trade and Its Remedy* (London, 1840), pp.98–9.

151 Oliver Ransford, *The Slave Trade: The Story of Transatlantic Slavery* (Newton Abbot, 1972), pp.62–3.

152 *Ibid.*, p.65.

153 *Ibid.*, p.61.

154 *Ibid.*, p.62, and Buxton, *op.cit.*, p.98.

155 *Ibid.*, p.109. Buxton (pp.99–113) gives horrifying descriptions of these marches. He quotes (pp.108–9) a letter from Dr Holroyd to him stating that 'these slave-hunts have produced a great depopulation in the districts where they are practised ...'.

156 *Ibid.*, pp.113–21.

157 Eltis, *op.cit.*, Table 1.1, p.9. Much higher figures for slave importations into the New World are given in other sources. Fogel and Engerman, *op.cit.* (p.16) state that 9,735,000 'Negro slaves' were imported to the New World down to 1870 (when slave importation to Brazil ceased), of whom 6.2 million came between 1701 and 1810. These figures appear to be exaggerations.

158 Eltis, *op.cit.*, Table 4.2, p.95.

159 Buxton, *op.cit.*, pp.126–7.

160 Ransford, *op.cit.*, p.90.

161 Fogel and Engerman, *op.cit.*, p.25.

162 Ransford, *op.cit.*, p.104.

163 This figure of about 6 million transported blacks accords well with much recent research, although some estimates are considerably higher. See 'Introduction' in J.E. Inikori, ed., *Forced Migration: The Impact of Export Slave Trade on African Societies* (London, 1982), esp. pp.19–38.

164 But not, perhaps, in the United States. In 1850 the average life expectancy for a slave was 36 years, compared with 40 years for a US white person (and 24 years for an inhabitant of Manchester, England in 1850) (Fogel and Engerman, *op.cit.*, p.125). This estimate has been questioned (together with much of their other relatively optimistic conclusions about American slave life) in Paul A. David *et al.*, *Reckoning With Slavery: A Critical Study in the Quantitative History of American Negro Slavery* (Oxford, 1976), especially Richard Sutch, 'The Care and Feeding of Slaves' (pp.231–301), which deals with longevity.

165 Eltis, pp.250–80, outlines a good deal of the current research on this much-debated issue.

166 On slavery in the Muslim and Arab worlds see Ronald Segal, *Islam's Black Slaves: The History of Africa's Other Black Diaspora* (London, 2001);

Humphrey J. Fisher, *Slavery in the History of Black Muslim Africa*
(London, 2001), Sir George MacMunn, *Slavery Through the Ages* (London,
1938), pp.44–82, 147–60, 181–224, 256–72; Stephen Clissold, *The Barbary
Slaves* (London, 1977); Robert C. Davis, 'Counting European Slaves on the
Barbary Coast', *Past and Present* (No.172, August 2001), pp.87–124; and
Paul E. Lovejoy, *Transformations in Slavery: A History of Slavery in Africa*
(Cambridge, 1983), esp. pp.23–43, 135–53, 184–219.

167 This was the estimate made in 1840 by Thomas Fowell Buxton (*op.cit.*,
p.72), who believed that about 150,000 slaves were taken into captivity
intended for the Christian world, and 50,000 intended for the Muslim
world.

168 *Ibid.*, p.63.

169 Davis, 'Counting European Slaves', p.118.

170 *Ibid.*

171 *Ibid.*, p.117.

172 Clissold, *Barbary Slaves,* p.155.

173 Sir William Henry Dillon, *A Narrative of My Professional Adventures
(1790–1839), Volume II, 1802–1839,* Michael A. Lewis, ed. (London, 1956),
p.215. Dillon's *Narrative* is a well-known British naval autobiography of
the Napoleonic era. Most readers may find this passage more disturbing
and horrifying than any other in this section, like reading about a man-
eating plant, a giant Amazonian snake which swallows a man whole, or
any other profoundly unnatural horror.

174 Cited in Segal, *op.cit.*, p.156.

175 *Ibid.*, pp.157–62; 199–233.

176 *Ibid.*

177 *Ibid.*, pp.152–6; Fisher, *op.cit.*, pp.332–43.

178 For instance, although a standard reference work such as Eric Foner and
John A. Garraty, eds., *The Readers' Companion to American History*
(Boston, 1991) contained enough space in its 1,226 pages for entries on
Woody Guthrie, labour organiser 'Mother Jones', and Andy Warhol, the
Tripolitan war is not so much as mentioned, probably the only American
war entirely omitted in this work.

179 James L. Sleeman, *Thug, Or a Million Murders* (London, 1933), p.232. (The
author of that book was the grandson of Sir William Sleeman who
suppressed Thuggee.) On the Thugs, see also George Bruce, *The Stranglers:
The History and Practices of the Thugs* (London, 1837); and Hiralal Gupta,
'A Critical Study of the Thugs and Their Activities', *Journal of Indian
History* (Vol.37, 1959), pp.167–77. Gupta argues that the Thuggee were

specific to the British takeover of India, ignoring their long history, and states (p.171) that they might have been anti-British in nature, although only Indians were their victims.

180 Sleeman, *op.cit.*, pp.19–20.

181 *Ibid.*, pp.25–6.

182 *Ibid.*, p.3.

183 *Ibid.*, p.8.

184 There were also some women Thugs, although these were very rare (*ibid.*, pp.152–69).

185 Sir William T.F. Horwood, 'Foreword', in *ibid.*, p.v.

186 A typical example of Behram (as he is called) listed in a popular book of superlatives is found in Mitchell Symons, *The Book of Criminal Records: Crime Lists, Figures and Amazing Facts* (London, 1994), p.12, where he is described as the second most prolific serial killer in history, just behind the (legendary and probably apocryphal) family of Sawney Bean, the Scottish cannibals in the reign of Scotland's King James I (1406–37), who are credited with '1,000' murders.

187 *Ibid.*, p.4.

188 *Ibid.*, p.237.

189 *Ibid.*, p.235.

190 *Ibid.*, p.117.

191 Bruce, *op.cit.*, p.212; Sleeman, *op.cit.*, p.238. About 500 of the worst Thugs were hanged.

192 *Ibid.*

193 It also contains the classic miscastings of Sam Jaffe as waterboy Gunga Din and of Cary Grant as a British army officer. The film is allegedly based on Kipling's famous poem, which, of course, was written many years after Thuggee was suppressed and has nothing to do with the Thugs.

194 James S. Donnelly Jr, 'Excess Mortality and Emigration', in W.E. Vaughan, ed., *A New History of Ireland, Vol.IV, Ireland Under the Union, I, 1801–70* (Oxford, 1989), p.351, citing Joel Mokyr, *Why Ireland Starved* (London, 1985), pp.253–68. Mokyr's figures, now generally accepted, are higher than the previously accepted figure of perhaps 860,000 excess deaths (*ibid.*, p.350).

195 *Ibid.*, p.353, citing Kerby A. Miller, *Emigrants and Exiles: Ireland and the Irish Exodus to North America* (New York, 1985), p.291.

196 This is, of course, the population of the whole island of Ireland, including what is now the Irish Republic and Northern Ireland: the island was not politically divided until 1922.

197 James S. Donnelly Jr, 'Famine and Government Responsibility', in Vaughan, ed., *New History of Ireland,* pp.272–3.

198 James S. Donnelly Jr., 'The Administration of Relief, 1847–51', in Vaughan, ed., *New History,* p.330; K. Theodore Hoppen, *The Mid-Victorian Generation, 1846–1886* (Oxford, 1998), p.571.

199 Donnelly, *ibid.*

200 Cited in *ibid.* Taylor's review was reprinted in his *Essays in English History* (Harmondsworth, 1976).

201 *Ibid.*

202 Apparently this requirement is not well-enforced, and the teaching of the Famine period has never been questioned. See 'The Great Irish Famine Curriculum' (on the website irishfamine.html).

203 See, for instance, Liz Curtis, *Nothing But the Same Old Story: The Roots of Anti-Irish Racism* (London, 1984), and C. Perry Curtis, *Apes and Angels. The Irishman in Victorian Caricature* (Washington, D.C., 1996).

204 Lord John Russell (later first Earl Russell, 1792–1878) introduced the Great Reform Act of 1832 into Parliament. He also certainly had a streak of progressive anti-Catholicism in his outlook, and responded, in the early 1850s, to the Pope's creation, for the first time in centuries, of English Catholic bishops, as 'papal aggression', probably the last outburst of British central government anti-Catholicism. Lord John Russell was the grandfather of Bertrand Russell, the famous philosopher.

205 For other recent balanced views on the Famine, see Alvin Jackson, *Ireland, 1798–1998* (Oxford, 1999), pp.69–86; Cormac Ó Gráda, *Black '47 and Beyond: The Great Irish Famine in History, Economy, and Memory* (Princeton, 1999); Christine Kinealy, *A Death-Dealing Famine: The Great Hunger in Ireland* (London, 1997); and Patrick O'Sullivan, ed., *The Meaning of the Famine* (Leicester, 1997).

206 Mokyr, *op.cit.,* p.292, cited in Jackson, *op.cit.,* p.768, and many other places.

207 Donnelly, 'Administration of Relief', p.309.

208 *Ibid.,* p.296.

209 See Graham Davis, 'The Historiography of the Irish Famine', in O'Sullivan, ed., *op.cit.,* esp. pp.32–7.

210 Cited in Woodham-Smith, *op.cit.,* p.162.

211 Ó Gráda, *op.cit.,* pp.89, 168.

212 See Kinealy, *op.cit.*, pp.130–4.

213 This figure is given in a wide range of sources, including many standard reference works. For instance, Melvin Small and J. David Singer, *Resort to Arms: International and Civil Wars, 1816–1980* (Beverley Hills, Cal., 1982) state (p.237) that among all civil wars 'the Taiping rebellion ranks first in severity', with 20,000,000 'battle deaths' (Table 13.2, p.224) out of a total Chinese population said to be 466.7 million at the opening of the Rebellion and 437.5 million at its close (*ibid.*). R. Ernest Dupuy and Trevor N. Dupuy, *The Collins Encyclopedia of Military History* (London, 1993) state (p.946) that the Taiping Rebellion 'was perhaps the most destructive war of the entire 19th century. It has been estimated that 20 million people died directly or indirectly due to the war between 1850 and 1864.' Similarly, Peter N. Stearns, ed., *The Encyclopedia of World History* (Cambridge, 2001) claims that 'all told, over 20 million perished in this conflict'. These three estimates, in normally very reliable standard sources, contain evident mutual contradictions, e.g. between 'battle deaths' and those 'directly or indirectly due' to Taiping.

214 Dupuy and Dupuy, *Collins Encyclopedia,* p.1083.

215 Jack Gray, *Rebellions and Revolutions: China from the 1800s to the 1980s* (Oxford, 1990), pp.75–6.

216 On Taiping see Ho Ping-Ti, *Studies on the Population of China, 1368–1953* (Cambridge, Mass., 1959); Jean Cheseneaux, *Peasant Revolts in China, 1840–1949* (New York, 1973); Teng Ssu-Yu, *History of the Taiping Rebellion* (London, 1863); Wolfgang Yu-Wen, *The Taiping Revolutionary Movement* (New Haven, Conn., 1973). Possibly the best English-language work on Taiping is Jen Yu-Wen, *The Taiping Revolutionary Movement* (New Haven, Conn., 1973). Franz Michael's three volume work, *The Taiping Rebellion: History and Documents* (London, 1966–71) contains much source material.

217 Gray, *op.cit.*, p.57. Hakka women did not bind their feet and worked more regularly than other Chinese women. They also practised local shamanistic religions.

218 *Ibid.*, p.55.

219 *Ibid.*, pp.63–76.

220 *Ibid.*, p.59.

221 *Ibid.*, p.71.

222 Jen Yu-Wen, *op.cit.*, p.531.

223 *Ibid.*, pp.541, 545.

224 For instance, Prescott Clarke and J.S. Gregory, *Western Reports on the*

Taiping: A Selection of Documents (Honolulu, 1982) contains only a handful of accounts of mass destruction, most notably by the German scientist Baron von Richtofen (pp.427–30) written in 1871, seven years after the defeat of Taiping. On the other hand, other eye-witness accounts (e.g. pp.373, 417) specifically deny that the Taipings were murderous, or assert that the number of inhabitants of Chinese towns has been exaggerated (e.g. p.344, where R.J. Forrest, writing in 1862, states that the population of Nanking was 'about 70,000 men [i.e. persons] as against the 100,000 spoken of by the authorities').

225   Ho, *op.cit.*, Table 40, p.241. It should be carefully noted, however, that many of the 'before' population figures are those from many years earlier, some from the late eighteenth century. (The 'after' figures date from 1865 to 1888.) Ho, however, believes that population growth just prior to Taiping means that the figures of population loss may be understatements.

226   *Ibid.*, p.240.

227   *Ibid.*, p.242.

228   *Ibid.*, p.246. This could, of course, have been caused by other aspects of China's turmoil, but seems to have specifically affected these regions. The population of Kiangsi province was 31 per cent lower in 1953 than in 1850.

229   *Ibid.*, p.245.

230   Frederic Wakeman Jr., *Strangers At the Gate: Social Disorder in South China, 1839–1861* (Berkeley, Cal., 1966), p.3.

231   T.H. Hollingsworth, *Historical Demography* (Cambridge, 1969), p.102.

232   Most historians believe that Taiping disappeared with little trace after 1864, while the Qing dynasty was strengthened for a generation or more.

233   Gilbert Phelps, *Tragedy of Paraguay* (London, 1975), citing R.B. Cunninghame-Graham's *A Vanished Arcadia* (1901). See also Charles J. Kolinski, *Independence or Death: The Story of the Paraguayan War* (Gainesville, Fla., 1965).

234   *Ibid.*, pp.25–31; W.H. Koebel, *Paraguay* (London, 1917), pp.164–70. Francia ordered all men in Paraguay to wear a hat, so it could be instantly doffed in his presence; after his death in 1840 'people still took off their hats and glanced anxiously about them at the mention of his name' (Phelps, *op.cit.*, p.31).

235   Phelps, *op.cit.*, p.242. According to George Thompson, an English officer serving in the Paraguayan army as a colonel, the Triple Alliance were resolved 'not to leave a Paraguayan of any age or sex alive' (*ibid.*).

236 Koebel, *op.cit.*, pp.200–1. Solano Lopez was killed by Allied forces in 1870, fighting in a guerrilla campaign after the war ended.

237 *Ibid.*, p.271. These figures, which have often been repeated, were first published in Max von Versen, 'Historia da Guerra do Paraguai', in *Revista do Instituto Historica e Geografico Brasileiro,* LXXVI, Part II (Rio de Janeiro, 1913). Von Versen was a young Prussian telegrapher who was present during the war.

238 Koebel, *op.cit.*, p.119.

239 Other, perhaps soberer, estimates of the Paraguayan slaughter exist. John Lynch states that Paraguay's population declined from 406,646 in 1864 to 231,000 in 1872 (John Lynch, 'The River Plate Republics from Independence to the Paraguayan War', in Bethell, ed., *Cambridge History of Latin America, Volume III: From Independence to c.1870* (Cambridge, 1985), p.673), while George Pendle estimates that 'at the beginning of the conflict the population was 525,000 and that by 1871 it had been reduced to 221,079. Of these survivors, 106,254 were [adult] women, 86,079 were children, and only 28,746 [adult] men' (George Pendle, *Paraguay: A Riverside Nation* (Oxford, 1967), p.22).

240 Phelps, *op.cit.*, pp.274–7. Of 77,000 troops sent by Bolivia into Paraguay at the start of the war, only 7,000 remained at the war's end, the others having deserted or been killed.

241 L.H. Gann and Peter Duignan, *The Rulers of Belgian Africa, 1884–1914* (Princeton, 1979), pp.13–24. The Belgian franchise was heavily restricted until 1893.

242 *Ibid.*, pp.24–40.

243 *Ibid.*, pp.53–8.

244 *Ibid.*, p.79.

245 *Ibid.*, p.100.

246 In 1910 it is estimated that there were 4,003 Europeans in the Belgian Congo (as it was known by then) (*ibid.*, p.156).

247 See, in particular, Adam Hochschild, *King Leopold's Ghost: A Story of Greed, Terror, and Heroism in Colonial Africa* (London, 1999), which has widely publicised the Congo atrocities and the role of E.D. Morel. See also Ruth Slade, *King Leopold's Congo: Aspects of the Development of Race Relations in the Congo Independent State* (Oxford, 1962) [the Congo Free State was sometimes also known as the Congo Independent State, although it was neither free nor independent]; *idem, English-Speaking Missions in the Congo Independent State* (1878–1902) (Louvain, 1958); Roger Anstey, *King Leopold's Legacy: The Congo Under Belgian Rule, 1908–1960*

(Oxford, 1966), pp.1–61; Neal Ascherson, *The King Incorporated: Leopold II in the Age of Trusts* (London, 1963); and Robert G. Weisbord, 'The King, the Cardinal and the Pope: Leopold II's Genocide in the Congo', *Journal of Genocide Research*, Vol.5, No.1 (March 2003).

248 Gann and Duignan, *op.cit.*, pp.121–40.

249 *Ibid.*, Table 13, p.123.

250 Slade, *op.cit.*, pp.257–305; Hochschild, *op.cit.*, pp.185 ff. On Morel, later a renowned anti-war campaigner and Labour MP, see Catherine Ann Cline, *E.D. Morel 1873–1924: the Strategies of Protest* (Belfast, 1980).

251 Hochschild, *op.cit.*, p.233.

252 *Ibid.*, p.226.

253 *Ibid.*, pp.226–7.

254 Edmund D. Morel, *King Leopold's Rule in Africa* (London, 1904), p.239. The Mongrella concession was a particular area in the Congo where rubber plantations existed in great numbers.

255 *Ibid.*, pp.229–33.

256 *Ibid.*, p.231.

257 'Congolese Sleeping Sickness Epidemic of 1895–1906', in George Childs Kohn, ed., *Encyclopedia of Plague and Pestilence from Ancient Times to the Present* (New York, 2001), p.66.

258 *Ibid.*

259 *Ibid.*

260 *Ibid.*

261 Hochschild, *op.cit.*, p.231.

262 Slade, *English-Speaking Missions*, p.185.

263 *Ibid.*, pp.178–9; Gann and Duignan, pp.151–5.

264 Gann and Duignan, *op.cit.*, p.135.

265 *Ibid.*, pp.134–5, 156–7.

266 On the Hereros see 'The Hereros of South-West Africa (Namibia)' in Chalk and Jonassohn, *History and Sociology of Genocide*, pp.230–48, which chiefly consists of an extract from Horst Drechsler, *'Let Us Die Fighting': The Struggle of the Herero and the Nama Against German Imperialism (1884–1915)* (London, 1980); Cocker, *op.cit.*, pp.269–357; and Torben Jorgensen and Eric Markugen, 'The Hereros, Genocide of', in Charny, ed., *Encyclopedia of Genocide,* pp.288–9.

267 Drechsler in Chalk and Jonassohn, *op.cit.*, pp.233–4; Cocker, pp.269–83.

268 Cocker, *op.cit.*, pp.282–3.

269 *Ibid.*, pp.314–21.

270 Drechsler, pp.235–6.

271 Drechsler, *op.cit.*, p.241.

272 Cited in *ibid.*

273 Cocker, *op.cit.*, pp.331–2.

274 *Ibid.*, p.341.

275 Drechsler, *op.cit.*, p.246.

276 *Ibid.*

277 *Ibid.*, p.243.

278 Cited in Cocker, *op.cit.*, p.318.

279 *Ibid.*, p.347.

280 The murder and enslavement of African tribes by African slaving middlemen and local kings, under European direction, might well also be described as genocidal in the commonly accepted sense.

CHAPTER 4

Genocide in the Age of Totalitarianism, 1914–79

The best-known and most infamous examples of genocide – some would say the *only* actual examples of genocide – occurred in what might be termed the 'Age of Totalitarianism', a period which began with the start of the First World War in 1914. To some historians, this era continued until the demise of European Communism around 1990: to others, it coincided with the ascendancy of Stalin and Hitler from about 1929 until 1953, centring on the decade or so between 1935 and 1945. In terms of genocide and mass murders, this chapter takes the 'Age of Totalitarianism' as lasting until the Pol Pot auto-genocide of 1975–9, probably the last mass murders carried out by ideologically motivated political fanatics who derived their beliefs from, in this case, a wildly extreme Asian form of Communism which can be traced back to Mao Zedong (Mao Tse-tung), to Stalin, and to the Bolshevik Revolution. The most infamous and universally known examples of genocide and mass murder in the modern world occurred during this period: the Armenian genocide of 1915, the Jewish Holocaust and other killings carried out by the Nazis, the Stalinist Purges and mass killings, and those carried out by Mao in China and Pol Pot in Cambodia. Indeed, the term 'genocide' was coined only in 1943, by the Polish Jewish writer Raphael Lemkin, for acts which were, in his view, 'a crime without a name'. It is surprisingly easy to forget that the genocidal mass killings of this period, with their millions of victims, occurred against a backdrop of millions of 'legitimate' violent deaths in the two world wars and innumerable lesser wars.

Three main characteristics distinguish the genocides of this period. First, they were, for the most part, ideological in their motivation, being carried out against victims arbitrarily so distinguished according to the precepts of the totalitarian ideology of that society. While these totalitarian ideologies resembled conventional religions (and often were expressed in quasi-messianic rhetoric), they were not religious in the normally acceptable sense, but secular doctrinal movements, products of the post-Enlightenment world. Second, for the most part the ideologically based political movements which carried out these genocides came to power as a direct or indirect effect of the collapse of the elite structure in central and eastern Europe as a result of the First World War. This was plainly true in the case of both Communism and (at a distance) Nazism. It is simply inconceivable that Hitler or Stalin would have come to power, or Bolshevism or National Socialism triumphed, had European politics continued on its normal course without the catastrophic interruption by the Great War: Lenin would have lived out his life in obscure central European street cafés frequented by equally obscure would-be revolutionaries; Stalin would surely have continued a step ahead of the law; Hitler would have remained in the demi-monde of Viennese flophouses and crackpot racialist periodicals. The Great War created a gap in the ordinary political life of Europe and in the recognised legitimate institutions of government, which otherwise marginal movements and leaders were able to fill. Third, the First World War, with its millions of casualties and bereavements and extended period of hardships and inhumanity, in and of itself ratcheted up the expectation of mega-deaths and extremist, violent solutions among ordinary Europeans in a way which, again, would have seemed impossible had the war not occurred. The results of the First World War had other negative effects as well which helped to engender genocide and mass murder, especially in making nationality, based on language and ethnicity, the sole legitimate basis for delimiting national boundaries, in place of the multi-ethnic empires which existed before, an outcome which was virtually certain to endanger ethnic minorities, especially in an atmosphere of economic depression and illiberalism.

For all these reasons, it is in my opinion historically accurate to view the genocides and mass murders of the whole period from 1914 to 1979 as forming a coherent and distinctive unit, set off from other instances of mass murder and genocide before or since. The genocides of this period were hallmarked by a European phase and then by an Asian phase, when fascism triumphed in Japan, followed, after Japan's defeat, by the triumph of a particularly fanatical version of Communism throughout most of east Asia. The genocides of this period should therefore be viewed as quite separate from, for instance, the bouts of 'ethnic cleansing' prevalent in the modern world since the nineteenth century but especially notable after 1945. These occurred largely as a result of the creation of new political boundaries and of the direct fruits of war, chiefly in the years 1944–8 and 1989–95 when boundaries were being redrawn, and were founded in primitive nationalistic hostilities rather than doctrinaire ideologies. They were more limited in scope and, as a rule, ended once the population transfers or expulsions were accomplished.

The Armenian genocide

Before turning to Nazism and Communism, however, what is generally regarded as the earliest and one of the most harrowing of modern genocides must be considered, the mass slaughter of the Armenians in the Ottoman Empire, during and just after the First World War, and especially in 1915. The Armenian genocide is rather difficult to fit into any typology, and much about it, especially on detailed analysis, remains rather mysterious: unlike the Jewish Holocaust, it is anything but straightforward.[1] Prior to the First World War, the Armenians were one of the very largest non-Muslim minorities in the Ottoman Empire, resident chiefly in the easternmost provinces of Anatolia (present-day Turkey), especially the 'six vilayets' (provinces) of Erzurum, Bitlis, Diyarbakir, Sivas, Mamuretulaziz and Van – remote, little-known areas south of the Caucasus, west of Iran, and adjacent to (and including territories now within) present-day Iraq and Syria. In 1914, other significant non-Muslim minorities within the Ottoman Empire included Greeks, Coptic and Nestorian Christians, and Jews; prior to the Balkan wars just before 1914, the Ottoman Empire still included significant areas in the Balkans with large non-Muslim populations.

The roots of the Armenian genocide of 1915–16 are to be found in the peculiar features of the Ottoman Empire, and its decline. In the early nineteenth century that empire was, at least nominally, one of the largest in the world, extending from Algeria to Hungary to Yemen to the borders of Persia. Although firmly under the control of Muslims, with a Turkish heartland, it was genuinely multi-ethnic, containing millions of Orthodox, Catholic and other Christians, Jews, and smaller religions, and dozens of different linguistic-ethnic groups. During the century after 1815, however, the Ottoman Empire suffered an almost unexampled reduction in its territories, a reduction which occurred as the European empires, Japan and the United States were rapidly expanding, and as nationalist movements grew throughout Europe. Between the 1820s and the First World War, the Ottomans lost Greece, which became independent in 1821–30; much of the Caucasus and eastern Anatolia (to Russia, 1829); Algeria (to France, 1830); Egypt (autonomous in 1840); Romania, Serbia, Montenegro (independent 1878), with Bulgaria autonomous (and fully independent in 1908); Cyprus (to Britain, 1878); Tunisia (to France, 1881); Thessaly and Epirus (to Greece, 1881); Crete (to Greece, 1897); Bosnia-Herzegovina (occupied by Austria in 1878 and annexed in 1908); Libya (to Italy, 1912); Albania (1912), and other minor territories. The Ottoman Empire was, it is generally agreed, kept alive only because Britain and France feared its annexation by Russia or Germany. Just before the First World War, there were also the first stirrings of a separate Arab nationalism, distinctive from an Ottoman-Islamic identity. The Balkan wars of 1912–13 proved utterly disastrous to the Ottomans, reducing their territories in Europe to a sliver around Constantinople. This constant diminution in Ottoman lands also removed many sources of taxation revenue; most importantly of all, it reduced the Empire to its Turkish-Anatolian heartland, only the remaining Arab areas (overwhelmingly Muslim, of course) constituting a large non-Turkish minority.

The Ottoman government had made many attempts to reform and modernise, with a European-based civil code in place in 1870–6 and the granting of a constitution in 1876 in place for a year or two before it was revoked by the Sultan. Like the somewhat similar case of Czarist Russia, the Ottoman Empire was renowned for its brutal autocracy. In 1826, troops loyal to the Turkish Sultan bombarded the barracks of the Janissaries (soldiers in the Sultan's guard in a corps established in the fourteenth century) in Constantinople, who had risen in revolt, killing several thousand soldiers inside. The corps of Janissaries was abolished and their destruction was celebrated in Ottoman history as the 'Auspicious Event' (*Vakayi Hayriye*), a landmark on the road to modernisation. In 1876 a revolt in Bulgaria, a part of the Ottoman Empire, was put down with such brutality by Ottoman forces as to become the subject of an anti-Turkish campaign by British Prime Minister William E. Gladstone against 'the Bulgarian atrocities'. Probably the worst outbreaks of ethnic mass murder in the later history of the Ottoman Empire (prior to the First World War) were the first Armenian massacres which occurred in 1894–6, when Armenian peasants around Sassoun in eastern Anatolia, resisting incursions by local Kurds, were attacked by both Kurdish and Ottoman troops. About 8,000 Armenians were killed. Soon afterwards occurred widespread massacres of Armenians throughout the Ottoman Empire, with somewhere between 50,000 and 300,000 killed.[2] These 1894–6 massacres, like those during the First World War, have been the subject of intense debate among historians, with some pro-Turkish historians suggesting that the killings were a response to deliberate provocation by Armenian nationalists and revolutionaries.[3] Most historians, however, regard the 1894–6 massacres as a grossly excessive response to rising Armenian nationalism.[4] It also left a persisting legacy of bitterness between Turks, Armenians and Kurds. The Turks themselves, it should also be noted, were also the victims of 'ethnic cleansing' on a large scale. With the autonomy or independence of the Balkans from the Ottoman Empire after the mid-1870s, no fewer than 1.5 million Muslims from the Balkans migrated to Anatolia (the Turkish heartland); thousands of Muslims from Crete also fled to Anatolia after 1881.

The rulers of the Ottoman Empire traditionally regarded themselves as the leaders of the Islamic world. In control of the primary Muslim holy places of Mecca, Medina and Jerusalem, from the early sixteenth century the Ottoman Sultan took the title of Caliph (successor to Mohammed) and Servitor of the Two Holy Sanctuaries (Mecca and Medina). The Sultanate evolved a complex system of government with a prime minister, the grand vizier, two principal ruling institutions, the army and the bureaucracy, and the *ulema*, Islamic ruling judges. But it was also renowned for the wide degree of autonomy given to the *dhimmis* (tolerated infidels), members of the non-Muslim monotheistic sects, who were given a recognised place in the Ottoman hierarchy in exchange for the payment of a tribute and acknowledgement of their essentially inferior status in comparison with Muslims. By 1914 there were 13 recognised *millets*, or organised and self-governing religious communities, in addition to the Muslim *millet*. These included the two Armenian groupings, Gregorian Armenians attached to a Patriarchate in Constantinople and Catholic Armenians, as well as the Greek Orthodox, Jews and others.[5] The religious leaders of these communities were responsible for their own communities in the eyes of the state: they collected taxes and had their own communal courts. In all other respects these *millets* were independent in their languages, religions and socio-economic life.[6] It is obvious that, in many respects, this was a remarkably enlightened system, far ahead of the West until the mid-eighteenth century at the earliest.

The Christian and Jewish *millets* acted as typical 'entrepreneurial minorities', virtually dominating much of the economy in the Ottoman Empire. As successful businessmen they far outnumbered Muslim Turks and others, and were also very disproportionate in the professional classes. The Greeks were the most important entrepreneurial element in the Ottoman Empire, followed by the Armenians, and then by the Jews and Levantese Christians.[7] Among 40 bankers listed in Istanbul in 1912, for instance, 12 were Greek, 12 Armenians, 8 Jews, 5 Levantese or Europeans: not one was a Turk. Among 122 bankers in the rest of the Ottoman realm outside the Arab provinces, 62 were Greeks, 30 Armenians, 12 Levantese or Europeans, 3 Jews, but only 2 were Turks.[8] In virtually every significant aspect of Turkish commerce and industry the same ethnic breakdown can be seen. Among 24,570 businesses in trade and industry in the Ottoman Empire in 1912, about 45 per cent were Greek, 25 per cent Armenian, 17 per cent other non-Turkish minorities, but only about 13 per cent were Turks.[9] Among 5,264 professional men or firms, 44 per cent were Greek, 22 per cent Armenian, 20 per cent other non-Turks, but only 14 per cent were Turks.[10] Survey after survey found the same distribution. Although originally excluded from the Ottoman civil service bureaucracy, by the early twentieth century the better-educated non-Muslim minorities became an ever-larger proportion of the state bureaucracy, making up about one-third of the Foreign Ministry bureaucracy by 1897.[11] Armenians were the largest single group here, followed by Greeks, and then by Jews and Arab Christians.[12]

The key economic and bureaucratic role of non-Muslim minorities in the declining Ottoman Empire coincided with the rise of militant Turkish nationalism. Turkish nationalism in the modern Western sense developed very late, and only after the cosmopolitan, multi-ethnic Ottoman Empire was being systematically reduced in size and stripped of its non-Turkish minorities in Europe and north Africa. Its precise nature was much disputed: in particular, nationalists could not decide whether they were Pan-Islamists, leading the international Muslim world; pan-Turkists (also known as pan-Turanians) seeking to unite the Turkish-language families of peoples in central Asia and Anatolia; or Anatolians, aiming at a small homogenous Turkey in roughly its present boundaries.[13] Gradually – but only gradually – a preference emerged among nationalist intellectuals for an Anatolian (the *Vatan*) Turkey, but one which retained its Arab Muslim domains. This *type* of Turkish nationalism was also heightened by the emergence of Armenian and Greek nationalism in Anatolia.[14]

The growth of modern Turkish nationalism crystallised into the formation of the Committee for Union and Progress (CUP), also known as the 'Ittihad' (i.e. Union), the revolutionary reformist movement known to history as the 'Young Turks', a term which, remarkably, has passed into the English language as a synonym for any group of youthful reformers. That the name of a group of reformers in far off Turkey would become proverbial is indicative of the chronological primacy of the movement, one of the few revolutionary reformist party movements to come to power before the outbreak of the First World War. The CUP was formed in Macedonia, chiefly among Turkish army officers and junior officials; it was chiefly drawn from the educated Turkish middle classes. It headed a rebellion in mid-1908 which spread quickly, aimed at restoring the short-lived 1876 Ottoman constitution. It took power in July 1908 by forcing the sultan to concede most of his powers and institute parliamentary elections.

The first Ottoman parliamentary election resulted in a victory for the CUP. A confused period followed, marked especially by the Italo-Turkish war of 1911–12, and the Balkan wars of 1912–13, utter disasters for the Turks. By 1913, however, the CUP was firmly entrenched in power. There can be no doubt that its central programme was one of extreme Turkish nationalism, entailing the 'turkification' of the educational and political systems, with 'Turkishness' replacing Islam as the basis of governing legitimacy.[15] This agenda became more visible as the Ottoman Empire lost its remaining European and north African territories. The CUP also flirted with pan-Turanism, seeking the unification of 'the Turkish race' throughout Asia. There is considerable evidence that extremist elements in the CUP increasingly sought the elimination of Armenians and Greeks from the Ottoman realms, in part because they were Christians, in part because great European powers, especially Russia, regarded their protection as a European responsibility, in part because of their dominant role in the economy.[16] Extremist Turkish ideologues developed a concept of Turkish integral nationalism very similar to that developed among other European right-wing groups, which sought, among other things, Turkish control of the economy in order to eliminate 'the Greeks [who] have taken possession of the harbours and coast towns of Anatolia [and] the Armenians who, thanks to their friendly relations with England, have become very rich'.[17] During the 1913 negotiations with Greece over the Aegean islands, an economic boycott of Greek shops by Turkish nationalists was organised, which was then extended, for no obvious reason, to Armenians.[18] The Greeks and Armenians in the Ottoman Empire, like the Jews in much of central and eastern Europe, were typical 'middle man minorities', especially vulnerable to nationalist pressures. As well, there was a steady growth at this time of overt Turkish racism, despite the highly multi-ethnic nature of the Ottoman state in previous times.[19]

All of this has been made clear by recent scholars, typically those writing specifically in order to analyse the Armenian genocide. Yet there is another side of the coin which also must be kept in mind. With hindsight, it is easy to view the pre-1914 Ottoman government as preparing for genocide, despite the evidence that the destruction of Turkey's Armenians was an *ad hoc* wartime measure. The last Ottoman parliament, elected in 1914 just before the outbreak of the war, included (out of 259 members) 144 Turks, 84 Arabs, 13 Greeks, 14 Armenians, and 4 Jews.[20] The number of Armenians in the 1914 parliament was exactly the same as in 1908. Early in 1914 both the Armenian and Greek communities carried out long negotiations with the CUP aimed at achieving a set level of proportional representation in future parliaments, based on their respective populations. After protracted discussions the CUP 'concede[d] to the quantitative demands of both communities'.[21] In other words, 'normal' politics, in no way discriminating against Armenians (but, it seems, rather the reverse) continued literally to the outbreak of the war.

While Turkish ultra-nationalism evidently grew just before 1914, a number of the more important figures in the CUP were actually Armenians, including Bedros Halacian, Public Works Minister in the CUP's Cabinet.[22] It is unnecessary to point out the crucial differences here between the pre-1914 CUP and the pre-1941 Nazi party: it is inconceivable that known Jews, after 1933, could have sat in Hitler's *Reichstag* or held important positions (or any other) in the Nazi government.

The outbreak of the First World War changed everything. Here again, however, there are stark differences between the evolution of the Armenian and Jewish genocides. After systematically persecuting Jews from the moment he came to power in 1933, Hitler shifted his stance with the invasion of the Soviet Union in June 1941 to one of deliberately killing Europe's Jews. The Nazi invasion of the Soviet Union in 1941 was carried out, in violation of the 1939 non-aggression pact between Germany and Russia, purely from ideological reasons, in large part to rid the world of 'Judeo-Bolshevism'. The deliberate killing of adult male Jews began with the invasion of Russia and, by no later than the autumn of 1941, evolved into a policy of murdering all Jews: following the Wannsee conference of January 1942, every Jew throughout Europe was marked for death. The Ottoman pattern was very different. Turkey obviously had no role in starting the First World War, which began when a Bosnian revolutionary assassinated the heir to the Hapsburg throne, setting off a chain reaction of war declarations and mobilisations. Turkey did not even enter the war until 29 October 1914, more than three months after the conflict began. Britain originally expected Turkey to remain neutral or even side with the Allies against Germany, and the alliance of the Ottomans with the Central powers (Germany and Austria-Hungary) was secretly pushed through the Turkish Cabinet by an extremist minority.[23]

As the weakest of the major powers the Ottoman Empire was ripe for dismemberment and, between 1915 and 1917, the Allies secretly agreed on the partitioning of the whole Empire following an Allied victory, with Russia to gain Constantinople, the Bosphoros and the areas of eastern Anatolia where most Armenians lived; Italy (which entered the war only in May 1915) southern Anatolia; Greece part of coastal Anatolia around Izmir (Smyrna); France south-central Anatolia and what are now Syria and Lebanon; and Britain the area stretching down from Baghdad along the Persian Gulf. The future Turkish state was to be limited to a portion of north-western Anatolia, perhaps one-third of its present size.[24] In February 1915 Britain launched the ill-fated Gallipoli campaign, designed to seize Constantinople and knock Turkey out of the war. This began with a naval bombardment of the Dardanelles on 18 March 1915. Even more serious, however, was the conflict on the Caucasus Front, that is, in the area in eastern Anatolia where most Armenians lived. Turkey entered the war hoping to regain the area around Kars and Batum which was seized by Russia in the 1870s. A military advance against the Russians by the Turks late in 1914 was repulsed and turned into a rout, with Russia seizing a large portion of north-eastern Anatolia. The head of the Turkish military forces in the Caucasus was Enver Pasha (1881–1922), one of the key leaders of the Young Turks and Turkey's Minister of War, although aged only 33. Enver was decisively defeated by the Russians at Ardahan and Sarikamish in January 1915, although the fighting continued in a bloody manner throughout the war.[25]

It was at this stage that the Turkish government launched its assault on the Armenians. In March 1915, it was initially decided to deport all Armenians from the areas of conflict in eastern Anatolia where most lived; the previous month, Armenians in the Turkish army had been removed from their units and placed in special labour units. Why the Armenians? With the Greeks, they were the largest and wealthiest non-Muslim minority (although 70 per cent were agricultural peasants and farmers); lacking a country of their own, they were particularly vulnerable. Much more importantly, they were seen as allies of Russia and treasonable opponents of the Ottoman Empire. Early in 1914, the Ottoman government had been forced into an international agreement protecting the Armenians. This was particularly offensive to the Young Turks, who viewed it as a prelude to the dismemberment of eastern Anatolia and the creation of an Armenian state. The Ottoman government renounced the 1914 agreement as soon as it entered the war. There is little doubt that much agitation for Ottoman reforms was spearheaded by Russia which, even pro-Armenians concede, had become champions of the Armenians, viewing them as a friendly Christian minority likely to be anti-Turkish.[26]

Initially, Armenians were ordered only to disarm. This was carried out in a brutal way, leading to an anti-Turkish uprising in Van in mid-April 1915.[27] The Van uprising was savagely suppressed and a general order given that all Armenians from eastern Anatolia be deported to desert regions in Mesopotamia (Iraq). This was often carried out by the 'Secret Organisation', a security body numbering around 30,000–34,000, established in 1914 by the Young Turks in order to deport Greeks from eastern Anatolia, and composed mainly of criminals and other riff-raff.[28] The deportations were carried out with historical brutality, in ways which were eerily like the Jewish Holocaust a generation later. In particular, Armenians were transported to the desert areas in sealed boxcars along the Baghdad-Berlin railway.[29] Many perished on the journey. Others died in forced 'death marches' to the desert: the mortality rate on these marches was estimated at 85 per cent.[30] Stragglers were brutally shot. Men, women and children were machine-gunned in pits. Many were murdered by Kurdish troops and bandits, who hated the Armenians. Rapes and the abduction of women were commonplace. The former homes and possessions of the Armenians in eastern Anatolia were systematically robbed by the Turks and Kurds. One important underestimated element in the Armenian massacres was religion. When Turkey entered the war, it declared a *jihad* (*cihad* in Turkish) against the Allied powers on behalf of Islam; eyewitnesses later said that the Christian Armenians were frequently attacked by fanatical Muslims.[31] Descriptions of the sufferings of the Armenians are harrowing beyond belief, and in this respect bear a close resemblance to the much more familiar accounts of the Holocaust. One eyewitness, a Venezuelan who became Inspector-General of the Turkish forces in Armenia, reported that

> *Among the women, almost all of whom were young, were some mothers with children, or, rather, childish skeletons, in their arms. One of them was mad. She knelt beside the half-putrefied cadaver of a new-born babe. Another woman had fallen to the ground, rigid and lifeless. Her two little girls, believing her asleep, sobbed convulsively as they tried in vain to awaken her, . . .*

and so on, with each description more horrifying than the last.[32]

The Armenian massacres of 1915 are often seen as the first true modern genocide. With a number of caveats and qualifications, this characterisation is probably accurate. Never before in modern history had an entire people been targeted for death, or death in wartime, purely on ethnic/religious grounds; the Armenian genocide thus marked a departure in modern history. Napoleon had conquered most of Europe without murdering a single civilian. Although up to 600,000 soldiers died in the American Civil War – the bloodiest of the nineteenth century – and the South was devastated for several generations, no civilians were deliberately killed. During the First World War itself, despite untold millions of deaths, no other civilian population was targeted in the same way. It must be noted, however, that the Turkish government and later pro-Turkish historians, have offered a number of reasons why the massacres of the Armenians have been exaggerated and do not constitute genocide. The deportation orders only affected Armenians in the eastern war zone: the Armenians of Constantinople and other parts of Turkey were unaffected, and remained where they were. Many Armenians died of disease, or were actually still alive at the end of the war in Russia or the Arab parts of the Ottoman realms. The rulers of Turkey appeared to have been genuinely shocked when they heard what had befallen the Armenians: in their view they had exiled the Armenians for legitimate reasons of war, in the midst of a dire national emergency, never wishing them to be killed, and attempted to alleviate their suffering. Hundreds of thousands of Muslim Turks were also killed in a particularly brutal war, sometimes at the hands of Armenians.[33] According to the pro-Turkish historian Mim Kemal Oke, official circulars sent to the governors of the provinces from which Armenians were to be deported made it clear that 'the deportation is not intended for the destruction of any individuals or groups, and the lives of the persons should be protected', that any Turkish troops engaging in murder, robbery or rape 'should be severely punished', and that 'guilty public officials should immediately be removed from office and court-martialled'.[34] CUP leaders later blamed the massacres on undisciplined troops and Kurdish irregulars who acted against the wishes of the government.[35]

There is probably an element of truth in all these claims, which deserve to be considered objectively. Armenians outside the war zone were not deported. According to Oke, the Ottoman circulars ordering the deportations of the Armenians made it clear that care should be taken of vulnerable individuals and protection should be given to Armenians against attacks, while 'the remaining Armenians besides those whose deportation has been determined should not be taken from their places of residence'.[36] Talaat Pasha (Mehmet Talaat, 1874–1921), one of the most important Turkish leaders, had four investigative commissions established and sent to Anatolia. These commissions turned 'the criminals [who carried out the massacres] over to local courtmartials'.[37] Nevertheless, all this, even if wholly accurate, misses the central point that the Turkish authorities had an absolute obligation to protect innocent life, especially civilian, and manifestly did not carry out this obligation. Most of the evidence suggests, on the contrary, that the Turkish authorities actively masterminded the mass killing of the Armenians as a deliberate policy. In considering the Armenian genocide, however, one is struck by the fact that a genuinely balanced and objective account of these terrible events by historians is lacking. Although some pro-Armenian historians have seen a secret plan as already in existence from as early as 1910 to rid Turkey of Armenians, no pre-1914 Ottoman government could have had foreknowledge of the outbreak of the First World War or the circumstances under which the deportations would be accomplished, while mainstream Ottoman politics included normal Armenian participation until war began.[38] Moreover, to suggest that the CUP government deliberately planned for genocide before 1914 implies that it intended to carry out the mass murder of an ethnic group, something for which there was no precedent in modern history, and that its actions would not have attracted intense international opposition, perhaps leading to an invasion of the Ottoman Empire by other European powers to stop the massacres. Viewed in this light, it seems most implausible that the genocide of the Armenians was pre-planned.

The deportation of the Armenians was accomplished at a time of grave national crisis when the existence of the state clearly hung in the balance. It was thus arguably comparable (on a vastly larger scale) to other tragic events which have occurred in somewhat similar circumstances, such as the deportation to the Isle of Man and, later, Canada and Australia of 'enemy aliens' (often Jewish refugees) by the British government in 1940 when a German invasion appeared certain, and the removal of thousands of harmless Japanese-Americans from the coastal counties of California to camps in Nevada following Pearl Harbor. Both of these were panic measures carried out by liberal governments and officials, not by ultra-nationalists. The removal of California's Japanese-Americans, for instance, was ordered by Governor Earl Warren, later the left-liberal American Chief Justice who, ironically, became the *bête-noire* of America's ultra-conservatives. A seemingly even clearer analogy is with

Stalin's deportation of many nationalities deemed anti-Soviet, such as the Chechen-Ingush peoples and Crimean Tartars during the Second World War.[39] Nor is it really accurate, except in hindsight, to term the Armenian deportations an example of 'ethnic cleansing', since Armenians were moved from one part of the Ottoman Empire to another (the Turks had no way of knowing, in 1915, that the desert regions to which they were brutally deported would be lost to the Ottomans) while not all Armenians were deported.[40] Nevertheless, the sheer and quite unprecedented scale of the deportations, even in the context of wartime crisis, went categorically beyond any conceivable military necessity. Additionally, there is good evidence that control of the Turkish government had been seized by extremist xenophobes who were bent on the slaughter of as many Armenians as possible. Henry Morgenthau, the American Ambassador to Turkey, reported Talaat Pasha as having said, when Morgenthau protested at the killing of the Armenians, that 'It is no use for you to argue, we have already disposed of three-quarters of the Armenians; there are none at all left in Bitlis, Van, and Erzerum. The hatred between the Turks and the Armenians is now so intense that we have to finish them. If we do not they will plan their revenge.'[41] The infrastructure of death, and the scale of the killings, was simply too great to be described as anything much short of genocide, by any definition. To reiterate, the Armenian slaughter appears to have been without real precedent in the modern Western world. Although the most notorious slaughter of the Armenians occurred in 1915, their persecution continued until the early 1920s. There were further terrible slaughters in 1916. In 1920 as many as 60,000 Armenians (mainly refugees) were killed by the armies of Mustafa Kemal (Ataturk, 1881–1938, the founder of modern Turkey) when they invaded and destroyed the independent Armenian republic that had been declared in 1918.[42] Much of the short-lived independent state was then absorbed by the Soviet Union, with Armenia remaining a 'republic' within the USSR until it finally achieved full independence in 1990–1.

There are a number of important unresolved questions about the Armenian genocide. One is the scale of death. Truly accurate statistics of great genocides are virtually impossible to ascertain and are subject both to wide margins of error and many definitional problems of attributing responsibility for causes of death. Even for the Jewish Holocaust, obviously the most frequently studied of all genocides, serious estimates of the number of Jewish deaths at the hands of the Nazis by serious scholars have ranged from 4.1 million (the lowest estimate by Gerald Reitlinger) to 6.1 million or more. Raul Hilberg, arguably the greatest of all experts on this topic, has placed the number of Jewish deaths at about 5.1 million, much lower than the invariably quoted figure of 6 million. Estimates of the total number of deaths at the hands of Stalin vary even more widely, and are subject to many more definitional issues. With the Armenian slaughter, these problems also occur in full measure, especially given the primitive and highly imprecise figures which exist for the number of Armenians in the Ottoman Empire at the outbreak of the First World War. European estimates of the number of Armenians in the Ottoman Empire on the eve of the First World War ranged from about 727,000 to 1,400,000.[43] Other responsible estimates are higher, ranging from 1.6 million to 2.1 million. Similarly, the number of Armenians actually deported, the numbers who perished, and the number of survivors are subject to wide variations among experts. A figure of 800,000 Armenians deported, of whom 600,000 perished, seems reasonable, with the proviso that further research may lead to a revision.[44] It is also likely that several hundred thousand more Armenians died, chiefly in massacres, between 1916 and 1923, making the total number of Armenian deaths at about 1 million. This was certainly the greatest massacre of civilians in what can be described as the Western world in modern times until that point, and one of the greatest slaughters in recorded history, as well as the first of the demonic slaughters of the twentieth century. Nevertheless, significantly higher estimates of the number of Armenians who perished, for instance the suggestions by R.J. Rummel that 'possibly 1.4 million' Armenians were deported in 1915 alone and that 2.1 million Armenians were killed in all, seem certainly exaggerated.[45] The Armenian population of the Ottoman Empire in 1914 was almost certainly much lower than figures of this range.

One must also note that pro-Turkish historians have presented much lower estimates for the number of Armenian deaths which, even if too low, deserve to be carefully considered. For example, Kamuran Gurun has pointed out that Dr Fridtjof Nansen (the head of the League of Nations Emigrants' Committee and winner of the Nobel Peace Prize) stated that about 400,000–420,000 Armenians fled from Turkey to Russia, while in 1921 the Armenian Patriarch of Istanbul estimated the number of Armenians in pre-Sèvres Turkey at 625,000.[46] Hundreds of thousands of Armenians apparently fled as refugees to other countries, including 100,000 to Syria, while the Armenian population of the Turkish republic at the time of its first census in 1927 was still 123,603.[47] From these figures, Gurun estimates the total number of Armenian deaths at about 300,000, including those who died of other causes besides the direct hostility of the Turks.[48] Of course, such a low figure (in comparative terms) might well be rejected out of hand as propaganda, but – as in so many other aspects of these peculiarly complex events – one wishes that an absolutely objective and painstaking analysis could be made.

Another disputed question is the extent of German influence on the Armenian genocide. To those who know little of these events, it may seem bizarre, and totally unexpected, that Germany (and, to a lesser extent, Austria-Hungary) should have had any connection whatever with events which seem to presage the Nazi Holocaust a quarter century later. Yet it is now regularly argued that this was the case. German influence in Turkey grew rapidly in the decades before 1914, and a wide variety of military, economic and political links grew up between the two states. Once Turkey declared war on Germany's side, this influence naturally increased, while the Allied powers lost any and all influence they previously possessed. During the Armenian massacres, it was argued in Britain and France that these events were the responsibility, if not the actual design, of German and Austrian diplomatic and military representatives in Constantinople.[49] Recent pro-Armenian historians have assembled an impressive array of evidence of German complicity in the 1915 Armenian genocide.[50] According to this view, Generalmajor Fritz Bronsart von Schellendorf, Germany's Chief of Staff at Ottoman General Headquarters, may well have been the actual instigator of plans for the genocide, at secret meetings between December 1914 and April 1915.[51] Other high-ranking German officers were also allegedly involved directly in instigating the genocide and helping to carry it out.[52] German officers and diplomats had allegedly also suggested the deportation of 100,000 Greeks from the coastal regions of Turkey to Greece in 1914.[53] A surprising number of major figures in Nazi Germany spent much of the First World War in Turkey as military leaders or advisers to the government, including Franz von Papen, Konstantin von Neurath, Hans von Seeckt and Karl Dönitz, while Rudolf Höss, later the infamous Commandant of Auschwitz, served with the German forces in Turkey.[54] Another German figure of note was Dr Max Erwin von Scheubner Richter, German Vice-Consul in Erzurum, who sent 15 reports to Germany on the deportations and massacres, apparently approving of them. In 1920 Scheubner Richter became an avid follower of Hitler and was killed in November 1923 at the abortive Nazi putsch in Munich, when he 'was marching with his arm linked with Hitler's'.[55] Hitler regarded him as 'irreplaceable'.[56]

Despite the very intriguing nature of these associations, it is probably drawing much too long a bow to view the presence of Germans in Turkey during the Great War as directly linked with the Jewish Holocaust. Apart from Höss (or Hoess), none of the major figures in the Holocaust had been in Turkey during the war, and Auschwitz was used as the primary Nazi extermination camp only after the pattern of death had been well established at other killing centres like Treblinka. More important, in all likelihood, was the influence of the example of the Armenian genocide on Hitler himself. Hitler was certainly well aware of the Armenian genocide, and, in particular, pointed out that the Turks 'got away with it', the fate of the Armenians largely forgotten. 'Who after all is today speaking of the destruction of the Armenians?' was Hitler's well-known comment in 1939.[57] One would, of course, like to know far more about this, especially whether the uncanny logistical resemblances of the two genocides were more than coincidental. Yet Hitler drew his inspiration from many sources, especially from his perceptions of Stalin's mass murders and even from the elimination of the American Indians and other native peoples from the path of European settlers. It is also the case that some historians have questioned the role of the Central Powers in encouraging Turkey's genocide (although they were apparently well aware of what was being done). German and Austrian diplomats apparently protested repeatedly at the Ottoman atrocities, especially as the Armenians were Christians.[58]

A third issue of interest is the remarkable facelessness of the leaders of the Armenian genocide. While Hitler is one of the best-known figures in modern history, the very archetype of the demented, raving dictator, the main figures in the CUP government responsible for the Armenian genocide remain virtually unknown. This anonymity is one important reason in my view why the Armenian massacres have not until recently received the publicity one might expect: great crimes require great criminals, and where the criminals are virtually invisible, there is a natural tendency to regard the crime as of lesser importance. Most historians regard three figures, sometimes referred to as the 'triumvirate', as the masterminds of the Armenian genocide: Ahmed Cemal (sometimes known as Djemal or Cemal Pasha, 1872–1922), Enver Pasha (1881–1922) and the previously mentioned Mehmet Talaat Bey (sometimes known as Talaat or Talaat Pasha, 1874–1921). Cemal and Talaat Pasha were assassinated by Armenians seeking revenge for the wartime genocide, while Enver was killed at Turkestan at almost the same time while fighting the Bolsheviks. Cemal, a colonel, was regarded as the senior member of the 'triumvirate', with Enver Pasha the most active member of the inner group, War Minister and Brigadier-General (at 34), whose incompetence on the Caucasian front in 1915 led to the deportation orders. Talaat, the Interior Minister, was responsible for pushing the deportation orders through Parliament and then ruling by decree. None of these three, it should be noted, was formally either head of the state of Turkey – which was still a monarchy under Sultan Mehmet V Rashad, or, at this time, the Grand Vizier (Prime Minister). Below these three, the actual soldiers and government officials responsible for deporting and killing the Armenians remain almost completely unknown, even in specialist works on this topic. While the major leaders and structure of the Nazi SS have been the subject of innumerable works, no English-language work apparently exists on the Special Organisation, which chiefly existed to 'solve' the Armenian question. For the most part, the Ottoman leaders of the Turkish genocide remain faceless men.

After the Armenians, it was the turn of the Greeks to be the victims of 'ethnic cleansing'. The cleansing of the Greeks was to have begun earlier. In November 1913 Greece and Turkey agreed to exchange hundreds of thousands of each other's citizens. Implementation of this agreement was prevented by the outbreak of the war but, in 1914–15, the Turkish government deported vast numbers of Greeks from the coastal areas bordering the Aegean to the interior where they did back-breaking labour: many died, in an episode similar to that resembling, in some respects, the suffering of the Armenians.[59] Why, then, did the Greeks in Turkey not suffer the full fate of the Armenians? Before the war, the Greeks were even more powerful than the Armenians in the Turkish economy and infrastructure, and ultra-nationalist hostility against the Greeks might have been expected to have been very strong. The reasons are not clear, but probably centre in the fact that Greece remained neutral in the Great War until 29 June 1917, when it declared war against the Central Powers. Previously, a major power struggle emerged between the Greek king (Constantine I, of German background), who was pro-German, and most of the country's political elite, who favoured the Allies and were certainly anti-Turkish. The Ottoman government thus did not see its Greeks as a threat in the same class as its Armenians, viewed as a Russian fifth column; pressure, too, might have been exerted by Germany to keep Greece neutral. Greece certainly harboured very strong ambitions to take over much of the Aegean area of Turkey, and in 1919, after the end of the war, Greece attacked Turkey and invaded western Anatolia. Between 1918 and 1922, a vast exchange of population took place between the two countries, one of the largest in European history up to that time. This built on the proposed 1914 exchange of population, interrupted by the war. It was driven by Turkish nationalists, bent on creating an ethnically pure Turkey, but was acquiesced in by Greece, which feared a massacre of Greeks in western Anatolia following the defeat of its invasion forces in September 1922.[60] The involuntarily exchanged populations were determined by religion rather than ethnicity or language, so that Greek Orthodox Turks and Muslim Greeks (there were some) were 'exchanged', in addition to those whose religion and ethnicity coincided. This exchange agreement was given official international recognition by the Lausanne Treaty of July 1923, which settled all the outstanding matters between Turkey, now headed by Mustafa Kemal Ataturk, and the West, much to Turkey's advantage. Between 1923 and 1925 more than 188,000 Greek Orthodox Turkish nationals were transferred from Turkey to Greece, and no fewer than 355,000 Muslims from Greece to Turkey.[61] At the time, virtually no one protested at this arrangement or regarded it as 'genocide'. With the Lausanne accord, the age-old Greek presence in Turkish society virtually came to an end.

Some might wonder why the Turks did not also vent their hostility on the group normally the first target of such campaigns, the Jews. In fact, the CUP had little hostility to the Ottoman Jews and many Jews were among the more prominent members of the early CUP.[62] The Turkish government regarded its Jews as very loyal, and did not perceive them as a grossly over-represented economic elite in quite the same way as the Greeks and Armenians.[63] As well, Jews were persecuted by Tsarist Russia and the newly created Christian states of the Balkans such as Romania and were thus perceived by the Turks as enemies of their enemies. Above all, Turkish Jews were obviously not pro-Russian, and longed for the defeat of Tsarism as much as did the Turks. Trouble only emerged over Zionism, and perceptions (obviously accurate) that the Zionist movement intended to establish an independent Jewish state in Palestine on Turkish territory.[64] A severe crackdown on Zionist activities in Palestine took place until the British conquered the region in 1917, although Turkish Jews were left alone. Under the Kemalist republic Turkey had, for the most part, a notably good record on Jewish refugees during the Holocaust period and, since 1948, has been one of the few Muslim nations to recognise Israel.[65] It is often argued that the good relations which exist between Israel and Turkey have been a major subtext in the alleged ability of the Turks to keep the Armenian genocide off the mainstream public agenda, especially in the United States. Certainly the relatively benign treatment of Jews by the Turks, in contrast to the barbaric treatment accorded to its other minorities (and often reserved for Jews), shows that while antisemitism may indeed be 'the world's oldest hatred', it is also a product of circumstance, and varies in intensity accordingly.

The Turkish state which emerged after the First World War was almost ethnically homogeneous, at least compared with the old Ottoman Empire. While the victorious Allies pledged themselves to establish an Armenian state, none ever came into existence. In 1920–1, the Turks, under their new leader Mustafa Kemal, with the cooperation of the new Soviet Union, combined to squelch hopes for an independent Armenia. The old CUP was mercilessly suppressed by Mustafa Kemal, who took the opportunity of an alleged assassination plot against him to eliminate potential opposition. An attempt, in 1919–20, to try some of those who took part in the Armenian genocide, proved abortive, chiefly due to the reluctance of the Allies to alienate the Turks and a lack of any precedence in international law for such trials.[66] A great deal of documentation of these crimes did take place, often because the post-1918 Turkish government also attempted to place the worst figures of the CUP on trial. A number of leading Ittihadists were sentenced to death *in absentia*, including Cemal, Enver and Talaat.[67] Nearly all escaped from Turkey before these were carried out. The phrase 'starving Armenians' entered the English language, but in general the Armenian genocide remained almost forgotten for many decades. Works like *The Forty Days of Musa Dagh*, Franz Werfel's famous novel of an Armenian uprising against Turkey during the Great War, first published in 1933, helped to keep memories of the Armenian genocide alive. Werfal was an Austrian Jewish author who fled to France and the United States. His book was immediately banned by the Nazis, while in the 1930s the Turkish government exercised successful pressure on Hollywood's MGM not to make the novel into a movie.[68]

With the growing centrality of the Jewish Holocaust in Western consciousness, awareness of the Armenian tragedy of the First World War as arguably the first authentic modern genocide gradually grew. This trend was augmented by the emergence of a new generation of articulate Armenian historians, especially in the United States, anxious to memorialise their tragedy in the same way as Jews have done with the Holocaust, and by the growth of 'genocide studies' as a recognised discipline. Giving centrality to the Armenian genocide has not, however, been unproblematical. It has, indeed, engendered a surprising degree of resistance. As noted, some scholars do not believe that the Armenian genocide constituted a premeditated episode of deliberate extermination similar to that of the Jews under Nazism. Some Jewish writers vociferously deny that any episode in modern history offers a true parallel to the Holocaust.[69] In other cases, a refusal to acknowledge the Armenian massacres as a deliberate genocide carried out by the Ottomans has been linked with support of the Turkish government. This was an element in the so-called 'Lewis Affair', which occurred in 1985 when Professor Bernard Lewis of Princeton University, one of the world's leading experts on modern Turkish history, signed a statement addressed to the American Congress concerning the inclusion of the Armenian genocide in a proposed 'National Day of Remembrance of Man's Inhumanity to Man'.[70] While asserting that vast numbers of Armenians were killed Professor Lewis has repeatedly denied that compelling evidence exists for a deliberate Turkish campaign of genocide. In 1994, he was successfully sued (*in absentia*) in a court in Paris for violating a 1990 law which makes the denial of a 'crime against humanity' illegal, and fined a token sum.[71] This verdict raises very far-reaching questions about intellectual freedom and debate.

Coming to terms with the Armenian genocide in an accurate way is surprisingly difficult, as has been noted several times. On the one hand, it appears certainly to have been the first instance in the twentieth century in which a whole ethnic group was targeted for death, and the number of its victims was unparalleled up to that time in modern Western history. On the other hand, it can be read as a botched wartime panic overreaction, with premeditation most unlikely and the scale of killings arguably exaggerated. Genuine argument and debate can reasonably exist on these questions. Those who have questioned the intention of the Turks to commit genocide and the number of Armenian victims are, often, excellent historians with some documentary evidence on their side. They are not necessarily being deliberately mendacious, and parallels with the obviously antisemitic propagandists and crackpots who enunciate 'Holocaust denial' can perhaps be strained.[72]

There is, as well, a good deal of ambiguity entailed in assigning the Armenian genocide to the schema suggested in this book, or to any other typology of genocide, for that matter. Plainly, the First World War created a 'new reality' in Turkey, especially the invasion of eastern Anatolia by the Russians and other threats to national existence. The norms of both peacetime law and universally accepted morality were replaced by an atmosphere in which mass murder of an ethnic group could be sanctioned and approved. While ultra-nationalist CUP hostility to the Armenians (and Greeks) predated the outbreak of the war, its virulence was greatly enhanced by the circumstance of the early phases of the conflict, the opportunities for destructiveness presented by the 'smokescreen' of the war, and the removal of international sanctions on anti-Armenian violence. The mechanisms of deportation and death created by the CUP against the Armenians, and the scale of the killings, even on the lowest estimates, strongly presaged later instances of genocide of the 1914–79 era. Yet the CUP never adopted an all-embracing secular, universalistic, quasi-messianic ideology in the sense of Nazism and Communism, remaining rooted in traditional (although modernising) nationalism and a vision of an Islamified Turkey. The Armenian genocide was the first of the modern genocides, but did not necessarily have direct descendants. Beyond that, there is still room for much research and debate.

The Jewish Holocaust, 1933–45

So much has been written on the Nazi extermination of the Jews that it might seem pointless to give it the detailed attention it deserves in a history of genocide.[73] The Jewish Holocaust was unquestionably the archetypal example of genocide in modern history, that to which all others are inevitably compared. By the early twenty-first century it had also become one of the most famous events of modern history: in terms of the number of written publications and media examinations, arguably the most famous (or infamous) event in modern history. It has been claimed that, whereas a few decades ago the Holocaust was a footnote to the Second World War, today the Second World War has become a footnote to the Holocaust. Anyone who lectures in modern history at a university will inevitably find that there is no easier way to augment student numbers than to offer a course on the Holocaust. In 2000 there were no fewer than 1,002 university courses (taught by 813 lecturers and professors) on the Holocaust in the United States, given in 324 different institutions.[74] It is doubtful if that many courses at American colleges were given on such subjects as, say, medieval history or modern French history, once among the staples of the curriculum. During the past 15 or 20 years, too, the Holocaust has become, in the Western world, a universally internalised symbol of evil, a universal tragedy and crime. In Washington DC a United States Holocaust Memorial Museum stands nearly adjacent to the Smithsonian Institution, the National Air and Space Museum and the Washington Monument, although the Holocaust was a crime which was committed in Europe by Europeans against other Europeans. In London, the Imperial War Museum, Britain's national museum devoted to the activities of the British forces in two world wars, recently opened a whole wing depicting the Holocaust, although Britain's only role in this event (apart from fighting Hitler) was to accept refugees and liberate some concentration camps.

Despite widespread fears among many Jews that claiming such centrality would lead to a backlash, none has occurred. In America, most of what little opposition there has been to the National Holocaust Memorial Museum has come from blacks and native Americans, concerned that their own tragic histories are not honoured by an appropriate museum. The museum attracts 2 million visitors a year, and is so popular that tickets have to be booked in advance. The Imperial War Museum opened its Holocaust exhibit after public questioning that it omitted depicting the Nazi genocide. Popular pressure, in effect, led to the opening of this exhibit, not to its closing. Many – not least of all many Jews – have questioned the current obsession with the Holocaust as unhealthy, and, even worse, a distortion of Jewish history, conceptualising Jewish history in teleological terms as inevitably leading to the Nazi genocide and virtually ignoring its positive elements.

There are a number of interrelated questions about the origins of the Holocaust which have led to much debate among historians. Among the most important are whether Nazi antisemitism was categorically different from previous waves and outbursts of antisemitism, whether Germany and German culture were inherently antisemitic, and whether Hitler bears the sole responsibility for instigating and masterminding the Holocaust.

It seems unquestionable that Nazi antisemitism was categorically different from previous waves of antisemitism in modern times, since its solution to the Jewish 'problem' was, eventually, mass murder, something which had not previously been advocated by anyone. When the basis of antisemitism had been religious, with Jews condemned for rejecting Christ, conversion was always a possibility for Jewish physical survival. In modern times, various ways of limiting Jewish influence in a society were advocated by antisemitic ideologues and parties: but physical extermination of the entire Jewish population of a country, let alone the European continent, was never advocated prior to Hitler.[75] To be sure, some ideological antisemites blamed the Jews for every conceivable evil, seeing them as one of the key motivating factors in everything wrong with the modern world, while nearly all post-1870 antisemites viewed the Jews as a distinctive racial group, different from 'Aryans' by heredity and group characteristics. To be sure, too, some well-known European antisemites of the pre-Hitler era did make what appear to be calls to violence and extermination against Jews, for instance Karl Lueger, the antisemitic Mayor of Vienna between 1897 and 1910 (when Hitler lived there), who claimed that antisemitism would 'perish when the last Jew perished' and, accused of saying that it was a matter of indifference to him whether Jews were hanged or shot, corrected the speaker by saying 'Beheaded! is what I said.'[76] The Russian pogroms which took place between 1881 and

1906 cost perhaps 30,000 Jewish lives. Nevertheless, prior to 1914, or even prior to 1933, there were distinctive limits to any programme of Western antisemitism. Explicitly antisemitic parties briefly enjoyed some limited electoral success in Germany and Austria, but never achieved power: they were actually fading in popularity in the period just before the Great War compared with a decade or so earlier.[77] By 1914, only Tsarist Russia still maintained major legal restrictions on Jews: most Jews (there were exceptions) were legally required to live in one of the provinces in western Russia, chiefly in what was later Poland, the Ukraine and Byelorussia, known as the 'Pale of Settlement'. Elsewhere in the Western world, nearly all legal and political restrictions on Jewish citizen rights and participation in public life had been abolished: antisemites were powerless before the overwhelming tide of nineteenth-century liberalism. The most important antisemitic incident in the generation before 1914, the Dreyfus Affair in France, split France down the middle, but resulted in a sweeping victory for the pro-Dreyfus left in French politics: as a result of the affair, for instance, the French Catholic church was disestablished in 1904, the Catholic church being seen by pro-Dreyfusards as an arch-reactionary instigator of antisemitism. In the English-speaking world, despite whatever economic and social antisemitism existed, no significant antisemitic party or movement ever emerged.

The First World War and its immediate aftermath, especially in the wake of the Bolshevik Revolution of 1917, destroyed much of the legal network of tolerance that had slowly been put in place throughout continental Europe in the 150 previous years. There is not the slightest doubt that the five years or so from 1917 witnessed an unparalleled upsurge of radical antisemitism. Much of this occurred in Germany, which lost the Great War, saw its ancient institutions destroyed overnight, and witnessed the near-victory of local Bolshevik forces in Bavaria in 1918–19 and elsewhere throughout Germany at the end of the war (and also the Bela Kun Marxist government in nearby Hungary), where a very disproportionate number of the revolutionary leaders were certainly Jewish.[78] Even in the English-speaking democracies, which were victorious in the Great War and whose institutions were intact, this period certainly saw a marked increase in antisemitism, with the dissemination of the *Protocols of the Elders of Zion*, the notorious antisemitic forgery, in England in

1919, and the publication of Henry Ford's *International Jew* in 1922. (This upsurge of antisemitism was not inconsistent with many counter-vailing trends: for instance, the Lloyd George Cabinet, 1916–22, contained five Jews and promulgated the Balfour Declaration in 1917.) As a reaction to the left-wing induced chaos in central Europe, extreme right-wing terrorist, vigilante and police groups and right-wing armies also temporarily flourished in the immediate aftermath of the war. Most were explicitly antisemitic, often ferociously and murderously so, with, for instance, probably 20,000 Jews murdered in the Ukraine in 1918–19 by the nationalist Ukrainian leader Simon Petlura (1880–1926).[79]

As most perceptive biographers of Hitler have noted, it was this phase of his life, his war service from 1914 and, especially, the year or two centring on the German armistice of November 1918 and the ensuing political chaos, which determined his subsequent political programme and uniquely extreme antisemitism.[80] It is now generally recognised that this era radicalised Hitler far more than his pre-war Vienna years, when he had Jewish friends and associates and lived the life of an unknown bohemian artist.[81] The apocalyptic mood engendered in Germany during and immediately after the Great War was especially traumatic to a front-line soldier like Hitler. The constant threat of death, a sudden and unexpected military defeat (after which Hitler apparently suffered a nervous breakdown), seemingly inexplicable except by a 'stab in the back' administered by traitors at home – Germany never actually surrendered in 1918 and was never invaded by victorious foreign troops, unlike 1944–5 – simultaneous with the overturning of all existing political institutions and a violent 'red revolution' throughout Europe, apparently led by Jews, determined Hitler's monomaniac hatred of Jews literally until the day of his death. Of course, Hitler had absorbed the Pan-Germanic antisemitism and anti-Slavism so common in pre-war Vienna, but, essentially, Hitler lived his life after the Armistice in the apocalyptic mood of 1918–19. To this must be added all the singular and bizarre aspects of Hitler's opaque personality with which so many biographers have wrestled – his utter lack of humane feeling in the conventional sense, his lack of a family or close friends, his not inconsiderable gifts as an autodidactical thinker, especially about history.[82] (In his historical musings Hitler invariably thought in terms of long periods of historical time as did most Marxist theorists: except for the odd 'hero', the individual person matters nothing in a long time-span, only the continuing racial 'germ' or *Volk*.) While only a minority of historians would argue that Hitler intended the mass murder of the Jews all along, all the elements were already in place in his psyche by the mid-1920s at the latest which led to this goal, especially a world-view centred around antisemitism at its most extreme, an utter relentlessness in carrying this out, and, most of all, a total lack of humanity or compassion.

Weimar Germany had been a functioning democracy which, by the height of the post-war boom around 1927–9, had achieved considerable legitimacy: virtually no one imagined, in 1928, that the regime would be overthrown only five years later, and from so unlikely a source. In the May 1928 German elections, the National Socialists won only 2.6 per cent of the vote, with only 12 seats in the *Reichstag*. The Depression, of course, in which millions of Germans were unemployed, coming on top of the defeat in the war, put Hitler in power. So, too, did the mediocrity of politics in Weimar, its lack of any national figures of stature, the fragmentation of political parties, aided by the Weimar constitution, and the assistance given to the destruction of Weimar democracy by the Communists, on Stalin's orders.

In power, the Nazis systematically and relentlessly discarded the entire apparatus of Western liberalism as it had evolved since the Renaissance, putting in place a regime thoroughly ideological in nature and totally devoted to creating a *volkish* (usually translated as 'ethnic', but 'racial national' is probably more accurate) German state, with race at the centre, directly or indirectly, of all policy.[83] Within this all-embracing doctrine of racial nationalism, Nazi Germany was, in its way, extremely radical in its opposition to class distinctions among the racially favoured. 'The National Socialist state knows no "classes", but politically speaking only citizens with absolutely equal rights and accordingly equal duties, and, alongside of these, state subjects who in the political sense are absolutely without rights,' Hitler wrote with startling frankness.[84] Needless to say, Jews were the primary group 'absolutely without rights'. As is too well-known to need any elaboration, Hitler's view of Jews was a Manichean one of absolute evil. 'The Jews inhabited Hitler's mind. He believed that they were the source of all evil, misfortune, and tragedy, the single factor that, like some inexorable law of nature, explained the workings of the universe,' Lucy S. Dawidowicz perceptively noted.[85] As many historians have pointed out, Hitler regarded the Jews as a kind of dark counter-elite to the 'Aryans', and a group which had kept itself intact and racially pure over the millennia, despite all vicissitudes, by rigorous inbreeding and racial 'hygiene' of exactly the kind Hitler wished the Germans rigorously to practise. By being present in Germany, Jews worked relentlessly to undermine 'Aryan' values through their pacifism, internationalism, championing of modernism in the arts, and mastery of both stock market finance capitalism and Marxist socialism. They represented a severe external threat as well, dominating the Soviet Union, France and the Anglo-Saxon powers, all enemies of Germany. Jews could not be absorbed into the 'Aryan' German population over time, regardless of their outward patriotism or seeming Germanness. Anyone with Jewish blood invariably reverted to type, and invariably worked to undermine the German *Volk*.

Because of the centrality of these doctrines and the thoroughness with which they defined Nazi policy, Hitler's antisemitism was categorically different from that found anywhere else. In the interwar period, virtually every country in eastern and central Europe turned to a policy of anti-semitism to a greater or lesser extent (often in response to the Nazi example), but their antisemitism was almost always different from that found under Hitler. Normally, Jews were seen as too successful in the national economic elite and professional classes, their success coming at the expense of the majority population who had the disadvantage of recently emerging from oppression and backwardness. The number of Jews in the economic elite and professional leadership of these countries was simply too great, and would have to be reduced, if possible, by humane means, such as the encouragement of emigration. (For this reason many continental nationalists were keen Zionists, especially in Poland.) As well, nearly all such antisemites recognised degrees and shades of difference between the Jews of their country, a very familiar division between 'good Jews' and 'bad Jews'. In general, highly accultur-ated Jews who had adopted the language, mores and patriotism of the majority group, especially in the capital city, were tolerated or even accepted. 'Bad Jews' were socialists, cultural modernists and the exotic Strictly Orthodox groups (although, since the Strictly Orthodox did not meddle in politics and were social conservatives, they were sometimes preferred), especially in remote and backward parts of the country.

European nationalist antisemitism often drew its main support from the churches, especially the Catholic church. This type of interwar anti-semitism, strongly emphasising the threat to the majority posed by an overly successful urban 'middleman' minority, was almost ubiquitous throughout central and eastern Europe at the time.[86] Despite obvious affinities with Nazism, it did not normally view Jews in strictly racial or wholly Manichean terms, always admitting to some exceptions among acculturated Jews, and was not normally single-minded in viewing 'inter-national Jewry' as the root of all evil. While acts of violence against Jews became commonplace in, for instance, Poland in the 1930s, all such ideologies and regimes drew the line at genocide or even organised pogroms. Antisemitism in other parts of the world at the time was even more of a milk-and-water affair. In the United States, unofficial quota sys-tems against the admission of too many Jews to elite private universities were common in the interwar period, as were many other forms of petty social and economic antisemitism, but everyone in the American main-stream remained committed to the values of democracy and nearly every-one was shocked by overt antisemitism of the Nazi kind.[87] Nazi antisemitism, at least in its fully developed wartime form, stood to these lesser forms of antisemitism roughly as the atomic bomb stands to a tor-pedo, or to a firecracker.

The notion that Germany was peculiarly antisemitic, or, before 1945, peculiarly attracted to authoritarianism, is an old belief, enunciated in the past by a variety of sources ranging from anti-German propagandists among the Allies in wartime to the Germans themselves. Certainly the notion that Germany adopted a 'special path' to modernity is so wide-spread among historians as to be almost ubiquitous.[88] The peculiarities of modern German history before 1945, especially its combination of a pre-modern militarist-oriented governing elite, unusually rapid industrialisa-tion, especially in heavy industries, and the lack of a successful liberal revolution which put in place liberal values, was unique, and set Germany apart from the historical experiences of Britain, France and the United States. Because Hitler exterminated the Jews with little overt opposition, it is also natural to search for the origins of Hitler's policies in a peculiarly virulent German tradition of antisemitism. It is not terri-bly difficult to construct a German authoritarian/malignantly antisemitic tradition around such national figures as Martin Luther, Frederick the

Great, Bismarck and Wilhelm II, and such cultural figures as Herder, Fichte, Hegel, Wagner, Wilhelm Marr (who coined the term 'anti-semitism') and other advocates of radical racial nationalism and anti-modernism. Recently, an even more extreme variant of this well-worn view achieved world renown in the form of Daniel Goldhagen's *Hitler's Willing Executioners* (1996). Goldhagen argued that 'eliminationist anti-semitism' had become virtually ubiquitous in Germany *before* the Nazis came to power, and that active participation in the Holocaust was far more extensive than previously argued, with 100,000 or more persons taking part in the Jewish genocide. In general (there are exceptions), Goldhagen's work has been treated with derision by most academic historians, and some of his evidence is very dubious.[89]

There may well be an element of truth in a component of Goldhagen's thesis, but it is certainly very questionable *in toto*. First of all, there is a great ambiguity, never frankly examined by Goldhagen, in discussing Germany as a single politico-cultural unit. 'Germany' did not exist prior to 1871; its boundaries were a matter of great contention throughout the nineteenth century and beyond; while the smaller German states were autonomous, even semi-independent, until 1918 or even 1933. Each component of 'Germany' had a separate pattern of historical evolution, with a liberal tradition certainly existing in the Hanseatic towns and parts of north-west Germany. The political emancipation of the Jews came at different times in different places. Cosmopolitan Berlin was as different from Thuringia as Boston, Massachusetts was from Birmingham, Alabama. It has also been repeatedly observed by historians of National Socialism that very disproportionate numbers of extremist Nazis came from Austria (starting, obviously, with Hitler, who was not even a German) and other border German-speaking areas adjacent to the areas where millions of Slavs, Czechs and Jews lived.[90] Then, too, Goldhagen's perceptions of German evolution is utterly contrary to the actual pattern of German history as it emerged between 1815 and 1933, which was indubitably one of ever-growing liberalism and constitutionalism, in which all barriers to Jewish participation in civil society were eventually removed. Indeed, the central dilemma for the Jews in Weimar Germany was that (in Nazi eyes) they were over-represented in the professional and economic German elite. Many have seen the role of Jews in Germany's elites as actually on the decline in Weimar compared with the

Wilhelmine period: such figures as exist apparently bear this out, although the decline was slight.[91] Intermarriage with German gentiles and assimilation by middle-class Jews was also notoriously rampant in Weimar, striking evidence that 'genocidal eliminationist' antisemitism was simply not common. Goldhagen also ignores the whole leftist tradition in Germany, as well as the growth of liberalism, cosmopolitanism and internationalism during the Weimar period, if not before. In 1930, for instance, the Berlin Municipal Council built an expensive country villa for its most distinguished living citizen, Albert Einstein.[92] Had the Depression not set in and changed everything, it seems almost inconceivable that Hitler would be known today except among scholars of post-1918 German extremist groups.

Goldhagen (and many others) also consistently exaggerates the importance of Jews in German politics and culture. Other lines of division in German society were far more important: Bismarck's *Kulturkampf*, for instance, pitted Protestants against Catholics; many Germans viewed the most important conflict in Europe as between 'Teutons' and Slavs (with Jews generally seen as allied to the 'Teutons'). Politics in Germany after 1880 chiefly revolved around the impact of the Socialist party and the trade unions on established society. Jews had nothing, or virtually nothing, to do with any of these lines of division in German society. Finally, no Jew in Germany prior to the rise of Hitler believed that he or she was living in a pre-genocidal society where 'eliminationist antisemitism' was rampant. If they had perceived Germany in these terms, none would have failed to emigrate. Germany's Jews led normal lives and engaged in normal politics; they were deeply divided (as most Jewish communities were at the time) among a wide variety of ideologies and parties. As Donald L. Niewyk has written, 'nothing short of clairvoyance' could have caused Germany's Jews to have foreseen what was coming.[93] If there is an element of truth in some of Goldhagen's contentions, it lies in the fact that Germany's defeat in 1918, alongside the Marxist revolution of the time, probably produced a greater antisemitic backlash than elsewhere. A figure like the ex-Kaiser, Wilhelm II, now made grossly antisemitic statements, and continued to make them during the rest of his life (although he attacked *Kristallnacht* in 1938).[94] Whether this wider backlash had any effect on the success Hitler enjoyed 15 years later is, however, questionable.

It seems completely contrary to the assumptions of modern historiography and sociology to attribute the responsibility for the Jewish Holocaust wholly or almost wholly to one man, Adolf Hitler, but no other reasonable conclusion is possible. 'No Hitler, no Holocaust' is the way one historian succinctly put it, a conclusion which seems perfectly valid. While antisemitism did increase markedly as a result of the Bolshevik Revolution and the collapse of the old regimes, by the prosperous mid-1920s for the most part antisemitism declined once more, even in countries which were to see a tidal wave of Jew hatred after 1933. The Italian fascist movement led by Mussolini was not originally antisemitic: it included many prominent Jews in government positions, while Mussolini categorically repudiated antisemitic racism during the 1920s.[95] Even in eastern Europe, the 'zone of antisemitism', radical measures attempting to limit the participation of Jews in public and professional life did not become endemic and commonplace until the 1930s, although antisemitic agitators and parties often flourished and many antisemitic incidents occurred. Even in Poland, for instance, the 1920s appeared in retrospect to many Jews 'as a kind of golden age of Polish democracy and tolerance', compared with the depressed 1930s.[96] Much the same was true throughout the rest of continental Europe.

While the immediate effect of the great Depression which began in 1929 was to increase calls for the removal of Jews from their position of 'over-representation' in the economic and professional elites of many European countries, really radical measures to achieve this end (such as those Hungary began to introduce from May 1938 on) invariably came in imitation of Nazi models or as a result of growing Nazi influence. Thus, while some historians have seen something like the Holocaust as 'inevitable', even if it did not take the extreme form it did, there is simply no credible evidence that antisemitism would not have been contained in normal patterns had, say, Hitler been killed in the trenches in 1916. Certainly in Weimar Germany after the early 1920s there was no significant political force or movement apart from the Nazis, even on the extreme right, which regarded the Jews or antisemitism as more than a fringe issue.[97] *Because*, however, Hitler saw antisemitism and German racial-nationalism of the most extreme kind as at the abiding core of his policies, and was, certainly after the death of President Paul von Hindenburg in August 1934, by law the absolute dictator of Germany, with a vast, violent and ruthless machine enforcing Nazi will at his command, he was able to put in place the policies which led to the Holocaust. Hitler's own bizarre personality, with his utter lack of human warmth or close human ties, also made the Holocaust more likely. Not only was Hitler totally lacking in pity, but, after the mid-1920s, by choice and policy he literally never met a Jew and had no Jewish contacts of any kind. (It would be interesting to know what Hitler's reaction would have been at the time of Munich if Léon Blum were still French Premier or Leslie Hore-Belisha Britain's Prime Minister. Would Hitler have agreed to meet these Jewish politicians?) No other conclusion seems sensible or convincing but that Hitler alone was responsible for initiating and carrying out the policies of extreme antisemitism associated with Nazi Germany. That others helped him and approved of these policies is beside the point: Hitler alone was responsible for their being put in place.

From the first moment the Nazis came to power in January 1933 the regime instituted discriminatory measures against the Jews. Nevertheless, there was what Karl Schleunes rightly described as a 'twisted road to Auschwitz', and it is a mistake to view Nazi policy towards the Jews as straightforward.[98] The well-known 'intentionalist' school of Holocaust historians, who view Hitler's genocidal intentions as implicit from the 1920s onwards, surely miss the point that Nazi policy towards the Jews changed radically as the possibilities open to Hitler grew. Hitler at all times intended to do the maximum possible harm to the Jews, but this progressively evolved and expanded. The main stages in Nazi policy towards the Jews from 1933–9 have been discussed many times and need little elaboration: in 1933, most Jews were removed from the civil service and the universities; in 1935, by the Nuremberg Laws, they lost their citizenship rights and were forbidden to intermarry with 'Aryans'; after *Kristallnacht* (9–10 November 1938), a Nazi-instigated pogrom in which 91 Jews died and hundreds of synagogues were destroyed, a huge fine was levied on Germany's Jews, Jewish businesses were 'aryanised', and it was made absolutely clear that all Germany's Jews would have to emigrate. All these stages were accompanied by a ruthless, barbaric campaign aimed at utterly marginalising Jews in Germany.[99] The forced emigration of Jews became the rule, slightly earlier, in Austria, which was occupied by Germany in March 1938 and forcibly incorporated into the German *Reich*. Over two-thirds of Austria's

Jews (about 126,000 of 185,000) emigrated by the end of 1939, only 21 months later. Only about 130,000 Jews, of 499,000 resident there in 1933 when Hitler came to power, remained in Germany in its 1933 boundaries when emigration finally became impossible in 1940–1. Although many historians have criticised the outside world, and especially democracies such as Britain and the United States, for 'closing their doors' to German Jewish refugees, in fact most German Jews were able to flee in time.[100] Neither Germany's Jews nor any foreign government knew what lay in store for those Jews who were unable or unwilling to flee.

To understand why these extreme and barbaric measures of anti-semitism, unknown in the Western world since the Middle Ages, were carried out in a way which was nearly uncontested even before the killing process began, it is necessary to keep a number of central points in mind. Jews, it must be noted, were not being *killed* in Nazi Germany or by the Nazi regime as a matter of deliberate policy prior to the invasion of the Soviet Union in June 1941. Several thousands probably died, in concentration camps or during *Kristallnacht* and other anti-Jewish assaults, but it was not Nazi policy to kill Jews, only to brutalise them and force their emigration. The synagogues remained open in Germany until *Kristallnacht* and the Nazis initially encouraged both Zionism (which had Jewish emigration to Palestine as its goal) and such forms of Jewish culture and publication that emphasised the differences between Jews and 'Aryan' Germans.

Successful opposition to Nazi policy by anti-Nazi Germans was impossible or virtually impossible, due to the systematic infrastructure of repression and totalitarianism that the Nazi government enacted, via the Gestapo and the SS, from the moment it came to power. The first 'concentration camps' – those like Dachau, Sachsenhausen and Buchenwald, all in Germany itself – were initially established for opponents of the regime, and by 1939 were widened to include such categories as 'asocials', the 'workshy', Jehovah's Witnesses and homosexuals. There were Jews (and gypsies) in the early concentration camps, but Jews were not sent there *en masse* and nor were these the mass killing centres, like Auschwitz and Treblinka, which came into existence from early 1942.[101] Although both types are known as 'concentration camps', this term is very misleading as they had different purposes. All organised opposition to the Nazi regime quickly became impossible, and any possible sources of anti-Nazi resistance, either from the left, trade unions, the churches, students or dissident conservatives, was ground down as a matter of urgent priority by the Nazi terror machine. In fact, no significant opposition to Hitler appeared before the War. More importantly, perhaps, the Nazi regime undertook a systematic, concentrated campaign aimed at eliminating all traces of Western liberalism, tolerance or constitutional normality throughout their entire political and legal operations. With the parallel assault on these institutions and values in the Soviet Union under Communism, these constituted the greatest attack on Western liberal norms, indeed the greatest attack on Western civilisation, in modern history. As Michael Burleigh has put it, 'the suppression of the rule of law' in Nazi Germany 'is not a side issue ... but *the* most important departure from civilised values engineered by the Nazi government'. Even apart from enacting a monstrous dictatorship, the rule of law in the normally accepted Western sense was replaced by a new concept of law, having much in common with that found in Stalinist Russia, in which the values of the 'national community', defined in racial-nationalist terms and by devotion to Hitler and the Nazis, became the sole determinant of legality.[102]

Although dissent from the Nazi 'new order' became so dangerous that virtually no one ever publicly dissented, the savagery of the Gestapo and the SS was not the only reason why Hitler was able to take the path which led to genocide. It was also unquestionably true that the Nazi government was popular with many, perhaps most, of the German people. Until 1941–2, Hitler's positive achievements were not merely considerable, but extraordinary: the restoration of full employment in place of mass unemployment, the return (to many) of national self-respect in place of the national humiliation of Versailles; the institution of a sense of national purpose; the banishment of the political mediocrity of Weimar; the unification of the German-speaking areas of central Europe; and the institution of German hegemony across the continent from the Pyrenees to the gates of Moscow. It is pointless to state the obvious, that these achievements were purchased at an incalculable cost in human misery and savage aggression – although, before the attack on the Soviet Union in June 1941, these costs were as nothing compared to what they would shortly become. To the average 'Aryan' German, Hitler, virtually unknown before 1930–2, must have seemed as something of a Divine

Deliverer (an image he carefully cultivated) and to deny this is to distort history. Until 1942, when the Soviet adventure began to go badly wrong, Hitler differed from all modern politicians: while they promised the earth, he actually delivered it.[103]

The fact that many, perhaps most 'Aryan' Germans could, in a sense, live vicariously through the success of the Fuhrer and the achievements of the Nazi regime points to a central point about totalitarianism, whether of the right or left, and its appeal: in contrast to democracy, totalitarian ideologies denied a rigorous division between the public and private spheres, and wished, perhaps above all, to make the individual subject feel a sense of unity with the regime and its ideals. While most democratic commentators have seen in this the very essence of Orwellian regimentation, it is also important to grasp the sense of purpose and idealism which this gives to the average man and woman of the regime, a sense of purpose almost always absent in a democratic society. Although most people in democratic societies presumably share many fundamental values, by definition they are divided into several, and often many, political parties which are inevitably in opposition much of the time, while all governments, even the most ideologically driven, are subject to severe legal, economic, institutional and customary restraints on what they can in practice accomplish. National unity and a sense of national purpose shared by the average person are normally achievable in a democracy only during a major war or emergency situation, especially one in which the life of the nation is at stake. The normal state of affairs in any democracy, however, is one of intense alienation of many, perhaps most, citizens, from their government, a pervasive sense of cynicism, and near-universal expectations that all politicians will prove to be self-seeking scoundrels or, at best, time-serving mediocrities.

At their heart, totalitarian ideologies seek to overcome this near-universal alienation from their governments which is the hallmark of all democratic regimes nearly all of the time, and replace it with a shared sense of purpose through universal support for a programme of national renewal and through vicarious participation in the life of the dictator and party notables. This was an obvious feature of Stalinist Russia, but was, if anything, carried even further in Nazi Germany, where 'the *Volk* community' – the 'community' of the whole 'Aryan' German people – became the most basic principle of the regime. Nor was this a cynical ploy: Hitler and the other leading Nazis believed it sincerely. Its pervasive enunciation as the regime's leading principle gave Nazi Germany a kind of dynamism – however evil and perverted – and energy lacking in most democratic governments of the time, as was also the case in the Soviet Union.

Hitler specifically excluded the Jews and a number of other groups, such as hard-core Marxists, from the German *Volk*, but it must be realised that their number was very small, not more than a few per cent of the total population. (Jews constituted less than 1 per cent of the German population in 1933.) Before 1941, their exclusion was, thus, hardly noticed by most Germans, who, in any case, assumed – if they gave the matter any thought at all – that the Jews emigrating from Germany were simply going to new, probably better and more prosperous homes in America, Britain and elsewhere. Seen in the light of totalitarianism as an inclusionary rather than exclusionary political ideal, the question of what role antisemitism played in Nazi Germany for the average German might also be addressed. Paradoxically, while fanatical antisemitism was at the core of Hitler's world-view, it probably played virtually no role whatever in the attitude of the typical 'Aryan' German towards the Nazi regime, which was (and was supposed to be) rooted in the sharing of a common, positive purpose embodying a German economic, political, military and 'spiritual' renaissance. Needless to say, the German people were constantly indoctrinated with venomous Nazi antisemitic propaganda, but the very pointlessness of this propaganda and the inability of the average German to relate to it with the same sense of positive achievement as he or she could towards the ending of unemployment or the *Anschluss* with Austria, probably meant that it was mainly disregarded, although, to be sure, a minority became (and needed little encouragement to become) murderous and committed antisemites. Diabolically, while Hitler regarded the removal of all Jews from Germany and then from Europe as at the centre of his policies, most Germans saw only the regime's positive features but were willing to acquiesce in Nazi policies towards a tiny minority.

Until 1940–1 the aim of the Nazi regime had been to force all its Jews to emigrate. Between 1940 and 1942 the emigration of Jews in Nazi-occupied Europe was forbidden, and, with the invasion of the Soviet Union in June 1941, the Nazis turned to genocide.[104] Why and precisely when

Hitler turned to genocide has been endlessly debated by historians. There are no easy answers, and one can only suggest the most likely sequence of events. The Nazis could not have realistically contemplated the genocide of Europe's Jews until most or nearly all came under their domain. Prior to the outbreak of the war, only the ever-diminishing Jewish population of the German Reich came under Nazi rule: the major Jewish population centres of eastern and central Europe were not yet under Nazi occupation. Hitler could thus not contemplate the mass murder of Europe's Jews until he had conquered most of the European continent, which he did between September 1939 and the Fall of France in June 1940. As a result of the Nazi-Soviet Non-Aggression Pact of August 1939, however, eastern Poland, the Baltic republics, Moldavia and other areas with large Jewish populations came under Soviet, not Nazi rule. To finish off European Jewry, it was thus necessary to invade and occupy the Soviet Union. It thus seems likely – but far from certain – that Hitler fixed on genocide, the actual physical extermination of the Jews, after the Fall of France in June 1940, when he began to contemplate the invasion and conquest of the Soviet Union, with its 5 million Jews. In February 1941 Hitler told a group of senior Nazis that he 'was thinking of many things [concerning the Jews] in a different way, that was not exactly more friendly'.[105] In the meantime, following the conquest of Poland, Nazis herded the captive Jews of Poland and elsewhere into notorious closed ghettos, where tens of thousands died of disease and malnutrition every month, while (as noted) forbidding emigration from Europe. Most historians believe that, before settling on genocide, the Nazis were actively contemplating transporting all Europe's Jews to Madagascar in the Indian Ocean. Plans to deport the 4 million Jews then under Nazi rule to Madagascar were drawn up by Adolf Eichmann (1906–62, then the head, within the SS, of the Central Office for Jewish Emigration).[106] Obviously this was never implemented, in part because the sea lanes to Madagascar were closed to the Germans, in part – almost certainly – because Hitler increasingly had even more radical plans in mind.

The mass murder of the Jews began with the invasion of the Soviet Union by Nazi Germany on 22 June 1941. As with so much else concerning the Holocaust, both the reasons for Hitler's decision to kill the Jews, and its precise timing and evolution, have been subject to fierce dispute. It is not entirely clear whether Hitler ordered the extermination of Soviet

Jewry to begin as soon as the invasion of Russia began or, as now seems more likely, a comprehensive programme of extermination was not fully put in place for several months.[107] By August 1941, however, mobile Nazi killing squads, the *SS Einsatzgruppen*, were killing all Jews, without exception, who came into their grasp. The most notorious single killing operation carried out by the *Einsatzgruppen* occurred on 29–30 September 1941, at Babi Yar outside Kiev, where nearly 34,000 Jews were killed by machine-gunning carried out by the SS with the help of Ukrainian militiamen.[108] A good many Jews managed to escape eastwards ahead of the Nazis, but Hilberg believes that the *Einsatzgruppen* and associated Nazi killing squads murdered up to 500,000 Jews in five months, that is, by the end of 1941.[109] The killings were often unpopular with the German troops, although virtually no single German soldier demurred from mass murder.[110] A further stage of *Einsatzgruppen* activity also began in the Baltic area in late 1941, in which they were assisted by the Order Police, often recruited from fairly ordinary Germans and from willing Balts, Ukrainians and Belorussians. Probably up to another 400,000 Jews were killed in this stage of the *Einsatzgruppen* activities, although even an approximate number is a matter for conjecture.[111] Hilberg gives a figure of 1.3 million as the total number of Jewish deaths carried out by the Nazis in 'open-air killings', including those carried out in Romania, Serbia and elsewhere.[112] Quite possibly this figure is too high, and even an approximate figure for *Einsatzgruppen* deaths remains one of the central demographic mysteries of the Holocaust: probably 750,000 open-air killings in the Soviet area is more likely than a higher figure.[113]

Owing to the psychological toll taken on German troops participating in these killings, their inefficiency, and the fact that open-air shootings could not readily take place in central or western Europe, the Nazi death machine next turned to new, more efficient ways of killing Jews (and others, but especially Jews): the extermination camps, where victims were (generally) killed in large numbers by poison gas in gas chambers, although others were worked or starved to death or killed in other ways. There were six major extermination camps: Chelmno (near Lodz), Belzec (in south-eastern Poland), Sobibor (in eastern Poland), Treblinka (northeast of Warsaw), Majdanek (near Lublin) and, most important of all, Auschwitz (in lower Silesia), as well as many minor camps. All were located in what had been Poland or were adjacent to Poland. None was in Germany or anywhere else in Europe, although German concentration camps (as opposed to extermination camps) existed by the score, like Bergen-Belsen and Dachau, and some killing centres existed in northern Romania and elsewhere. Chelmno (or Kulmhof, in Germany), a relatively small camp, was established in December 1942. Belzec, Sobibor and Treblinka were purely killing centres, from which virtually no one escaped alive. Majdanek (where most of the prisoners were Poles or Soviet prisoners of war) was both an extermination and a labour camp. So, too, was Auschwitz, where over 90 per cent of the victims were Jews. Auschwitz is by far the most infamous of the extermination camps, and has become synonymous with modern evil. In part this was because it was the largest of these camps, with the most victims but, paradoxically, also because as a labour camp it had the most survivors. Additionally, it continued to function closer to the end of the war than the other camps, meaning that its inmates were more likely to be liberated (many Auschwitz inmates died on Nazi 'death marches' at the very end of the war). The three 'Operation Reinhard' camps, as they are known (because of the Nazi action against most of Poland's Jews, termed 'Operation Reinhard'), Belzec, Sobibor and Treblinka, functioned earlier than Auschwitz, from early 1942 until the autumn of 1943, when they were closed down. In contrast, Auschwitz continued to function until late 1944.[114]

The extermination camps began their operation early in 1942 (although preparations were made earlier). The relationship of the infamous Wannsee Conference of 20 January 1942 to the extermination process remains controversial. This conference, held near Berlin, was believed to have apparently taken the cryptically worded decision to exterminate all Europe's Jews, but most historians now believe it merely gave the SS an opportunity to announce already determined policy, especially towards part-Jews, to a number of senior German civil servants.[115] It was attended by Reinhard Heydrich (1904–42), the sinister head of the Reich Security Main Office and chiefly responsible, at that stage, for carrying out the Holocaust, and by Adolf Eichmann, but not by Heinrich Himmler (1900–45), the true head of the SS who had actually been charged by Hitler with executing the 'Final Solution', nor by any important head of a death camp. It appears likely that about 2.7 million

Jews (and 500,000 others) were killed in the extermination camps: 960,000–1 million in Auschwitz (plus at least 100,000 others), 550,000–600,000 in Belzec, 200,000–250,000 in Sobibor, up to 750,000 in Treblinka and 150,000 elsewhere. Apart from the conveyor-belt empire of death, unprecedented in history, the camps have become universally infamous for many other aspects of satanic hellishness which have become ingrained upon the modern consciousness: the hideous sealed trains, the selection process at the gates, the medical experiments, the piles of clothing, the smoking chimneys and a hundred other images from Dante's Inferno, come into existence in twentieth-century Europe. The Jewish Holocaust represented, truly, the moral nadir of humanity in modern history.

While the precise degree of Hitler's involvement in masterminding the Holocaust is often unclear, there is no doubt that only Hitler had the authority to turn to a policy as radical and unprecedented as genocide. It is inconceivable that the comprehensive mass murder of the Jews could have 'welled up' from army commanders and SS men in Russia, or that so many resources could have been diverted from the war effort to kill the Jews without Hitler ordering it. In a famous part of his testimony at his trial in Jerusalem, Eichmann stated that Himmler told him 'two months' or 'three months' after the invasion of the Soviet Union, 'the Fuhrer has ordered the physical extermination of the Jews', that is, in August or September 1941.[116] Hitler certainly intervened directly with Admiral Horthy, the Regent of Hungary, in April 1943 to have the Jews of Hungary deported to their deaths.[117] He directly intervened again in March 1944.[118] In November 1941 he had promised Haj Amin Husseini, the Grand Mufti of Jerusalem, that Germany was committed 'to the annihilation of the Jews living under British protection in Arab lands'.[119] Hitler, in other words, took an immediate and continuing interest in the extermination of the Jews. Broad policy, it seems, was decided in secret face-to-face meetings between Hitler and Himmler, of which no transcripts survive: the logistical details were, however, apparently left entirely to Himmler.

Why did Hitler kill the Jews? Answering this is difficult since we are discussing a psychopath, and there is probably no single answer. Hitler did offer, however, a perfectly straightforward answer to this question in his will, drawn up a few hours before he committed suicide, that if millions of 'Aryans' died in the war, millions of Jews (who had started the war) would also have to die, so that they could not emerge triumphant, on the ruins of Germany, as they had in 1918. '[M]illions of children of Europe's Aryan peoples would not die of hunger, millions of children of grown men would not suffer death, and hundreds of thousands of women and children would not be burned and bombed to death in the towns, without the real culprit having to atone for his guilt, even if by my more humane means.'[120] That Hitler had started the war, not the Jews, was somehow here overlooked. Many other factors seem to have played a part in Hitler's decision, especially his perception of Jews as a permanent Fifth Column., but the dictator seems, above all, to have been centrally motivated by a desire that the experience of the First World War would not be repeated, when millions of Germans and other 'Aryans' had died but the Jews had emerged triumphant via Western capitalism, modernism, internationalism and Bolshevism.[121]

The number of Jews killed at the hands of the Nazis is invariably given, in shorthand terms at any rate, as 6 million, a figure which has, of course, entered the common consciousness and is endlessly repeated.[122] It appears likely, however, that this number is too high by a considerable amount, as some careful Holocaust scholars such as Gerald Reitlinger and Raul Hilberg have pointed out. Reitlinger's early (1953) but carefully argued estimate of between 4,194,000 and 4,581,000 Jewish deaths is certainly the lowest ever offered by a serious historian; Hilberg's more recent, but even more carefully argued estimate of 5,100,000 Jewish dead appears to be the next lowest among reputable scholars.[123] Without entering here into an inappropriately lengthy discussion of this question, it appears to this historian that Reitlinger's figures are probably most nearly correct, with the figure of Jewish victims of the Holocaust numbering about 4.7 million, although there is a wide margin of imprecision. Given that about 2.7 million Jews perished in the six major extermination camps, a figure of 6 million Jewish dead necessarily means that 3.3 million perished in other ways: this is very difficult to believe and is almost certainly an exaggeration. In demographic terms, there are two ways of approaching this question: to compare the number of Jews in Nazi-occupied countries in September 1939 with those alive in May 1945 (bearing in mind such other factors as the escape of refugees and battle deaths), and to provide an estimate of the number of Jews who perished by method of death – in the extermination camps, at the hands of the *Einsatzgruppen*, etc. Both are fraught with difficulties, especially the former method. Because of the many boundary changes between 1938 and 1945, there is a continuing ambiguity about the initial size of each country's Jewry, and a danger of double counting, for instance, of attributing the deaths of the Jews of Transylvania both to Romania (Transylvania having been part of Romania before 1940 and after 1945) and Hungary (which incorporated Transylvania within its borders in 1940 and from where Eichmann deported tens of thousands of Jews to Auschwitz during the campaign to exterminate Hungarian Jewry in 1944). Anyone who is familiar with country-by-country figures for Jewish deaths in most histories of the Holocaust will be aware that this double counting is frequently encountered.

The other method (employed by Hilberg) of estimating Jewish losses by mode of death is also subject to probably significant margins of error. The number of Jews who perished at the hands of the *Einsatzgruppen*, for instance, is simply not known: estimates range from 600,000 to 1.3 million. That a surprisingly large number of Soviet Jews managed to flee in time is evident from the 1959 Soviet Census (the first post-war Soviet census), which showed quite significant Jewish populations in the areas of the western Soviet Union where the *Einsatzgruppen* operated; most were presumably post-1945 returnees to their old homes.[124] The other major source of demographic difficulty in this approach rises from estimating the number of Jews who died in ghettos and other places of incarceration prior to deportation to a death camp. Hilberg's estimate of 'over 600,000' seems high, although obviously the number was enormous.[125] In sum, a figure of 4.7 million Jewish deaths at the hands of the Nazis is not too low and may, indeed, be too high, suggesting that 2 million Jews were killed by the Nazis in ways other than by deportation to the death camps. To *this* figure, however, must be added another 400,000 or so to account for Jews who perished in the war in 'normal' ways, especially battle deaths in the Soviet army and those who died in the Siege of Leningrad and other Soviet sieges. Thus, there was a decline in European Jewry's numbers of around 5.2 million between September 1939 and May 1945.[126] This was the price of Adolf Hitler's existence.

Although at Wannsee the Nazis promised that 'Europe will be combed from west to east' in order to carry out 'the practical execution of the

Final Solution', the rate of Jewish survival varied very considerably from country to country.[127] As a general rule – there were exceptions – the slaughter was more thorough as one approached the Polish-Soviet area, which Hitler regarded as the very epicentre of the 'Judeo-Bolshevik' threat. In Western Europe and the Balkans, occasionally surprisingly large numbers of Jews survived. In France, for instance, about 75,000 of perhaps 225,000 Jews perished; in Belgium 24,000 of 65,000. (Next door in the Netherlands, however, only about 35,000 of 140,000 Jews managed to escape death or deportation.) In parts of the Balkans the figures were even more striking: all of Bulgaria's 50,000 Jews survived. In Romania (in its pre-1940 and post-1945 boundaries, ie excluding Moldavia but including Transylvania) Jews had numbered 427,042 in the 1930 Census, and 456,624 in the 1947 Census.[128] In general, countries with semi-independent 'quisling' regimes managed to protect their Jews better than the Polish-Soviet area, where there was no Nazi-recognised native puppet government, only brutal Nazi direct administration. Since even fascist and traditionally antisemitic allies of the Nazis drew the line at genocide, governments whose leaders were not philosemites but fero-cious antisemites occasionally emerged looking in relative terms like humanitarians, as Romania's dictator Ion Antonescu did after an initial period of instigating murderous pogroms against the Jews.

This, as much as anything, highlights the fact that the doctrines of Nazism went utterly beyond the outermost boundaries of what Western man regarded as permissible, even in the most extreme of other regimes and ideologies. Compared with Hitler brutal and antisemitic fascist dic-tators such as Romania's Antonescu looked like moderates, as did more traditional fascists and authoritarians such as Mussolini (until 1943), Horthy and Franco. Hitler and the Nazis were outside the pale of Western civilisation. It also highlights again the sheer unnaturalness of genocide, the inability of most people to continue to kill the innocent in cold blood apart from ideologically driven struggles. Still, it is not clear why nearly all Jews in the Regat ('Old Romania') survived while more than half in Hungary, with a similar type of government, perished. In particular, it is not clear why the SS did not deport Romania's Jews as they did the Jews of Hungary. Had the war lasted longer, of course, it seems certain that every Jew in Nazi-occupied Europe would have perished. Within each country, each ghetto, each transport to a death camp or concentration camp, blind luck often played an important element in survival: some survived and others perished for no obvious reason, as later testimonies asserted time and again.

The Jewish Holocaust was assuredly the closest approximation to a comprehensive example of genocide in the sense this term normally connotes that there has ever been in modern history. By any criteria, it fits the archetypal definition of genocide as this is understood by the ordinary person: intent to kill an entire group, in this case a well-defined, historically reviled ethno-religious minority, a specific infrastructure of death and murder organised for that purpose; a success rate which, in parts of eastern Europe, approached 100 per cent and which was forestalled from achieving complete success throughout a continent only because its organisers were themselves destroyed in a war. So much has been written on the Jewish Holocaust that little in the way of relatively new and important points can be made by the historian, but a few such observations are in order. The Jewish Holocaust was one of the few great massacres in history in which female victims probably (there are no comprehensive statistics) outnumbered male victims.[129] In most massacres down the ages, some pity was often shown to women and children, who were less dangerous than the men. Women were normally raped and taken captive, to become part of the victorious tribe or warring nation, while men were slaughtered. This pattern, comprising what has recently been termed 'gendercide', has only lately been identified or studied by scholars.[130] It is, in other words, the reverse of what one might have expected: the strong are killed, the weak often survived. More men than women are killed in all wars, and in other infamous recent examples of mass murder – Stalin's Purges, for example. The Nazis, whose ideology was based wholly in Social Darwinism at its most extreme and uncompromising, reversed that historical pattern: more women perished. Women less often had the labour skills which might save a man in a concentration camp; they were less able to flee to the forests and fight as partisans; as bearers of Jewish children, they were even more dangerous than the men. Absorption into the dominant German group by abduction and concubinage was, needless to say, utterly ruled out by the Nazis' racial laws forbidding sexual contact with Jews.

The Nazi genocide of the Jews was based in hatred of a biologically defined ethnic group. Surprisingly, this is not as common among modern genocides and mass slaughters as one might suppose: most killings in modern mass murders have probably been based in class rather than ethnic hatreds. Certainly most of the millions who perished at the hands of the Communists did so because of their 'dangerous' class backgrounds, not their ethnic origins. That 'genocide' is normally construed by the average person as being based in ethnic hatreds, largely because of the Jewish Holocaust and an array of other ethnically based massacres from the Armenians to the Rwandans, has disguised this fact.

While some rather desultory efforts were made at the end of the First World War to try a small number of those who carried out the Armenian genocide, the Jewish Holocaust was also distinguished by the fact that, immediately after the end of the Second World War, it became the centrepiece of the first and most famous of all war crimes tribunals, the Nuremberg Trials which began in October 1945 and lasted for nearly a year.[131] The 22 indicted Nazi leaders were charged on four counts: crimes against peace; war crimes; crimes against humanity; and a conspiracy to commit such crimes. The first article of indictment was thus not one of committing genocide against the Jews or atrocities against any other group, but for 'planning, preparation, initiation or waging of a war of aggression, or a war in violation of international treaties'.[132] Perhaps for this reason the principal defendant at Nuremberg was Hermann Goering, technically the number two man in Nazi Germany, but during the war the head of the *Luftwaffe*; Goering had nothing to do with the persecution of the Jews once the war began, although he was closely involved in *Kristallnacht* in 1938. In any case, although Hitler certainly started the war for no reason other than German aggrandisement, the Soviet Union, one of the four powers conducting the Trials, in 1939-40, as a consequence of the Nazi-Soviet Pact, eagerly joined in, annexing eastern Poland, the Baltic states, Moldavia and other areas. The Soviet Union was, in other words, trying the top Nazis for crimes of which it was itself guilty; similarly, while Nazi 'crimes against humanity' were punished at Nuremberg and elsewhere, Stalin's heinous atrocities never were. Because of the feeling by both the Americans and the Russians that the whole of the Nazi government be shown to be criminal, a number of top Nazis were placed on trial at Nuremberg who had nothing or virtually nothing to do with the Holocaust or other atrocities, such as Franz von

Papen (who was acquitted) and Admiral Karl Dönitz (Hitler's temporary successor; he received ten years).

Indeed, though all shared in the guilt of the Nazi regime in a general way, not more than perhaps one-half of the Nuremberg defendants, by any reasonable assessment, had any direct responsibility for murdering Jews; the real perpetrators of the Holocaust, Hitler, Himmler and Heydrich, were, of course, dead (as were Joseph Goebbels and Martin Bormann), while Eichmann was on the run. Moreover, the Nuremberg defendants notably failed to include any of the heads of extermination camps, the *Einsatzgruppen*, or other bodies which actually implemented the 'Final Solution'. Rudolf Höss (or Hoess), the commandant of Auschwitz, was tried separately and hanged (on the gallows in Auschwitz) in March 1947, while a variety of the most fiendish of the Nazi perpetrators of genocide were hanged, or sentenced to long terms of imprisonment, in separate trials which continued for several decades.[133] (Amon Goeth, infamous as the commandant in *Schindler's List*, was typical of those who met justice. He was tried by the Polish supreme court, convicted and hanged in 1948.) Even by the early 1950s (if not before), however, it was clear that most steam was running out of the drive for continuing prosecutions. As the Cold War got under way and West Germany, back on its feet as a pro-Western democracy, was needed as an ally, there was a sense that the past should be buried. While the West German government, sovereign once more, continued to try its guilty residents through the mid-1960s, they seldom received condign punishment and often got away virtually scot-free.[134]

Additionally, there are serious questions as to how far down the ranks punishment should extend. Initially, only the senior Nazis were considered for trial: the 'little men', who may have personally murdered thousands, were considered as simply minor cogs in the machine, carrying out orders they could hardly disobey. As a result, they were simply ignored. Walter Foster (*né* Fast), an Austrian Jew who emigrated to Britain in 1938 and wound up, in 1946, a British soldier identifying war criminals for trial, later recalled:

> The first thing we did was to screen out the big Nazis from the small ones, the war criminals from the fellow travellers ... The most important detail was that anyone below a senior rank, anyone below major at

least, and anyone less than 35 was not even looked at; they were sent home. We said 'These are too young, too stupid; they were not in a key position – send them home!'[135]

For these reasons and others, tens of thousands of participants in the Holocaust escaped justice while the war was a fresh memory. The celebrated trial in Jerusalem of Adolf Eichmann (who, like many others, had escaped to South America) in 1960–2 was both probably the last trial of a really top administrator of the Holocaust, and the event which brought the genocide of the Jews into the centre of public attention, breaking something of a taboo on presenting or discussing it, at least with the intensity and frequency later commonplace.[136] From the 1970s, however, as the Jewish Holocaust gradually became universally internalised in the Western world as the ultimate symbol of evil, a new, concerted drive took place in many countries to bring the remaining Nazi killers to justice. Laws were passed in many countries to facilitate this, often in the teeth of considerable opposition.[137] A few important remaining war criminals, such as Klaus Barbie (1913–91), convicted in France in 1987, were tried at this late date, and several hundred war criminals (often Ukrainians or Balts) who emigrated to the United States were stripped of their citizenship and deported. On the other hand, travesties of justice also occurred, such as the trial of John Demjanjuk, allegedly 'Ivan the Terrible' of Treblinka, whose conviction in Israel was quashed by the Israeli Supreme Court. By the early twenty-first century, there was a nagging sense that justice had not dealt fully with the perpetrators, but also a widespread sense that further prosecutions, of very old men 60 years after their crimes, was futile.

The Holocaust also sparked the best-known 'denial' movement, however much it has been confined to the fringe of crackpots and propagandists. 'Holocaust denial' – embodying such claims as that the Nazis killed no Jews at all or very few, that there were no gas chambers in the camps, that the *Diary of Anne Frank* and other well-known Holocaust texts are fraudulent, and so on – began surprisingly early: indeed, almost as soon as the war ended.[138] It remained virtually unknown until the mid-1970s, when the movement's activists began to attract some attention. Its main proponents, such as Arthur Butz and Robert Faurisson, published scholarly-looking works with many footnotes, ostensibly based on serious research, and a so-called 'Institute of Historical Review' in California became prominent in publicising 'Holocaust revisionism'. Claims that the Nazis killed no Jews, but that Jews are lying about their wartime experiences, are singularly shocking, especially to Jews who do not understand that no academic could possibly fail to see that such claims are worthless and mendacious, their obvious intention twofold: to white-wash Hitler and to further humiliate the Jews, especially Holocaust sur-vivors. Much of the redoubled effort to publicise the facts of the Holocaust among the general public has probably stemmed from fear, arguably misplaced, that belief in 'Holocaust denial' would become widespread. 'Holocaust denial' is now illegal in many European coun-tries. The movement in fact returned to semi-obscurity until 2000, when its claims received world-wide publicity in the libel suit brought in London by David Irving, the right-wing historian, against American aca-demic Deborah Lipstadt and her book *Denying the Holocaust*.[139] The suit was contested in brilliant style by Lipstadt's publisher Penguin Books. The result was a comprehensive defeat for David Irving, who was declared bankrupt. A surprising number of commentators on the lawsuit, especially in Britain, were disturbed by the outcome, fearing it rep-resented an attack on free speech. Incredibly, some writers believed that Lipstadt and the 'Jewish lobby' had brought the suit against Irving, whereas it was Irving who was suing Lipstadt for libel.[140]

Denial of mass murder is not unknown or even uncommon: some pro-Turkish historians have denied the Armenian genocide; many Japanese play down or deny Japan's atrocities during the 1930s and 1940s. Many Communists and pro-Communists routinely dismissed allegations of mass murder in the Soviet Union until Krushchev publicly admitted them in 1956, or even later. Yet 'Holocaust denial' seems to be in a class by itself in being orchestrated in the main by propagandists who are using it in part as a weapon to further torment the survivors of the crime itself. That anyone in his senses would argue that the Holocaust did not occur, despite the simply overwhelming and irrefutable evidence that it did, is a sign of just how deeply the Holocaust has entered into the con-sciousness of the West.[141] This can be charted – and criticised too – in other ways, for instance by the growth of the so-called 'Holocaust industry' which has convinced foreign governments – such as Switzerland – to agree to pay literally billions of dollars in compensation, purportedly for victims and survivors, although much of it has gone to Jewish organisations and, especially, to lawyers and bureaucrats.[142] As almost always, the Holocaust is unique, the nadir of evil and archetype of genocide.

Explaining the Holocaust is as difficult today as when it occurred, and no truly satisfactory explanations of how such an event could have occurred have yet emerged. Many writers on the Holocaust have sought to place it in a theological or philosophical framework: none seems especially satisfactory.[143] One of the best-known attempts to set the Holocaust in an explanatory context was made by the Polish-born British sociologist Zygmunt Bauman, in his *Modernity and the Holocaust* (1989). Bauman emphasises the allegedly 'modern' features of Nazism and the Holocaust – the regime's freedom from traditional restraints and institutions, its belief in racial 'science', its constant adaptation of efficient, up-to-date technology to the machinery of death. Bauman also introduced the useful metaphor of Nazi racial 'scientists' viewing themselves as gardeners eliminating garden 'weeds' and pests and producing stronger, more beautiful plants through dedicated social engineering. By implication, at least, Bauman apparently views 'modernity' as engendering mass murder in the interests of general improvement.

While there is clearly much to commend this view, and even assuming that one can agree as to what constitutes 'modernity', Bauman's thesis surely explains both too much and too little. The West was 'modern' in 1910 and in 1960, but neither date saw mass murder and genocide in the Western world, certainly not anything which resembled the Holocaust. America, Britain, the Commonwealth, among other nations, were more 'modern' than Germany but did not produce a Holocaust. Many historians, indeed, have argued that the United States and a handful of other English-speaking settler societies such as Australia and Canada, were 'born free', without any pre-modern 'atavisms' (throwbacks to an earlier age) in their social structure but with a thorough commitment to 'modern' political modes. Whatever the fate of the aboriginal natives of these countries, none produced a Holocaust but, instead, fought against Hitler in part at least because Nazism was viewed as utterly barbaric. 'Modernity' in the Western world has seen the steady, relentless and seemingly inexorable expansion of democracy and citizenship rights, and their extension to previously excluded groups.

How, then, to explain Hitler? The best explanation, surely, is that which forms the basis of the historical argument presented here: that the First World War, by weakening and destroying the elite structure of most of Europe and undermining its social structure, built up over centuries, allowed extremist ideologies to come to power which would, assuredly, have been excluded from power and consigned to permanent marginality and obscurity had the First World War not occurred. Both Nazism and Soviet Communism were, indeed, committed in a sense to 'modernity', to the extension of the benefits of science and technology to the (ideologically defined) masses, and to the ending of institutions and elites from the old regime, obviously so in the case of Soviet Communism. By espousing a 'modern'-sounding ideological programme they gained popularity and, in the case of the Nazis, came to power more or less legally after parliamentary elections. But their doctrines differed categorically from those ascendant in the democratic and liberal states while, in the context of their own societies, they represented fringe movements led by marginal leaders, who would almost certainly have been excluded from government and confined to the minority extremes but for the catastrophe of 1914–18. German National Socialism uniquely combined modern Europe's most successful and ruthless demagogue with the modern world's most evil doctrines and programmes. Hitler was not a normal by-product of 'modernity' but a unique creation of the time and place from which he emerged. One may hope that his like will never be seen again, in my opinion with every reasonable expectation that it never will.

Non-Jewish victims of the Nazis

The Nazi regime had many other targets besides the Jews. It is often stated that Hitler's regime murdered about 11 million people, of whom 5 million or more were non-Jews.[144] Very much less is known of the non-Jewish victims of the Nazi regime than of the fate of the Jews, although in recent years there has been a revival of interest in the wartime suffering of groups such as the Gypsies, Slavs and homosexuals under Nazism. This is itself a reversal of historical presentation: during the Second World War, the press and media in the democracies stressed that the Nazis were persecuting virtually every group in occupied Europe (although, it should be carefully noted, almost nothing was said about such groups as the Gypsies). Lidice, the town in Czechoslovakia where 1,300 persons, including 200 women, were murdered in cold blood and the other inhabitants deported to concentration camps in June 1942 in retaliation for the assassination of Reinhard Heydrich, became infamous throughout the democratic world as a symbol of Nazi barbarism. Indeed, the publicity given in the West to non-Jewish persecution and suffering (the facts often derived from governments-in-exile in London and elsewhere) may well have been responsible, until the last stages of the war, for an underestimation of Jewish suffering and an unwillingness to believe that it was categorically and fundamentally greater than that visited on other groups. With the post-war centrality of the Jewish Holocaust, and also because much of the 'other' suffering took place among nationalities cut off behind the Iron Curtain, relatively little was heard of these groups until recently. Even today, indeed, there is no authoritative general study of the suffering of other groups under the Nazis, and some very fundamental matters, such as the number of non-Jewish Poles killed by the Nazis, remains a matter of great dispute.[145] For the historians of genocide, the primary question in any discussion of these groups is whether the Nazis intended genocide – that is, the comprehensive physical destruction, by deliberate murder or other means, of these groups – in other words, whether the fate of the Jews awaited these other groups had the war lasted longer or if Hitler had won the war. The question of 'other victims' of the Nazis is also controversial from the viewpoint of (especially) many Jewish writers on the Holocaust who have, in some cases, ferociously denied that modern history offers any parallel to the Jewish Holocaust.[146] Many Jews fear that any general identification of a separate but similar group of victims of the Nazis necessarily detracts from the uniqueness (in their view) of the Nazis' attempts to murder *all* European Jews, and ultimately plays into the hands of 'Holocaust deniers'.[147] The question of 'other victims' of the Nazis is thus unclear and disputed in terms of available evidence and hotly debated in terms of interpretation. This section will attempt to examine the evidence in the case of 'other' groups most often said to have been the chief victims of the Nazi death machine, especially as to whether the term 'genocide' in its ordinary meaning is an accurate description of their fate, or intended fate.

Of the groups persecuted by the Nazis, probably *the Gypsies* are most often seen as constituting a case most similar to that of the Jews, that is, a group marked out for extermination. Many historians now regularly link the fate of the two groups. On the other hand, the contention that the Gypsies were to share, and did share, the same fate as Europe's Jews has been anything but unproblematical, and has been contested and denied by many eminent historians, often in ways which Gypsy spokesmen find offensive, as do other historians. The facts are anything but clear, and despite recent research far less is known about the Gypsies during the Second World War than about the Jews.[148]

The Gypsy peoples apparently originated in India, reaching Europe in the late Middle Ages.[149] The English-language term Gypsy, which is a corruption of 'Egyptian', is often regarded today as pejorative. It is more common at present to divide the Gypsies into the *Sinti* tribe and the *Roma* tribe, the latter of south-eastern European descent. (The term 'Gypsy' is only used in English: elsewhere Gypsies are known by such terms as *Zingari* (in Italian).) Even more than the Jews, the Gypsies were hated and despised wherever they went. A near-permanent nomadic people, travelling around Europe in Gypsy 'caravans', they were almost universally regarded as little more than an outlaw band of thieves, carnival musicians, fortune-tellers and the operatives of performing animals in circuses. By folk repute, they kidnapped children and practised sorcery. Levels of literacy remained extremely low among Gypsies until the very recent past.

Although it is perfectly clear that Gypsies were widely despised and feared, Nazi hostility to them was, in many ways, quite different from Nazi hatred of the Jews. There is no question why the Nazis hated the Jews: because Hitler, the *Führer* of Nazi Germany, had a maniacal and all-consuming hatred of the Jews, whom he regarded as an incredibly powerful and malevolent 'counter-elite' to the Aryans, a people who controlled Wall Street and the Kremlin, and who also dealt Germany a 'stab in the back' in 1918. Hitler could literally not go for ten minutes without raving dementedly about the Jewish peril. The Jewish Holocaust occurred because of Hitler's dementia. In complete contrast, Hitler referred to Gypsies only twice in anything he wrote or said, both times in connection with Gypsies serving in the German military.[150] *Mein Kampf* does not mention the Gypsies: Hitler 'appears to have had no interest' in them.[151]

Additionally, the socio-economic profile of the German (and other) Gypsies was utterly different from that of the Jews, as were the prejudices which flowed from these differences. Jews were, unquestionably, dramatically over-represented in the economic and professional elites of Germany, and had been an important part of the German cultural scene for 150 years before Hitler. In contrast, Gypsies were perceived as among the dregs of society. There was, in all likelihood, not a single Gypsy professional person in Germany in 1933. Indeed, perhaps the only European Gypsy of the 1930s who had acquired a public reputation in any field whatever was Django Reinhardt, the jazz guitarist.[152] Gypsies were, however, the only Asian, non-white group present in any numbers in Europe at the time. Although many Gypsies were no darker than many Italians or Spaniards, their language, culture and continuing separateness from the rest of society betrayed their exotic origins. Gypsies also shared with Jews the fact that they had no obvious homeland, but were everywhere nomadic itinerants, always (to many) slightly sinister and dangerous. Indeed, they were in this respect even less linked to a homeland than the Jews, whose religion and culture had always revolved around a return to Palestine. In contrast, Gypsies were permanent wanderers, perpetually on the move.

There was unquestionably a great deal of popular hostility to Gypsies which hardly abated over the years. The Weimar government, and local governments in Weimar Germany, liberal as they were, enacted a series of laws against the 'Gypsy Menace'.[153] Under Nazism, little changed for the Gypsies from the previous years. Gypsy camps were actually set up in several cities, for instance in Frankfurt in 1937.[154] Whatever crackdown there was against Gypsies in these years was chiefly because of their status as 'asocials' or 'workshy', and not necessarily because of their status as an 'alien' race.[155] Much official hostility to Germany's Gypsies came from the criminal police (the 'Kripos') rather than from the Gestapo.[156]

Nevertheless, Gypsies, as an 'alien' race, were slowly but surely brought into the Nazi racial net. They were included in the notorious Nuremberg Laws of 1935, and subject to a series of other demeaning measures.[157] Although there were only 26,000 Gypsies in Germany (compared with 500,000 Jews), a typical Nazi racial pseudo-scientific apparatus grew up to deal with the 'Gypsy Plague', such as a far-reaching decree issues by Himmler in December 1938, 'Combating the Gypsy Plague'.[158] The Nazis also wished to deal with the large number of German itinerants (similar to the pseudo-Gypsy 'travellers' in Britain today) who had attached themselves to real Gypsy caravans or posed as Gypsies.[159] Since (so far as we know) Hitler took no interest in Gypsies, it would appear that Himmler was the driving force in both the persecution of the Gypsies and the bizarre exceptions to this persecution, but perhaps responding in part to local anti-Gypsy pressures.

For the Gypsies, the war brought a steady deterioration in an already negative situation, leading to mass murder. Gypsies were among the first racial groups sent to German concentration camps. In January 1940, 250 Gypsy children were murdered in Buchenwald; some historians see this as the first act of racial genocide of the Holocaust.[160] Over the next five years large numbers of Gypsies were murdered by the Nazis, a catastrophe known among them as the 'Porrajmos' ('the Devouring' in Romany). Gypsies were included with Jews and Soviet 'commissars' among the groups to be liquidated by the *Einsatzgruppen*. Thousands of German Gypsies were deported to ghettos and reservations in the General-Government of Poland, starting in May 1940.[161] In December 1942 came a general order from Himmler to deport all Gypsies to concentration camps, although with some notable exceptions.[162] Remarkably, many pure-blooded Gypsies (about 10 per cent of Germany's *Roma*) were spared. This was because of Himmler's bizarre but logical belief that pure-blooded Gypsies were 'Aryans', which they surely were, from 'Aryan' northern India.[163] As Levy points out, this was the reverse of the Jewish situation: the Nazis considered pure-blooded Jews worse than mixed-bloods.[164]

Most other German Gypsies were not as lucky. Large numbers were sent to concentration camps. About 2,000 were sent to their deaths in Treblinka.[165] It has been estimated that about 30,000 were murdered by the *Einsatzgruppen*.[166] Statistics on Gypsy deportations to Auschwitz, which began in 1943, are somewhat more reliable: about 21,000 were sent there, of whom most perished.[167] Many thousands were also shot elsewhere, while large numbers were sent to the German concentration camps such as Dachau.[168] Almost everywhere, Gypsies were the victims of particularly sadistic treatment, and were among the chief fodder for the infamous 'medical experiments' carried out by Mengele and his ilk. Many were involuntarily sterilised. In terms of torture, their treatment might well have been worse than that of the Jews. There are several reasons for this. Unlike the Jews, who were normally marked out for either instantaneous death or work as slave labourers, Gypsies were often held in a kind of limbo, sometimes in 'family camps' which were marked by inhuman conditions. As relatively 'long-term' prisoners, but racially inferior, they were perfect victims for Nazi sadism. As well, there was probably a great deal of innate hostility felt towards the Gypsies, which probably (*contra* Goldhagen) exceeded pre-existing levels of antisemitism, and which probably needed little encouragement to erupt into barbaric cruelty.

The question of how many Gypsies perished at the hands of the Nazis remains unknown and is subject to a very large margin of error, perhaps a greater margin of error than for any other group discussed here. According to Ian Hancock, in 1997 the US Holocaust Memorial Museum placed the number of Gypsy victims at 'between half and one and a half million'.[169] Henry R. Huttenback also estimates the number of Gypsy casualties 'from a conservative low of 250,000 to a possible high of 500,000'.[170] Such figures are almost certainly wild exaggerations.[171] Rummel suggests that the Nazis 'exterminated at least 200,000 Gypsies, probably some 258,000'.[172] In the first comprehensive study of this question, in 1972, Kenrick and Puxon put the number of Gypsies killed at 219,700 out of a pre-war Gypsy population in Nazi-occupied Europe of nearly 1 million.[173] In 1989 Kenrick provided a lower estimate, of 196,000 killed from a Gypsy population of 831,000.[174] In 1997 Michael Zimmerman, the leading German expert on the Gypsies under the Nazis, provided an even lower estimate, of 'at least 90,000 killed in the territories controlled by the Nazis'.[175] In my view, based on all the available evidence, it seems clear that a lower figure, in the range of 90,000–150,000 (and probably in the lower part of this range) is most likely, although this estimate may certainly be revised upwards if new information becomes available, especially concerning the activities of the *Einsatzgruppen*. There is simply no apparent evidence to suggest a much higher figure. It is even harder to estimate the total number of Gypsies in Nazi-occupied Europe. Most estimates are in the range of 800,000–1 million, but the itinerant nature of Gypsy society, and the fact that many were almost certainly not counted in national censuses, makes any firmer estimate impossible.[176]

In all, it would thus appear that about 20 per cent of the total number of Gypsies in Nazi-occupied Europe were killed, but about 80 per cent survived. There are several reasons for this relatively high survival rate. Most Gypsies were probably located in the Balkan area, especially in Romania, where there were no deportations of Jews, and Hungary, where mass deportations of Jews occurred only for a very brief time (15 May– 8 July 1944). Presumably, too, many Gypsies fled to these safer regions if they were able. Nazi intentions towards the Gypsies, although murderous, were never as ideologically important as their aim of wiping out 'the biological bases of Jewry in Europe', as Hitler put it. Hitler's apparent lack of intense interest in the Gypsies probably also spared them the worst effects of the comprehensive death machine created to deal with his central enemy, the Jews.

Gypsy suffering in the Holocaust should in no way be minimised. The deliberate murder, often in sadistic and ghastly circumstances, of over 100,000 people, was one of the most appalling events of its time. These people were killed because they were Gypsies and for no other reason, and it is thus entirely accurate to describe the Gypsy Holocaust as genocide. Yet it is also clear that Gypsies did not invariably share the fate of Europe's Jews, that the number killed, although vast, was not as great as most much higher estimates, and that the majority of Europe's Gypsies survived the Nazi period. Had the war continued longer, or if the Nazis had won, it is entirely possible that most or all would have perished, but as of May 1945 most had survived.

Next to the Jews and possibly the Gypsies, *the Poles* and most other Slavic nations were the ethnic groups most detested by Nazi ideology. It is a commonplace claim that, next to the Jews, more Poles were killed by the Nazis than any other group. 'In the six years of the war, the population of the former Polish Republic was reduced by 6,028,000,' Norman Davies, the eminent historian of Poland, has summed up a figure repeated in many other sources.[177] Of these, 2.9 million were Jews, the rest – a majority – were Polish gentiles.[178] About 10–15 per cent of Poland's gentile population died during the war, compared (for example) to 1 per cent of Britain's total population. Whatever the accuracy of the death toll, it was chiefly driven and determined by the Nazis' racialist hatred of the Poles. In September 1939 Hitler announced in secret talks with army and intelligence officers that he intended to 'exterminate' the

Polish nobility, gentry and other elite groups.[179] To the Nazis, Poles were invariably seen as *Untermenschen* (sub-humans) occupying what was naturally a territory which ought to be colonised by Germans as 'living space'. 'The destruction of Poland is our primary task,' Hitler told his senior military officers just before the German invasion. 'The aim is not the arrival at a certain line but the annihilation of living forces . . . Be merciless! Be brutal . . . This is to be a war of annihilation.'[180] Himmler, the main agent of the Holocaust, was, if anything, ever blunter. 'All Poles will disappear from the world . . . It is essential that all the great German people should consider it as its major task to destroy all Poles.'[181] During the Polish Warsaw uprising in mid-1944, Himmler told Hitler that as a consequence 'Warsaw, the capital, the head, the intelligence of this former 16–17 million Polish people will be extinguished – this people that has blocked the east for us for 700 years . . . Then the Polish problem will historically no longer be a big problem for our children and all who come after us, nor indeed for us.'[182] The Polish territory annexed by Germany 'had to be cleared of Jews, Polacks, and other trash [*Polacken und Gesindel*],' Hitler told Alfred Rosenberg and General Wilhelm Kertch in September 1939. 'It would be necessary to conduct a brutal racial war [*Volkstumskampf*] which would admit no legal restrictions.'[183] Innumerable other blood-chilling remarks of this kind were repeatedly made by the leading Nazis. The scale of the destruction wrought by the Nazis in Poland was indeed colossal, possibly greater than against any other group except the Jews.

It is, however, necessary to take a number of factors into consideration in considering what actually occurred. Nazi policy towards the Poles did not, at least during the period when it occupied most of Poland, entail the immediate and deliberate genocide of the entire Polish people, Himmler's remarks notwithstanding. Second, vast numbers of Poles suffered, and many died, under the Soviet occupation of eastern Poland in 1939–41. Third, it is extremely difficult to ascertain in an accurate way the actual number of Poles who died under Nazi occupation, perhaps more difficult than any other single demographic question of the Nazi enslavement of Europe.

While Hitler obviously detested Poles on racialist grounds, prior to the war he treated Poles and Jews in very different ways. Hitler's central hatred of the Jews figured in virtually every speech and statement he ever made while Germany's Jews were targeted for oppression from the first days of Nazi power. In contrast, Hitler made no public pronouncements against Poland or Poles until just before the war.[184] In 1934, Germany actually concluded a non-aggression pact with the Polish government. Germany and Poland enjoyed normal diplomatic relations and the right-wing Polish government appeared, if anything, to be a natural ally of Germany against 'Bolshevism'.[185] Polish officials and diplomats were repeatedly received, even cordially, by leading Nazis. For instance, in January 1939 Hitler met Poland's Foreign Minister Joseph Beck in Berlin, attempting to win territorial concessions from Poland.[186] In contrast, as noted, Hitler never met a single Jewish representative during his years of power. It is, for instance, simply inconceivable that Hitler would have received Zionist leader Chaim Weizmann, or even agreed to meet a renowned Jewish journalist such as Walter Lippmann. Within Nazi Germany, there is no evidence that Poles were ever discriminated against prior to the war, again in complete contrast to the persecution of the Jews and the elaborate superstructure for ascertaining 'Aryanness' which the Nazis erected.

With the conquest of western Poland by the Nazis in September 1939, and of the entire former territories of Poland with the invasion of Russia in June 1941, Nazi intentions towards Poland became much clearer. Unlike many other parts of Nazi-occupied Europe, Poland was not allowed to form even a puppet government. The remnant of central Poland not directly absorbed by Nazi Germany, the so-called Government-General, was ruled by the high-ranking, ruthless Nazi Hans Frank, not by a Polish quisling. Frank ruled from Cracow, not Warsaw, through an almost wholly German administrative apparatus.[187] Some minor Polish collaborationist office-holders were allowed, but there was never any question of granting even limited powers to a Polish entity. In the meantime, as a result of the Nazi-Soviet pact, the Soviet Union occupied eastern Poland, where it remained for two years, until the German invasion of the Soviet Union in June 1941. Polish casualties under *Soviet* rule were very great, and our assessment of them is one of the most important difficulties in an accurate assessment of Polish suffering in the war. Eight pre-1939 Polish provinces, with 13 million people, were forcibly incorporated into the Soviet Union.[188] During this occupation, between 1.2 million and 1.7 million Polish citizens (of all nationalities, including Poles, Ukrainians, Jews, Russians, etc.) were forcibly deported (in four massive waves) to the Soviet Union, where many died.[189] The number is not precisely known, but Davies claims that 'almost half' were 'already dead' by the time the Soviet government granted 'amnesty' to these deported Poles in 1941.[190] Davies also claims that '100,000 Polish Jews, headed by the Chief Rabbi of Warsaw, Moses Shore', were among the dead.[191] About 15,000 Polish officers and prisoners of war were murdered on Stalin's orders in the notorious massacre at Katyn in April 1940. Many other Poles were certainly killed by the Soviet forces when they reoccupied the country in 1944–5, with more than 50,000 Poles arrested in the Lublin area alone in 1944–5.[192] If these figures are reasonably accurate, it would appear that at least 700,000–800,000 Poles were killed by Stalin during the Second World War.[193]

The Nazi reign of terror, unleashed on western Poland in September 1939 and on eastern Poland in June 1941, was even more brutal and murderous, as befitted their belief in Polish subhumanity. Apart from the total and automatic extermination of all Polish Jews and many Gypsies, the Nazis at least threatened the lives of all gentile Poles and destroyed much of its infrastructure. Most significantly, the Nazis engaged in Poland on ethnic cleansing on a grand scale and, it seems, fully intended to expel tens of millions of ethnic Poles from Poland to Siberia to make way for German colonists.[194] Soon after conquering Poland, the Nazis actually expelled 630,000 Poles from the areas of western Poland they annexed, another 265,000 from Germany itself (a total of 923,000 persons) to the General Government.[195] About 200,000 'Aryan'-looking Polish children were kidnapped and brought to Germany by Himmler's orders. As well, during the war about 2.3 million Poles were deported to Germany to do forced labour.[196] The Nazis systematically murdered the Polish elite, killing 45 per cent of physicians, 57 per cent of lawyers, 40 per cent of professors and 18 per cent of the clergy.[197] Probably over 200,000 gentile Poles (and perhaps far more) were killed in extermination and concentration camps, including 74,000 at Auschwitz, where they constituted the second largest group of murder victims.[198] About 100,000 Poles died in the Warsaw uprising of 1944.[199] The overall number of gentile Polish dead at the hands of the Nazis has generally been estimated at about 2 million.

This figure (like so many others) seems high, although anything in the way of a better estimate appears extremely difficult to achieve with the sources available to us. There is, for instance, no evidence that more than, at most, several hundred thousand gentile Poles died in the extermination camps, and nor is there any evidence of the general mass murder of gentile Poles equivalent to the killing of the Jews by the *Einsatzgruppen*, although very large numbers of ethnic Poles were certainly murdered by the Germans, often for no reason. It seems reasonable to assume that perhaps 500,000–700,000 gentile Polish civilians were deliberately killed by the Nazis during the war, with, say, 300,000 dying while doing slave labour in Germany; thus, upwards of 1 million gentile Poles perished at the hands of the Nazis, to which must be added up to several hundred thousand more at the hands of the Soviets.[200] These figures do not begin to cover the scale of damage done to Poland during the Second World War. About 84 per cent of the buildings in Warsaw were destroyed, and the city was, at the end of the war, almost literally uninhabited.[201] By any standards, and even if the number of victims is scaled down from considerably higher figures, this was an appalling slaughter. With the possible exception of the western Soviet Union, Poland plainly suffered more than any other nation during the Second World War.

But perhaps another group, yet to be considered, suffered even more, *Soviet prisoners of war*, who fell into the hands of the Germans. It seems likely that more Soviet prisoners of war died in Nazi captivity than any other group except for the Jews. It appears that no less than 5,160,000 Soviet soldiers were captured by the Germans, of whom 3,222,000 died while prisoners of war.[202] If accurate, or even approximately accurate, this figure is higher than the total number of Jews who died in extermination camps such as Auschwitz. There is some evidence, however, that the death toll is an *underestimate*, since other authoritative German files reveal the number of captured Soviet troops to have been 5,754,000, suggesting that *3,816,000* Soviet troops died while prisoners of war.[203] While there may be some exaggeration in these figures, especially from inflation in the number of Soviet soldiers allegedly captured in reportage to their superiors, in general (and unlike other groups in this chapter) these figures are probably accurate enough. The German army captured vastly more Soviet soldiers soon after invading the Soviet Union than it had expected – probably 3.4 million in 1941 and 1.4 million in 1942 – and had no facilities for dealing with them. Hitler specifically ruled out any humane treatment of Soviet prisoners, except for *Volksdeutsch* (Germans living elsewhere, in this case in the Soviet Union) and other 'Aryans'.

Thousands of prisoners were literally starved to death, or died of the cold. Jews and other 'subhumans' were often murdered. Since the Germans had no reliable means of identifying Jews, they often killed any circumcised soldier. Thousands of non-Jews (including many Muslims) were killed in this way.[204] Asian soldiers were often killed as well, as were, routinely, all 'commissars' (Communist party officials and *apparatchniks* found in all platoons in Stalin's army).[205] From 1942, the Germans, in desperate need of manpower for their factories, sent tens of thousands to Germany as slave labourers.[206] No fewer than 875,000 Soviet soldiers managed to survive the war in this way: 83 per cent of all captured Soviet soldiers were still alive in 1945.[207] Thousands also joined the anti-Bolshevik army of Andrei Vlasov, a former Soviet general captured by the Germans in July 1942, who organised a 'Free Russia' movement under Nazi tutelage.[208] The enormous number of dead Soviet POWs in Nazi hands dwarfed anything seen in any other army in modern times.[209] Virtually all POWs captured by other armies, and certainly by the Anglo-American forces, survived the war.[210]

The deaths of Soviet POWs and, indeed, of Soviet Jews at the hands of the Nazis are widely seen as the tip of an enormous iceberg of mass murder and death wrought by the Nazis on the peoples of the Soviet Union. It is widely believed that *20 million* people of the Soviet Union died as a consequence of the Nazi invasion, a figure apparently first popularised in the 1950s by Khrushchev.[211] Other figures are even higher, ranging up to *37.5 million*, a figure given by the American sociologist N.S. Timasheff in 1948.[212] As is so often the case, it is likely that these figures are exaggerations: it now seems probable that the actual number of Soviet deaths totalled about 8.3 million civilians (including Jews and others deliberately murdered) and 8.0 million Soviet soldiers (including prisoners of war), about 16.3 million people in all.[213] This was, almost certainly, the greatest loss of life ever suffered in any single country in any war in history.[214]

Nazi Germany is also notorious for its so-called '*euthanasia programme*', a euphemism to describe Nazi mass murders of handicapped and 'asocial' persons who fell foul of its ideology of producing 'Aryan supermen'. In Nazi Germany, most of these victims were 'Aryans', although the programme was extended to Poles and others.[215] An extreme 'eugenics' movement had long been a part of mainstream German culture, as it was (probably in a less extreme form) in many other countries. Its aim was to decrease the number of 'inferior' peoples in Germany, eliminating eastern Europeans and 'inferior' types wherever possible.[216] Although not necessarily antisemitic, it normally went almost automatically with doctrines of Aryan superiority but also with the elimination of the physically and mentally unfit at home, which its proponents disguised with such euphemisms as offering 'mercy deaths' and, in much more sinister vein, the elimination of those 'unworthy of life'.[217] Hitler rapidly put into place some of its doctrines, promulgating a far-reaching Sterilisation Law in July 1933 which allowed the forced sterilisation of nine categories of persons, including those suffering from 'congenital feeblemindedness', 'schizophrenia', 'severe hereditary physical deformity' and even 'severe alcoholism on a discretionary basis'.[218]

Between 1934 and the end of 1936, about 157,000 persons were involuntarily sterilised in Nazi Germany (over half of whom were 'feeble-minded'), with possibly 300,000 in all during the 12 years of Nazi rule.[219] Between 1938 and 1940 (and chiefly in the middle of 1939) Hitler took a far-reaching decision to kill many of the persons who came under the coverage of the Sterilisation Laws. This programme is known as 'Operation T4', from the address of the building in central Berlin from which it was directed. A vast bureaucracy grew up to implement this programme, which is, in many ways, of historical importance both in Nazi Germany and in wider society. T4 represented the first time the Nazis had deliberately killed any large group of people defined by an ideological and arbitrary categorisation: perhaps, indeed, the first time that any modern government had killed a group of people who did not (in its view) represent a military or internal subversive threat to its rule, and the first time that women and children were murdered in large numbers. It also represented the first time that the Nazis killed people with poison gas (although other methods were employed), and the first time that professional men and women, including doctors and nurses, were used to murder people. The Nazis had no trouble finding recruits for its programme, and established six killing centres in Germany itself.[220] In all, about 80,000 persons were murdered in the T4 programme. Although the programme was secret, news leaked out, and – even in wartime Nazi

Germany and almost uniquely in Hitler's regime – public protests emerged, especially a famous sermon denouncing the programme by the Roman Catholic Bishop of Munster, Clemens von Galen, in August 1941. Fearing unrest at home (after all, the victims had thousands of living relatives), Hitler ordered an end to the programme, although it continued unofficially throughout the war.[221] Indeed, it spread to the east, where handicapped Germans, Jews and Poles were killed. As many as 275,000 persons may have been murdered in the 'euthanasia programme', although Jews and some Poles would presumably have been killed anyway.[222]

Since the Nazi regime was wiped off the earth in May 1945, we have no way of knowing how general the 'euthanasia programme' might have become had Germany won. It seems almost inconceivable that any modern Western society would accept the involuntary killing of its own members (as opposed to outsider 'subhumans') as a matter of course, but so much about Nazi Germany is outside Western experience that the inconceivable might have happened, as it did in so many other diabolical ways. It is also unclear whether the programme would have spread to other 'disabled' or allegedly inferior groups, or whether some semblance of normality might have returned with peace.

Many people believe that the Nazis murdered *homosexuals* in vast numbers. Claims that 'as many as 2,500,000 homosexuals were killed in Nazi death camps' have been made by pro-homosexual sources.[223] According to Rummel – who first states that Himmler 'estimated that there were 1,000,000 [homosexuals] in Germany. Perhaps the Nazis killed as many as this overall' – a 'more prudent' estimate of the number of homosexuals murdered by the Nazis is '220,000, an estimate of the Protestant Church of Austria'.[224] This figure is 'often cited in Gay Liberation circles'.[225] At present, homosexuals are routinely included in lists of those categories of persons marked out for extermination by the Nazi death machine.

Such claims as these appear to have virtually no factual basis whatever. Contrary to widespread belief, there was no *general* campaign aimed at the extermination of homosexuals by the Nazis, and most careful historians now estimate the number of homosexuals who died in Nazi concentration camps and prisons at about 10,000.[226] Some estimates are even lower. Günter Grau, who has written widely on this subject, has stated that about 5,000 homosexuals were deported to German concentration camps, of whom 'about 3,000 were murdered or died'.[227] This figure – about 3,000 – appears most accurate to me: indeed, from the tables given in Grau's work, the actual figure might well have been even lower, in the hundreds or low thousands. It might be useful to address the question of why the Nazis opposed homosexuality: the answer is not as straightforward as might be imagined. One might offer four main reasons: homosexuality violated traditional moral values, especially of conservative Christians; the homosexual demi-monde was redolent of the 'degenerate' Weimar regime, especially in Berlin, and also of such milieux as the pre-1914 royal courts, despised by the Nazis; homosexuality stood in opposition to the aim of rapid population increase, part of the Nazi agenda; and homosexuality was 'effeminate', the absolute reverse of the image of ruthless, pitiless warrior masculinity central to Nazi ideology. All of these obviously are important elements in the formulation of Nazi policy towards homosexuals, with, for instance, Himmler using each of these arguments in his attacks on them.

On the other hand, and in complete contrast to this, Nazism, pervasively misogynistic, also had a strand in it which, in common with many misogynistic-militaristic regimes back to Greek times, regarded homosexuality as a 'higher' form of sexuality among warriors, especially if stripped of its effeminate 'nancy boy' component. Nazi 'art' and sculpture was almost overtly homoerotic, with a repeated emphasis on the male nude figure, in conscious imitation of Greek and Roman art. Hitler's 'court sculptor' Arno Brecker (1900–1) was commissioned by Albert Speer to create two monumental male nudes, *Torch Bearer* and *Sword Bearer*, to stand at the entrance of the New Reich Chancellery, in Berlin, the very centre of the Nazi government.[228] Brecker's figures were universally praised by leading Nazis, with Alfred Rosenberg describing them as 'a representation of the "force and willpower" of the age'.[229] Hitler was repeatedly photographed at exhibits featuring muscular male nudes, which he contrasted with 'degenerate' modern art. Many early critics of Nazism, in fact, argued that it was a movement dominated by homosexuals, with Samuel Igra, a Jewish historian who fled Germany in 1939 noting, for instance, that Hitler was 'the condottiere [leader] of a band of evil men united together by a common vice [homosexuality]'.[230] That Ernst Rohm, the senior Nazi leader and head of the SA assassinated by

Hitler in 1934, was an overt homosexual, is well-known from all histories of the Nazi regime. Recently Lothar Machtan, a German historian, argued in *The Hidden Hitler* that Hitler himself was a practising homosexual who had Rohm and others killed in the 'Night of the Long Knives' in 1934 because Rohm threatened to go public with the vast amount of evidence he had accumulated about Nazi homosexuality.[231] Although *The Hidden Hitler* obviously sounds like a sensationalist potboiler, it is a deeply researched work: Machtan is a professor at Bremen University, not a journalist. Machtan also suggests, even more suggestively, that the crackdown on German homosexuals initiated by Hitler and Himmler in 1934–5 may have been chiefly designed to frighten or imprison anyone who remembered Hitler as a homosexual from his pre-1933 days; it was not chiefly a component of Nazi anti-homosexual ideology.[232]

Homosexuality had been a crime in Germany since 1871 under Article 175 of the Penal Code. Upon seizing power, the Nazis cracked down on the homosexual organisations and bars which had grown up in the liberal conditions of Weimar. From 1935, Article 175 was made tougher, widening the definition of sexual offences and increasing imprisonment to ten years, especially for sex with under-age males. The number of convictions for homosexuality rose sharply, from 948 in 1934 to 8,562 in 1938.[233] There was a further crackdown during the war, with the death penalty applied to homosexual offences among men in the SS and the police.[234] From 1937 some convicted homosexuals were sent to the Buchenwald concentration camp, where they often suffered inhuman conditions and sadistic punishments, including castration. Famously, they had to wear a 'pink triangle'. Some were killed by guards or worked to death. Homosexuals found very little sympathy from other prisoners, and probably received worse treatment than any other group. It was at these German concentration camps that the so-called 'genocide' of German homosexuals occurred. To reiterate, this description, regardless of how often it has been repeated, appears extremely misleading. It is not clear how many homosexuals in all were actually sent to German concentration camps, but the number is much lower than many imagine. In 1944, for instance, there were only 189 homosexuals in Buchenwald, out of a total population of 63,048 prisoners.[235] So far as is known, no homosexual was ever sent to Auschwitz, or any other extermination camp (those used to the notion of a 'homosexual Holocaust' may well find this very surprising). So far as is known, lesbians were never sent to concentration camps. In 1940–1, the Nazis conquered a number of countries, such as France and the Netherlands, where no, or few, laws against homosexuality existed. There, tough Nazi laws were applied, but prosecution remained the responsibility of local authorities, who virtually ignored the laws.[236]

Elsewhere, the Nazis made little attempt to enforce any laws against homosexuality. In the Polish General-Government, for instance, Polish homosexuals were not prosecuted if no Germans were involved.[237] It is believed that, from late December 1941 onwards, Polish homosexuals 'would come in for special SS measures and be shipped off to a concentration camp', but no direct evidence on this exists.[238] If only 1 per cent of adult German males were homosexuals, their number would have totalled over 300,000, with millions more throughout Nazi-occupied Europe. In Manhattan alone, after a concerted crackdown against homosexuals began with the repeal of the liquor Prohibition Laws in 1933, the number of men arrested for homosexual solicitations rose from about 700 a year in the 1930s to more than 3,000 a year in the late 1940s.[239] To include the plight of homosexuals in Nazi Germany, as brutal as it often obviously was, with the suffering of the Jews throughout Nazi-occupied Europe is plainly absurd, and there is surely an element of truth in the claim made by anti-homosexual writers that the 'success of the "gay holocaust" myth' has been a deliberate attempt to gain sympathy for their movement by distorting history.[240]

The plight of the *Jehovah's Witnesses* ought also to be mentioned here. A small Protestant sect, strictly fundamentalist and eschatological (seeing the end of the world as at hand), it was founded in the United States in the 1870s and introduced into Germany in the 1890s.[241] They had about 20,000 followers in 1933, mainly drawn from the lower classes. During the Weimar period, they were already under surprisingly fierce attack by the German far right as pro-Communist and pro-Jewish (which they were not), and were attacked as well by the mainstream churches. From the institution of Nazi power in 1933 they were distinguished as the only organised group of any kind which refused to show obedience to the Nazi state, to join any Nazi organisations, or be conscripted into the army. Small religious sects of this kind, such as the Quakers, had always existed in the English-speaking world, and provision was made for them as conscientious objectors from the draft, but no such provision ever existed in Germany, let alone under the Nazis, and the entire weight of Nazi oppression was brought against them almost at once. [242] (The Jehovah's Witnesses, it should be noted with gratitude, offered a kind of resistance to the Nazi regime not demonstrated by political parties or trade unions with millions of members.) Virtually all aspects of their activities were banned, many were beaten up by the Gestapo, and hundreds were among the first thrown into concentration camps.[243] A mass rally of 7,000 Witnesses in Berlin in June 1933 protesting at the violation of their religious freedom was, possibly, the largest anti-Nazi demonstration held in Hitler's Germany. Conditions for Jehovah's Witnesses became progressively worse, with 7,000 imprisoned in concentration camps in 1939, over 10 per cent of all inmates.[244] Witnesses, who were 'Aryans', were given the chance to be released from camps if they resigned from the movement and agreed to join the military, but many remained true to their convictions. During the war, about 10,000 were imprisoned in German concentration camps, where about 2,500 died.[245] It is said that about one-quarter of Jehovah's Witnesses died in the German camps.[246] The Witnesses were the only victims of Nazism who had the choice of escaping persecution, an option few took. If the majority of Germans had behaved like the Jehovah's Witnesses, the Holocaust would not have happened and the German nation would have escaped from the burden of guilt which still hangs over it.

Coming to terms with Hitler's legacy in genocide and democide is rather difficult. There is no doubt that, in modern times, he was in a class by himself, the worst mass murderer of the modern age. Even employing any conservative estimates of deaths at the hands of the Nazis, it seems unlikely that many less than 30 million people were killed in Europe during the Second World War (some estimates are far higher), not one of whom, in all likelihood, would have died in conflict or as a result of conflict had Hitler not lived.

Murder and death on this scale was inconceivably horrible, but to what extent was it genocide? Plainly, in the case of European Jewry both the intention and actuality of Nazi policy was genocide in its purest sense, the physical extermination of European Jewry. With other groups, both the intention of the Nazis in committing genocide and their success in carrying out their intentions, are more questionable, while in the case of homosexuals, there appears to have been no intention of committing genocide. Had the Second World War continued longer, or if the Nazis had won, this summary would probably be in need of revision. In particular, the Poles, and probably other Slavic groups, would have become victims of 'ethnic cleansing' and perhaps mass murder on a colossal scale. Nazism represented the most extreme example of pitiless Social Darwinism being put into practice with no regard for human life or the humane values of Western civilisation. Yet it is important to remember that Hitler, whose creation Nazism was, was centrally obsessed with the Jews and most clearly and comprehensively left the accepted norms of law and morality behind only in dealing with the Jews and, perhaps, with Soviet 'Judeo-Bolshevism'.

Axis allies: Italy, Croatia, Japan

Nazi Germany was the most important of the Axis powers, the fascist grouping of 'anti-Bolshevik' and anti-democratic states. But there were other Axis nations, and it is worth examining their record in genocide and mass murder compared with that of the Nazis. Italy was headed by Benito Mussolini, the senior fascist leader, in power in Italy from 1922 until 1943 and then in the so-called 'Salo Republic' (a Nazi puppet state in northern Italy) for two more years until his execution by Partisans. While Mussolini was no angel, his record until the mid-1930s was surprisingly free of massacre or slaughter, and, although the head of a one-party dictatorship, killed few of his opponents. Probably the most notable exception to this pattern (until Mussolini became a stooge of Hitler's in 1943) came at the 'Massacre of Lake Ashangi' during the unprovoked Italian invasion of Ethiopia, in April 1936, when thousands of Ethiopian troops were massacred by aerial bombardment, mustard gas and the poisoning of the local lake.[247] During the Second World War, however, Mussolini refused to deport Jews to extermination camps: they were relatively safe until German troops occupied Italy in 1943. Italians notably failed to cooperate with Germany in the killing of Jews and others, in part because there was little in the way of native Italian racialist antisemitism, in part because of widespread anti-German feeling, but in large measure because of the prevalent Italian culture of routinely subverting authority and orders from the government.[248]

In complete contrast was the nation which was probably Hitler's bloodiest puppet satellite, Croatia, led by its *Poglavnik* (Führer), Dr Ante Pavelic (1889–1959), head of the Ustashe ('Insurrection') an extremist right-wing fascist and terrorist body. Pavelic's Croatia was so extraordinarily murderous and genocidal that it requires a separate mention, in contrast to Hitler's run-of-the-mill brutal quislings. There had been no independent state of Croatia until April 1941, when Germany and Italy invaded Yugoslavia, divided the former nation into three smaller states, and put Ustashe in power in Croatia. The Pavelic government, strongly backed by Hitler, continued to rule until May 1945, occupying most of northern Yugoslavia (Croatia, Bosnia, Herzogovina) with its capital at Zagreb. Under the previous kingdom of Yugoslavia, Ustashe, which had advocated the dismemberment of the state, had been outlawed. Most of its leaders had been in exile in Italy.[249] Its population of 6.3 million included only 3.3 million Croatians, the others being Serbs (1.9 million), who were Orthodox Christians in religion, while the Croatians were Catholics; 700,000 Muslim Croats, 40,000 Jews, 30,000 Gypsies and 350,000 members of other minorities. The Ustashe was remarkable in regarding all non-Croatians as their absolute enemies, especially the Serbs, whom they detested and vowed to destroy. 'In this country, nobody can live except Croatians,' one Croatian nationalist (a Catholic priest) put it.[250] Another Ustashe ideologue claimed that 'the bell tolls. The last hour of those foreign elements, the Serb and the Jew, has arrived. They shall vanish from Croatia.'[251] The Serbs and Croats were racially and linguistically almost identical, differing only in religion, but Pavelic insisted in conversations with Hitler that the Croatians were not Slavs, stating that 'they were descendants of the Goths, and the Panslav idea has been forced upon them'.[252] Hitler accepted this view, treating them as near-Germans, despite the fact that they were indeed Slavs.[253] Pavelic proceeded to institute a constitution eliminating all non-Croats from the government and all positions of power, and virtually conceding hegemony in all aspects of Croatian policy to Nazi Germany. Croatia was also compelled to give up most of the Adriatic coast to Italy, and had (nominally, since he never set foot in the country) to accept an Italian prince as Croatia's king.[254]

After eliminating all non-Croats from the governance of the country, the Ustashe proceeded to kill as many of them as possible. Pavelic's regime carried out genocide against the Serbs, Jews, Gypsies and others, regarding Serbs as their principal enemy. It is claimed that about 200,000 Serbs were killed in the first year of the regime, generally by savage public killings which included hacking to death, burning alive, mutilation (both before and after death) and machine gunning.[255] So horrifying did this butchery become that the Ustashe enjoyed the unique distinction of being criticised by local Nazi diplomats for excessive brutality![256] The Ustashe established a particularly dreadful concentration camp at Jasenovic, where killings were carried out by revolvers, rifles, machine guns, bombs, knives, axes, hatchets, wooden hammers, iron bars, by trampling, freezing and burning alive, among other methods.[257] According to pro-Serbian sources, Pavelic made a collection of the eye-balls of his victims, gouged out after they were killed.[258] Another 200,000 Serbs were forcibly expelled to Serbia, while the Croatian regime, which had a considerable clerical-conservative base, forcibly converted thousands of Serbs and Muslims.[259] Most of Croatia's Jews were taken to local concentration camps, especially Jasenovic near Zagreb, where thousands died, along with thousands of Serbs and Gypsies. About 7,000 Croatian Jews were deported to Auschwitz.[260] In one pogrom against Serbs in the Kozara district in 1942, 60,000 persons were driven to the Jasenovic camp, where most died.[261] Thousands of Gypsies were also killed, almost all by the Ustashe, possibly a higher percentage than anywhere in Europe.[262] Pavelic's regime was bitterly unpopular with almost all sections of the population, and most of the country had been lost to Tito's Communist insurgents by 1943–4.[263] After the war, with a reunified Yugoslavia, thousands of Ustashe supporters fled abroad, while Croatia did not recover its short-lived independence until 1991.[264]

The Empire of Japan was Nazi Germany's great ally in the Far East. Although nominally a democratic constitutional monarchy of sorts, from 1931, and emphatically from about 1937, it was dominated by a clique of militarists who embarked on a deliberate policy of conquering as much of the East Asia–Pacific area as possible. Their value system, emphasising absolute obedience to the Emperor, Japanese racial superiority, military might and the like, offered close parallels to Nazi doctrine, although they were a part of the Japanese national psyche long before.[265] Unlike Nazism (or Soviet Communism) Japanese ultra-nationalism was not a product of the First World War, although it gained absolute hegemony in the 1930s in large part in imitation of the growth of Nazi Germany and as a result of the apparent discrediting of liberal democracy by the Depression and the worldwide rise of dictatorship. Imperialist Japan was not genocidal in the strict sense. Although its aim, in organising the so-called 'Greater East Asia Co-Prosperity Sphere', was to enslave and exploit most of the peoples of Asia, it had no intention as such to exterminate its helot peoples. Nor did it engage in 'ethnic cleansing', except perhaps in Manchuria, where over 330,000 Japanese were settled.[266] As Ienaga points out, even in wartime Japan, there were no concentration camps or mass killings of opponents or minorities. Rather remarkably, it appears that only one person was executed for treason in wartime Japan.[267] Nevertheless, throughout the East Asia-Pacific region, Japanese military conquest and rule became a byword for murderous brutality. The total number of civilian deaths caused, directly or indirectly, by the Japanese during the war has probably never been accurately calculated but must be very large. In French Indochina (invaded by Japan in 1940) 'many rice paddies were converted to jute, and part of the rice crop was shipped to Laos and stored for contingency use. A severe food shortage occurred; nearly 200,000 Vietnamese reportedly starved to death after the war.'[268] In Malaya 'several thousand' overseas Chinese were murdered by mass drowning.[269] About 90,000 Filipino civilians were murdered by the Japanese.[270] In China, the numbers killed by the Japanese is incalculable. One estimate is that 2,600,000 'unarmed Chinese' were murdered.[271]

Best known in the West, of course, was Japanese brutality to Allied prisoners of war, in penal colonies, as slave labourers on the Burma Railway, on 'death marches' and in other barbaric ways.[272] The treatment of British, Commonwealth and American POWs during the war is strongly reminiscent of the Nazis' treatment of captured Soviet troops. About 27 per cent of captured Allied troops died in captivity, compared with only 4 per cent of British and American troops captured by the Germans or Italians.[273] As at Nanking (described below) the sadism and brutality which were the hallmark of the Japanese military beggars belief. In several well-documented cases, Japanese troops low on rations killed and ate (*sic*) captured American flyers.[274] Cannibalism by Japanese troops apparently became widespread on the Pacific islands.[275] After the war, 25 Japanese leaders and particularly brutal military commanders were tried by the Allies at Tokyo, headed by wartime Prime Minister

Hideki Tojo. The 'Japanese Nuremberg' resulted in 6 death sentences and 16 sentences of life imprisonment.[276] As in the case of Nazi Germany, it is not easy to predict what the future would have held for the captive peoples of Japan's Asia-Pacific empire, but it could hardly have been very pleasant.

As appalling as Japan's numerous crimes were, probably the most infamous single event in the 14-year history of Japanese militarist aggression was the 'Rape of Nanking', carried out in the months following Japan's capture of Nanking on 13 December 1937. In July 1937 Japan used an incident between Japanese and Chinese troops at the Marco Polo Bridge near Beijing to launch an all-out attack on China. Japan quickly sized Beijing and many other cities in northern China, and, on 8 November, conquered Shanghai, China's great international seaport. The Japanese employed a relentless bombing campaign against China's cities which allegedly killed up to 250,000 Chinese. Japan's attack (12 December) on the *Panay*, an American ship near Nanking, increased tensions between the two countries, setting the stage for Pearl Harbor four years later.

After the initial advance, however, conquering China, with its vast population, proved no walkover for the Japanese, who were greatly outnumbered by local troops, and the battle for Nanking, China's temporary capital on the Yangtze upriver from Shanghai, proved very difficult. Japan's military leader in this campaign was the newly appointed Prince Asaka Yasuhiko, uncle of the Emperor, a 30-year military veteran but also a military extremist. For reasons which are obscure and disputed, a secret order was given, under Asaka's personal seal, to kill all captives once the city surrendered.[277] This order was circulated among all Japanese officers, who had no way of feeding the 300,000 troops likely to surrender.[278] The Chinese soldiers and civilians surrendered peacefully, expecting reasonable treatment. The next day, the Japanese began shooting all the Chinese troops they had captured. They then went on an orgy of killing, raping, torturing and mutilating Nanking's civilian population on a scale possibly unknown in warfare up to that point in modern history.[279] This orgy of evil lasted for six weeks, until late January 1938. Even to case-hardened historians used to reading about the enormities of the Nazi Holocaust and other sadistic slaughters, the forms of torture and mass killings employed by the Japanese at Nanking simply beggars belief: the burying alive and burning alive of civilians were only some of the most commonplace methods.[280] Women were routinely raped, tortured and murdered in numbers which numb the mind in their horror. The number of victims killed by the Japanese at Nanking has been estimated by one Chinese historian at over 227,000, to which another 150,000 or even more, secretly buried by Japanese troops, must be added, bringing the total to about 377,000.[281] Most other reliable estimates are also in the 300,000–400,000 range.[282] Some Chinese escaped by taking shelter in the city's international zone, which the Japanese left alone.[283] Although the outside world knew a great deal about this horror, it has only recently become common knowledge in the West. A War Crimes Trial was held in Nanking in 1946–7, three of the worst murderers were hanged, but the overwhelming majority escaped justice.[284] Ever since, however, the 'Rape of Nanking' has festered in the Chinese memory. As so much else in its history of aggression, the facts of the 'Rape' have been consistently denied or downplayed by the Japanese.[285] It has also been pointed out that Japan's troops were drawn from the dregs of society and were taught, from earliest childhood, both absolute obedience to the Emperor and murderous hostility to others; as well, the capture of Nanking had taken four months, during which an unexpectedly fierce Chinese resistance had resulted in higher Japanese casualties than expected: Nanking was their revenge.[286] The 'Rape of Nanking' has become a defining moment in the evolution of modern China, and was used by the emergent Communist movement as proof of the incompetent supineness of the Nationalists.[287] Comparisons with the Nazi Holocaust have inevitably been made, especially in Western discussions of Nanking. Obviously, in terms of the scale of victims the two events cannot be compared, yet, in terms of the cruelty and barbarism employed, anyone who has read about the Rape of Nanking must see that the comparison is not misplaced.

Soviet Communism

For many, perhaps most, historians and commentators, repression and mass murder in the Soviet Union represent the opposite side of the coin from Nazi Germany and its allies, a left-wing totalitarian system which also produced innocent victims by the millions in blind, inhuman furtherance of an abstract ideology. While Soviet Communism lasted far longer than German National Socialism – 74 years rather than just 12 – it, too, eventually collapsed with such finality that today, barely a decade after its downfall, it has become very difficult to recall its omnipresence in world politics; like Nazism, Soviet Communism left little in the way of a permanent legacy besides a great many graves. There are many other parallels between the two systems as well, especially the role of Stalin which in many (not all) ways offers a close likeness to Hitler.

For the historians of genocide, however, the history of the Soviet Union presents many conceptual and other problems. While millions died in the Soviet Union, there is a real and fundamental question about how these deaths should be categorised. If the notion of 'genocide' is restricted to the mass killings of an ethnic or religious group, it is clear that only a part (arguably a small part) of those killed by Stalin and other Soviet leaders will be included as victims of genocide. In the Soviet Union and the other Communist regimes, most of the millions who died as 'enemies of the people' were 'class enemies', defined as a rule by their belonging to, or acting on behalf of, the bourgeoisie, the kulaks, or some other allegedly anti-working class component of the population. There were exceptions to this: during the Second World War, Stalin deported allegedly pro-German ethnic groups like the Chechen-Ingush and the Crimean Tartars (among others) to Siberia, while his onslaughts against the Ukrainians in the 1930s and the Jews after 1945 can be seen as ethnic hostility in the normal way. Yet, plainly, any definition of 'genocide' or 'democide' in the modern world, and especially during the era of totalitarianism, must include mass killings based on 'class' as well as ethnicity within it, or most of the millions who perished under Communism will somehow be written out of the history of genocide. Regrettably, this has characterised some recent works on genocide.[288] Yet in the twentieth century, it seems likely (though not certain) that many more people were killed as a result of their alleged 'class' than because of their ethnicity. Certainly the numbers involved (and often the two are conflated and confused) would not be radically dissimilar.

Another important difficulty in assessing Soviet democide lies in the evolution of our knowledge of Soviet, especially Stalinist, crimes, and the changes which have occurred over the decades in the ways in which we commonly perceive these crimes. Until the beginning of the Cold War in the later 1940s, Stalinist Russia and the Soviet Union split Western observers and the Western intelligentsia into passionately differing camps. To an extent only seldom appreciated today, Stalin and his regime were enthusiastically admired and supported by much of the leftist and left-oriented Western intelligentsia, who closed their eyes to his crimes, justified them as the unfortunate results of imposing socialism on backward Russia, where so many oppositionist forces remained, or simply dismissed reports of mass killings and an unprecedented network of terror as reactionary propaganda.[289] There always were, to be sure, a steady stream of iconoclastic and damning works about Soviet Communism from its foundation, but these were often (sometimes rightly) dismissed as emanating from the right-wing fringe of Russian exile groups, pro-fascists and extremist crackpots. During the 1930s, it should be remembered, support for the Soviet Union became one of the central *leitmotifs* among the Western world's young intellectuals, especially during the Spanish Civil War. Stalinist Russia actually appeared to many intellectuals – at the height of the Great Purges – to be a superior society, a real glimpse of the future, the only state to have ended unemployment and to be fighting fascism.[290]

The onset of the Cold War saw the emergence of a new genre of fiercely anti-Soviet memoirs and accounts, some by renegades from the USSR such as Victor Kravchenko, some by disillusioned Communists and leftists such as Arthur Koestler and George Orwell. Only in the late 1960s, however, a decade or so after Khruschchev's celebrated 1956 denunciation of Stalin, did the apparently true scale of Stalin's crimes and enormities become widely known (and accepted) among Western intellectuals. Probably the key work in this process was Robert Conquest's seminal *The Great Terror* (1968), a magisterial and truly horrifying account of Stalin's reign of terror, which has often been compared with the works of historians such as Raul Hilberg on the Jewish Holocaust, although no single work on the Holocaust (with the possible exception of *The Diary of Anne Frank*) did as much as Conquest's book to inform anyone with an interest in Stalinist Russia about its enormities. Conquest was joined by similar works by Soviet dissidents such as Roy Medvedev, and by many other Western historians and demographers. By the 1980s the notion that Stalin murdered truly astronomical numbers of people, certainly 20 million, perhaps 50 million, were commonly held in the West.[291] Since the opening of former Soviet archives to Western scholars, beginning in the 1980s, something of a reaction has set in. Recent academic works on Stalinist Russia, while in no way apologising for Stalin's enormities, have considerably scaled down the number of his victims.[292] With recent evidence from the Russian archives, it now appears highly likely that the truly astronomical figures of deaths under Stalinism suggested by writers in the 1960s and 1970s were greatly exaggerated, as appalling as they obviously were. In this section, the evidence and current state of knowledge in this ongoing debate can only be summarised and set out.

Stalin's crimes and enormities actually consisted of several separate, only indirectly related campaigns of democide, most notably the arguably man-made Ukrainian famine of the early 1930s, the Great Purges (or *Ezhovschina*) of the later 1930s, and the mass relocation of minority peoples, deemed likely to be opposed to the Soviet war effort, during the Second World War. As well, there were other specific criminal acts, such as the deportation of thousands of Poles and others after the Soviet Union occupied significant parts of eastern Europe as a result of the Nazi-Soviet pact of 1939, and, behind everything, the constant, continuous background of terror, repression and imprisonment which became an everyday feature of Stalinist Russia.

Lenin and the early Bolsheviks were no angels, and an appalling period of 'Red Terror' occurred during the post-revolutionary interval of civil war and foreign invasion. At least 10,000–15,000 people were killed in the 'Red Terror' in 1918 alone, while at least 70,000 persons were imprisoned in Communist labour and concentration camps (already an established feature of the regime) in September 1921.[293] Mass killings – often aimed at striking workers who failed to recognise Leninism as introducing an earthly paradise – continued throughout Lenin's life, with up to 10,000 persons shot or drowned in the town of Astrakhan alone in 1919–20, according to recent detailed research.[294] In the latter stages of the Russian civil war, even larger massacre totals became the order of the day, with at least 50,000 civilians killed by the Bolsheviks in one notorious massacre in the Crimea area in November-December 1920.[295] Vast numbers of inhabitants of the Soviet Union certainly died in the great famine of 1921–2. Their number has been estimated at 5 million.[296]

While the number of persons killed by the regime or dying as a result of its policies thereafter declined steadily until Stalin's ascendancy to power in the late 1920s, the Soviet Union was already a society whose government demonstrated utter ruthlessness and disregard for life. Its secret police and other implements of repression were already in place.[297]

Stalin's first great acts of alleged genocide – probably, in retrospect, his greatest crime – were the Ukrainian famines of 1930–3, and especially that which occurred in 1933. This has been described by many historians and commentators as a 'holocaust', equivalent in the number of victims to the Jewish Holocaust, or nearly so.[298] After becoming supreme Soviet leader in 1928–9, Stalin embarked on an all-out programme of Soviet industrialisation. To pay for the purchase or construction of heavy industry equipment, Stalin and his henchmen began the mass collectivisation of Soviet agriculture, hoping to seize, and sell overseas, all surplus grain and other agricultural produce from the Soviet peasantry, especially the 'kulak' class of so-called 'rich peasants'. This was pursued with the utmost brutality and uncompromising single-mindedness which revealed the hallmarks of one of the worst totalitarian regimes in modern history. The peasants resisted collectivisation by any means possible, including, most notably, the slaughter of livestock on a grand scale. In turn, this engendered a series of annual famines reaching its climax in the spring of 1933, when literally millions starved. Stalin's inhumanity was worst in the Soviet Ukraine, where the crackdown on the peasants was combined with an attempt to uproot what Stalin perceived as excessive Ukrainian nationalism, leading to the execution of many prominent Ukrainian cultural and national figures.[299]

Many of the features which became common aspects of Stalin's reign of terror first originated in the famine period. For instance, in 1932 Lazar Kaganovich, one of the most odious of Stalin's henchmen, was sent to the North Caucasus (suffering from the same policies) to put down a strike of Kuban Cossacks who refused to cultivate their land. The entire population of 16 Cossack villages in the North Caucasus were deported to Siberia.[300] Whole villages in the Ukraine were placed on a blacklist, for allegedly sabotaging grain procurements, resulting in the closing of all state and cooperative stores and the ending of all trade, including the trade in bread.[301] Millions, facing starvation, took to the roads, where enormous numbers died. According to pro-Ukrainian sources, at the height of the famine about 25,000 people died every day.[302] To reiterate, Stalin's brutality appeared in particular to be directed against the Ukraine, since Russia did not experience a famine.[303] It is this feature which has caused the Ukrainian famine to be described as 'genocide', in that it was primarily directed against one national group. The famine did, however, also affect other parts of the Soviet Union, especially the Kuban and Don regions, inhabited chiefly by Ukrainians and Cossacks, and Kazakhstan in central Asia. Apart from his already well-entrenched mechanism of terror and authoritarianism, Stalin was also able to play on Communist and urban fears of the peasantry, especially the 'kulaks', and on memories of Ukrainian and Cossack hostility to Bolshevism during the Civil War of 1917–21.[304] From April 1933, however, even Stalin was forced to call something of a halt to the more extreme features of the collectivisation process, characteristically blaming (in a directive to party operatives) 'Polish agents and enemies of the Soviet regime'.[305]

How many died during the Soviet famine of the early 1930s has been hotly debated. Estimates by reliable historians and statisticians range from 3 million to 7 million.[306] In contrast to the death figures from the Great Purges of the late 1930s, recent historians, writing with access, post-Communism, to suppressed Soviet data, have tended to raise rather than lower the scale of mortality. Wheatcroft, with access to comprehensive Soviet data, has raised his estimate of the death toll in the 1932–3 famine from '3 to 4 million' to a figure which 'might be as high as 4 to 5 million'.[307] (Nevertheless, Wheatcroft specifically takes issue with historians such as Conquest who have placed the death toll much higher, at up to 8 million; such figures are 'impossible to accept'.[308]) Nove has also drawn attention to the fact that, slightly earlier, the famine, as well as disease and the destruction of livestock through fanatical collectivisation, also affected Kazakhstan in ways as horrifying as the Ukraine. Apparently, 1.5–1.7 million Kazakhs died in 1931–3, up to 42 per cent of the entire Kazakh population.[309]

In all, the death toll caused by Stalin's collectivisation policies in the early 1930s was probably the greatest non-military demographic catastrophe in the Western world in the twentieth century, likely exceeding, in absolute numbers, the death toll in the Jewish Holocaust. To be sure, the percentage of Ukrainians who perished was clearly much lower than the percentage of European Jews who died in the Holocaust (but causing a large part of the decrease in the total population of the Ukraine from 31.2 million to 26.4 million between 1926 and 1937), but the percentage of Kazakh deaths, if accurate, began to approach the Jewish death percentage in Nazi-occupied Europe as a whole.

However, all this begs the question of whether the Soviet famines were a case of genocide, as opposed to an appalling human catastrophe. There is, of course, no evidence that Stalin wished to exterminate the Ukrainian people, as opposed to cowing them into obedience. The Soviet famines were the entirely unnecessary byproduct of an ideologically driven social planning on a grand scale, not of deliberate mass murder. This is of small comfort to the millions of its victims, but it is important that historians distinguish accurately among these categories of horrors.

Stalin's Great Purges of the later 1930s, especially the *Ezhovschina* of 1937–8, consisted of the intentional killing of hundreds of thousands of innocent victims, and was much more clearly an example of deliberate mass murder than the famines of a few years earlier. Like the famines, it was ideologically driven and, above all, based in Stalin's megalomaniacal attempts to centralise power in his own hands. Nevertheless, recent historians have questioned some of the traditional assumptions which are commonly held about the Great Purges. It is normal to date the outset of Stalin's true reign of terror with the murder of Sergei Kirov, the Communist boss of Leningrad, in December 1934, probably at Stalin's behest. Over the next three years, most of the 'Old Bolsheviks' were tried on absurd charges of treason and executed, among them Zinoviev, Kamenev, Radek, Bukharin, Rykov and virtually everyone who was a high official of the Soviet Union under Lenin. In June 1937 Stalin executed his best general, Marshal Mikhail Tukhachevski, and seven other generals, on equally absurd charges of treason. The period from December 1934 until the beginning of 1937 was termed the 'vegetarian' period of the Terror by the famous poet Anna Akhmatova, when thousands, rather than millions, perished, generally 'Old Bolsheviks' and anyone who appeared unlikely to give total obedience to Stalin as dictator. September 1936 marked the beginnings of the Great Terror proper, a period which is normally seen as continuing until November 1938, coinciding with Nikolai Ezhov's (or Yezhov's) term as head of the NKVD, the Soviet security force and secret police.[310] The *Ezhovschina*, the 'Reign of

Ezhov', is seen by many as being equalled in modern European history only by the reign of Hitler's SS in occupied Europe. Of course Ezhov (1895–1938), a stooge of Stalin, functioned as the Soviet dictator's puppet.[311] Unlike Hitler, Stalin deliberately gave the impression that his rule was a collective one, and that he shared power with other leading Soviet officials. During the Terror, many ordinary Soviet citizens sincerely believed that Stalin was being kept in the dark about what was actually going on, and the excesses of the Terror would stop if he learned the truth.[312] In actual fact, Stalin personally approved many of the thousands of executions in this period, including lists containing 44,000 names, of whom 39,000 were executed, in 1938 alone.[313]

Much about the Great Terror remains very mysterious. It appears, however, that, beginning in early 1937, a chain reaction of denunciations and counterdenunciations began among ordinary Soviet citizens who were themselves accused of crimes during the crackdown. To escape the death penalty (seldom successfully), each accused person, brought before the NKVD and often tortured, would then name 40 or 50 'Trotskyites, White Guardists, and wreckers' (or the like) known to him or her, each of whom would then be brought in, following the dreaded 'knock on the door' after midnight. They would then name 40 or 50 more, in turn, and so on. This procedure had much in common with the witch hunts of medieval Europe and, indeed, for Kafkaesque irrationality there was little in modern Western history to compare with the *Ezhovschina*. After torture, or to escape the death penalty, the accused would confess to monstrous absurdities: Jews were accused of working for the Gestapo, lifelong Communists of conspiring with exiled monarchists and fascists. Most of the 'conspiracies' were *a priori* preposterous. According to V.M. Molotov, speaking in 1937, Soviet heavy industry was infested by 'Japanese-German-Trotskyite' agents, plus 'Bukharinist and Rykovist wreckers of the right'.[314] This was, of course, very much the world of Orwell's *1984*: Orwell drew much of his inspiration from a penetrating awareness of the realities of Stalinism, the nature of which he appreciated long before many other Western intellectuals. The *Ezhovschina* spread outward like a forest fire to engulf ever-wider areas of Soviet society, apparently defying rational explanation. In one popular joke of the period, a prisoner newly arrived in the Gulag is asked how long his term of imprisonment was to be. 'Twenty-five years.' 'For what?' 'For nothing.' 'Impossible,' comes the reply, 'for nothing you get ten years.'[315] At the height of the *Ezhovschina*, the Politburo set quotas of persons to be 'repressed'. On 2 June 1937, for instance, it set a quota of 35,000 persons to be 'repressed' in Moscow, of whom 5,000 were to be shot. The following month, the Politburo provided each region with quotas of persons to be arrested, of whom 70,000 were to be executed without trial.[316]

All this sounds a good deal like Nazi Germany, but there were many differences. Nazi Germany was a *volkish* society, founded on the racial unity of the German people. If one did not belong to the regime's ethnic enemies – Jews, Gypsies or Slavs – had no record as a hard-core Communist, and did not make trouble politically once Hitler took power, probably nothing adverse was likely to happen to you. About 95 per cent of the German population was thus probably safe from 'repression'. As well, until the very end Hitler never turned on his comrades in the Nazi leadership, the execution of Ernst Rohm in 1934 (probably because he was attempting to blackmail Hitler) being virtually the only exception. Hitler never held a show trial for Goering, Hess and Kaltenbrunner, where they confessed to being 'agents of Zionism, British imperialism, and the Third International' before being shot, and nor did Hitler announce one day that the German aircraft industry and the entire Nazi party apparatus in Baden and Hanover were riddled with 'Bolshevik spies and wreckers', executing most of its officials, although Stalin did the equivalent of this scores of times. To Stalin, increasingly paranoid, everyone was a potential enemy: his foes were everywhere, constantly conspiring. To most Western observers and historians, it appeared that literally no one was safe. Hitler detested only small, select groups: in contrast, Stalin hated everyone impartially.[317]

Although the *Ezhovschina* was fundamentally irrational, many historians have attempted to portray it as rationally motivated. Obviously it had the effect of eliminating all rivals and potential rivals to Stalin's unchallenged rule as a dictator with powers exceeding virtually any despot in ancient or modern history, and left the whole population in abject fear of satisfying his every whim. By eliminating the 'Old Bolsheviks' and the cadre of Soviet managers who held office in the 1920s and early 1930s, Stalin also created a vacuum for the upwardly mobile. Many of his newly risen managers were genuinely of worker or peasant background and were, of course, utterly loyal to Stalin, who had directly benefited them. Soviet society was remoulded, and some historians have dated the 'real' Russian revolution from Stalin's time rather than from 1917.[318] Stalin's ascendancy to supremacy has also struck some Western historians as virtually a revival of the Tsarist system with a Marxist terminology. Stalin turned himself into an imitation of Ivan the Terrible (whom he admired), restored some of the symbolism and titles (as among military officers) of the former regime, and created what Tucker has described as a 'new service nobility' similar to that which existed under the Tsars.[319] Ultra-nationalism, especially Great Russian chauvinism, became a *leitmotif* of the Soviet regime from the mid-1930s, in striking contrast to Marxism's alleged cosmopolitanism and internationalism. Expenditure on the military and heavy industry, in order to build up Soviet power at home and abroad, became the driving force of Soviet 'socialism' from the mid-1930s until the collapse of the regime 55 years later. The Purges also arguably had a profound effect on the group psychology of the Soviet people, instilling hysteria, fear and paranoia into millions of ordinary Russians in a way which persisted into the 1980s, over 30 years after Stalin's death.[320] This mood of fear was amplified by the pre-modern social outlook still prevalent throughout much of rural Russia, which was receptive to mass hysteria and moods of paranoia similar to western Europe during the witchcraft crazes of the Middle Ages.[321]

The Purges also assumed the dimensions they did, some recent historians argue, because of the inherent contradictions between the demands placed by a command economy, via its centrally directed Five Year Plans, on factory managers, and actual realities: when quotas could not be fulfilled (which was often the case), factory managers, suppliers and local party officials would blame and denounce each other, with mass arrests and executions following once the Purges became institutionalised.[322] This tendency was greatly augmented by the fundamental premise of Stalinism that nothing happened by accident: when a planned production quota was not met, this was blamed on the actions of 'wreckers' and anti-Soviet elements, not on inefficiencies in the system. The philosophy that 'nothing happened by accident' was especially prevalent in areas such as transport (where there were innumerable railway accidents) and throughout the entire productive part of the manufacturing sector. It augmented other points of conflict which were also present in the Stalinist system.[323]

Recent historians have thus tended both to broaden the nature of the Great Terror, viewing it as often instituted (for specific reasons) from below, in an effort by officials and others to cope with the Stalinist system, but have also narrowed its scope, seeing it as directed centrally to highly specific groups. According to these historians, while everyone was indeed vulnerable, certain groups were especially prone to arrest and severe punishment, chiefly 'Old Bolsheviks' and dissenters of various kinds, and also the managerial elite.[324] According to this view, only Communists and other members of the managerial elite were genuinely at risk. Thurston cites a joke from the purges: the NKVD [secret police] bangs on the door of an apartment in Leningrad in 1937. 'Who's there?' 'NVKD – open up!' 'No, no – you've got the wrong apartment – the Communist lives upstairs.'[325] He also cites a prisoner in the camps who noted that after 1937 'a situation existed ... in which the higher the post occupied in Soviet society, the greater the chances of arrest'.[326] According to this view, Stalin and the secret police actually believed that a vast anti-Soviet conspiracy existed, but was centred in highly specific components of Soviet society rather than generally dispersed.[327]

Recent historians of *Ezhovschina* (and other aspects of Soviet terror) have presented some intriguing evidence about the comparatively limited nature of the Great Purges. According to Getty and Chase, the 'incidence of purges' among different at-risk groups among the Soviet elite of the 1930s showed great variations among different categories, with 62 per cent of those who took part in the 1917 Revolution purged, 69 per cent of the senior military, and 61 per cent of the economic elite, but only 17 per cent of the intelligentsia, and 31 per cent of scientific researchers defined as a part of the elite.[328] Sheila Fitzpatrick, a noted historian of Stalinism, rather cleverly compared telephone subscribers listed in the Moscow phone book in 1937 and 1939, to ascertain the 'drop out rate' caused by the Great Terror of 1937–8. She found a remarkably low rate of disappearance among many occupations (the Moscow phone book listed the occupations of individual subscribers), including a 12 per cent 'drop out' rate among engineers, 16 per cent among teachers and only 3 per cent among doctors. Among senior officials of the Commissariat of Heavy Industry of the USSR, however, no fewer than 60 per cent of those in the 1937 directory had vanished by 1939.[329]

This raises the key question of how many people died in the Great Purge of 1934–8. As noted, older estimates, made during the Cold War before relevant Soviet archives became accessible, were often astronomical. R.J. Rummel suggested 4,345,000 deaths in the period 1936–8, including 1 million executed and the others in labour camps.[330] This he regards as a median estimate between a low figure of 2,044,000 and a high one of 10,821,000.[331] More recent estimates, based on newly released Soviet sources, have *all* tended to be much lower. According to Alex Nove, 786,098 persons were shot 'for counterrevolutionary and state crimes' in the entire period 1931–53, of whom 353,074 were shot in 1937 and 328,618 in 1938.[332] The number thereafter declined markedly. Another estimate, made in a confidential letter to Khrushchev, was that 642,980 persons were shot in the period 1921–53.[333] Deaths among prisoners in the Gulag in 1937–9 totalled 166,424, with 90,546 dying in 1938. Thus, it would appear that about 850,000 persons died during the *Ezhovschina*, not some vastly higher figure. Even if this figure is an underestimate, particularly with regards to the number of deaths in the Siberian camps, it seems unlikely that, unless much new evidence is forthcoming, figures in the millions have a factual basis. Obviously, by any conceivable standards except those one might expect from a monster like Stalin, a figure like 850,000 deaths (over 100,000 more than the entire total of British casualties in the First World War) is almost beyond comprehension, and is almost certainly without precedent in previous Western history. It is also obvious that 99 per cent of those who died were no more 'wreckers', 'spies' or 'agents of Trotsky and the Japanese' than the millions of Jews who died at the hands of the Nazis had been quietly 'stabbing Germany in the back'. All these, like millions of others, were victims of totalitarian ideologies in which there were no restrictions or restraints on carrying out the will of the dictator. The recent figures, moreover, are for those who died in the Great Purges, not those who were imprisoned in the Gulag, which was vastly higher. Nove suggests that 2,671,000 persons arrived in the many Soviet Gulags and labour camps in the three years 1937–9.[334]

Imprisonment in labour camps and Gulags continued until Stalin's death in 1953 (and beyond). Indeed, the best evidence available today suggests that more Soviet citizens were imprisoned after 1940 than before. In 1950, there were apparently 2,561,000 persons in Soviet labour camps, including 'counterrevolutionaries', ordinary citizens of the so-called 'punished peoples' such as the Chechens and Crimean Tartars, deportees from the Baltic states, former Vlasov army (anti-Soviet fighters on the side of the Axis, headed by ex-Soviet agent Andrei Vlasov) veterans, and many others.[335] This total was considerably higher than the number of camp inmates in the late 1930s. 'Only' 1,224,000 persons were imprisoned in labour camps in 1938, for instance.[336] By the 1950s fewer were shot, which paradoxically accounts for the rise in numbers.

The third and separate aspect of Stalin's criminal record concerns the deportation of peoples deemed disloyal to the Soviet regime, and likely to support the Nazi invaders, during the Second World War. This subject has received a good deal of scholarly debate in recent years.[337] Between 1937 and 1944 the central Soviet government deported 12 separate nationalities from their homelands to areas of 'internal exile' in central Asia and Siberia.[338] During the period of growing conflict with Japan in the late 1930s, 172,000 Koreans were deported to Kazakhstan and Uzbekistan, while the Volga Germans and Leningrad Finns were deported soon after the war began, in August 1941, as were the Karachai (a Turkish-speaking people in the north Caucasus), in November 1941. Most of the others, especially the Muslim nationalities affected, were deported in 1943 or 1944, after it became clear that the war was certainly going to be won. (These nationalities had been conquered by the Nazis during the early phases of the war and then recaptured. Under German rule they had briefly enjoyed semi-autonomy.[339]) The Crimean Tartars were deported on 18 May 1944, after D-Day. In all, extraordinary numbers of people were affected, with the NKVD (the Secret Police) recording 1,810,361 such persons as deportees.[340] Other sources suggest even higher figures. At least 1,209,000 Volga Germans, for instance, were deported in 1941–2 alone.[341] They were invariably sent to harsh and remote areas, often in conditions of great brutality. According to Pohl, the NKVD recorded 263,908 deaths among the affected groups between 1944 and 1948, reducing the numbers of each group by 15–30 per cent.[342] As well, the Stalinist government attempted to destroy the entire cultures of these nations, outlawing the use of their native languages.[343]

The deportations were as clear-cut a case of 'ethnic cleansing', in the worst sense of the term, bordering on overt genocide, as one can imagine. The Soviet government was, it seems, genuinely worried about the loyalties of these peoples, who were viewed as either likely to defect to the Germans or, in the case of the Muslim nationalities, likely to become prey to separatist Muslim tendencies. The Soviet government chose its targets with some care, according to its own internal logic. For instance, while the Crimean Tartars were deported, the Volga Tartars were regarded as loyal, with significant numbers receiving military decorations.[344] Other states, including the United States (in the case of California Japanese-Americans) and Britain (in the case of 'enemy aliens', many Jewish refugees) demonstrated the same harsh panic measures at the outset of the war, but none of the anti-Axis coalition went to Stalin's lengths to deport potential security threats.[345] Men, women and children were deported, often in sealed box-cars or on cattle trucks. In central Asia or Siberia, the deportees were assigned to collective farms or local industries. Many went without shelter. None of this was reported in Soviet newspapers or in any works published in Stalin's time.[346] Penalties against the deported groups were rigorously enforced until Stalin's death.[347]

After the death of Stalin and the beginning of a 'thaw' in Communist rigour, the survivors were gradually allowed to return, although the process only gathered force in 1956–7. For instance, the Chechen and Ingush Autonomous Republic, abolished during the war, was re-established in 1957: the returning Chechens and Ingush often forcibly drove out the inhabitants who had taken over their homes.[348] (The origins of the post-USSR conflict in Chechnya is obviously to be found in these deportations.) Some of the affected peoples were, however, never given permission to return during the existence of the USSR. For instance, while the Crimean Tartars were officially cleared of collaborating with the Nazi invaders in 1967, they were never formally given permission to return to Crimea.[349]

These facets of the brutality of Stalinism probably only scratch the surface and touch only on the highlights.[350] In all, on even the most conservative possible estimate, at least 7 million people were either directly killed by Stalin or perished directly because of his brutally enforced policies. The actual figure may well be much higher, and many historians and observers believe that the 'cost of Stalin' was 20 million dead.[351] Even if these very high figures prove to be exaggerated, it is clear that Stalin was, in many respects, an altogether worthy rival to Hitler.

This brings us to the two most fundamental factors in any consideration of Stalinism, the personality of the dictator and the nature of Soviet totalitarianism. It is apparent that, although cunning and crudely intelligent, Stalin was a paranoid megalomaniac who trusted no one and regarded literally everyone as a potential enemy. Even more than Hitler, perhaps, Stalin craved blind obeisance. The 'refusenik' Mark Azbel pointed out that in the late 1940s the Soviet government released a series of 78rpm records (each lasting about five minutes), containing one of Stalin's speeches. The final record consisted of nothing but applause! From the early 1930s until Stalin's death, it was considered daring to omit Stalin's name from any paragraph of a Soviet newspaper. Coexisting with this slaveocracy was the arguably more humane socialist system founded by Lenin but then transformed by Stalin. Lenin died at the age of only 54: it appears (that is all one can say) that he was in the process of moderating the Soviet system into something more pluralistic and more closely resembling a Western mode of government, rather than a totalitarian system which rejected Western models virtually *in toto*.[352] It is likely that Lenin would have preferred as his successor Nikolai Bukharin, a moderate (in the Soviet sense) who might well have made the Soviet Union into something like Titoist Yugoslavia.[353] In 1923, just before Lenin died, most of the Soviet economy, including almost its entire agricultural sector, was still in private hands, with Lenin's blessing. The victory of Stalin in the late 1920s meant the brutally imposed transformation of the Soviet Union into a total 'command' economy, with no private sector remaining in either industry or agriculture. Stalin's aim was to transform backward Russia into a powerful state, but also to introduce 'modernity' into a culturally backward, almost medieval, society as quickly as possible, at whatever cost. Like Nazism, Soviet Communism also attempted to end the division between the public and private spheres, making each citizen a part of the Communist-dictated public effort at national development, eliminating private motivations almost entirely.

Much has been written on whether Nazism and Soviet Communism were mirror images of one another.[354] In many respects they were, with 'race' (or *Volk*) and 'class' being used respectively in the two societies in similar ways. Yet there is general agreement that this is not the whole story, and there are many difficult paradoxes here. Stalinist Russia probably retained a greater belief in something like human rights in the Western sense than did Nazi Germany: although, for instance, there was 'ethnic cleansing' of many minorities, there was never anything like the Jewish Holocaust. Yet Stalinist Russia was probably fairly consistently more dominated by an apparatus of terror than was Nazi Germany, at least in peacetime, and its citizens, after the early 1930s, were more fearful than were most Germans under Nazism.

Centrally, both systems were direct products of the First World War, which allowed marginal and extremist ideologically based movements to come to power after the existing European elite and constitutional structure had collapsed. In both cases, the really extreme component of the movements' totalitarianism did not emerge at once, but after a period of years: in the German case, only after 15 years of Weimar and then (by subsequent standards) the relatively 'moderate' phase of the Nazi regime until about 1938; in the Soviet case, only after the complete ascendancy of Stalin in the early 1930s. In other words, both regimes became progressively more extreme, steadily detaching themselves from Western norms. Thus, neither regime moderated as it became entrenched, as one might have expected them to have done: both regimes – probably because of the interplay between the dictators' personality and belief-systems, and the totalitarian nature of their dominant ideologies, from which dissent became increasingly difficult – became progressively more extreme. After enacting their legacies of evil, both regimes disappeared (in the Soviet case, of course, over 35 years after Stalin's death), leaving no trace. Western liberalism survived to bury both systems.

Asian Communism, 1945–79
Mao's China

After the Second World War, Communism, in its most extreme and fanatical form, came to power throughout much of east Asia. As a result, millions perished, while the last manifestation of fanatical Asian Communism to come to power, Pol Pot's Cambodia, became synonymous with post-war genocide. Except for North Korea, all these regimes have greatly moderated or, in the case of the Khmer Rouge, disappeared. Nevertheless, the record of post-war Asian Communism in the killing stakes is certainly not as well-known as other modern totalitarian governments, with many well-informed people probably unaware of the mass murders carried out in Maoist China. In this section, the records of mass killings in Maoist China, North Korea and Pol Pot's Cambodia will be examined.

That the People's Republic of China, headed from October 1949 until his death in September 1976 by Mao Zedong (1894–1976; more commonly known in the West during his lifetime as Mao Tse-Tung), was, in the eyes of many, one of the most murderous regimes in all history, is certainly not common knowledge. Many excellent accounts of genocide, even those which discuss Stalinist Russia and Pol Pot's Cambodia, simply omit any mention of Maoist China.[355] Yet, according to several influential observers, Maoist China might well have been the worst regime of all, dwarfing both Nazi Germany and Stalinist Russia in the number of its victims. According to Professor Richard K. Walker, the total number of 'casualties to Communism' in China through 1971 (including victims who perished at the hands of the Communists between 1927 and 1949) can be estimated at between 34.3 million and 63.8 million, of whom 15–30 million perished in the 'Political Liquidation Campaigns' of 1949–58 and another 15-30 million in 'forced labour camps and frontier development'.[356] R.J. Rummel, writing in 1994, placed the likely figure of those 'murdered' in 'the Communist Chinese Anthill' at 35.2 million.[357] Even higher totals are suggested by Jean-Louis Margolin in his essay on China in *The Black Book of Communism*.[358] Some official sanction for estimates of deaths in this range is given by *The Guinness Book of Records*, which lists the deaths in the People's Republic of China under the heading 'Greatest Claimed Mass Killings', again surpassing Hitler and Stalin. These figures are extraordinary, and certainly require a careful analysis.

Maoist Communism came to power in 1949 on a platform of unremitting Communist totalitarianism, and went to work eliminating, from the first and without exception, all domestic opposition to its ideological system. What Stalin could only initiate 16 years after the October Revolution, Mao made a part of his regime from its first day. His aim was the total, comprehensive transformation of society into 'socialism', hallmarked by abject subjugation to the state, the elimination of all opposition, and the removal of most of China's traditions (especially its religions and culture), in the interests of establishing a peasants' and workers' state along Stalinist lines in the Asian context. Perhaps the most striking feature of pre-1949 China to remain, however, was Chinese ultra-nationalism, and Maoism was also bent on ending the centuries of Chinese 'humiliation' by the West and Japan, eliminating all foreign influence (except, initially, Soviet influence), and rebuilding China as an independent, self-sufficient great power.[359] Maoist ideology was an utterly simplistic doctrine of right and wrong, invariably enunciated in black-and-white terms, in which the West, especially America, was always wrong.[360] Enemies of the regime were always painted black, in truly Orwellian terms strongly reminiscent of *1984*. The 'terrible simpli-fiers' had come to power even more comprehensively than in Nazi Germany or Stalinist Russia.

It is therefore not surprising that human life meant little or nothing to Maoist China, with enemies of the regime executed in large numbers from the first day; indeed, even before Day One, since it has been argued that vast numbers of persons were killed by the Chinese Communists in the regions they controlled before 1949. Rummel estimates their number as somewhere between 'almost 1,800,000 to almost 11,700,000 people, most likely close to 3,500,000'.[361] Walker estimates the number of pre-1949 Communist 'casualties' at between 2,050,000 and 3,800,000.[362] Although widely accepted, these figures have also been disputed by some authors: as we shall see, a common pattern with deaths under Mao.[363]

When the Communists came to power they initiated a wave of execu-tions in carrying out their comprehensive land reform campaign and their political campaign against 'class enemies'. Communist cadres went into innumerable villages throughout China, taking over the land of the 'rich peasants' (generally defined as the wealthiest 15 per cent) and set-ting the 'poor peasants' against them, with executions routinely follow-ing in virtually every village.[364] This was done to make the facts seem to conform to Marxist dogma, which 'required' that an exploiting feudal class existed and had to be eliminated. As R.H. Tawney pointed out, how-ever, pre-1949 China did *not* possess a neo-feudal class of landowners, but of land-holding peasants hardly richer than their poorer neighbours; the situation was simply not comparable with that in Tsarist Russia or, say, Latin America.[365] Nevertheless, since such a class of rural exploiters was required by Marxist dogma, one was identified and 'eliminated'. The question is how many 'rich peasants' were killed by the Communists during their first years in power, 1949–51. Most Western anti-Communist sources place the numbers at about 1.5 million or more, apparently extrapolating from local examples.[366] As well, 'counter-revolutionaries' and 'bandits' were also ruthlessly eliminated in the early years of the Maoist regime. Mao himself was quoted in differing sources as stating that between 500,000 and 800,000 persons were 'liquidated' between 1949 and 1954, while Chou En-lai, the regime's Premier and Number Two man, placed the figure for the same period at 830,000.[367]

While some Western observers have consistently questioned such very high figures, even they concede that the number killed by the Maoist regime in its early years was of this order of magnitude. Shalom, a consistent (and often very compelling) critic of very high Western estimates of Maoist genocide, nevertheless states that 'a total figure of perhaps a million for all killings in the first few years of Communist rule seems reasonable'.[368] There seems little reason to question this figure (although it may be an underestimate): probably over 1 million people were killed by Maoist China in its first five years or so as class enemies or 'counter-revolutionaries', mainly 'rich peasants'. Beyond this, however, one simply cannot go: as is so often the case, vastly higher death totals, for instance Walker's estimate of 15–30 million deaths in the period 1949–58, do not appear to be substantiated by reliable evidence. Part of these astronomical numbers appears to stem from estimates, made in American anti-Communist circles, for deaths *predicted* to occur in a great famine expected in mainland China in 1950, but which in fact did not actually occur.[369] Similarly, the 'inactivation' of hundreds of thousands of 'bandits' by the Communist regime was widely interpreted as their killing, without further evidence.[370] There is no compelling evidence that the total number of killings by the Communist Chinese regime between 1949 and 1954, for any reason, exceeded the figure of 1 million noted above – horrendous, and attributable almost wholly to crude ideological fanaticism, but far below the estimates widely accepted in the West.

It does appear very likely, however, that an enormous demographic catastrophe occurred in China during the 'Great Leap Forward' of 1958–61, when Mao attempted an even more radical transformation of Chinese society, initiating 'people's communes' throughout rural China where farmers were taken from their land to make steel in backyard furnaces. This ideologically driven insanity ruined much of Chinese agriculture for several years. It is quite possible that 10 million people starved to death as a result, especially in 1960–1. Certainly at least 1 million died of starvation, and official demographic statistics imply an excess of 20 million deaths over the normal level of the years preceding.[371] The resemblance between the 'Great Leap Forward' and the Soviet famine of the early 1930s is obvious, both having their origins in totalitarian ideological rigidity. Mao, like Stalin, was forced to cancel this campaign in January 1961. On the other hand, Walker's figure of 15–30 million deaths in 'forced labour camps and frontier development' appears greatly exaggerated. Shalom makes a convincing case that the total figure for people who 'died at various forms of forced labour in China from 1950 to 1970, beyond the death rate of the population at large' was 'perhaps one million people'.[372] The exaggerated figures adduced by Walker and others apparently resulted from overestimates of the numbers of labour camp inmates and false analogies from mortality statistics in the Soviet Gulag.[373] In contrast to this, however, Walker's estimate of 250,000–500,000 deaths in the 'Great Proletarian Cultural Revolution' of 1965–8 and its aftermath may well be too low, especially in regard to armed clashes between Red Guards and others during a period of near-anarchy and chaos. It is likely that about 1 million people were killed in the period 1965–76, half in the 'Cultural Revolution' period.[374]

Another aspect of mass killing in Maoist China was that carried out against China's national minorities, especially the Tibetans. Although Tibet was invariably considered to be a component province of China (and was so regarded by all Chinese regimes, including the Nationalists), the Chinese Communist occupation of Tibet in 1951, and more comprehensively, in 1959 (when, following revolt by Tibetans, their spiritual head the Dalai Lama fled to India), is regarded everywhere in the West as one of the greatest crimes committed by the Maoist government, even by most persons normally friendly to mainland China. Nevertheless, there are convincing reasons for believing that Walker's estimate of 500,000–1 million victims among China's minorities, especially in Tibet, is a wild exaggeration. There is no evidence that more than about 15,000 Tibetans were killed during the 1959–60 Tibetan revolt, rather than the figure of 65,000 (or far higher) often suggested.[375] Whatever crimes Maoist China has committed against Tibet, 'genocide' in the sense of deliberately murdering large numbers of their nationals cannot realistically be levelled against it – or so the best evidence would suggest. The continuous occupation of Tibet, the denial of its self-determination and traditional culture, and the settlement of large numbers of non-Tibetans there are, however, great crimes against which the world rightly protests.

In summary, Maoist China can be accused, based on the best available evidence, of directly murdering perhaps 2 million people, and being directly responsible for the deaths of at least 11 million more, of whom 10 million (at least) perished in an ideologically generated and wholly unnecessary famine. This still puts Mao and his regime in or near the first rank of mass killers, although the vastly higher numbers of deaths attributed to the Chinese Communists appear untenable. Nor can mere statistics reflect the Orwellian nature of Maoist society, whatever gains to the ordinary Chinese person through the removal of innumerable ills present in pre-1949 Chinese society, from warlordism to rampant drug addiction to prostitution, which the regime certainly brought about.

North Korea and North Vietnam

A number of other Asian Communist regimes have been accused of committing deliberate mass murders against their own peoples on a vast scale. Before coming to Pol Pot and Democratic Kampuchea, the cases of North Korea (officially, the Democratic People's Republic of Korea) and North Vietnam (the Democratic Republic of Vietnam) ought to be considered. North Korea, the state founded in the late 1940s by the arch-Stalinist Kim Il Sung (1912–94), continues to exist as the most repressive and mysterious state in the world, despite some superficial attempts at moves towards disarmament and towards opening to the outside world under his son and successor Kim Jong-il. As a result, claims about the scale of death in North Korea cannot be verified apart from weighing anecdotage, reports from refugees, and accounts in the press of South Korea, its bitter enemy. North Korea goes to unique lengths to exclude access to independent information about the country and its competing elites, and also has no large group of well-informed exiles.[376] The regime itself is uniquely repressive:

> Officials open and read personal mail before sending it on. The party
> prints all ... magazines and books ... and it fills virtually printed
> material with the 'great' sayings and doings of Kim Il Sung. The party

even so fixes radios and television sets that no foreign broadcasts can be heard, and it continuously inspects the receivers so that they cannot be altered.[377]

Rummel also cites an account of a schoolteacher whose student 'accidentally dropped a portrait of Kim Il Sung while cleaning the classroom'. The student's parents were taken to a forced labour camp at a coal mine while the teacher was expelled from the Communist party and also sent to a labour camp.[378] The question therefore poses itself of how many persons the North Korean regime has killed. Rummel's best estimate (made in 1994) is 1,663,000.[379] That North Korea, like most other Communist regimes, purges its high-ranking officials, is not in doubt. From, 1945 to 1971, Kim Il Sung executed 41 vice premiers, 16 division military commanders and 9 directors of operations against South Korea.[380] Whether a vast number of North Koreans have been killed by the regime, especially in its early days, remains unknown. 'How many people died in this [Chegdomyn] and other [labour] camps is a guess,' Rummel notes, but he estimates their number at '260,000 [or] possibly even nearly three times this'.[381] Tens of thousands of South Korean prisoners of war certainly died in captivity in North Korea.[382] In all, Rummel gives a median estimate of nearly 1.7 million dead at the hands of the regime, of whom – according to him – 983,000 died in 'corvée/hard labor' periodically enforced by the government.[383] Whether this figure is accurate remains unknown and will presumably remain unknown until the regime disappears or alters radically. In addition, it is now widely accepted that up to 2 million North Koreans died in its great famine of the later 1990s; North Korea's infant mortality rate is 88 per 1,000 births, compared with 8 in South Korea, while average male lifespan in the North is 49 years compared with 70 in the South.[384]

Professor Rummel has also made similar claims about killings at the hands of the North Vietnamese: '1,670,000 murdered' by 'the Vietnamese war state'.[385] As he clearly notes, this is among 'the most difficult' mass killings 'to unravel and assess', given the complexity of the situation in Vietnam between 1945 and the late 1980s, especially during the Vietnam War. He suggests, however, that 1,669,000 persons were deliberately killed by the North Vietnamese, through the familiar process of suppressing all opposition, killing 'landlords' and 'capitalists', purging opponents, forced labour and the effect of famines.[386] In addition, many thousands of South Vietnamese anti-Communists certainly perished following the fall of Saigon in 1975.[387] To this number, however, must be added 2.5 million deaths (1,062,000 of which are attributed to the North Vietnamese and Viet Cong) during the Indo-China and Vietnam wars, 90,000 civilian deaths by the South Vietnamese government, and 54,000 by 'others', of which 6,000 he attributes to the actions of the United States.[388] Most observers will surely regard the figure attributed to the United States as much too low, omitting, at the very least, probably hundreds of thousands killed in American bombing raids. Rummel here insists, however, with cogent evidence, that the number of civilians deliberately killed by American soldiers (including such events as the My Lai massacre, in which 347 women and children were murdered), did not exceed about 6,000.[389] As with the North Korean case, the numbers who perished at the hands of the Vietnamese Communists remain unclear. Given the nature of Asian Communism and the bitterness of the very long Vietnamese conflicts, the numbers were, presumably, very sizeable, although it seems too early to provide anything but a rough guess, if that.

Pol Pot and democratic Kampuchea, 1975–9

It is appropriate that we conclude this survey of genocides and democides in the Age of Totalitarianism with one of the most infamous of all, the massacres and killings carried out by the appalling Pol Pot regime in Kampuchea (Cambodia) between April 1975 and January 1979. It seems reasonable to assert that if the average well-informed person were asked to name a genocide and its perpetrator apart from Hitler and the Jewish Holocaust, Pol Pot and Kampuchea are likely to be mentioned. Cambodia, like much of south-east Asia, was a Buddhist enclave with a rather mysterious monarchy centred, traditionally, at the Khmer temple of Angkor Wat, the largest religious building in the world.[390] France took over the whole of Indo-China, including Cambodia, between about 1862 and 1887. Cambodia was administered by a typical French colonial class, ruling through the Cambodian monarch and a growing local educated class. Japan ruled Indo-China between July 1941 and August 1945, although it worked through the largely French administrative apparatus until February 1945, surprisingly late in the war, when it staged a *coup*

d'état which weakened the French and allowed Indo-Chinese nationalists and Communists to come to the fore. Japanese confiscations of goods
and destruction of property led to a horrible famine in 1944–5, in which
hundreds of thousands died. When the French regime returned, they confirmed Norodom Sihanouk (b.1922) – who had earlier proclaimed
Cambodia independent – as puppet King of Cambodia; most remarkably,
despite all the catastrophic changes which have come over Cambodia
since then, he remained head of state in the early twenty-first century. In
the period between the French defeat in Indo-China in 1954 and the overthrow of the pro-American Khmer Republic in October 1970, Sihanouk
steered an unpredictable, but effective, course aimed at remaining neutral and avoiding being sucked into the Vietnamese maelstrom, using
Communist China as his Great Power patron. In 1970, American and
South Vietnamese forces briefly invaded Cambodia in order to destroy
North Vietnamese and Viet Cong bases, and, in October 1970, a pro-
Western Republic was set up under General Lon Nol. Over the next few
years, America conducted intensive bombing raids on Cambodia, which
proved so unpopular at home in the context of mounting hostility to the
Vietnam War that they were halted by Congress at the end of 1973. These
raids have been blamed by many Western sources, especially among leftists, for alienating much of Cambodia's population, destroying the countryside, and opening the way for the Khmer Rouge.[391]

The Khmer Rouge was founded in 1960 and by the 1970s had become
a highly secretive and well-organised body which espoused what was
probably the most extreme form of Communism ever advocated by any
regime which ever came to power. In many respects, the Khmer Rouge
was the most extreme example of a fanatical ideology ever to come to
power in modern history, and represented the final distillation of the
post-1914 extremist ruling ideologies which first appeared when Lenin
gained control of Russia, whose primary exemplars were Hitler, Stalin
and Mao. Within Marxism, Richard Pipes has written, 'just as the
Holocaust represented the quintessential nature of National Socialism, so
did the Khmer Rouge ... represent the purest embodiment of
Communism: what it turns to when pushed to its logical conclusion'.[392]
Similarly, in its automatic disregard for human life, and its willingness to
kill anybody and everybody regarded as enemies of the regime, it represented the culmination of the twentieth-century ideologically based

genocides and democides which arguably began with the Armenian massacres in 1915.

The Khmer Rouge horrors were largely the responsibility of the leader of the movement, Saloth Sar (1925–98), who, after early 1976 (but not before), was known as 'Pol Pot', the name by which he is infamous. Born to a fairly well-off peasant family who acquired royal connections (his sister and cousin were consorts of the king), he lived in a Buddhist monastery for six years, and studied radio electronics in Paris in 1949–53, where he acquired the circle of Cambodian Communist associates who were to lead the Khmer Rouge.[393] He taught at a private school in Phnom Penh (Cambodia's capital) from 1954–63, while at the same time becoming secretary of the Cambodian Communist Party. While pseudo-Buddhist and French left-wing elements have been detected in his ideology, Pol Pot's extremism certainly owes much more to Maoism, especially that of Mao's most extreme phase during the Great Leap Forward and the Cultural Revolution of the 1960s. It also owes a good deal to Stalin's Terror.[394] As well, race and ethnicity also figured so strongly in Khmerist ideology as its main driving force that, in Kiernan's view, it 'overshadowed ... class'.[395] As a result, the Khmer Rouge murdered tens of thousands of non-Khmers in Cambodia. Nevertheless, it seems undeniable that ultra-extreme Marxist ideology lay at the core of the Khmer Rouge's murderous reign, in particular its determination to have 'leaped' from feudalism 'to a socialist society straight away'.[396]

The murderous reign of the Khmer Rouge began when it entered Phnom Penh on 17 April 1975, two weeks before the fall of Saigon to the Viet Cong. The Khmer Rouge forced the whole of the capital's population of 2 million to evacuate the city and march to the countryside, there to work as agricultural labourers. Tens of thousands died in the process. For the next three and a half years, a regime as oppressive and Orwellian as any in history held sway. Hundreds of thousands were killed, often for no reason. All intellectuals, Buddhist monks, civil servants, teachers and the entire middle class became automatic targets of the regime, in an effort to purge totally all relics of the previous regime. 'What is infected must be cut out ... It isn't enough to cut down a bad plant, it must be uprooted,' were among the slogans used on radio and at meetings.[397] As is well-known, persons wearing spectacles were often murdered for being 'intellectuals'. Many thousands were killed in Tuol Sleng (known at the time as S-21), the chief prison-execution facility in Phnom Penh. Torture, to obtain 'confessions', was a way of life.[398] Of 16,000 prisoners held there, only seven survived. The traditional lifestyle of Cambodia was totally reorganised, with peasants turned into what might be fairly described as worker-ants, their individuality entirely erased. Widespread famine was the result, in which, in rice-rich Cambodia, probably hundreds of thousands perished. From mid-1977 Pol Pot carried out an even wider purge of the whole country, hunting down, torturing and killing hundreds of thousands of 'enemies' in a widening maelstrom of mass paranoia.[399] The tortures routinely employed in killing the regime's enemies were horrifying beyond description. Buddhist monks were a particular target, with an estimated 68,000 out of 70,000 being killed.[400] As noted, Khmer ultra-chauvinism was a major component of its ideology, with non-Khmers (estimated at over 20 per cent of the Cambodian population) systematically persecuted. The Cham, an Islamic sect of Malayo-Polynesian ethnic origin, were singled out for special oppressions, with an estimated 36 per cent being killed, 90,000 out of 250,000.[401] Even higher death percentages were recorded among other minorities – 50 per cent of urban Chinese (215,000 of 430,000), and, in particular, the Vietnamese, a specially hated enemy of the Khmer Rouge. Kiernan has estimated that *all* Vietnamese in Cambodia, 20,000 persons, were killed by the Khmer Rouge.[402]

The best estimate available to us is that the Khmer Rouge killed 1,671,000 persons out of a Cambodian population of 7,890,000, or 21 per cent of the entire population.[403] For once, there does not appear to be much room for doubt about this figure which may, if anything, be an underestimate: it is possible that 2 million perished under the Khmer Rouge.[404] This was, certainly, the highest *percentage* figure of mass killing ever inflicted by a government against its own people in modern times and probably in history. Stalin killed (on our very conservative estimate) about 7 million Soviet citizens of a population of about 170 million in 1939, or 4.2 per cent, one-fifth of the Khmer Rouge percentage. Even if Stalin killed 20 million of his own people, as is often suggested, this amounted to but 11.8 per cent of the Soviet population, barely half of Pol Pot's total in only three years of rule. The Pol Pot genocide, it should be noted, was carried out in peacetime, and did not (unlike the Nazi or Ottoman Turk mass killings) take place behind a smokescreen of war or the 'need' to eliminate wartime enemies. On the contrary, the experience of the Khmer Rouge regime shows that class-based mass killings can be just as deadly as ethnic massacres, bearing in mind what has been said about the ethnic hatreds of 'Democratic Kampuchea'.

Like all such regimes, the Khmer Rouge generated numerous internal purges and faction-building, and these, plus the invasion of eastern Cambodia by Vietnamese troops in 1978–9, led to the regime's downfall early in 1979. Images of piles of Cambodian skulls and bones, victims of Pol Pot, quickly became part of the iconography of the late twentieth century, graphically continuing the photohistory of mass murder which began with the piles of emaciated corpses at Dachau and Belsen.[405] The subsequent history of Cambodia has been just as bizarre as what went before. Early in 1979, the Khmer Rouge leadership fled to the Thai border, and a pro-Vietnamese government was installed, a virtual puppet of its larger neighbour. This state of affairs continued until the mid-1980s when the end of the Cold War saw a willingness to install a moderate, broadly based government. In 1993, astonishingly, Cambodia reverted to its former status as a monarchy, with Norodom Sihanouk back in power as king. The remnants of the Khmer Rouge continued in hiding until the 1990s, when they began to disintegrate, with many rejoining the Cambodian mainstream. While some efforts were made to try Pol Pot for crimes against humanity, nothing came of them, and he died in Thailand in 1998, possibly a suicide. Most of his closest associates died in purges, although some defected to the Cambodian government.[406] Kang Khek Iev, known as Deuch, former commandant of the Tuol Sleng torture and extermination prison, became a Christian. 'I'm interested in my children, my stomach, and God. There is no future for the Khmer Rouge, they're finished,' he was reported to have said, shortly before his arrest in April 1999 for genocide.[407] The Khmer Rouge regime indeed ended not with a bang but with a whimper.

Conclusion

This survey of genocide and democide in the Age of Totalitarianism, 1914–79, concludes with the record of Asian Communist regimes which were, if anything, more ideologically driven and extreme than those totalitarian governments which preceded them. Yet, on the schema presented in this book, they were the last of their kind: Pol Pot was the last of his kind, and has had no real successor. Obviously there have been massacres galore, but these were not based in killing people for the sake of an abstract political ideology. Such genocides as those in Rwanda and former Yugoslavia, it will be argued, were qualitatively different from those described here.

The Age of Totalitarianism was also *par excellence* the Age of Genocide, comprising the most infamous examples. Both race and class became the instruments of mass murder, at heart because the normal evolution of Western civilisation in the direction of liberalism, law and tolerance, was derailed, in much of Europe, by the effects of the First World War. That this derailment did not become a permanent and fixed component of the Western world's experience was largely due to, above all, one factor: the steadfastness of the English-speaking democracies, especially the United States, in maintaining the liberal values of Western man, normally in triumphalist fashion. Because of the steadfastness of the English-speaking democracies, both fascism and Communism were eventually vanquished and disappeared. Too many died before this happened, but, without Western democracy, the death toll would have been far higher.

Another major theme we have identified in this chapter (and similar to that found earlier) is that in many – not all, but many – genocides and democides in this period, the death toll was actually lower than is commonly believed. This phenomenon has many causes: deliberate exaggeration by partisans, the genuine lack of accurate figures, the discovery of realistic statistics only in recent years. Even in the worst regimes in history it seems clear that the drive to kill, as opposed to enslave or oppress, demanded by the dictator, his clique and party, cannot be continued indefinitely, and that the apparently natural instinct not to kill sooner or later takes hold. In cases where there were no limits to the killing mania of the totalitarian regime, for instance in the case of Nazi Germany and the Jews, a halt came when the regime was defeated and destroyed, in this case by the forces of Anglo-American liberalism and also of Soviet Communism. Viewed from a wider perspective, this may also be seen as a form of the natural process wherein mass killings are not natural, produce revulsion and, for this reason, are sooner or later brought to a halt.

Notes and references

1   Important books in English on the Armenian genocide include: Feroz Ahmad, *The Young Turks: The Committee of Union and Progress in Turkish Politics, 1908–1914* (Oxford, 1969); Niyazi Berkes, T*he Development of Secularism in Turkey* (Montreal, 1964); Benjamin Braude and Bernard Lewis, eds., *Christians and Jews in the Ottoman Empire: The Functioning of a Plural Society* (2 vols., London, 1982); Vahakn N. Dadrian, *The History of the Armenian Genocide: Ethnic Conflict from the Balkans to Anatolia to the Caucasus* (Oxford, 1997); *idem, Warrant for Genocide: Key Elements of the Turko-Armenian Conflict* (New Brunswick, N.J., 1999); Kamuran Gurun, *The Armenian File: The Myth of Innocence Exposed* (London, 1985); Richard G. Hovannisian, ed., *The Armenian Genocide: History, Politics, Ethics* (Basingstoke, 1992); *idem*, ed., *The Armenian People: From Ancient to Modern Times, Volume II* (Basingstoke, 1997); *idem*, ed., *Remembrance and Denial: The Case of the Armenian Genocide* (Detroit, 1999); Bernard Lewis, *The Emergence of Modern Turkey* (Oxford, 1961); A.L. Macfie, *The End of the Ottoman Empire, 1908–1923* (London, 1998); Justin McCarthy, *Death and Exile: The Ethnic Cleansing of Ottoman Muslims, 1821–1922* (Princeton, N.J., 1995); *idem, Muslims and Minorities: The Population of Ottoman Anatolia and the End of the Empire* (New York, 1983); Robert Melson, *Revolution and Genocide: On the Origins of the Armenian Genocide and the Holocaust* (Chicago, 1992); Norman M. Naimark, *Fires of Hatred: Ethnic Cleansing in Twentieth-Century Europe* (Cambridge, Mass., 2001), esp. pp.17–56. Mim Kemal Oke, *The Armenian Question, 1914–1923* (Oxford, 1988); R.J. Rummel, *Death by Government* (New Brunswick, N.J., 1994); esp. pp.209–40. Stanford L. Shaw and Ezel Kuval Shaw, *History of the Ottoman Empire and Modern Turkey, Volume 2* (Cambridge, 1977). Most of these books include extensive bibliographies. Only a number of important articles can be cited here. They include: Vahakn N. Dadrian, 'The Role of the Special Organization in the Armenian Genocide During the First World War', in P. Panayi, ed., *Minorities in Wartime* (Oxford, 1993), and *idem*, 'The Secret Young-Turk Ittihadist Conference and the Decision for the World War I Genocide of the Armenians', *Holocaust and Genocide Studies* 7(2), 1993. Alan S. Rosenbaum, ed., *Is the Holocaust Unique?: Perspectives on Comparative Genocide* (Boulder, Col., 1996), contains two essays on the Armenian genocide, Robert F. Melson, 'The Armenian Genocide as Precursor and Prototype of Twentieth-Century Genocide' and Vahakn N. Dadrian, 'The Comparative Aspects of the Armenian and Jewish Cases of Genocide: A Sociohistorical Perspective'. See also by V.N. Dadrian, 'The Armenian Question and the Wartime Fate of the Armenians As Documented By Officials of the Ottoman Empire's World War I Allies: Germany and Austria-Hungary', *International Journal of Middle East Studies*, Vol.34, No.1 (February 2002).

2 Melson, *Revolution and Genocide*, p.47. As with most figures, this statistic cannot really be verified, but is cited in most accounts.

3 See, for instance, Shaw, *op.cit.*, pp.203ff.

4 Melson, *Revolution and Genocide*, pp.51–3.

5 The other recognised *millets* were the Catholics or Latins, who were remnants of Genoese and Venetian merchants; Syrian Catholics attached to a Patriarchate in Mardin; Chaldean Catholics; Syrian Jacobites; Protestants; Melchites; Bulgarian Catholics; Maronites; and Nestorians. (Oke, *op.cit.*, p.49. See also Berkes, *op.cit.*, pp.10–19.)

6 *Ibid.* Nevertheless, they suffered from some disabilities; for example they could not carry arms or ride horses. Hugh Poulton, *Top Hat, Grey Wolf and Crescent: Turkish Nationalism and the Turkish Republic* (London, 1997), p.46.

7 Charles Issawi, 'The Transformation of the Economic Position of the *Millets* in the Nineteenth Century', in Braude and Lewis, eds., *op.cit.*

8 *Ibid.*, pp.262–3.

9 *Ibid.*, p.263.

10 *Ibid.*, p.263.

11 Carter V. Findlay, 'The Acid Test of Ottomanism: the Acceptance of Non-Muslims in the Late Ottoman Bureaucracy', in *ibid.*, p.345.

12 *Ibid.*, p.344.

13 Poulton, *op.cit.*, pp.50–75; Bernard Lewis, *The Emergence of Modern Turkey*, pp.317–55.

14 Poulton, *op.cit.*, p.63.

15 Poulton, *op.cit.*, p.80.

16 See, e.g. Stephan H. Astourian, 'Modern Turkish Identity and the Armenian Genocide: From Prejudice to Racist Nationalism', in Richard G. Hovannisian, ed., *Remembrance and Denial*, esp. pp.35–41.

17 *Ibid.*, pp.36–7, quoting the Turkish ideologue Tekin Alp.

18 *Ibid.*, p.37.

19 *Ibid.*, pp.38–41. See also Feroz Ahmad, 'Unionist Relations with the Greeks, Armenian, and Jewish communities of the Ottoman Empire, 1908–1914', in Braude and Lewis, *op.cit.*

20 Feroz Ahmad, *The Young Turks*, p.155.

21 *Ibid.*, p.145.

22 Ahmad, *op.cit.*, p.171.

23 A.L. Macfie, *The End of the Ottoman Empire, 1908–1923*, pp.119–27, gives a good account.

24 *Ibid.*, pp.151–60 and Map 4, p.252.

25 For the military solution, see W.E.D. Allen and Paul Muratoff, *Caucasian Battlefields: A History of the Wars on the Turco-Caucasian Border 1828–1921* (Cambridge, 1953), pp.221ff., although the Armenian deportations and massacres are virtually ignored.

26 Naimark, *op.cit.*, p.29.

27 See, e.g., Dadrian, *The History of the Armenian Genocide*, p.194.

28 Vahakn Dadrian, 'The Role of the Special Organisation in the Armenian Genocide during the First World War', in Panayi, *op.cit.*, esp. pp.61–4.

29 *Ibid.*, p.31, and Hilmar Kaiser, 'The Baghdad Railway and the Armenian Genocide, 1915–1916: A Case Study in German Resistance and Complicity', in Hovannisian, *op.cit.*, pp.67–172.

30 Naimark, *op.cit.*, p.34.

31 Dadrian, *op.cit.*, p.240.

32 Rummel, p.220, citing Rafael De Nogales, *Four Years Beneath the Crescent* (New York, 1926), pp.130–1.

33 See, for instance, Shaw and Shaw, *op.cit.*, pp.315–16; Oke, *op.cit.*, pp.125–36 and *passim*; and Justin McCarthy and Caroline McCarthy, *Turks and Armenians: A Manual on the Armenian Question* (Washington, D.C., 1989). The last work was published by the Assembly of Turkish American Associations.

34 Oke, *op.cit.*, pp.134–5, citing an Interior Ministry circular of 29 August 1915.

35 *Ibid.*, p.135.

36 *Ibid.*, p.134. On the other hand, it must clearly be noted that by the second half of 1915 the Turkish government seemed certainly bent on genocide. An infamous telegram sent by Talaat Pasha stated unequivocally that the aim of the Turkish government was 'to destroy completely all Armenians living in Turkey ... an end must be put to their existence'.

37 *Ibid.*, p.135.

38 See Dadrian, 'The Secret Young-Turk Ittihadist Conference', *op.cit.*, and *Warrant for Genocide*, pp.96–101 for claims of such pre-1914 plans. The CUP government certainly hoped to rid itself of the 1914 agreement which imposed international guarantees on its treatment of the Armenians, but it is an enormous gap between that and planning for genocide.

39 On these deportations, see Naimark, *op.cit.*, pp.85–108.

40 The discussion of these points by Naimark, *op.cit.*, pp.35–8, is useful.

41 Henry Morgenthau, *Ambassador Morgenthau's Story* (New York, 1919), pp.337–8, cited in Macfie, *op.cit.*, p.133. Most Turkish documentation relating to the Armenian genocide was deliberately destroyed by the Turks at the end of the war.

42 Naimark, *op.cit.*, p.39; Levron Marshalian, 'Finishing the Genocide: Cleansing Turkey of Armenian Survivors, 1920–1923', in Hovannisian, *op.cit.*, pp.113–46.

43 Justin McCarthy, *Muslims and Minorities: The Population of Ottoman Anatolia and the End of the Empire* (Studies in Near Eastern Civilization 10, New York, 1983), p.63. Most of these estimates were for the 'nine vilayets' (provinces) where the majority of Armenians lived. The estimate of Ludovic de Contenson in 1913 was that there were 1,150,000 Armenians in 'Asiatic Turkey' and 250,000 in 'European Turkey' (*ibid*).

44 See the discussion in Naimark, *op.cit.*, pp.40–1.

45 Rummel. *op.cit.*, pp.221–5.

46 Gurun, *op.cit.*, p.217.

47 *Ibid.*, p.218.

48 *Ibid.*, p.219.

49 Macfie, *op.cit.*, p.134.

50 Most comprehensively in Dadrian, *The History of the Armenian Genocide*, *op.cit.*, pp.248–302.

51 *Ibid.*, p.263.

52 *Ibid.*, pp.260–5.

53 *Ibid.*, p.256.

54 *Ibid.*, pp.424, 427.

55 *Ibid.*, p.412.

56 *Ibid.*

57 Cited in *ibid.*, p.403.

58 Macfie, *op.cit.*, pp.134–5.

59 See the discussion in Naimark, *op.cit.*, pp.42–4.

60 Macfie, *op.cit.*, pp.209–11.

61 *Ibid.*, p.211.

62 Macfie, *op.cit.*, pp.34–6.

63 Stanford J. Shaw, *The Jews of the Ottoman Empire and the Turkish Republic* (London, 1991), pp.206–38.

64 *Ibid.*, pp.229–38; Isaiah Friedman, *Germany, Turkey and Zionism, 1897–1918* (Oxford, 1977), and *idem*, ed., *The Rise of Israel: Germany, Turkey and Zionism, 1914–18* (New York, 1987).

65 The fullest treatment of the 1933–45 period is Stanford J. Shaw, *Turkey and the Holocaust* (New York, 1943).

66 Dadrian, *History*, pp.303–16.

67 *Ibid.*, p.331.

68 Yair Auron, 'The Forty Days of Musa Dagh: Its Impact on Jewish Youth in Palestine and Europe', in Hovannisian, ed., *Remembrance and Denial*, pp.147–64; Roger W. Smith, 'The Armenian Genocide: Memory, Politics, and the Future', in Hovannisian, ed., *The Armenian Genocide*, p.11.

69 See the essays in Rosenbaum, ed., *op.cit.*

70 Yves Ternon, 'Freedom and Responsibility of the Historian: The "Lewis Affair" ', in Hovannisian, *Remembrance and Denial*, pp.237–43.

71 *Ibid.*, pp.243–6.

72 For an exposition of the parallels, see Richard G. Hovannisian, 'Denial of the Armenian Genocide in Comparison with Holocaust Denial', in *idem*, ed., *Remembrance and Denial*, pp.201–36.

73 Only a handful of the thousands of works on the Holocaust can possibly be cited here. General, comprehensive surveys include Raul Hilberg, *The Destruction of European Jewry* (three volumes, New York, 1985), regarded as the most complete account; Lucy S. Dawidowicz, *The War Against the Jews, 1933–45* (London, 1987); Martin Gilbert, *The Holocaust: The Jewish Tragedy* (New York, 1987), is particularly harrowing; Gerald Reitlinger's early history, *The Final Solution: The Attempt to Exterminate the Jews of Europe, 1939–1945* (London, 1953), is still enormously valuable; Leni Yahil, *The Holocaust: The Fate of European Jewry* (Oxford, 1990), is a detailed account. Donald Niewyk and Francis Nicosia, *The Columbia Guide to the Holocaust* (New York, 2000) is a valuable reference work with an up-to-date annotated bibliography of some (by no means all) significant works. There are three general encyclopedias of the Holocaust: Israel Gutman, ed., *Encyclopedia of the Holocaust* (four volumes, New York, 1990); Walter Laqueur, ed., *The Holocaust Encyclopedia* (New Haven, Conn., 2001); and Robert Rozett and Shmuel Spector, eds., *Encyclopedia of the Holocaust* (Jerusalem, 2000). The two atlases of the Holocaust (which, remarkably, take different approaches) are graphically valuable: Martin Gilbert, *The Dent Atlas of the Holocaust* (London, 1993), which has appeared under a number of different titles; and [United States Holocaust Museum] *Historical Atlas of the Holocaust* (New

York, 1996). Robert J. Wistrich, *Who's Who in Nazi Germany* (London, 1982), is excellent in offering well-informed biographies of those who carried out the Holocaust. Michael R. Marrus, *The Holocaust in History* (London, 1987), contains shrewd assessments of the historiographical debates which have arisen (as of the mid-1980s) over the Holocaust.

74 Information provided by Dr Robert M. Ehrenreich, Director, University Programs Division, US Holocaust Memorial Museum.

75 Innumerable books have been written on modern antisemitism. Good introductions include Albert S. Lindemann, *Anti-Semitism Before the Holocaust* (London, 2000), and *idem, Esau's Tears: Modern Anti-Semitism and the Rise of the Jews* (Cambridge, 1997); Richard S. Levy, *Antisemitism in the Modern World: An Anthology of Texts* (Lexington, Mass., 1991); and Robert Wistrich, *Antisemitism: The Longest Hatred* (New York, 1991).

76 Ian Kershaw, *Hitler, 1889–1936: Hubris* (London, 1998), p.35, citing Brigitte Hamman, *Hitler's Vienna: A Dictator's Apprenticeship* (Oxford, 1999). Although Lueger was one of Hitler's heroes and role models, he was a pro-Hapsburg pro-Catholic, not a German racial nationalist as were Hitler and the Nazis.

77 Peter Pulzer, *The Rise of Political Anti-Semitism in Germany and Austria* (New York, 1964); Richard S. Levy, *The Downfall of Anti-Semitic Parties in Imperial Germany* (New Haven, Conn., 1975).

78 Kershaw, *op.cit.*, pp.110–16; Peter Pulzer, *Jews and the German State: The Political History of a Minority, 1848–1933* (Oxford, 1992), pp.201–14.

79 On this general topic see Mark Levene, 'Frontiers of Genocide: Jews in the Eastern War Zones, 1914–1920 and 1941', in Panikos Panayi, ed., *Minorities in Wartime*, esp. pp.98–105.

80 Kershaw, *op.cit.*, pp.87–128; Lindemann, *Anti-Semitism*, pp.75–94.

81 Kershaw, *op.cit.*, pp.27–71; Brigitte Hamann's excellent *Hitler's Vienna: A Dictator's Apprenticeship* (Oxford, 2001) is an illuminating study of Hitler's Vienna days.

82 On Hitler's psychology see especially Robert G.L. Waite, *The Psychopathic God: Adolf Hitler* (New York, 1993), which remains the best such study. Another good study is Fritz Redlich, *Hitler: Diagnosis of a Destructive Prophet* (Oxford, 1999).

83 The best interpretation of Nazi Germany from this viewpoint is Michel Burleigh, *The Third Reich: A New History* (London, 2000).

84 *Hitler's Table Talk, 1941–1944* (London, 1953), p.548. See also Rainer Zitelman, *Hitler: The Policies of Seduction* (London, 1998), a recent book which stresses Hitler's radicalism.

85 Lucy S. Dawidowicz, *The War Against the Jews, 1933–45* (London, 1986), pp.47–8.

86 Probably the best comparative discussion is in Ezra Mendelsohn's excellent *The Jews of East Central Europe Between the World Wars* (Bloomington, Ind., 1983).

87 Normally the unofficial Jewish quota at such universities as Harvard was 10 per cent of every freshman class. One of the best studies of this subject, on Yale University, is Dan A. Oren, *Joining the Club: A History of Jews and Yale* (New Haven, Conn., 1985). Criticised by a rabbi, the dean of admissions at Yale emphatically denied that a Jewish quota existed, rather cleverly pointing out that every freshman class at Yale probably contained the same percentage of 'fat boys' (as he put it), but no one ever claimed that Yale operated a quota based on weight! In September 1941 Charles Lindbergh, the famous aviator and a leading isolationist, made a notorious speech in which he accused American Jews of being one of the most important groups attempting to get America to enter the war, a group whose 'danger . . . lies in their large ownership and influence in our motion pictures; our press, our radio, and our Government'. As a result, Lindbergh became a political pariah, and was attacked in venomous terms by virtually every newspaper in the country.

88 For an up-to-date series of essays on the dimensions of modern German history, including its historiography, see Mary Fulbrooke, ed., *German History Since 1800* (London, 1997). Other sophisticated works on modern German history include Gordon A. Craig, *Germany 1866–1945* (Oxford, 1981), Gordon Martel, ed., *Modern Germany Reconsidered, 1870–1945* (London, 1993); David Blackbourn, *The Fontana History of Germany, 1780–1918: The Long Nineteenth Century* (London, 1997); and Richard J. Evans, *Rethinking German History: Nineteenth-Century and the Origins of the Third Reich* (London, 1987).

89 For instance, he claims (p.445, citing the 1963 German doctoral thesis of Klemens Felden, which has never been published), that 'fully two-thirds of the prominent antisemitic polemicists proposing "solutions" to the "Jewish problem", who were examined in one study, agitated during this period [1875–1900] explicitly for a genocidal assault against the Jews'. What does this mean? That they wanted to comb Europe from one end to the other and put them in gas chambers? Since this 1963 dissertation remains unpublished, the accuracy of this assertion cannot be examined. Goldhagen also has great difficulty in accounting for the fact that antisemitism has declined so markedly in post-1945 West Germany (as he admits it has) and resorts (p.606, n.53) to such 'explanations' as 'after the war, Germans were reeducated . . . Germans, moreover, were subjected to counter-images of Jews, first under allied occupations and then when they regained sovereignty ... the Nazified view of Jews, because it was so at odds with reality, was also fragile; its hallucinatory components were difficult to maintain without institutional reinforcement', although evidently this was somehow easy before 1933.

90 See, for instance, Robert S. Wistrich, *Between Redemption and Perdition: Modern Antisemitism and Jewish Identity* (London, 1990).

91 Pulzer, *Jews and the German State*, pp.271–86.

92 Ronald W. Clark, *Einstein: The Life and Times* (London, 1973), p.388.

93 Donald L. Niewyk, *op.cit.* (Manchester, 1980), p.199. Although the takeover of student groups by pro-Nazi elements is well-known, Niewyk emphasises the resistance to overt antisemitism in German universities at this time, as well as in other areas of German society (*ibid.*, pp.63–81).

94 Wilhelm II (who died in the Netherlands in 1941) stated about the Bolshevik Revolution that the Russian people had been 'turned over to the vengeance of the Jews, who are connected to all the Jews of the world'. (Richard Pipes, *The Russian Revolution* (New York, 1991), pp.585–6). On the post-1918 escalation of the ex-Kaiser's (already intense) antisemitism, see also John C.G. Rohl, *The Kaiser and the Court: Wilhelm II and the Government of Germany* (Cambridge, 1996), pp.190–212. Much of his hostility to Jews was combined with extreme anti-British feeling.

95 Meir Michaelis, *Mussolini and the Jews: German-Italian Relations and the Jewish Question in Italy, 1922–1945* (Oxford, 1978), pp.10–56.

96 Mendelsohn, *op.cit.*, p.43.

97 See the discussion of the German Nationalist People's Party (the Nationalists), the mainstream right-wing party in Weimar Germany prior to the rise of the Nazis in 1930, in Niewyk, *op.cit.*, pp.49–52.

98 Karl A. Schleunes, *The Twisted Road to Auschwitz: Nazi Policy Towards German Jews, 1933–1939* (Urbana, Ill., 1970).

99 Saul Friedlander, *Nazi Germany and the Jews: Volume I, The Years of Persecution, 1933–1939* (London, 1997), provides a gripping account of this process.

100 William D. Rubinstein, *The Myth of Rescue: Why the Democracies Could Not Have Saved More Jews from the Nazis* (London, 1997), pp.15–62.

101 Burleigh, *op.cit.*, pp.198–205.

102 *Ibid.*, pp.158–77; M. Stollesis, *Law Under the Swastika* (Chicago, 1998).

103 Ian Kershaw, *Hitler, 1936–45: Nemesis* (London, 2001), pp.xxxv–xliv; Rainer Zitelman, *Hitler: The Politics of Seduction* (London, 1998), is an interesting interpretation of Hitler as a radical populist of a kind; Peter

Fritzsche, *Germans Into Nazis* (Cambridge, Mass., 1998) sees the popular appeal of Hitler in the hopes and optimism the Nazi government generated among ordinary Germans. See also the interesting essays in John Lukacs, *The Hitler of History* (London, 1997), especially 'Reactionary and/or Revolutionary' (pp.76–112), Lukacs (p.98) notes that the number of suicides in Nazi Germany declined by *80 per cent* between 1932 and 1939, from 1,212 to 290.

104 Concerning the Nazi ban on Jewish emigration see Rubinstein, *op.cit.*, pp.80–4.

105 Christopher R. Browning, 'Nazi Resettlement Policy and the Search for a Solution to the Jewish Question, 1939–1941', in Browning, *The Path to Genocide: Essays on Launching the Final Solution* (Cambridge, 1992), p.23.

106 Gotz Aly, *'Final Solution': Nazi Population Policy and the Murder of the European Jews* (London, 1999), pp.88–104.

107 As has been argued, in a fairly convincing way, by Philippe Burrin in *Hitler and the Jews: The Genesis of the Holocaust* (London, 1994). Apparently, only adult male Jews, especially Communist operatives, were initially killed: Jewish women and children were, in the very first stages, initially spared.

108 The clearest discussion of the *Einsatzgruppen* probably is still to be found in Hilberg, *op.cit.*, Volume One, pp.271–390.

109 *Ibid.*, p.298.

110 *Ibid.*, p.390.

111 *Ibid.*, pp.320–34.

112 *Ibid.*, p.1219.

113 Hilberg's rather inconsistent figures clearly suggest a lower estimate (*ibid.*, pp.1213–5, 1218). Reitlinger's usually very sensible figure is 700,000–750,000 for the pre-1939 Soviet Union and the Baltic states (p.499).

114 On the three 'Operation Reinhard' camps see Yitzhak Arad, *Belzec, Sobibor, Treblinka: the Operation Reinhard Death Camps* (Bloomington, Ind., 1999). On Auschwitz see Yisrael Gutman and Michael Berenbaum, eds., *Anatomy of the Auschwitz Death Camp* (Bloomington, Ind., 1994) and Robert Jan van Pelt, *The Case for Auschwitz: Evidence from the Irving Trial* (Bloomington, Ind., 2002).

115 Mark Roseman, *The Villa, the Lake, the Meeting: Wannsee and the Final Solution* (London, 2002) is the latest and clearest discussion.

116 Cited in Burrin, *op.cit.*, p.125, and many other sources. The date of September 1941 is now widely accepted as when Hitler turned unalterably to genocide.

117 Gerald Fleming, *Hitler and the Final Solution* (Berkeley, Cal., 1984), p.157. The Hungarian Jews were not actually deported for over a year.

118 *Ibid.*, p.158.

119 *Ibid.*, p.104.

120 Cited in Kershaw, *op.cit.*, p.822.

121 For the array of motives, Kershaw, *ibid.*, pp.459–96 gives a wide-ranging up-to-date account.

122 It appears that this figure first became published at the Nuremberg Trials, which produced an estimate of 5,700,000 Jewish deaths.

123 Reitlinger, Appendix I, *op.cit.*, pp.489–501; Hilberg, 'Statistics of Jewish Dead', pp.1201–20.

124 The most graphic account of this can be found in the map (p.148) in Alec Nove and J.A. Newth, 'The Jewish Population: Demographic Trends and Occupational Patterns', in Lionel Kochan, ed., *The Jews in Soviet Russia Since 1917* (Oxford, 1978). This compares the Jewish populations of *oblasts* in the Soviet Ukraine and Byelorussia according to the 1926 and 1959 Soviet censuses. (The suppressed 1939 census was not yet available.) While the Jewish population of these areas, all occupied by the Nazis, had usually declined, often drastically, it was still often surprisingly large. For instance, the Jewish population of the Odessa *oblast* declined from 198,000 to 121,000; the Crimea *oblast* from 40,000 to 26,000; of the Kiev *oblast* from 203,000 to 168,000. In several *oblasts* the Jewish population actually rose, e.g. in Donetsk, from 37,000 to 43,000. Even in *oblasts* occupied by the Nazis for over two years there was still an appreciable Jewish population. In Minsk, the Jewish population declined from 116,000 in 1926 to 48,000 in 1959; in Gomel (south of Minsk) from 91,000 to 45,000. Quite evidently many thousands of Jews managed to escape from the *Einsatzgruppen* killers in 1941, and returned after the war. Hilberg's estimate (p.1215) is that 700,000 Jews were killed by the *Einsatzgruppen*.

125 Hilberg, p.1215. About 83,000 Jews died in the Warsaw ghetto prior to the deportations to the death camps (*ibid.*, p.268).

126 This figure is very comparable to global estimates of Jewish numbers provided by well-informed independent sources. Arthur Ruppin, the distinguished Jewish demographer, estimated the world's Jewish population at the end of 1938 at 16,717,000 (*The Jewish Fate and Future* (London, 1940), p.35). In *The American Jewish Year Book 1950* (New York, 1950), the standard reference work, Leon Shapiro and Boris Sapir estimated (p.246) the world Jewish population total in 1949 at 11,303,350. Depending on the accuracy of these figures, this would indicate a deficit of

5.4 million between 1938 and 1949, *The Year Book*'s figures almost certainly understate the Soviet Jewish population, which they place at 2 million. This would balance the 1945–7 increase because of the 'baby boom'. The figure of Jewish victims in the Holocaust accepted by Rummel (who often, in my opinion, exaggerates the number of victims in the slaughters he has studied), of 5,291,000, also seems fairly accurate, or even a slight overstatement (R.J. Rummel, *Democide: Nazi Genocide and Mass Murder* (New Brunswick, N.J., 1992), p.30).

127 'Translation of the Protocol' [of the Wannsee Conference], in Roseman, p.113.

128 Tamas Stark, *Hungarian Jews During the Holocaust and After the Second World War, 1939–1949: A Statistical Review* (Boulder, Cal., 2000), p.99. As large numbers of Transylvanian Jews were deported to their deaths when it was a part of Hungary, many of those counted in the 1947 census were refugees from other countries. Stark (p.137) believes that 50,000–100,000 fewer Jews perished in the Hungarian phase of the Holocaust than previous estimates. His lower figure is apparently accepted by most recent specialist historians.

129 William Anderson, 'Women to the Right – Discrimination on the Ramp: Some Reflections on the Higher Mortality Rate of Women Victims During the Holocaust' (unpublished conference paper, Australian Association for Jewish Studies Conference, February 2002), summarises the known facts. At Auschwitz, for instance, of Jews selected for labour (i.e. not gassed on arrival) only 32.54 per cent were women (Mary Lowenthal Felstiner, *To Paint Her Life: Charlotte Salomon in the Nazi Era* (New York, 1995), p.206).

130 Adam Jones, 'Gendercide and Genocide', in *Genocide Research* (Volume 2, Number 2, 2000), and the 'Special Issue' of *ibid.* (Volume 4, Number 1, 2002) on 'Gendercide and Genocide'.

131 The development of the concept of trials for war crimes and for 'crimes against humanity' is discussed in the final chapter of this work.

132 'Chart of the International Military Tribunal', in Telford Taylor, *The Anatomy of the Nuremberg Trials: A Personal Memoir* (London, 1993), Appendix A, p.648.

133 Hilberg, *op.cit.*, Volume III, pp.1060–109, gives a full account.

134 At the 'Auschwitz Trial' of 1965, however, six SS staff members were sentenced to life imprisonment. Of 91,000 West Germans tried for 'war crimes', fewer than 1,000 came after 1951 (Niewyk and Nicosia, *op.cit.*, p.39).

135 Adi Wimmer, ed., *Strangers At Home and Abroad: Recollections of Austrian Jews Who Escaped Hitler* (Jefferson, N.C., 2000), p.153.

136 For instance, it is notorious that Hollywood, despite its large Jewish presence, never made a film about the Nazi persecution of the Jews at the time or for many years afterwards, *The Diary of Anne Frank* (1959) being one of the few exceptions. Shortly after Eichmann's capture, Stanley Kramer's *Judgement at Nuremberg* began what became a flood of Holocaust movies, followed by *The Pawnbroker* in 1965. During the years when Hitler was in power, only Charlie Chaplin's *The Great Dictator* (1940), made by a non-Jewish British radical from an independent studio, even began to confront Hitler's antisemitism.

137 For the British aspect of this effort see David Cesarani, *Justice Delayed: How Britain Became a Refuge for War Criminals* (London, 1992). On America see Allen A. Ryan, *Quiet Neighbours: Prosecuting Nazi War Criminals in America* (New York, 1984).

138 Deborah Lipstadt, *Denying the Holocaust: The Growing Assault on Truth and Memory* (New York, 1993), chapters 2–5. Another useful study is Michael Shermer and Alex Grobman, *Denying History: Who Says the Holocaust Never Happened and Why Do They Say It?* (Berkeley, Cal., 2000), which refutes the 'arguments' made by the 'Holocaust deniers'.

139 Probably the most interesting work on the trial is Richard J. Evans, *Telling Lies About Hitler: The Holocaust, History and the David Irving Trial* (London, 2002). Evans' work is chiefly a devastating critique of Irving's historical argumentation concerning Hitler, the Jews and such events as the Allied bombing of Dresden in 1945. Irving is a curious case. He is admittedly a first-rate researcher and military-oriented historian whose works are frequently cited by mainstream academic historians. With virtually anything touching on Hitler and the Jews, however, Irving's works appear deliberately flawed, invariably in the direction of playing down the extent of the Holocaust and Hitler's direction of it. As a right-wing gadfly and contrarian, however, he is admired (often silently) by a surprisingly wide audience, especially in Britain.

140 Evans, *op.cit.*, pp.28–33.

141 See Peter Novick, *The Holocaust in American Life* (Boston, 1999), for detailed explication of this process in the United States.

142 Norman Finkelstein's *The Holocaust Industry* (London, 2000) became an international *cause célèbre*. However exaggerated (and wrong-headed in linking the Holocaust 'industry' with support for Israel) it contains a strong element of truth.

143 Yehuda Bauer, *Rethinking the Holocaust* (New Haven, Conn., 2001), pp.14–38, 186–212; Dan Cohn-Sherbok, ed., *Holocaust Theology: A Reader* (Exeter, 2002).

144 This widely quoted figure of 11 million deaths at the hands of the Nazis (which is cited repeatedly on websites and the like) was apparently originated by Simon Wiesenthal, the celebrated Nazi-hunter (Michael Berenbaum, 'The Uniqueness and Universality of the Holocaust', in *idem*, ed., *A Mosaic of Victims: Non-Jews Persecuted and Murdered by the Nazis* (New York, 1990), p.20).

145 The first, and even today one of the few general studies of these groups, is Berenbaum, ed., *A Mosaic of Victims*, which contains papers from a conference on 'The Other Victims: Non-Jews Persecuted and Murdered by the Nazis' held in Washington D.C. in 1987. On Nazi racial theory and intentions towards Nazi-occupied Europe, see Norman Rich, *Hitler's War Aims* (two volumes, London, 1973 and 1974).

146 See the essays in Rosenbaum, *Is the Holocaust Unique?*

147 See David E. Stannard, 'Uniqueness as Denial: The Politics of Genocide Scholarship', in *ibid.* Stannard takes issue (in the strongest possible terms) with those who allegedly hold this view, especially Deborah Lipstadt.

148 The most comprehensive recent account is Guenter Levy, *The Nazi Persecution of the Gypsies* (Oxford, 2000). Some pro-Gypsy historians, especially Professor Ian Hancock, have found this work disturbing in its (in their view) downplaying of Gypsy suffering compared with that of the Jews. See also Henry Friedlander, *The Origin of Nazi Genocide: from Euthanasia to the Final Solution* (Chapel Hill, N.C., 1995), esp. pp.246–62; Donald Kenrick and Grattan Puxon, *The Destiny of Europe's Gypsies* (London, 1972); David Crowe and John Kolsti, eds., *The Gypsies of Eastern Europe* (London, 1991); Jiri Lipa, 'The Fate of Gypsies in Czechoslovakia under Nazi Domination', in Berenbaum, ed., *Mosaic of Victims*, pp.207–15; Ian Hancock, 'Roma: Genocide of Roma in the Holocaust', in Charny, *op.cit.*, pp.501–8; Yehuda Bauer, 'Gypsies', in Yisrael Gutman, ed., *Encyclopedia of the Holocaust*, pp.634–8; and *idem*, 'Gypsies', in Gutman and Berenbaum, eds., *Anatomy of the Auschwitz Death Camp*, pp.441–55; Donald Kenrick and Grattan Puxon, eds., *Gypsies under the Swastika* (Hertford, 1995); Donald Kenrick, ed., *The Gypsies During the Second World War, Vol.2: In the Shadow of the Swastika* (Hartford, 1999); and Raul Hilberg, 'Gypsies', in Walter Laqueur, ed., *The Holocaust Encyclopedia*, pp.271–7.

149 Jean-Paul Clébert, *The Gypsies* (London, 1963), pp.26–42.

150 Levy, *op.cit.*, p.38.

151 *Ibid.*

152 Charlie Chaplin (who was often supposed, incorrectly, to be Jewish) apparently had a Gypsy grandmother.

153 Levy, *op.cit.*, pp.4–10.

154 *Ibid.*, p.21.

155 *Ibid.*, pp.28–35.

156 *Ibid.*, p.25.

157 *Ibid.*, p.42–3.

158 *Ibid.*, pp.53–4.

159 *Ibid.*, p.54.

160 Ian Hancock, 'Genocide of the Roma in the Holocaust', p.3, on 'The Patrin Web Journal-Roma (Gypsy) Genocide' [website].

161 Levy, *op.cit.*, pp.77–81.

162 Arad, *op.cit.*, p.151.

163 Levy, *op.cit.*, pp.136–40.

164 *Ibid.*, p.55.

165 Arad, *op.cit.*, p.153.

166 Donald Kenrick and Grattan Puxon, *The Destiny of Europe's Gypsies* (London, 1972), p.150.

167 Bayer in Gutman and Berenbaum, *op.cit.*, pp.449–50; Van Pelt, p.115. Some estimates are slightly higher, about 24,000.

168 For instance, hundreds of Gypsies were shot by the Nazis in Serbia. In 1942, 'thousands' of Gypsies were rounded up by the Croatian fascist government and transported to the Jasenovic concentration camp 'where the large majority eventually perished' (Hilberg in Laqueur, *op.cit.*, p.277). In Romania, about 25,000 Gypsies were transported to camps in Transnistria, of whom probably 19,000 perished through 'misery, disease, hunger, cold, and maltreatment' (Michelle Kelso, 'Gypsy Deportations from Romania to Transnistria, 1942–44', in Kenrick, ed., *In the Shadow of the Swastika*, p.130). In 1930 there were 262,501 Gypsies in Romania, excluding 'nomadic Gypsies'. This figure shrank to 208,700 in 1942, due to boundary changes (*ibid.*, p.98).

169 Hancock, 'Genocide of the Roma', p.3. See also Ward Churchill, *A Little Matter of Genocide: Holocaust and Denial in the Americas 1492 to the Present* (San Francisco, 1997), who states (p.37) that 'it was known at least thirty years ago that between 500,000 and 750,000 [Gypsies] died in [Nazi] camps'. The footnote references in Churchill's books are usually impressively erudite. But his source (*ibid.*) for this claim is *The Morning of the Magicians* by Louis Powells and Jacques Bergier (London, 1971), a potboiler on Nazism and the occult. No credible evidence exists, in my opinion, for a death toll in this range.

170 Henry R. Huttenbach, 'The Romanian Porajmos: the Nazi Genocide of Gypsies in Germany and Eastern Europe', in Crowe and Kolsti, *op.cit.*, p.45.

171 About 960,000 Jews died at Auschwitz, an estimate based on such sources as train timetables and carrying capacities. Any claim that up to 50 per cent more Gypsies were killed by the Nazis than the number of Jews who died in Auschwitz ought to provide such information as where and how these people were killed and the evidence on which these claims are based. If the US Holocaust Memorial Museum indeed has such evidence, it certainly ought to publish it. In addition, it was certainly the case that very large numbers of Gypsies lived in continental Europe after the Holocaust. There were, for instance, 219,554 Gypsies in Czechoslovakia in 1970, and (officially) 25,663 in Hungary in 1960, where 'unofficial estimates placed the figure at 200,000' (Crowe and Kolsti, *op.cit.*, pp.109, 120).

172 Rummel, *Democide*, p.44.

173 Kenrick and Puxon, *op.cit.*, pp.183–4.

174 Levy, *op.cit.*, p.222, citing a letter written by Kenrick to *Holocaust and Genocide Studies*.

175 Levy, *ibid.*

176 These difficulties may be illustrated by the number of Gypsies counted in the Soviet national censuses of 1926 and 1959, which were, respectively, 60,000 and 132,000 (*after* the Holocaust). Both figures are regarded as underestimates (Kenrick and Puxon, *op.cit.*, p.150).

177 Norman Davies, *God's Playground: A History of Poland in Two Volumes – Volume II, 1975 to the Present* (Oxford, 1981), p.463.

178 *Ibid.*

179 Norman Rich, *Hitler's War Aims: Volume II, The Establishment of the New Order* (London, 1974), p.74.

180 Cited in Richard C. Lukas, *Forgotten Holocaust: The Poles Under German Occupation, 1939–1944* (New York, 2001), p.4.

181 Cited in *ibid.*

182 Cited in Kershaw, *op.cit.*, Volume II, p.725. The Warsaw uprising of 1944, by gentile Poles, is not to be confused with the Warsaw Ghetto uprising by Jews in April–May 1943.

183 Cited in Rich, *op.cit.*, p.75.

184 *Ibid.*, p.74.

185 Poland actually participated in the carve-up of Czechoslovakia in 1938–9, grabbing some of its territory at the same time that Germany organised the 'Protectorate' of Bohemia-Moravia.

186 Kershaw, *op.cit.*, p.166.

187 Rich, *op.cit.*, pp.84–94; Jan Tomasz Gross, *Polish Society Under German Occupation: The Generalgouvernement, 1939–1944* (Princeton, N.J., 1979), *passim*, esp pp.117–44.

188 Tadeusz Piotrowski, *Poland's Holocaust: Ethnic Strife, Collaboration with Occupying Forces and Genocide in the Second Republic, 1918–1947* (Jefferson, N.C., 1998), p.9. See also Jan Gross, *Revolution from Abroad: The Soviet Conquest of Poland's Western Ukraine and Western Belorussia* (Princeton, N.J., 1988); Richard C. Lukas, 'The Polish Experience During the Holocaust', in Berenbaum, *op.cit.*, pp.88–95, and Israel Gutman, 'The Victimisation of the Poles', in *ibid.*, pp.96–100.

189 Piotrowski., *op.cit.*, p.13. There is some recent evidence (*ibid.*, p.397, n.48) that the number deported was actually much lower, a total of 320,000 plus those induced into the Soviet army and POWs. Gross now apparently accepts a much lower figure than 1.2–1.7 million.

190 Davies, *op.cit.*, p.451. As he notes, this 'amnesty' was 'for crimes that had not been committed'.

191 *Ibid.*

192 Piotrowski, *op.cit.*, p.19.

193 But see footnote 46 above, for a suggestion that this figure is an exaggeration. In my view, it is almost certainly an exaggeration, with the actual figure in the range of 100,000–300,000.

194 Piotrowski, *op.cit.*, p.22; Lukas, pp.17–27.

195 Piotrowski, *ibid.*

196 *Ibid.*

197 Lukas, *op.cit.*, p.9.

198 Van Pelt, *op.cit.*, p.116.

199 Piotrowski, *op.cit.*, p.305.

200 *Ibid.*

201 As well, 70,000 Polish troops were killed during the Nazi invasion of Poland, and 300,000 taken prisoner.

202 Alexander Dallin, *German Rule in Russia 1941–1945: A Study of Occupation Policies* (London, 1981), Table, p.427. The figure of 3,222,000 was obtained by subtracting those 'released to civilian or military status' (818,000) / 'escapes' (67,000) / and 'surviving as prisoners of war' (1,053,000) from 5,160,000.

203 *Ibid.*

204 *Ibid.*, p.418.

205 *Ibid.*

206 *Ibid.*, p.421.

207 *Ibid.*, p.427.

208 *Ibid.*, pp.523 ff. Vlasov was not (as is often claimed) a 'White Russian' fascist, but a liberal who refused to include an antisemitic plank in his platform (*ibid.* p.633). Many Nazis regarded him as an unrepentant Communist. Repatriated to Russia in 1945, he was hanged by Stalin the following year. Although many have claimed that Stalin sent virtually all repatriated Soviet POWs to Siberia in 1945 for having 'failed' Russia, in fact it appears that no action was taken against over 80 per cent of those returned to the Soviet Union at the end of the war.

209 For instance, even in Germany itself, of 231,000 captured British and American soldiers only 8,348 (3.6 per cent) died in captivity (Christian Trent, 'The Fate of the Soviet Prisoners of War', in Berenbaum, *Mosaic of Victims*, p.142).

210 On Soviet prisoners of war in Nazi hands see also Alfred Stein, 'International Law and Soviet Prisoners of War', in Bernd Wegner, *From Peace to War: Germany, Soviet Russia and the World, 1939–1941* (Providence, R.I., 1997), pp.293–308; Omar Bartov, *The Eastern Front, 1941–45, German Troops and the Barbarisation of Warfare* (Basingstoke, 1985); Gerhard Hirschfeld, ed., *The Policies of Genocide: Jews and Soviet Prisoners of War in Nazi Germany* (London, 1986); Theo J. Schulte, *The German Army and Nazi Policies in Occupied Russia* (Oxford, 1989); and Gerald Reitlinger, *The House Built on Sand: the Conflicts of German Policy in Russia, 1939–1945* (London, 1960), esp. pp.98–127 and 446–9. Reitlinger, an outstanding historian whose figure of 4.1–4.6 million Jewish deaths in the Holocaust is the lowest ever advanced by a mainstream historian, also accepts that the figure of over 3 million Soviet POW deaths 'can be regarded as roughly established' (*ibid.*, p.446).

211 R.J. Rummel, *Lethal Politics: Soviet Genocide and Mass Murder Since 1917* (New Brunswick, N.J., 1996), p.1151.

212 *Ibid.*

213 Georgily A. Kumanev, 'The German Occupation Regime on Occupied Territory in the USSR (1941–1944)', in Berenbaum, *Mosaic of Victims*, p.140. The civilian figures are based on newly released Soviet documents. They would, presumably, include all deaths in eastern Poland, the Baltic states, Moldavia and other areas annexed by the Soviet Union in 1939–41 as well as civilian deaths in the siege of Leningrad and other sieges.

214 Germany lost about 6,960,000 soldiers and civilians in the Second World

War (Bartov, *op.cit.*, p.153), although other estimates are lower. Despite the Blitz and the fact that it was at war for six years, Britain's total dead in the Second World War totalled just 464,000. It should be noted that Reitlinger's estimate of total Soviet losses, made in 1960, is very much lower than any other figure: 12 million dead, consisting of 8 million soldiers, 3 million civilians and 1 million Soviet Jews and Partisans (Reitlinger, *House Built on Sand*, pp.448–9). Although anomalously low, Reitlinger's figures in my view are usually uncannily accurate and deserve respect and careful analysis. His estimate of the number of German deaths (*ibid.*) is also much lower than any other source.

215 On the 'euthanasia programme' see Michael Burleigh, *Death and Deliverance: Euthanasia in Germany, 1900–1945* (originally Cambridge 1994; London 2002); *idem, The Third Reich*, pp.345–406; and *idem* and Wolfgang Wippermann, *The Racial State: Germany, 1933–1945* (Cambridge, 1991), pp.136–99; Gita Sereny, *Into That Darkness: From Mercy Killing to Mass Murder* (London, 1991); Robert J. Lifton, *The Nazi Doctors: Medical Killing and the Psychology of Genocide* (New York, 1986); Henry Friedlander, *The Origins of Nazi Genocide: From Euthanasia to the Final Solution* (Chapel Hill, N.C., 1995), *idem*, 'The Exclusion and Murder of the Disabled', in Gellately and Stoltzfus, eds., *Social Outsiders in Nazi Germany*, pp.145–64; and *idem*, 'Euthanasia', in Lacquer, ed., *op.cit.*, pp.167–72; Hans-Heinrich Wilhelm, 'Euthanasia Program', in Gutman, ed., *op.cit.*, pp.451–4.

216 Friedlander, 'Exclusion of the Disabled', pp.146–8.

217 *Ibid.*, p.147.

218 *Ibid.*, p.148.

219 *Ibid.*, p.149.

220 *Ibid.*, p.153.

221 Wilhelm, *op.cit.*, p.453.

222 Wilhelm, *op.cit.*, p.453. This figure was the estimate given at the Nuremberg Trial. According to Wilhelm (*ibid.*), 'it may be assumed that in the strict sense, 200,000 persons were murdered in the Euthanasia Programme'. While I have frequently criticised estimates of deaths at the hands of the Nazis as inflated, there is no reason to suppose that a figure of 200,000 or so is inaccurate. Physically handicapped persons were also murdered in large numbers by the Nazis.

223 *Outworld*, July 1996, cited in 'International Committee for Holocaust Truth: 1996 Report #1' [website], p.1.

224 Rummel, *Democide*, p.45.

225 *Ibid.*, citing Frank Rector, *The Nazi Extermination of Homosexuals* (New York, 1981), p.113. On the Nazis and homosexuals, see Gunter Grau, ed., *Hidden Holocaust?: Gay and Lesbian Persecution in Germany, 1933–45* (London, 1995); Richard Plant, *The Pink Triangle: The Nazi War against Homosexuals* (New York, 1986); Jack Nusan Porter, *Sexual Politics in Nazi Germany: The Persecution of Homosexuals* (Newton, Mass., 1998); Elisheva Shaul, 'Homosexuality in the Third Reich', in Gutman, *op.cit.*, pp.687–8 and Geoffrey J. Giles, 'The Institutionalisation of Homosexual Panic in the Third Reich', in Robert Gellately and Nathan Stoltzfus, eds., *Social Outsiders in Nazi Germany* (Princeton, N.J., 2001). For a contrary view see Scott Lively and Kevin Abrams, *The Pink Swastika: .Homosexuality in the Nazi Party* (Keizer, Ore., 1996).

226 Jack Nusan Porter, 'Homosexuals: Genocide of Homosexuals in the Holocaust', in Charny, *op.cit.*, p.340.

227 Günter Grau, 'Homosexuality', in Laqueur, *op.cit.*, p.313.

228 Jonathan Petropoulos, *The Faustian Bargain: The Art World in Nazi Germany* (London, 2000), p.224. See also Frederic Spotts, *Hitler and the Power of Aesthetics* (London, 2000), esp. pp.18–186, for other examples of homoeroticism in Nazi 'art'.

229 *Ibid.*, p.225.

230 Samuel Igra, *Germany's National Vice* (London, 1945), p.26, cited in 'International Committee for Holocaust Truth: 1996 Report #2' [website], p.4.

231 Lothar Machtan, *The Hidden Hitler* (Oxford, 2001), pp.181–230. According to Machtan (p.215) Goebbels said that the reason for the 'Rohm Purge' was that the SA leaders 'were on the point of exposing the entire leadership of the Party to suspicions of shameful and loathsome sexual abnormality'. Machtan also claims (pp.91–2) that Hitler's failure to be promoted above the rank of lance corporal, despite winning the Iron Cross, was because of his known homosexuality; it was virtually unheard of for a lance corporal not to be promoted after several years' battlefield experience, let alone a winner of the Iron Cross. The specific act for which Hitler won the Iron Cross remains unknown and, curiously, was never detailed by Nazi propaganda during Hitler's lifetime. Machtan claims further (pp.169–71) that Hitler's relationship with Eva Braun, his 'mistress' from 1932–45 (and his wife for a few hours before both committed suicide), was purely asexual, designed to thwart rumours of Hitler's homosexuality. Machtan suggests that Hitler probably never had normal sexual relations with any woman. The range of men murdered in the 'Rohm Purge', which has long puzzled historians, was, according to Machtan, designed to eliminate anyone with access to knowledge of Hitler's homosexuality.

232 Machtan, *op.cit.*, pp.225–6.

233 Grau, *op.cit.*, p.154.

234 *Ibid.*, pp.192–4.

235 *Ibid.*, p.270. 47,982 inmates were political prisoners.

236 *Ibid*, p.202. From 1940 to 1943 proceedings were initiated in the Nazi-occupied Netherlands against 138 alleged homosexuals, of whom 90 were convicted by Dutch courts.

237 *Ibid.*, p.201.

238 *Ibid.*

239 George Chauncey, *Gay New York: The Making of the Gay Male World, 1890–1940* (London, 1995), p.360. During the more tolerant 1920s when the American Prohibition Amendment (which prohibited the sale of any alcoholic beverages) was in force, a vast network of unregulated homosexual 'speakeasies' grew up. After Repeal, the licensing of all bars for the sale of liquor became the duty of the New York State Liquor Authority, which relentlessly cracked down on 'gay bars' until the late 1960s.

240 'International Committee for Holocaust Truth: 1996 Report #2' [website], p.1. Using the curious logic that less is more, Jack Nusan Porter notes that 'Gay leaders and writers insist on higher figures [such as 'one million dead'] in order to legitimate their claim of special pleading. Yet, why indeed are 10,000 killed less tragic than one million? (Porter, 'Homosexuals', in Charny, *op.cit.*, p.340). Surely one answer (among others) is because it is not 'genocide'. Many of the recent writings on the treatment of homosexuals by the Nazis are clearly written with post-1960s eyes, ie, in a Western world in which homosexuality is increasingly tolerated. They fail to situate Nazi hostility to homosexuals in the context of a world where virtually everyone regarded it as abnormal and 'depraved'.

241 Sybil Milton, 'Jehovah's Witnesses', in Laqueur, *op.cit.*, pp.346–50; Christine King, 'Jehovah's Witnesses Under Nazism', in Berenbaum, *op.cit.*, pp.188–93.

242 Pacifists in Nazi Germany who refused to serve in the German army in wartime were routinely executed. See Gordon C. Zahn, 'Pacifists During the Third Reich', in Berenbaum, *op.cit.*, pp.194–9.

243 Milton, *op.cit.*

244 *Ibid.*, p.349.

245 *Ibid.*, p.350.

246 King, *op.cit.*, p.190. According to Irena Strzelecka, some women Jehovah's

Witnesses were sent to Auschwitz, beginning in March 1942. Many died in the camp's appalling conditions, but none, it seems, was gassed. Irena Strzelecka, 'Women', in Gutman and Berenbaum, *op.cit.*, pp.397–8. Something should also be said here of the suppression of Freemasons in Nazi Germany (and other totalitarian regimes). The 'Jewish-Freemason Conspiracy' was a stock-in-trade of right-wing ideologues at that time. The dimensions of the suppression of Freemasonry in Nazi Germany remains poorly explored.

247 Angelo Del Boca, *The Ethiopian War, 1935–1941* (Chicago, 1969), pp.174–85. Numerous massacres were certainly committed by both sides in the Spanish Civil War of 1936–9, in which Italy enthusiastically supported Franco's right-wing insurgents.

248 Jonathan Steinberg, *All Or Nothing: The Axis and the Holocaust, 1941–43* (London, 1990).

249 Menachem Shelah, 'Genocide in Satellite Croatia During the Second World War', in Berenbaum, *op.cit.*, pp.74–9 and *idem*; 'Croatia' in Gutman, *op.cit.*, pp.323–9; Vladimir Dedijer, ed., *The Yugoslav Auschwitz and the Vatican: The Croatian Massacre of the Serbs During World War II* (Buffalo, N.Y., 1992), Rich, pp.273–82; Yeshayahu A. Jelinek, 'Yugoslavia' in Laqueur, *op.cit.*, pp.706–13; Stevan K. Pavlowitch, *A History of the Balkans, 1804–1945* (London, 1999), pp.274–82, 307–30; and Marcus Tanner, *Croatia: A Nation Forged in War* (New Haven, Conn., 1997), pp.141–67.

250 Cited in Shelah, 'Genocide', p.74.

251 Cited in *ibid.*

252 Cited in Rich, *op.cit.*, p.277.

253 *Ibid.*

254 *Ibid.*

255 Steinberg, p.30; Dedijer, *passim.*

256 Shelah, 'Genocide', p.76. The Germans feared that the highly unpopular Ustashe government would lose all support and that guerrilla activities would be encouraged. Hitler rejected this view, recommending a policy of 'national intolerance' for 50 years.

257 Dedijer, *op.cit.*, pp.231–67.

258 *Ibid.*, p.251.

259 Shelah, 'Genocide', p.78.

260 Shelah, 'Croatia', p.329. Rather remarkably, Pavelic's wife was Jewish (Reitlinger, *op.cit.*, p.365). The Ustashe was widely believed to have many

members with Jewish ancestry (Shelah, *ibid.*). Many Jews were saved by fleeing to Italian-controlled Croatian territory, from which there were no deportations.

261 Shelah, 'Genocide', p.78.

262 *Ibid.*

263 Rich, *op.cit.*, p.281; Reitlinger, *op.cit.*, p.369.

264 Pavelic fled to Argentina, living there until 1957, when he went to Spain, where he died. The Ustashe continued to be popular in Croatian emigré circles. In Melbourne, Australia (where I lived for many years) the Croatian community centre was, in the 1970s and 1980s, named 'Ante Pavelic House' (and may still be). This is not so very different from a German community centre being named 'Hitler House'. There is (as almost always) a good deal of dispute about how many people were killed by the Ustashe. While estimates of 750,000 Serbs and others as Pavelic's victims are common, other estimates are much lower (and more credible). Tanner (*op.cit.*, p.152) cites a range of recent estimates of from 80,000 to 215,000 victims, of whom about two-thirds were Serbs.

265 Subero Ienaga, *Japan's Last War: World War II and the Japanese, 1931–1945* (Oxford, 1979). Ienaga notes (p.49) that the Japanese army criminal code of 1908 forbade all soldiers from either surrendering or becoming prisoners of war. Even during the relatively liberal period of the late 1920s and early 1930s, Ienaga states (pp.25–32) that as a school child he was constantly bombarded with textbooks preaching obedience, Emperor-worship, Japanese national superiority, the duty of dying for one's country, etc.

266 *Ibid.*, p.233.

267 Namely Ozaki Hotsumi, a spy for the Sorge spy ring (*ibid.*, p.114). One hallmark of Nazi ideology which was certainly not shared by the Japanese was antisemitism. The Japanese actually went out of their way to help Jewish refugees, allowing unrestricted Jewish immigration to Shanghai, and resisting Nazi pressure to allow their deportation. Sempo Sugihara, the Japanese consul at Kovno, Lithuania, on his own authority gave 3,500 transit visas to Jews fleeing the Soviet (not Nazi) armies in 1940 bound for Shanghai. In 1985 he was officially designated a 'Righteous Gentile' by Israel's Yad Vashem.

268 *Ibid.* On other appalling aspects of Japan's wartime inhumanity, see Yuki Tanaka, *Hidden Horrors: Japanese War Crimes in World War II* (Boulder, Col., 1996).

269 *Ibid.*, p.173.

270 Rummel, *Death by Government*, p.147.

271 *Ibid.*, p.146. Rummel's estimates of mass deaths in the twentieth century are arguably often (but not always) exaggerations, and, in the case of China, subject to enormously wide margins of error. Rummel claims (p.143) that the Japanese 'murdered' 5,964,000 people between 1937 and 1945, including POWs and slave labourers.

272 Probably the most gripping description of these (and other Japanese) brutalities remains Lord Russell of Liverpool, *The Knights of Bushido: A Short History of Japanese War Crimes* (London, 1958).

273 *Ibid.*, p.57.

274 *Ibid.*, pp.235–40.

275 *Ibid.*, pp.239–40. Japanese soldiers apparently developed a taste for human flesh and, in Lord Russell's words (p.240), cannibalism 'was practiced when there was other food available, that is to say, from choice and not of necessity'. See also Tanaka, *op.cit.*, pp.111–34.

276 Arnold C. Brackman, *The Other Nuremberg: The Untold Story of the Tokyo War Crimes Trials* (London, 1989), pp.454–62.

277 Iris Chang, *The Rape of Nanking: The Forgotten Holocaust of World War II* (London, 1997), p.40. Chang's work, which became a best-seller in America, is the most vivid guide to this appalling horror story; she is the American daughter of survivors of Nanking.

278 *Ibid.*, p.41.

279 *Ibid.*, pp.42–7.

280 *Ibid.*, pp.87–9.

281 *Ibid.*, pp.101–3.

282 *Ibid.* These figures have been repeatedly questioned by Japanese historians, it should be noted. Dafing Yang, 'The Challenges of the Nanking Massacre: Reflections on Historical Inquiry', in Joshua A. Fogel, ed., *The Nanjing [sic] Massacre in History and Historiography* (Berkeley, Cal., 2000), pp.138–49.

283 One unlikely hero of Nanking was John Rabe, an ardent German Nazi, who was Chairman of the International Committee for the Nanking Safety Zone. Rabe, who expected the Nazis to be sympathetic, was arrested by the Gestapo on his return to Germany, and thereafter led a life of near-poverty. After the war, he was given the equivalent of $2,000 (a considerable amount at the time) by Nanking survivors, and died in 1950, long before his actions in Nanking became widely known (Chang, *op.cit.*, pp.187–95).

284 *Ibid.*, pp.170–2. A fourth man, Matsui Iwane, commander of Japan's Central China Expeditionary Force, was hanged for crimes at Nanking at the separate International Military Tribunal for the Far East (*ibid.*, pp.172–5).

285 Takashi Yoshida, 'A Battle Over History: The Nanjing Massacre in Japan', in Fogel, *Nanjing Massacre*, pp.70–132.

286 Mark Eykholt, 'Aggression, Victimization, and Chinese Historiography of the Nanjing Massacre', in *ibid.*, pp.16–17.

287 *Ibid.*, pp.24–8. Ironically, however, the Chinese commander at Nanking, Tang Sheng-Chih, became a high-ranking Chinese Communist official, a revered national hero until his death in 1970 (Chang, *op.cit.*, p.184).

288 See, for instance, Alexander Laban Hinton, ed., *Genocide: An Anthropological Reader* (Oxford, 2002), a collection of reprinted essays and extracts which almost totally ignores the Soviet Union (Stalin does not have an entry in the index), and mentions the Maoist Cultural Revolution on only two pages. The Khmer Rouge does 'better', being accorded half an essay (pp.265–75).

289 See David Caute, *The Fellow Travellers: Intellectual Friends of Communism* (New Haven, Conn., 1988). A comprehensive study of support for Stalinism on the Western left remains to be written. It is interesting to contrast the lack of interest in this subject by historians with the many studies of Western pro-Nazis, for instance the innumerable works on Sir Oswald Mosley and the British Union of Fascists, although support for Mosley was confined to a tiny fringe. The massive (and often quite interesting, even valuable) work by Sidney and Beatrice Webb, *Soviet Communism – A New Civilisation?* (1936) is often regarded as the *ne plus ultra* of Soviet-glorification among Western fellow travellers and Soviet admirers.

290 In 1938, for instance, the Socialist Club (ie the pro-Communist club) at Cambridge University had 1,000 members out of 5,000 undergraduates. T.E.B. Howarth, *Cambridge Between Two Wars* (London, 1978), p.158.

291 R.J. Rummel, *Lethal Politics: Soviet Genocide and Mass Murder Since 1917* (New Brunswick, N.J.), summarises all the demographic evidence about Soviet (especially Stalinist) democide. See also Stéphanie Courtois *et al.*, *The Black Book of Communism: Crimes, Terror, Repression* (Cambridge, Mass., 1999) for an extremely detailed and up-to-date account of the crimes of all Communist regimes.

292 Among the recent works scaling down the scope of Stalin's terror are J. Arch Getty and Roberta T. Manning, eds., *Stalinist Terror: New Perspectives* (Cambridge, 1993), a useful collection of essays by leading scholars; Robert W. Thurston, *Life and Terror in Stalin's Russia, 1934–1941* (New Haven, Conn., 1996); and Chris Ward, ed., *The Stalinist Dictatorship* (London, 1998).

293 Courtois *et al.*, pp.78, 80.

294 *Ibid.*, p.88.

295 *Ibid.*, p.100. This figure is derived from anti-Communist sources.

296 *Ibid.*, p.123. Wheatcroft, using recent demographic evidence, places the number of deaths in the 1921–2 famine at 3–4 million (Stephen G. Wheatcroft, 'More Light on the Scale of Repression and Excess Mortality in the Soviet Union in the 1930s', in Getty and Manning, p.280).

297 Rummel estimates the likely number of deaths in the Soviet Union in 1917–22 at 3,284,000 (*Lethal Politics*, p.33), with another 2,200,000 'victims' during the NEP [New Economic Policy, an era of relative liberalism] period of 1923–8 (*ibid.*, p.610). Both figures seem very high, with the latter implausibly high.

298 On the Ukrainian famine see Robert Conquest, *Harvest of Sorrow: Soviet Collectivization and Terror-Famine* (Oxford, 1986); Barbara B. Green, 'Stalinist Terror and the Question of Genocide: The Great Famine', in Rosenbaum, ed., *Is the Holocaust Unique?*; and Wasyl Hryshko, *The Ukrainian Holocaust of 1933* (Toronto, 1983). Green's outstanding essay objectively examines the issues concerned with the famine as 'genocide' and contains a comprehensive English-language bibliography.

299 Hryshko, *op.cit.*, pp.89–91.

300 *Ibid.*, p.185.

301 *Ibid.*, p.187.

302 *Ibid.*, p.101.

303 *Ibid.*, p.103.

304 Green, *op.cit.*, esp. pp.174–6, and Hryshko, p.103.

305 Green, *op.cit.*, p.187.

306 Green, *op.cit.*, p.172.

307 Stephen G. Wheatcroft, 'More Light', in Getty and Manning, *op.cit.*, p.280.

308 *Ibid.*

309 Alec Nove, 'Victims of Stalinism: How Many?', in *ibid.*, p.265.

310 Nicholas Werth, 'A State Against Its People: Violence, Repression, and Terror in the Soviet Union', in Stéphanie Courtois, *op.cit.*, pp.184–202.

311 Robert C. Tucker, *Stalin in Power: The Revolution From Above, 1928–1941* (New York, 1990), p.377.

312 *Ibid.*, p.443.

313 Martin McCauley, *Stalin and Stalinism* (London, 1995), p.39.

314 Cited in Tucker, *op.cit.*, p.423.

315 Cited in Richard Pipes, *Communism: A History* (New York, 2001), p.68.

316 *Ibid.*, p.64.

317 On this theme, see Ian Kershaw and Moshe Lewin, eds., *Stalinism and Nazism: Dictatorships in Comparison* (Cambridge, 1997).

318 Chris Ward, ed., *The Stalinist Dictatorship*, pp.205–12.

319 Tucker, *op.cit.*, pp.319–37.

320 Pipes, *op.cit.*, p.67.

321 Lynne Viola, 'The Second Coming: Class Enemies in the Soviet Countryside, 1927–1935', in Getty and Manning, *op.cit.*, pp.97–8.

322 Roberta T. Manning, 'The Soviet Economic Crisis of 1936–1940 and the Great Purges', in *ibid.*

323 See Robert Thurston, 'The Stakhanovite Movement: The Background to the Great Terror in the Factories', in *ibid.* and Fitzpatrick, *op.cit.*, *passim.*

324 Probably the most forceful exposition of this viewpoint is in Thurston, *op.cit.*, but see also the essays in Getty and Manning.

325 Thurston, *op.cit.*, p.145.

326 *Ibid.*

327 *Ibid.*, esp. pp.84–98.

328 J. Arch Getty and William Chase, 'Patterns of Repression Among the Soviet Elite in the Late 1930s: A Biographical Approach', in Getty and Manning, *op.cit.*, pp.236–8.

329 Sheila Fitzpatrick, 'The Impact of the Great Purges on Soviet Elites', in Getty and Manning, *op.cit.*, pp.252–3.

330 R.J. Rummel, *Lethal Politics*, pp.109–25.

331 *Ibid.*, p.116.

332 Nove, *op.cit.*, p.270.

333 *Ibid.*, p.271.

334 *Ibid.*, p.270. Of this number, 869,000 were also released in this period, about 32.5 per cent.

335 *Ibid.*, p.272. See also Edwin Bacon, *The Gulag at War: Stalin's Forced Labour System in the Light of the Archives* (Basingstoke, 1996), p.24, for a year-by-year breakdown of camp numbers.

336 *Ibid.*, p.270.

337 On this subject see 'Soviet Deportation of the Chechens-Ingush and the Crimean Tartars', in Naimark, *op.cit.*, pp.85–107; the Special Issue (Volume 4, Number 3, September 2002) of the *Journal of Genocide Research* on

'Stalin's Policy of Mass Deportations as Genocide', edited by J. Otto Pohl; Samuel D. Sinner, *The Open Wound: The Genocide of German Ethnic Minorities in Russia and the Soviet Union 1915–1949* (Fargo, N.D., 2000); J. Otto Pohl, *Ethnic Cleansing in the USSR, 1937–1949* (Westport, Conn., 1999); Robert Conquest, *The Nation Killers* (London, 1970); and *idem*, 'Stalin's Genocide Against the "Repressed Peoples"', *Journal of Genocide Research*, Volume 2, Number 2 (2000), pp.267–93; Bryan Glynn Williams, 'The Hidden Ethnic Cleansing of Muslims in the Soviet Union: The Exile and Repatriation of the Crimean Tartars', *Journal of Contemporary History*, Vol.37 (July 2002); Ann Sheehy, *The Crimean Tartars, Volga, Germans and Meskhetians: Soviet Treatment of Some National Minorities* (Minority Rights Group, Report No.6, 1973); William Fleming, 'The Deportation of the Chechen and Ingush Peoples: A Critical Examination', in Ben Fowkes, ed., *Russia and Chechnia: The Permanent Crisis* (Basingstoke, 1998).

338 J. Otto Pohl, *Ethnic Cleansing*, p.5. The 12 nationalities were the Koreans (in 1937), Volga Germans, Leningrad Finns, Karachays, Kalmayks, Chechens, Ingush, Balkars, Crimean Tartars, Georgian Kurds, Hemshins, and Ahiska (Meskhetian) Turks. Other sources name seven deported nationalities (Fleming, *op.cit.*, p.65). The list in Pohl's 'From the Guest Editor', in *Journal of Genocide Research* (2002), p.323, is slightly different.

339 Courtois, *op.cit.*, p.220; Naimark, *op.cit.*, *passim*.

340 Pohl, 'From the Guest Editor', *ibid.*; Courtois *et al.*, p.218.

341 Courtois, *op.cit.*, p.218. Pohl (*Ethnic Cleansing*, p.5) suggests an overall figure of 1,982,142 deportees for all nationalities, including 172,000 Koreans deported in 1937.

342 Pohl, 'From the Guest Editor', *ibid.* These figures may well also be understatements (Courtois, *op.cit.*, p.223). In his *Ethnic Cleansing* (p.8) Pohl places the number of deaths from 1941–8 at 309,100.

343 *Ibid.*

344 Alexander Werth, *Russia At War, 1941–45* (New York, 1964), p.531.

345 At the start of the war, Stalin also deported vast numbers of other potential security risks, including nearly 1 million 'Kulaks' (Courtois, *op.cit.*, p.225).

346 Naimark, *op.cit.*, p.98. For a more balanced view of the deportations, citing local leaders who blamed the deaths on the fact that food, clothing and other goods did not reach the deported nationalities in time (often because of embezzlement or misappropriation), see Fleming, *op.cit.*, esp. pp.78–82.

347 Fleming, *op.cit.*, pp.81–2.

348 *Ibid.*, p.99.

349 *Ibid.*, p.104. Apart from these groups, the Stalinist government also expelled thousands of Bulgarians, Armenians and Greeks from the Crimea, probably for reasons of national security.

350 For instance, nothing has been said of the deportations and executions of possibly hundreds of thousands of Poles, Balts and others to Siberia in 1939–41, following the Soviet takeover of eastern Poland, the Baltic states and other areas, nor of the brutality of the Stalin regime after 1945 (when, for instance, Alexander Solzhenitzin was sent to Siberia), nor of Stalin's increasingly paranoid antisemitism, leading to the 'Doctors' Plot' just before his death in 1953.

351 Rummel, in *Lethal Politics*, sets the overall death toll of persons 'systematically killed' by Stalin at 61.9 million.

352 See the useful discussion in Tucker, *op.cit.*, pp.25–44.

353 See Stephen F. Cohen, *Bukharin and the Bolshevik Revolution: A Political Biography, 1888–1938* (Oxford, 1980).

354 See the essays in Kershaw and Lewin, eds, *op.cit.*

355 For instance, Frank Chalk and Kurt Jonassohn, *The History and Sociology of Genocide* (New Haven, 1990), a useful history of past genocides and democides, devotes 32 pages to Stalin and 10 to Cambodia, but simply fails to mention Maoist China.

356 Richard L. Walker, 'The Human Cost of Communism in China', Senate Committee on the Judiciary, Internal Security Subcommittee; 1971, Committee Print, p.16, cited in Stephen Rosskamm Shalom, *Deaths in China Due to Communism: Propaganda Versus Reality* (Center for Asian Studies, Arizona State University, 1984), Occasional Paper No.15, p.7.

357 R.J. Rummel, *Death By Government* (New Brunswick, N.J., 1994), p.91. Rummel has also written an entire work on genocide in China, *China's Bloody Century: Genocide and Mass Murder Since 1900* (New Brunswick, N.J., 1991).

358 According to Margolin, 'China: A Long March Into Night', in Courtois *op.cit.*, *The Black Book of Communism*, pp.463–4, another 20 million died in 1959–61 in the 'Great Leap Forward'.

359 See, among many others, Richard L. Walker, *China Under Communism: The First Five Years* (London, 1956) and Peter S.H. Tang and Joan M. Maloney, *Communist China: The Domestic Scene, 1949–1967* (South Orange, N.J., 1967).

360 See, eg, Walker, pp.50–76, 177–213, 301–21. As with both Nazism and Soviet Communism, this entailed, in an even more extreme form, the elimination of the private sphere in favour of public direction. As Tang

and Maloney put it (p.237), 'The root assumption in the Communist view of individual freedoms and rights is that the interests of the individual are inseparable from and identical with the interests of the state as a whole. In Liu Shao-Chi's words: "Under the system of people's democracy and socialism, the masses of people can see for themselves that personal interests are indivisible from the public interests of the country and society; and that they are one and the same."'

361 Rummel, *Death By Government*, p.96.

362 Cited in Shalom, *op.cit.*, p.7.

363 *Ibid.*, pp.6–13.

364 Walker, *China Under Communism*, pp.128–41.

365 *Ibid.*, pp.130–1, citing R.H. Tawney, *Land and Labour in China* (1932).

366 See, eg, Walker, p.12. Walker also placed the figure at 'several millions' (Shalom, p.37).

367 Shalom, *op.cit.*, pp.34–5.

368 *Ibid.*, p.41. Shalom's other works include titles such as *The United States and the Philippines: A Study of Neocolonialism* (1981) and *Socialist Visions* (1983), and his *Deaths in China Due to Communism* contains a good deal of gratuitous criticism of American policy. Nevertheless, as noted, it is often convincing in pointing out the exaggerations of many observers of Maoist China, especially those connected with what he terms the 'China lobby' of the 1950s and 1960s.

369 Shalom, *Deaths in China*, p.23. The *New York Times* of 25 June 1950 carried a story stating that 'in February [1950] it had been predicted that at least 10 million Chinese would starve to death this spring' (*ibid.*). There is simply no evidence that any such famine occurred.

370 *Ibid.*, pp.27–31.

371 *Ibid.*, p.61.

372 *Ibid.*, p.109.

373 *Ibid.*, pp.89–109.

374 *Ibid.*, pp.87–8.

375 *Ibid.*, p.65.

376 'Introduction' to Hazel Smith *et al.*, eds., *North Korea in the New World Order* (Basingstoke, 1996), pp.xiv–xv. This work, in my view, goes overboard in trying to explain North Korea as a 'normal' if eccentric society, and its essays hardly touch on the regime's oppression. See also Kongdan Oh and Ralph C. Hassig, *North Korea: Through the Looking Glass* (Washington, D.C., 2000), esp. 'Social Control', pp.127–47.

377 Rummel, *Death By Government*, pp.366–7.

378 *Ibid.*, p.368.

379 *Ibid.*, p.365.

380 *Ibid.*, p.370.

381 *Ibid.*, p.373.

382 *Ibid.*, p.376.

383 *Ibid.*, p.377.

384 Pipes, *op.cit.*, p.152.

385 *Ibid.*, p.241. See also Jean-Louis Margolin, 'Vietnam and Laos: The Impact of War Communism', in Courtois, *op.cit.*, pp.565–76.

386 Rummel, *Death by Government*, *op.cit.*, p.243.

387 Margolin, *op.cit.*, pp.572–5.

388 Rummel, *Death by Government*, pp.272–8.

389 *Ibid.*, pp.272–3. Rummel also claims (pp.273–4) that 'scrupulous care' was taken by the American military to avoid killing civilians, contrary to popular belief. He believes that about 65,000 civilians (p.274) were killed in American bombing raids.

390 David P. Chandler, *A History of Cambodia* (Boulder, Col., 1993).

391 See Kiernan, pp.16–25, for an exposition of this view.

392 Pipes, *op.cit.*, p.132.

393 Ben Kiernan, *The Pol Pot Regime: Race, Power, and Genocide Under the Khmer Rouge, 1975–79* (second edition, New Haven, Conn., 2002), pp.9–16.

394 Kenneth M. Quinn, 'Explaining the Terror', in Karl D. Jackson, ed., *Cambodia, 1975–1978: Rendezvous With Death* (Princeton, 1989), esp. pp.219–31, 234–6; Karl D. Jackson, 'Intellectual Origins of the Khmer Rouge' in *ibid.*; François Pouchaud, *Cambodia Year Zero* (London, 1978); David P. Chandler, *Brother Number One: A Political Biography of Pol Pot* (Boulder, Col., 1992) and *idem*, *History of Cambodia*, pp.209–25; Jean-Louis Margolin, 'Cambodia: The Country of Disconcerting Crimes', in Courtois, *op.cit.*, pp.577–635; and Rummel, *Death By Government*, pp.159–207.

395 Kiernan, *op.cit.*, p.26.

396 Cited (from Khmer Rouge documents) in *ibid.*, p.26.

397 Cited in Quinn, *op.cit.*, p.185.

398 *Ibid.*, pp.197–200.

399   *Ibid.*, pp.200–5.

400   Ben Kiernan, 'The Cambodian Genocide and Its Leaders', in Israel Charny, *op.cit.*, p.132.

401   Kiernan, *op.cit.*, Table 4, p.458. The Cham dominated the Cambodian fresh-water fishing trade. Charles H. Twining, 'The Economy', in Jackson, *op.cit.*, pp.135–6.

402   Kiernan, *op.cit.*, p.458.

403   *Ibid.*, Rummel's estimate (*Death By Government*, p.160) is higher still: 2,400,000.

404   Kiernan, *op.cit.*, pp.456–63, for a detailed examination of the figures. The only expert opinion about the death toll which appears to be markedly lower is that by Michael Vickery (740,000), which Kiernan (p.457) offers cogent reasons for rejecting. All other expert opinion supports the conclusion that about 1.7 million perished.

405   David Hawk, 'The Photographic Record', in Jackson, ed., *Cambodia, 1975–8*, pp.209–14.

406   Kiernan, *op.cit.*, p.x.

407   *Ibid.*

CHAPTER 5

Genocide in the era of ethnic cleansing and Third World dictators, 1945–2000

The Age of Totalitarianism was hallmarked by genocides and demo-cides on an unprecedented scale. While totalitarian regimes, especially the revolutionary governments of Asian Communism, continued to slaughter by the millions, most of the well-known examples of what many would term 'genocide' in the post-1945 period were of an entirely different kind, typified not by ideologically motivated massacres but by what is termed 'ethnic cleansing' and by mass killings of their own peoples, for reasons largely unrelated to ideology, by Third World dictators and others. This chapter explores some of the best-known examples of the post-war period. Some, like the 'ethnic cleansing' carried out by the Serbian government in parts of the former Yugoslavia, are well-known and continuously reported in the world's media, while others remain less well-known.

Many of these are examples of what is now termed 'ethnic cleansing', the involuntary and forced transfer of an ethnically distinct component of a population outside their area of former residence by an invading or occupying power. Neither the term 'ethnic cleansing' nor its reality is – surprisingly – very old. In popular English-language usage the term dates only to 1992, when it was adopted by Serb leaders and paramilitary forces in Bosnia and given widespread popularity as a result in the

American media.[1] It had, apparently, previously been used just after 1945 by Poles and Czechs in the process of expelling their Germans and Ukrainians, and has affinities to the Nazi use of the term *Säuberung*.[2] Nevertheless, had the present book been written even 20 years ago, the term would probably not have been used and would not have been notorious. Although in one sense 'ethnic cleansing' is as old as history, there were, rather strangely perhaps, few authentic instances of large-scale 'ethnic cleansing' until the twentieth century, with the provisions of the Lausanne Treaty of 1923, in which 1.5 million Greeks and Turks were compelled to leave for their ethnic majority homeland, often being seen as the earliest example of modern 'ethnic cleansing'.[3] 'Ethnic cleansing' in its modern sense has almost always accompanied or followed closely upon significant changes in national boundaries, especially after a major war. In the nineteenth century, when many of Europe's larger states – such as Austria-Hungary and Russia – were organised on a multi-national basis, 'ethnic cleansing' was less easy to imagine, even in repressive societies, than in the twentieth-century world where national boundaries are based chiefly on such attributes of ethnicity as language, religion and shared culture. Under the UN Convention on Genocide of 1948, what is denoted by the term 'ethnic cleansing' was not defined as 'genocide' and, unless it entailed deliberate mass murder, would not be regarded by most people as 'genocide' in the same sense as a mass murder *à la* Hitler or Pol Pot. While many died in the examples of 'ethnic cleansing' described in this chapter, seldom did the scale of killing approach those described in the previous two chapters.

One notable feature of 'ethnic cleansing' is that until perhaps the 1970s legally constituted mass population transfers seemed to many to be humane and rational, and in no way criminal or genocidal. Such transfers promised to reduce the sources of international conflict and provide long-term humanitarian solutions for intractable problems arising from the presence of minority ethnic and religious groups in ethnically defined nation-states. Thus, as will be examined, Winston Churchill, Clement Attlee, Mohammed Ali Jinnah and many other democratic leaders advocated the involuntary transfer of very large numbers of minority nationality groups to new homes. At the time, they were seldom criticised for their stands, and were not denounced as advocates of 'genocide' by any left-liberal or humanitarian lobby or international organisation, as they surely would be today. The 'War of the Yugoslav Succession' of the 1990s (as it is sometimes termed) appears, in fact, to have been the first time that 'ethnic cleansing' was either identified as such or widely attacked and demonised by *biens-pensants* or by international humanitarian bodies. In considering the three examples of 'ethnic cleansing' of the 1944–8 period discussed here, it perhaps cannot be emphasised too strongly that these events were simply not seen in the same light as they would be today, barely half a century later.

Ethnic cleansing among Germans and Eastern Europeans, 1944–8

Between 1944 and 1948 about 16 million Germans, Poles and Ukrainians were resettled in other parts of Europe, chiefly owing to boundary changes and the alterations of regimes accompanying the end of the Second World War.[4] Perhaps about one-third of this vast number was voluntary, at least in the sense that those involved deliberately fled their traditional homelands ahead of the Red Army: the other two-thirds of these resettled millions were involuntarily expelled as a result of treaties arrived at by the victorious powers in the war, treaties fully supported by Britain and the United States. This was arguably the most glaring example of 'ethnic cleansing' in the history of the modern Western world. Eleven million of this number were Germans, who left or were expelled from their traditional homes in East Prussia, from those regions of eastern Germany which were ceded to Poland in 1944–5, and from the Sudetenland component of Czechoslovakia, as well as smaller German minorities from other countries in east-central Europe. The remaining 5 million or so expellees were Poles, transferred from the areas of pre-1939 eastern Poland ceded to the Soviet Union or into the former areas of Germany taken over by Poland, or were Ukrainians or Belorussians transferred out of Poland. Until very recently, these mass expulsions received virtually no publicity whatever in English-language accounts of twentieth-century genocide and ethnic cleansing, presumably because they were carried out chiefly among Germans immediately after the Holocaust and largely behind the Iron Curtain.[5] Even now, despite some recent studies, it is safe to say that many readers will simply never have heard of them.

These enormous eastern European population transfers might be divided into three parts. Initially, several million Germans voluntarily fled the advancing Soviet army in the closing stages of the war, fearing Communism, and the murders, pillaging and rapes which Nazi propaganda insisted would accompany the Red advance. Many of these fears were well-justified, with (in particular) pillaging and rapes carries out on a mass scale. Probably thousands of Germans were killed by the advancing Soviet troops. In February 1945, for example, German soldiers found 300 murdered German civilians in one village they temporarily recaptured from the Soviets, with most of the women raped and most bodies mutilated.[6] In Konigsberg 'mountains of bodies made up of *ca.* 3000 women, girls, and only a few men' were found at about the same time.[7] Throughout eastern Europe, however, vastly larger expulsions of Germans were carried out following international treaty agreement, especially at Potsdam, the last great 'Big Three' conference of the war, held in July-August 1945. By Article XIII of the Potsdam Protocol, America, Britain and the Soviet Union formally agreed that 'the transfer to Germany of German populations, or elements thereof, remaining in Poland, Czechoslovakia and Hungary, will have to be undertaken', provided that they should 'take place ... in an orderly and humane manner'.[8] Even before this, and even among leading democratic politicians, there was widespread approval for the mass transfer of German civilians from other countries to Germany. On 5 December 1944, for instance, Winston Churchill told the House of Commons, 'A clean sweep will be made. I am not alarmed by the prospect of the disentanglement of populations, nor even by these large transferences, which are more possible in modern conditions than they ever were before.'[9] Churchill specifically referred to the 'success' of the transfer of Greek and Turkish minorities authorised by the Lausanne Treaty.[10] In March 1945 Britain's Deputy Prime Minister Clement Attlee, a staunch socialist, claimed that the Germans affected 'are not entitled to appeal on the basis of the moral laws they have disregarded or the pity and mercy that they have never extended to any other'.[11]

The Western Allies would probably not have insisted on the most numerous of these mass transfers, Germans from those areas of eastern Germany ceded to Poland in 1944–5, except to appease Stalin. He insisted on literally moving the boundaries of Poland to the west, with the former easternmost areas of Poland in its 1918–39 borders ceded to the Soviet Union and with it receiving, in compensation, much of East Prussia, Pomerania, East Brandenburg and Silesia in exchange, areas which had always been German. To facilitate this movement westward of Poland, whole populations had to be transferred as well, something which the democratic West was in no mood to rule out (even if they had been in a position to thwart Stalin, which they were not), with the horrors of Belsen and Dachau just revealed. The Polish government-in-exile was forced to accept these changes as *faits accomplis;* naturally, however, it, too, favoured the mass transfer of ethnic Germans out of Poland's newly acquired territory.[12]

In Czechoslovakia, the non-Communist democratic government headed by Edward Benes, installed in power in May 1945, expelled 3 million Sudeten Germans to occupied Germany. This mass transfer of the Sudeten German population had been Czech government-in-exile policy before the war ended, as early as 1942.[13] By late 1947 virtually all Sudeten Germans had been expelled, with most going to West Germany but over 1 million transferred to the Soviet zone.[14] A number estimated by historians at between 19,000 and 40,000 died in the process, although there is much dispute at the actual figure.[15] Some estimates are vastly higher, but these are certainly exaggerated.[16] Smaller numbers of Germans were also expelled from other eastern European countries such as Romania and Yugoslavia. In addition and thirdly, over 2 million Poles were expelled westward from the former eastern regions of Poland into Poland's new frontiers, over 500,000 Ukrainians and Belorussians were transferred from Poland to the Soviet Union, chiefly the former. This came about as a result of an agreement enacted in September 1944 between Nikita Khrushchev, representing the so-called Ukrainian Soviet Socialist Republic, and the Lublin (ie pro-Soviet) Polish government-in-exile.[17] Resistance to these transfers was widespread, with at least 6,000 persons killed in the process.[18]

The reaction of many, perhaps most, readers to this 'ethnic cleansing' on a vast scale is likely to be one of what psychologists term 'cognitive dissonance', the holding of two contradictory attitudes simultaneously. On the one hand, few will fail to sympathise with the plight of millions of ordinary people uprooted from the homelands where they had lived for centuries, and few will fail to deplore the undemocratic attitudes of the democracies in what occurred. On the other hand, more than a few readers – the majority, in all likelihood – are very likely to believe that the German expellees got what they richly deserved, a small sample of what their government inflicted on so many millions of innocents, and to sympathise with Clement Attlee's observation that these Germans had no right to complain, in 1945, about the absence of pity, compassion or democracy among the wartime victors. At the time, too, the Czechoslovak government naturally viewed the Sudeten German minority with the deepest suspicion, as a disloyal minority whose agitation led to the dismemberment of the Czech state at Munich.[19]

Similarly, few eastern European Slavic groups were likely to have the slightest sympathy for the plight of the expelled Germans, given the horrors Germany had just inflicted on Slavs, as well, of course, as on Jews, Gypsies and others. While it was perfectly true that the majority of those Germans affected were women, children and the elderly, and this was unfortunate, Germans and *Volksdeutsch* had, with a handful of exceptions, fully accepted Hitler's rule and had no objections to his policies while Germany's armies were victorious. Moreover, in the newly-created Federal Republic of Germany (but not in East Germany) these expellees found new lives as citizens of a prosperous democracy and became largely reconciled to their new positions.[20] They were, in fact, certainly better off than they would have been as members of minority ethnicities in some wretched Soviet satellite. Moreover, the disappearance of large German minorities throughout eastern Europe probably diminished national hostilities. 'It is possible to argue that forced migration, in this case, worked to end old national conflicts and prevent future conflicts,' Ana Siljak observes.[21] While some irridentist groups have existed among the displaced Sudeten Germans, theirs is obviously a lost cause: with the end of Communism and the entry of many of the former Soviet satellite states into the EC, too, it will presumably be possible for the expellees to return to their old homelands if they wish. It is notable that few of those commentators who unhesitatingly condemn 'ethnic cleansing' have had anything to say about the mass expulsion of the Germans. Most have simply ignored it, suggesting that it has at least their tacit approval.

Israel and the Palestinians

Shortly after the resettlement of the Germans and others, one of the most controversial and intractable examples of large-scale population transfer occurred in the Middle East in 1948, when a very large number of Palestinian Arabs left their home areas in the portions of the Palestine Mandate which became the State of Israel and moved elsewhere, chiefly to other parts of the Palestine Mandate or to adjacent Arab countries. Virtually everything about these events is both hotly contested by both Israelis and Arabs, and extraordinarily controversial. Unlike other examples of what might, justly or unjustly, be termed 'ethnic cleansing', this population transfer remains without a generally accepted resolution, and is among the main reasons why the Arab-Israeli dispute remains unresolved.

After years of increasingly futile efforts to control the contending forces of Arab nationalism and Zionism (the movement to re-establish a Jewish homeland) in Palestine, war-weakened Britain turned the future of the Palestine Mandate over to the newly formed United Nations. Britain had also come under intense pressure from the United States, where Zionist lobbying was strong, to allow more Jewish survivors of the Holocaust into Palestine, which it had previously refused to do. At this juncture, too, the Soviet Union (almost always unsympathetic to Zionism) decided to support the creation of a Jewish state in part of the Palestine Mandate. On 29 November 1947 the United Nations voted to partition the Mandate into a Jewish state, a Palestinian Arab state and an international zone encompassing Jerusalem and Bethlehem.[22] This decision was reluctantly accepted by the *Yishuv* (the Jewish community in Palestine), but rejected *in toto* by the Arab League (the international body of Arab states) and by nearly all the dominant factions among the Palestinian Arabs. The 1947 Partition scheme was similar to one proposed by the British in 1937, but not acted upon following opposition by both sides. Under the UN Plan, the Jews were to receive 57 per cent of the Mandate and the Palestinians 43 per cent.[23] These figures exaggerate the Jewish share, since most of the territory allotted to the Jews was in the virtually uninhabited Negev desert area, with only a coastal strip and an area around the Sea of Galilee representing developed land allotted to the Jews. The Palestinians were to have the entire central area of Palestine (what is now termed the West Bank, but much larger), the Gaza area and the northern Galilee, as well as the coastal town of Jaffa, adjacent to Tel Aviv. Included in the Palestinian area were dozens of Zionist settlements and *kibbutzim*. The Palestinians were, moreover, soon to have something they had hitherto lacked in their history, an independent state of their own.

Although some factions among the Palestinians, especially those looking to Jordan for leadership, might have accepted Partition, however reluctantly, as noted the entire Arab world (at least officially) rejected it, as did the dominant Palestinian leadership. It is genuinely tragic that the Palestinians rejected Partition, which might have given them independence without bloodshed. Instead, the Arabs insisted, over and over again, on independence for the whole of the Mandate as a single state, with the Jews continuing in a permanent minority status and Jewish immigration effectively ended. This was obviously unacceptable to the Zionists, although the UN Partition plan gave them far less than they believed they were entitled to under the Balfour Declaration, Britain's 1917 promise of a Jewish national home in Palestine.

The subsequent course of events, and the traumatic events which overtook so many Palestinians, was also caused in large measure by the nature of the political leadership of the Palestinians at the time: to describe it as execrable would be flattering. The recognised leader and spokesman of the Palestinians was Haj Muhammed Amin Al-Hussani (*c*.1895–1974), the Grand Mufti of Jerusalem and President of the Arab Higher Council, the Palestinian leadership body. Al-Hussani became notorious during the Second World War for his open support of Hitler, leading up to an infamous meeting between the two in November 1941, at which Hitler promised to bring about the 'annihilation of the Jews living under British protection in Arab lands', and Al-Hussani claimed that 'the Arabs were prepared to collaborate wholeheartedly with Germany'.[24] Noting Al-Hussani's blue eyes, Hitler also stated that he must have had 'more than one Aryan among his ancestors and one who may be descended from the best Roman stock'.[25] Through his international and domestic intrigues, Al-Hussani also managed to alienate the Iraqis, the Jordanians and Britain, as well as the Palestinian middle classes, which regarded him as a rabble-rouser. The conduct of the Palestinian leadership during the closing days of the Mandate was marked by mistake after mistake. It boycotted the UN's special committee convened in early 1947 to decide on the future of Palestine, thus allowing the Zionists to make the running.[26] More seriously, perhaps, despite repeated urging by westernised Palestinians, until September 1948 it declined to institute a state structure or administrative apparatus to govern Arab Palestine following the end of the Mandate, when the Israeli military had gained the upper hand.[27]

During the crucial period of 1947–8 there was thus no Palestinian negotiating partner with whom the new State of Israel could deal. (In contrast to the situation among the Palestinians, the Jews of the *Yishuv* already had a remarkably sophisticated governing apparatus in place.) Palestinian politics were, in fact, still quasi-feudal, with locally based notables and powerful clans and families still constituting the dominant elite.[28] Although political parties existed, they had no internal elections and continued to be based on clan loyalty. As is so common in the Arab world, extremist factions marginalised the moderates.[29] This was the opposite of the situation in the *Yishuv*, where a wide range of sophisticated, secularised parties spanning the political spectrum long existed and where pro-socialist Labour Zionism, led by David Ben-Gurion, constituted the dominant faction.

Shortly after the UN Partition vote, Britain announced that it intended to leave Palestine on 14 May 1948. In the interim it did virtually nothing to keep order, and a situation of near-anarchy ensued marked by ever-increasing violence and the formation of Jewish and Arab armies. The aim of the Jewish forces, the Haganah and other underground organisations, was to secure the continued existence of the *Yishuv*. The Arab forces, on the other hand, intended to crush the Jews and 'drive them into the sea'. Fighting began in earnest at the end of 1947 and continued with no quarter given. Initially, the war went badly for the Jews but, after about April 1948, the tide turned in their favour and the Jews increasingly gained areas not assigned to them by the UN. On 15 May 1948 an independent State of Israel was proclaimed, but, as noted, no equivalent State of Palestine was announced by the Arabs. It was in 1948, too, that the Palestine refugee problem became a reality. In early 1948, the first wave of Palestinians fled from places like Haifa and Jaffa.[30] Many fled simply to escape violence. In 1936–7, during a previous period of communal violence, many had also fled and later returned, and it seems clear that they imagined the same would happen again. Initially Al-Hussani did not oppose their flight and did little to stop it.[31] Most who fled represented the Palestinian middle classes and leadership elite. A much larger, mass exodus occurred in April-June 1948, as the Jews gained the upper hand. The most balanced accounts of this wave stress that they were caused literally by panic among the leaderless Palestinian masses, who were afraid of Israel's military forces: there was a general sense of 'falling apart' which permeated Palestinian society.[32] The loss of a homeland and the dispersion of a large fraction of the Palestinian population became overwhelmingly pervasive themes in Palestinian culture and writing. Since 1948, Palestinian writing has centred on 'images of tangible objects: olive trees, orange groves, pomegranates, grapes and stony fields ... A key theme is the difficulty or impossibility of becoming a complete person when one is living as an alien.'[33]

It is now known that the oft-repeated Zionist claim that they fled in response to Arab radio broadcasts urging them to leave is false. In the latter stages of the civil war – but not before – considerable numbers appear to have deliberately been forced out of their villages by the Israeli forces, and it is well-documented that Israel's leaders shed few tears over these remarkable events which not only gave them a state, but one with an overwhelming Jewish majority. Nevertheless, the notion sometimes put by Arab and radical Israeli and Jewish historians that the expulsions were part of a preconceived plan steeped in Zionist ideology also appears false.[34] The Zionist leadership could have had absolutely no foreknowledge of the course the Israeli War of Independence actually took, whose outcome depended upon wholly unpredictable contingent factors of international politics and the day-to-day evolution of the conflict. Another crucial point which seems to have escaped virtually all commentators on the birth of the Palestine refugee problem is that the great majority fled *to areas designated by the UN as the Palestinian Arab State*, which, had it come into existence, would presumably have absorbed large numbers of Palestinians who left the new State of Israel voluntarily.

In all, probably somewhere between 600,000 and 760,000 Palestinian refugees fled from areas which became the State of Israel.[35] Of these, probably over 500,000 went to what is now the West Bank or the Gaza Strip.[36] In mid-1949, Israel offered to take 100,000 refugees back, although it is likely that this offer was made merely as a gesture it was immediately rejected by the Arabs.[37] Possibly with the example of post-1944 German mass migration in mind, and certainly with the Greek-Turkish transfers of the 1920s well-known, from the start the Western powers accepted the flight of the Palestinians as a *fait accompli* and did not realistically expect the Israelis to take back more than a minority. Dean Acheson, America's Secretary of State, told Israeli representatives in April 1949 that America might expect Israel to allow back 'say a fourth of the refugees', a number believed at the time to be about 200,000 persons.[38] Even as early as 1949, there was thus a widespread sense that the flight of most of the Palestinians was likely to be permanent. Had a Palestinian state come into existence at the time, the subsequent despair and poverty of these refugees might still have been avoided in a state of their own. As is well-known, however, the West Bank was annexed by Jordan and Gaza by Egypt, so that no Palestinian state was ever created. Israel conquered these areas in the Six Day War of June 1967, at about the same time as modern Palestinian nationalism was formed, and the Israeli-Palestinian conflict took on the dimensions with which the world has become all too familiar. The failure to create an independent Palestinian state in 1947–8, as was intended by the UN, turned what could have been an example of a settlement in Mandate Palestine which was peaceful, creative and mutually liberating into a tragedy which remains unresolved after more than half a century. Over the subsequent decades, too, the political leadership of the Palestinians has remained grossly inadequate: as Abba Eban put it, seldom missing an opportunity to miss an opportunity.[39]

Population transfer in India and Pakistan, 1947–8

The third post-war example of massive population transfer across newly created international boundaries occurred in the Indian subcontinent in 1947–8, when vast numbers of non-Muslims fled Pakistan for India from the newly created Muslim state of Pakistan at the same time as enormous numbers of Muslims left India for Pakistan. This situation, which produced suffering and bloodshed on a fantastic scale, emerged because of the insistence by Muslim Indian nationalists on the creation of a separate Muslim state in the Muslim-majority areas of British India which would achieve independence as a separate entity from the rest of India. The leader of the movement for an independent Pakistan – as the Muslim state became known – was Mohammed Ali Jinnah (1876–1948), the son of a Karachi merchant and, like many other leaders of Indian nationalism, a barrister trained in London, a product of Lincoln's Inn. Jinnah was a peculiar and unlikeable man whose grandfather was a Hindu (from the same caste and region as Mohandas Gandhi) who, for unknown reasons, converted to Islam.[40]

A successful lawyer in London and India, Jinnah was known for flouting most Muslim conventions: he ate pork, seldom visited a mosque, and knew less of the Koran than did Gandhi. He was also known for his elegant dress and monocle.[41] Jinnah was imperiously vain and, once determined on a course of action, became more stubborn and less amenable to compromise than virtually any political leader of his time. He gradually built up a unique ascendancy among British India's 94 million Muslims, a minority compared with 295 million Hindus, Sikhs, Jains and others.[42] From 1933, Jinnah came to the conclusion that, when Britain granted dominion status to India – as seemed to increasing numbers to be inevitable, although when this would occur was unclear – a separate Muslim state should be created, divided off from the Hindu-majority areas of India.[43] Jinnah, increasingly authoritarian in his manner and perhaps unbalanced, 'delighted in touring India's Moslem cities in princely processions, riding under victory arches on a kind of Rose Bowl style float, preceded by silver-harnessed elephants and a band booming out "God Save the King" because, Jinnah observed, it was the only tune the crowd knew'.[44] Jinnah was also increasingly alienated from the Hindu-dominated Indian Congress Party, which did little or nothing to share power with Muslims when it won provincial elections.

Coming on top of decades of nationalist agitation led by Gandhi, Jawaharlal Nehru and other Indian leaders and activists, the Second World War fatally weakened Britain's hold over the subcontinent. During the 1930s, it was taken for granted by most moderates in Britain's ruling National government, including Stanley Baldwin, the leader of the Tories, that India would sooner or later become an independent, self-governing Dominion within the Commonwealth. (Prior to becoming leader of the anti-Appeasement forces in Britain, during the 1930s Winston Churchill was most famous as the fringe leader of Britain's right-wing politicians who totally opposed Indian independence.) After the war, with the election in 1945 of a Labour government with an enormous majority, the only question became how quickly Indian independence could be achieved. Britain's Labour government was ideologically committed to granting Indian independence, while Britain, virtually bankrupt and facing the threat of Soviet expansionism in Europe, could simply not afford to pour resources into holding India, an effort which would have made America's Vietnam involvement 20 years later look like nothing. Britain's Labour Prime Minister Clement Attlee hit upon the seemingly brilliant decision of appointing as Viceroy of India (the supreme ruler of British India) Lord Louis Mountbatten (1900–79), a young, charming, highly successful admiral who had been Supreme Allied Commander of South-East Asia in 1943–6. A better choice to cushion the fatal blow to Britain's Indian empire could hardly be found, since he was the king's cousin and closely related to Europe's royal families. He was also, by inclination, something of a socialist. Mountbatten's wife, Lady Edwina Ashley, was a charming, glamorous socialite who was the granddaughter of Sir Ernest Cassel, an enormously wealthy merchant banker, and was independently wealthy in her own right. Early in 1947, Attlee unexpectedly appointed Mountbatten viceroy. Mountbatten's clear orders were to oversee the process of Indian independence as quickly as possible. Therefore he was virtually forced to concede Jinnah's plans for an independent Pakistan, as well as other controversial aspects of independence, such as the end of the pro-British princely states, which Britain would probably not have wished to concede.

Granting independence to a separate state of Pakistan unleashed a torrent of religious and ethnic hatred almost unparalleled in the post-1945 era. There were several reasons for this sudden upsurge of group hatred. The boundaries between the Muslim and non-Muslim areas of British India were often quite unclear, and drawing new national boundaries meant partitioning several provinces of British India where both communities lived, especially the Punjab in the west and Bengal in the east. Even after partition, in 1948 India still contained a population of 45 million Muslims while Pakistan held 21 million non-Muslims.[45] East and West Pakistan were part of a state which, uniquely, comprised two separate areas 1,500 miles apart. The messiness of partition, and the fact that Pakistan was deliberately created as a religiously defined Muslim state, strongly implied a large-scale transfer of those population in the 'wrong' religious area but near to the area of the nation in which they were the majority. There were, as well, the economic and social dimensions to religious conflict: in general, Hindus (as well as Sikhs and Parsees) formed most of British India's economic elite and most of its administrative leadership strata, somewhat similar to the role of Jews, Greeks and Armenians in the Levant. Hindus were widely disliked by Muslims as moneylenders, while Muslims tended to remain as peasants, with an upper class of landlords.[46] Nevertheless, under the British relations between the communities were generally peaceful, and few could have predicted the orgy of violence which was to follow.

Probably the first outbreak of communal violence occurred in Calcutta on 16 August 1946, when, as a result of a proclamation by the Moslem League of 'Direct Action Day' in favour of an independent Pakistan, mobs of impoverished slum-dwelling Muslims began murdering any Hindu they could find; Hindu mobs then retaliated with equal fury. In one day, 6,000 people were murdered in Calcutta.[47] This was apparently the trigger for an ever-growing wave of communal violence and of the voluntary exodus of the religious minority in border regions. Within two years, a refugee tidal wave of incredible dimensions had left their homes: about 6.5 million Muslims left India for Pakistan, while 6 million non-Muslims left Pakistan for India.[48] One column of refugees in the Punjab consisted of an estimated 800,000 people, the largest such group of refugees in history.[49] In some areas the evacuation was almost complete: almost no non-Muslims, for instance, remained in the West Punjab, the Northwest Frontier Province or Bahalwalpur (south of Lahore).[50] Nearly all of this flood of peoples was spontaneous, the product of well-grounded fears that those left behind would be massacred. In December 1945 and November 1946 Jinnah actually proposed a deliberate exchange of populations, but this was rejected by the Hindu-dominated Congress Party and by Mohandas Gandhi as 'unthinkable and impractical'.[51]

The spontaneous transfer of populations was accompanied by massacres and killings of a truly appalling kind, in which perhaps 200,000 people were killed. Collins and Lapierre recount many of these horrors in graphic fashion: in one typical case, a horde of Muslim killers brandishing clubs, spears and hatchets swept down on a stationary train packed with 2,000 Hindus: only 100 managed to survive.[52] In another case, a train carrying hundreds of Muslims formerly employed by the Viceroy's establishment in Simla was attacked by Hindus and Sikhs. Only one Muslim survived.[53]

> *A man's executioner could be a friend or a stranger. Every day for fifteen years, Nivanjan Singh, a Sikh tea merchant . . . had served a pot of Assam tea to the Moslem leatherworkers who [now] came rushing to his shop one August morning [in 1947]. He was setting the man's ration on his little brass balance when he looked up to see his customer, his face contorted in hate, pointing at him and screaming 'Kill him, kill him!'*
>
> *A dozen Moslem hoodlums raced out of the alley. One severed Singh's leg at the knee with a sword. In an instant they had killed his 90–year-old father and his only son. The last sight he saw as he lost consciousness was his 18-year-old daughter, screaming in fright, being carried off on the shoulders of the man to whom he had been serving tea for fifteen years.*[54]

Although the worst of the violence ceased by 1948, it lingered on in some areas until about 1950, while it still persists today in the disputed Kashmir area and elsewhere. Despite attempts to offer a rational explanation for this murderous orgy, none really exists. 'Our people have gone mad,' Liaqat Ali Khan, Pakistan's first Prime Minister, told Nehru in the Punjab in August 1947. Perhaps no better explanation exists. One can, of course, offer reasons for these horrors. In the power vacuum created by the almost overnight disappearance of the British Raj after several centuries of rule, amidst successor states based explicitly or implicitly on religious lines of division and patterns of authority, it was understandable that the masses among all communities would flee to the realms where they would be safest. Communal hatreds and jealousies, pent up for centuries by British rule, plainly existed in the most destructive of forms. Yet these explanations are probably insufficient to account for the sheer murderous enmity which exploded in 1947. Perhaps no rational explanations exist which fully explain these events.

Both governments did their best to accommodate the millions of refugees, but the legacy of these events deeply affected the development of both countries, even in very mundane ways. For instance, among India's vast railway staff, about 73,000 non-Muslims left Pakistan for India, while 83,000 Muslims left India for Pakistan. They were not necessarily balanced by occupation, meaning that the railways of both countries were disrupted for several years.[55] British India's libraries were deliberately divided up between the two countries. In some cases sets of the *Encyclopedia Britannica* were divided in two, alternative volumes going to India and Pakistan. Some dictionaries were divided in two, A-K going to India, L-Z to Pakistan.[56] India, it seems, made no protest at Pakistan getting extra letters. 'Delhi and Karachi took on the character of refugee cities which they have never lost,' Ian Talbot observes.[57] Much of the subsequent histories of the two countries, especially the continuing violence over Kashmir, and the terrorism associated with the Sikh community (which did not achieve an independent homeland, although Sikhs occupy a geographically distinctive area of the Punjab), arose out of the events surrounding independence.[58] In 1971, the poorly constructed Islamic state created in 1947 came apart, when the largely Muslim area of East Bengal known as east Pakistan declared its independence from west Pakistan, where the capital and most of the country's political elite were located. Known as Bangladesh, the new state came into being in a brutal civil war in which it has been alleged hundreds of thousands, perhaps millions, of people were killed and a further 10 million people fled to India.[59]

Idi Amin and Saddam Hussein

Apart from these examples of 'ethnic cleansing' and mass population transfers in the immediate post-1945 period, examples abound of mass murder and alleged genocide typically practised by recent Third World dictators. There is obviously no shortage of candidates for providing examples of recent mass killers: the problem, indeed, is how to compress the material which exists into the space available. Here, we will look at two of the most notorious of recent Third World murderous dictators, Idi Amin Dada (b. c.1925 or 1935–2003) of Uganda and Saddam Hussein (b.1937) of Iraq. Amin was born in Uganda's West Nile district, of a family of subsistence farmers; unusually, his family became Muslims.[60] His father became a sergeant in the Uganda Police and – although his background remains very obscure – Idi Amin joined the King's African Rifles, served in Burma in the Second World War, and then in the British suppression of the Mau Maus in the 1950s.[61] Amin was an enormous man, six feet four inches tall and weighing 250 pounds; he became Ugandan heavyweight boxing champion. He was much respected by the British authorities, although he was also already known for his sadism, cruelty and embezzlement of large sums.[62] By 1971 Amin was a Major-General serving in the regime of Milton Obote, which had been widely seen as one of the better African governments, though mired in the usual morass of poverty, tribal hatreds, corruption, the rise of new elites and a power vacuum increasingly filled by the army.[63]

In its later stages, the Obote government became increasingly author-itarian, and instituted a move to the left in economic policy. Much of Uganda's trading sector was in the hands of an increasingly unpopular Asian minority from the Indian subcontinent. In January 1971, while Obote was overseas, Amin and senior officers seized power, instituting a reign of terror which quickly became internationally infamous. In part this was because of Amin's persona as a grotesque, murderous buffoon, which won him an attentive audience among the world's media eager for a bizarre quote and seldom failing to get one. Amin was quoted as stating that 'Hitler was right to burn six million Jews', that 'Some Asians in Uganda have been painting themselves black with shoe-polish. ... If anyone is found painting himself with black polish, disciplinary action will be taken against him.' He sent President Julius Nyerere of Tanzania a telegram in 1972 proclaiming 'I want to assure you that I love you very much, and if you had been a woman, I would have considered marrying you, although your head is full of grey hairs, but as you are a man that possibility does not arise.' He sent President Nixon (while still in office) a telegram wishing him 'a speedy recovery from Watergate', and once demonstrated at a meeting of the Organisation of African Unity how to suffocate someone with a handkerchief.[64] What David Martin termed 'an unending stream of idiocies' from Amin made him, during the 1970s, into arguably the best-known and most recognisable African leader in the Western world, perhaps the best-known leader of any Third World state.[65]

Initially, the Amin regime was friendly to South Africa, England, Israel and other future enemies (at this stage, for instance, Israel – later Amin's *bête noire* – gave Amin strong support). From late 1971, however, Amin cut ties with his allies and initiated an increasingly repressive mili-tary regime. In 1971–2 virtually all Asian merchants and shopkeepers (about 49,000) were expelled from the country.[66] Thousands of persons now 'disappeared' or died violently, including innumerable prominent Ugandans, among them the country's Chief Justice, the head of the Bank of Uganda and the Anglican archbishop.[67] From 1972 until Amin was finally overthrown in 1979, a general reign of terror ensued, in which thousands died. The usual estimate is that at least 300,000 persons were killed by Amin, but Jorgensen, on the basis of low numbers of refugees and 'the absence of more substantial evidence', provides a much lower number, 'from 12,000 to 30,000' in addition to 16,000–20,000 'ordinary' murders.[68] Large-scale killings in torture chambers, mass rapes, and the night-time dumping of bodies in mass graves became commonplace. In mid-1976 occurred the celebrated Entebbe raid by the Israeli air force to rescue Israeli civilians on a plane hijacked by Arab and German terrorists and flown to Uganda, where the terrorists were given safe haven. All the captives were rescued with the exception of Mrs Dora Bloch, a hospitalised British woman, who was murdered by Amin's soldiers. In April 1979 the psychopathic Amin was finally overthrown by a force of Tanzanian and Ugandan soldiers. Amin fled to Libya and then to Saudi Arabia, where, reportedly, he lived in some luxury until his death in 2003. It seems extraordinary that the West did not vigorously demand his deportation and trial at an international court.

Saddam Hussein became prominent in Iraqi affairs from 1968, when, in collaboration with his cousin Ahmed Hasan al-Bakr and others, he overthrew the existing government and established the Ba'ath party in power, whose ideology was a fairly typical one of extreme Arab nationalism, socialism, fervent Islam (although this was neglected for many years), anti-Westernisation and anti-Zionism.[69] A small clique, chiefly from the town of Takrit along the Tigris River, came to dominate the government, which found itself in conflict with local Shi'ite Muslims, Kurds and Western oil interests. In July 1979 Saddam became Iraqi president, and in September 1980 Iraq invaded Iran to settle a long-standing border dispute. It met little resistance at first, but Iran quickly rallied and the war dragged on until 1988. An estimated 800,000 people were killed; it ended in a stalemate with Iraq vaguely getting the better of Iran.[70]

The charge of genocide against Saddam is, however, most commonly voiced concerning his treatment of Kurds in northern Iraq. Vast numbers of Kurds were certainly killed by Saddam, especially in the period

1987–9, when an estimated 75 per cent of Kurdish villages were destroyed and thousands were killed by chemical weapons.[71] About 500,000 Kurds were forcibly removed from their villages, many 'to places which were little more than concentration camps'.[72] Countless thousands of Iraqis were murdered and tortured, especially among Shi'ite Muslims, marsh-dwelling Arabs and Saddam's political opponents. One estimate, made by John F. Burns in the *New York Times* in January 2003, was that the number of Iraqis dying under the Saddam regime may have been as high as 1 million.[73] In 1990–1 came Saddam's invasion of Kuwait – the first time that a member state of the UN had been invaded and conquered by another state – and the subsequent Gulf War in which a vast international force, led by the United States and Britain, liberated Kuwait but left Saddam in power. In 2003 Saddam and his regime were removed from power by an invading force led by the United States with the support of Britain and a number of other powers. Mass graves, including one containing the bodies of 15,000 Shi'ite Muslims killed by Saddam's regime following an uprising in 1991, were found after his overthrow.

Many other recent Third World dictators could relevantly be examined here – the 'Emperor' Bokassa of the Central African Republic and many other African dictatorships, regimes in Argentina, Haiti, the Dominican Republic and other Latin American states, most of the governments of independent Burma, the Taliban in Afghanistan, and numerous others – but these two regimes will do nicely as exemplars of contemporary Third World brutality and barbarism.[74] Many experts would regard most of these regimes as guilty of genocide.

Biafra and Bangladesh

Two civil war-type conflicts of the post-war era involved casualties on such a scale, directed specifically against particular groups, that they have been described as 'genocide': the Biafran War (also known as the Nigerian Civil War) of 1964–70, and the Bangladesh conflict of 1971–2. The origins of the Biafran War lay in the unstable and inchoate nature of the large Nigerian state which achieved independence from Britain in 1960.[75] Originally a democracy, from 1966 the country became increasingly unstable, leading, in May of that year, to a military coup by army officers from the country's North (where there is a large Muslim population). Southerners, especially the Ibo (or Igbo) peoples of the south-east, feared northern domination and, in May 1967, declared their independence as the Republic of Biafra. The Ibos were among the most successful of Nigeria's peoples, and feared military domination by the more backward north. The central Nigerian government immediately launched a concerted military action to restore national unity, its army being described as 'a monstrous agglomeration of over 855,000 men armed to the teeth with modern weapons, whose government has had uninhibited access to the armouries of at least two major Powers and ... [been] endowed with limitless supplies' of arms.[76] On the Biafran side was 'a volunteer force representing less than one in ten of those who have presented themselves at the recruiting booths for service'.[77] Massacres of Ibos began even before Biafran independence: in July 1966, following a previous coup, as many as 8,000 Ibos were murdered by the army.[78]

The civil war, lasting 18 months, was fought with the utmost bitterness. Although at first Biafra, surprisingly, got the upper hand, the fortunes of the war continued to switch back and forth, and in January 1970 Biafra surrendered. It is often stated that about 2 million Biafrans died in the civil war, reducing its population from 12 million to 10 million.[79] Other estimates are relatively lower, but still horrendous: between 600,000 and 1 million Biafrans dead.[80] Although massacres were common, the majority apparently died of starvation, which became a deliberate policy of the Nigerian government. 'Starvation is a legitimate weapon of war, and we have every intention of using it against the rebels,' one Nigerian diplomat stated in July 1968.[81] An estimated 500,000 Biafran children died as a result.[82] Overt massacres also occurred, as for example in January 1968 at the Ibo town of Asaba 'where 700 Ibo males were lined up and shot'.[83] The Ibos also reportedly engaged in massacres and atrocities against neighbouring peoples.[84]

During the whole of the Biafran conflict, the Nigerian government was given continuing *de facto* support by Britain and most other major governments, with British Prime Minister Harold Wilson's role questioned by many. The *Spectator* (a pro-Tory British weekly magazine) claimed on 31 May 1968 that 'for the first time in our history Britain has become an accomplice in the deliberate slaughter of hundreds of thousands of men, women, and children, whose only crime is that of belonging to a proscribed nation: in short, an accomplice in genocide'.[85]

The war over Bangladesh presents many parallels to Biafra. Pakistan was created in 1947 as a state in two parts, its eastern component fashioned from the Muslim areas of Bengal. Apart from religion it had little in common with Pakistan's other component a thousand miles to the west, which was wealthier and came to dominate the nation's elite structure. Most inhabitants of the densely populated Bengal region spoke Bengali, whereas the inhabitants of west Pakistan spoke Urdu or Punjabi. Even the climate of the two components is entirely dissimilar, with the arid west in stark contrast to the monsoon-swept east, regularly wreaking havoc. In November 1970, just before the civil war, a major cyclone struck, killing hundreds of thousands in one of the worst natural disasters of the century. The following month, a Bengali nationalist movement, the Awami League, led by Sheik Mujibur Rahman, won a major victory in the Pakistani national election. In March 1971, Bangladeshi independence was declared, and a fierce civil war raged for the next nine months.[86] The west Pakistan governing elite sent an army to put down the rebellion. One of its goals was the forced emigration of east Pakistan's 10 million Hindus: this, and the prospect of crucially weakening its archrival Pakistan, led to the involvement of the Indian army, which decided the civil war in favour of the Bengalis in December 1971. In Bengal, the west Pakistani army committed innumerable atrocities against ordinary Muslim Bengalis, especially women, and against local Hindus. The educated elite was also targeted, and routinely killed in large numbers.[87]

Much of the responsibility for these enormities rests with west Pakistan's leader, General Yahya Khan. It has been estimated that between 1 million and 3 million people were killed, with no fewer than 10 million Bengalis fleeing to India as refugees.[88] Rape was widespread and, as 25 years later in Yugoslavia, was employed on a deliberate basis by the west Pakistani army, with especially heinous psychological results in a Muslim country.[89] In February 1974, west Pakistan agreed to recognise Bangladeshi independence, and the new country entered the United Nations the same year. In 1975 its founding father, Sheik Mujibur, was assassinated by young army officers. Its next president, Major-General Ziaur (or Zia) Rahman, was also assassinated, in 1981.

Indonesia: the fall of Sukarno, 1965 and East Timor, 1974–9

Two instances of what has widely been described as genocide occurred in Indonesia, or at the hands of Indonesia, in recent decades. In 1965, very substantial numbers of pro-Communist and pro-Sukarno supporters were killed during an anti-Sukarno, anti-Communist coup in that country which brought General Suharto to power. During the mid-late 1970s, large numbers of East Timorese were killed following the Indonesian takeover of that Portuguese colony, while large numbers have been killed since.

The events leading to the massacres following the overthrow of Sukarno in 1965 are complicated.[90] Indonesia is a largely Muslim island state off south-east Asia which achieved independence from the Dutch in 1945–9. Its leader during the first 20 years of independence was Sukarno (1901–70), of aristocratic Javanese origin.[91] Sukarno became head of the Indonesian National Party in the late 1920s and was recognised as the great nationalist leader of the Dutch East Indies. As president of Indonesia, his power base was in the army, but he had to contend with a variety of rival groupings which sought power, especially the Indonesian Communist Party (the PKI) and two Muslim religious parties. Sukarno also became known for his increasingly left-leaning, pro-Communist and anti-American foreign policy, especially in the 1960s, although the United States retained a good deal of influence in the country. In 1962 Indonesia gained control of West Irian, the western half of New Guinea, which had been retained by the Dutch, and in 1963 was declared President for Life. During this time, the PKI grew enormously in strength, and had over 2 million members by 1965. Although these events remain very murky, on 30 September-1 October 1965 some military factions launched a coup against Sukarno's own core supporters in the Indonesian army, apparently with the aim of seizing power. They were allegedly backed by the PKI, and the PKI was widely perceived as being behind the coup. Although six generals were killed during the coup attempt, its leaders spared General Suharto, who emerged as the leader of the conservative anti-PKI elements within the Indonesian elite, and a rival to Sukarno; over the next three years Suharto became *de facto* ruler of Indonesia and was Indonesia's president from 1968 to 1998.

From October 1965 until March 1966 conservative and Muslim forces in Indonesia launched a violent purge of the PKI, killing enormous numbers of its followers and others. 'Disloyal' Chinese were also attacked, as were westernised 'atheists', by Muslim fundamentalists. As well, many were killed in vendettas against personal enemies.[92] Although the army remained firmly in control, there was a real danger of anarchy, and by March 1966 the army placed an effective halt on further killings. In the meantime – and especially between October and December 1965 – an enormous bloodbath had occurred. Estimates of the numbers killed range from 60,000 to 1 million or more. Hughes' conclusion, based on a careful weighing of the evidence, is that probably 250,000 were killed, although many other estimates are far higher, with 400,000–500,000 being a figure often seen.[93] 'The nation ran amok,' is his summary.[94] Most killed were Communists, chiefly in Bali and Java.[95] The army consistently argued that 'It was the Communists or us. If we hadn't killed them, they would have killed us,' a view apparently accepted by Hughes and some other commentators.[96] Chalk and Jonassohn repeatedly refer to these massacres as 'genocide', although this seems a misuse of the term, however bloody these events were.[97]

The elimination of the PKI and then of Sukarno, and the coming to power of a conservative-military regime oriented towards the West, had profound long-term consequences for east Asia. It was particularly welcomed by the West at a time when the whole of the area appeared to be heading for a takeover by Communists and America had just begun a systematic escalation of its forces in South Vietnam. Nevertheless, Western and American influence on the anti-Communist coup appears to have been remarkably slight, even non-existent, and, indeed, rather curiously the Indonesian coup seldom figures in any discussions of the geo-politics of East Asian Communism during this period, although it was evidently an event of the first importance.[98]

The other recent large-scale massacre involving Indonesia occurred in East Timor, which occupies parts of an island south of Celebes and north of Australia, with an area of 7,336 square miles (slightly smaller than New Jersey) and a population of 689,000 in 1974 and about 800,000 in 2002. Unlike the rest of the island nation, which had been a colony of the Netherlands and is largely Muslim, East Timor was a possession of Portugal and is chiefly Roman Catholic. Portugal did everything possible to retain its far-flung colonies long after the rest of Europe had decolonised, and East Timor remained a colony, separate from Indonesia, until the 1970s. The country is mountainous and remote. Portuguese rule was harsh and backward, probably more so than in colonial Indonesia.[99] During the Second World War East Timor was occupied by the Japanese, and then reoccupied by Portugal. In 1974, a left-wing revolution occurred in Portugal which spelled the end of its empire, and Indonesia increasingly eyed East Timor for takeover and incorporation within its regime. Most Timorese desired independence, although a minority favoured integration with Indonesia. The local nationalist movement, Fretilin, declared independence in November 1975. Fretilin's actions triggered an invasion of East Timor by Indonesia and, in May 1976, its incorporation into Indonesia. Indonesia's invasion was tacitly supported by both the United States and nearby Australia, keen to see the right-wing Suharto government of Indonesia in charge of East Timor rather than a left-wing, possibly Marxist, separatist government. In East Timor, however, a guerrilla campaign got underway which was met by the Indonesian military in an unusually brutal way. By 1988, it was widely claimed that 200,000 Timorese had been killed by the Indonesian invasion, both directly and indirectly through the uprooting of the population and a deliberate policy of starvation.[100] Torture and involuntary sterilisation were widespread and the population was terrorised.[101] (This figure, of 200,000 dead, appears to be generally accepted by most authorities.)

Although East Timor became something of a *cause célèbre* in leftist circles in Australia and possibly elsewhere, its plight gained little international recognition despite the repeated condemnation of Indonesia by the United Nations. East Timor's remoteness, and the perceived necessity to appease Indonesia, were important factors in this wall of silence. In 1996, however, the Nobel Peace Prize was awarded to two East Timorese activists (one the local Catholic bishop) and a sea-change occurred in East Timorese affairs with the resignation of President Suharto in May 1998. His successor, Bacharuddin Habibie, reversed decades of Indonesian policy by announcing that a referendum on its future would be held in East Timor. This took place in August 1999, resulting in a 79 per cent vote for independence amidst Indonesian-sparked violence. The UN put in place an interim government in September 1999, leading to full independence in April 2002. Also in 2002 the Indonesian former governor of

East Timor, Abilio Soares, was convicted in the Indonesian court of crimes against humanity for failing to control army forces during the 1999 independence referendum. East Timor is another example, it seems, of how local and international pressure towards democratisation has proved to be effective, at least in the long term.

Serbia and the wars of Yugoslav succession, 1990–2000

The campaigns of 'ethnic cleansing' and mass murder in parts of the former Yugoslavia during the 1990s quickly became infamous around the world, indeed introducing the term 'ethnic cleansing' into the international vocabulary. The response of the international community to the slaughters in former Yugoslavia is especially instructive, for it demonstrates how attitudes had dramatically shifted in the space of a generation.

Although the internal tensions and hatreds which eventually tore Yugoslavia apart are often said to be ancient and time-honoured, such a description is true only in a limited sense.[102] Yugoslavia, of course, did not exist until late 1918, when it came into being as the 'Kingdom of the Serbs, Croats, and Slovenes' at the end of the First World War. Prior to 1914, its component units had gradually achieved independence from the Ottoman Empire, and had looked to either Germany or Russia for great power patronage: only in the loosest sense did these lines of division prefigure the sources of ethnic conflict which erupted in the 1990s. To be sure, ethnic conflict was a serious undercurrent in Yugoslav politics down to Tito's accession to power at the head of a Communist state at the end of the Second World War, but this revolved above all around the rivalry between Serbs and Croats, the two largest groups in Yugoslavia.

Under the rule of Josef Broz Tito (1945–80), Yugoslavia was technically a federal republic consisting of six local republics – Slovenia, Croatia, Bosnia and Hercegovina (or Herzegovina), Serbia, Montenegro and Macedonia. Serbia, the most populous federal republic, also contained two autonomous regions with more limited powers than the republics – Vojvodina in the north and Kosovo in the south. After Yugoslavia's famous break with Moscow in 1948 and more emphatically from the adoption of constitutional changes in 1963–8, the local republics assumed greater powers: in 1971, while Tito was still alive, further constitutional changes meant that the presidency of Yugoslavia rotated among representatives of the six republics. This system worked fairly well at first but proved to have fatal flaws which led to endemic violence after the fall of Communism. Each of the republics had already achieved something like full autonomy, even semi-independence, by the time Communism ended, and were ripe for breaking away to full independence, while Yugoslavia lacked a charismatic or legitimate national ruler to succeed Tito and hold the country together. To compound these difficulties, some of Yugoslavia's republics lacked anything like ethnic homogeneity, but were hodge-podges of ethnic groups; unfortunately, these ethnic groups did not dwell in geographically contiguous and discrete local areas, but were often to be found in villages arranged, in ethnic terms, in crazy-quilt pattern, making it almost impossible to redraw the republican boundaries to take account of ethnic realities. For Serbia, too, there was the separate problem of the two autonomous regions, Vojvodina and Kosovo, which increasingly aspired to republican status. The problem of ethnic diversity was particularly acute in Bosnia-Herzegovina, where 40 per cent of the population were Muslims, 33 per cent Serbs and 18 per cent Croats, and in Macedonia, which had a one-third Macedonian minority. On the other hand, in the Kosovo autonomous region 90 per cent of the population were ethnic Albanians, with only 10 per cent consisting of Serbs and others.[103]

The centrifugal forces which eventually led to the complete breakup of Yugoslavia in the 1990s were also assisted by the rise of ultra-nationalist local leaders whose long-term effect was to frighten other components of Yugoslavia into declaring their independence. The most notorious of these was Slobodan Milosevic (b.1941), the president of Serbia between 1989 and 2000. Milosevic, the son of Montenegrin Serbian parents who both committed suicide, rose to power in the Yugoslav Communist party as a Serb ultra-nationalist and party hard-liner.[104] Milosevic achieved the highest offices in Yugoslavia just at the time when the state was in the process of disintegration.

The course of the wars and atrocities which occurred in parts of former Yugoslavia between 1991 and 1999 is extremely complicated, and this bewildering complexity has added greatly to the difficulty in resolving these conflicts. To simplify an often bewilderingly complex sequence of events, the following are the major highlights as to why many regard these events as genocide. In February 1991 the Serbs in Croatia (about 12 per cent of the population) declared their independence from the (still-Yugoslav) republic of Croatia. The Yugoslav (ie, chiefly Serbian) army intervened, leading to deaths in clashes between Croatian Serbs and Croatian police in Plitvice near Zagreb. In June 1991, both Croatia and Slovenia declared their independence from Yugoslavia. The Yugoslav army then attempted, unsuccessfully, to abort Slovenia's independence in a brief war which it lost. (Slovenia, the northernmost Yugoslav republic, contained only a tiny number of Serbs and had long had major links with neighbouring Austria and Italy.) Croatia, Serbia's traditional rival, also declared independence on the same date, leading to Serbian attacks on Kijevo and, especially, Vukovar, which surrendered to Serbia in September 1991 after an estimated 2,000 deaths. Bosnia-Herzegovina declared its independence from Yugoslavia in March 1992. Bosnia then became the scene of the most brutal events of the Yugoslav conflict, especially those carried out by Radovan Karadzic, the military leader of the self-proclaimed 'Serbian Republic of Bosnia-Herzegovina'. It was then, in Bosnia, that the term 'ethnic cleansing' first gained world-wide currency, as a term to describe the policy of the Serbs (and, to a lesser extent, the Croats) towards the Bosnian Muslims and towards one another. Slaughters and massacres occurred, such as that of Muslims at Mostar in November 1993. What were widely described as 'concentration camps' for Muslims were established, where murder and torture were rampant. By the end of 1992, it was estimated that up to 2 million Bosnians had been displaced from their homes.[105]

Despite repeated cease-fires arranged by NATO and other international bodies, slaughters continued to occur. In particular, the killing of 71 persons by Serb shell-fire in Tuzla (May 1995) and the apparent mass murder of several thousand Muslims by Serb forces in Srebrenica (July 1995) became internationally infamous. Although continuous fighting scaled down after the Dayton Accords of December 1995, perhaps the worst single incident of all occurred in the largely Albanian province of Kosovo, technically a part of Serbia, but long contested by its Albanian majority, who wanted independence, and its Serb minority, who perceived themselves as targets of Albanian 'ethnic cleansing' and looked to

Serbia for help.[106] There, due to Serb 'ethnic cleansing' and fears of a general war between NATO and Serbia, by May 1999 the flight of vast numbers of Albanian Serbs to border regions and Albania became synonymous with 'ethnic cleansing'. One UN estimate placed the number of refugees at 863,000.[107] Many were killed: estimates range from 10,000 to more than 100,000, although – as almost always – these may well be exaggerations.[108] After 1999, and especially with the fall of Milosevic in 2000, some measure of stability returned to the region. It is very difficult to know how many died in the former Yugoslavia in 1991–7: 'hundreds of thousands' according to the careful historian Norman Naimark, although a figure of, say, 30,000–80,000 seems more plausible to this writer.[109]

Another notable feature of the war in Yugoslavia was the frequency with which rape was used as a deliberate instrument of terror and debasement.[110] Rape by conquering soldiers is a tragic feature of virtually all wars, especially brutal ones, but in Yugoslavia (as in Bangladesh) this appears to have been an instrument of policy, encouraged by the commanding officers among the Serbs. In part this was to humiliate Muslim women, whose religion regards them as especially defiled by rape; in part this was to produce 'Serbian' babies and thus reclaim these infants from Bosnian Muslims who were looked upon as originally Serbs who had been forced to convert to Islam.[111] 'Rape houses' were a feature of Serbian 'ethnic cleansing' in Bosnia, while – perhaps for the first time in history – rape as a criminal act featured strongly in the indictments brought against the Serbs at the Hague tribunal after the war.[112] While Serbia's Slobodan Milosevic and his forces were seen as the chief offenders in terror throughout the war, Croatia's Franjo Tudjman and his armies also committed widespread atrocities. Bosnia's Muslims, on the defensive throughout the war, only periodically engaged in the murder of non-Muslim civilians, and certainly on a much smaller scale than either the Serbs or the Croatians.[113]

The atrocities which occurred in the former Yugoslavia between 1991 and 1999 were, of course, the worst of their kind in Europe since the Second World War. It is noteworthy that many other boundary changes, especially the breakup of the former Soviet Union into independent states, occurred at this time, following the end of the Cold War, with no violence at all and no 'ethnic cleansing'. To some extent this was arguably because other parts of eastern Europe were ethnically homogeneous, at least in a relative sense, with (as we have seen) considerable 'ethnic cleansing' having occurred at the end of the Second World War. In these states, too, democratic and relatively stable governments nearly always succeeded the former Communist regimes: in Yugoslavia alone, and especially in Serbia, ultra-nationalist leaders such as Milosevic and Tudjman remained in power after their regimes had ceased to be Communist dictatorships.

The response of the outside world to events in Yugoslavia during the 1990s is especially interesting, and shows how world opinion had shifted and become much more sensitive to these events and the issues they raised than even a few decades before. At some point between the late 1940s and the 1990s, 'ethnic cleansing' became intolerable as an option for resolving an endemic struggle between hostile ethnic groups sharing the same land, something which, as the previous discussion shows, was certainly not the case just after the Second World War. The evidence suggests that this occurred surprisingly late. As recently as 1972, the British government headed by Edward Heath actively discussed a secret plan for the repartition of Northern Ireland which would have entailed compulsorily transferring up to 500,000 Catholics living in Northern Ireland to the Republic of Ireland, and to 'bring 200,000 Protestants out of the ceded areas to the rest of Northern Ireland'.[114] This report noted that 'such a massive movement would not be peacefully accomplished' and also stated that 'compulsion would be a breach of the European human rights convention', but did not *ipso facto* rule it out.[115] The Heath government, it should be noted, was by no means wholly supportive of the Northern Ireland Protestants. In the same year, it passed an act suspending Stormont (the Northern Irish Parliament, dominated by Protestants) and initiating direct rule from Westminster, and also actively negotiated with the Irish government towards a solution of the Ulster dispute, to the enormous chagrin of Northern Ireland's Protestants. That it would have even contemplated such a population transfer was extraordinary, and – so far as is known – no subsequent British government has ever discussed this possibility.

By the 1980s, it seems likely that the ubiquity of the notion of 'genocide' (stemming, in all likelihood, from near-universal internalisation of the Jewish Holocaust), and a much greater degree of seriousness with which governments took the many international agreements outlawing genocide, made even the discussion of involuntary population transfers *a priori* illegitimate, notwithstanding the fact that these had been encouraged by democratic governments only a few decades earlier. Some hint of the previous attitude, however, remained even in the 1990s. In 1995, the Dayton (Ohio) Peace Agreement brokered by the American government and intended to settle the Yugoslav conflict divided Bosnia into two 'entities', a Muslim-Croat Federation, which controlled 51 per cent of Bosnia's territory, and a Bosnian Serb entity, which controlled 49 per cent.[116]

The 1990s also witnessed a range of international efforts to halt the violence in Yugoslavia, and in particular to end any brutal inter-ethnic clashes which could be seen as 'genocide'. The Dayton Accord also established a NATO Implementation Force to enforce the brokered cease-fire. It had mixed results, and was frequently criticised, but it represented arguably the first such international peace-keeping force aimed in large part at halting genocide.[117] Even critics of the NATO force, however, conceded that its presence might well have saved hundreds of thousands of lives.[118] More strikingly still, as a result of these accords a UN International Criminal Tribunal for the former Yugoslavia was established, receiving much publicity as probably the first continuing tribunal ever established. In the later 1990s, many Bosnian Serbs, including Radovan Karadzic and General Ratko Mladic, the commander of the Bosnian Serb military forces, were indicted for war crimes. In 1997 Dusan Tadic, a Bosnian Serb charged with torturing and murdering Bosnian Muslims and Croats at Osmarksa prison camp in Prijedor, Bosnia in 1992, was convicted and sentenced to 20 years in prison. In 1998 the UN established a Permanent International Criminal Court to try individuals for genocide, war crimes and crimes against humanity. It seems clear that these efforts represented a major shift in international attitudes, assisted by the end of the Cold War and by the ever-increasing centrality of 'genocide' as acts which the international community ought to have at the forefront of its agenda. These shifts in opinion and response were very recent, and it remains to be seen whether the circumstances which allowed them to dominate the resolution of the Yugoslav situation will be repeated elsewhere.

Rwanda 1994

One of the most horrifying and destructive post-war genocides occurred in the central African republic of Rwanda in 1994. It is also one of the most difficult satisfactorily to categorise, presenting many features which make it unique among recent genocides.

Rwanda is a very small landlocked central African state, about the size of Vermont and slightly larger than Wales. It was occupied by Germany in the 1880s and, after 1918, was controlled by Belgium until it was given independence in 1962 along with neighbouring Burundi. In many respects, however, Rwanda is not a typical African state.[119] Known as the 'land of 1,000 hills', it is temperate and extremely densely populated. Its population totalled 7,128,000 in 1989, giving it a density of 270 persons per square mile, compared, for example, with Tanzania's 109 per square mile.[120] Rwanda also has probably the highest percentage of its population resident in rural areas of any country in the world. In 2002, only 6 per cent of its population was resident in an urban area, compared with 32 per cent in Tanzania. It thus has had little in the way of unchecked urban growth nor of the edge-of-city shanty towns so common in the Third World. Its economy is heavily dependent on livestock and on its chief export crop, coffee.

As is well-known, Rwanda's population consists of two distinct groups, the Hutu and the Tutsi, who between them comprise 99 per cent of the population. They are not precisely distinctive 'ethnic groups' in the normal sense of the term, as they speak the same language and are not separate tribes; as well, they follow the same traditions and, in pre-colonial times, acknowledged the same Tutsi king.[121] In some respects, they correspond more to separate castes with, traditionally, the Tutsis being dominant. Intermarriage was discouraged but not forbidden. Traditionally, the Tutsis were hereditary cattle-raisers and the Hutus, comprising about 80 per cent of the population, were farmers.[122] Apparently, however – to complicate matters – there are ethnic differences between the two groups, the Tutsis being, in stereotype, taller and thinner than the Hutus, with, some anthropologists have argued, a remote Ethiopian Hamitic origin.[123] In contrast, the Hutus are shorter and typically Bantu people.

Over the centuries, the Tutsis achieved a political ascendancy over the Hutus, with, by the twentieth century, the supreme king and nearly all of

Rwanda's chiefs and local chiefs being Tutsis.[124] The ascendancy of the Tutsis over the Hutus was long favoured by both the Germans and the Belgians, who regarded them as a superior race, although it is also important to realise that this ascendancy had been established long before the colonial period.[125] From the early 1950s, however, Belgium completely reversed its former policy of favouring the Tutsis and deliberately promoted Hutus. In part this was a response to Hutu nationalism and in part to the impact of a new generation of leftist administrators and missionaries who favoured the Hutus as underdogs.[126] In 1959, just before independence, rioting against the Tutsi chiefs by the Hutu majority resulted in 20,000 deaths and the exiling of large numbers of Tutsis to neighbouring countries.[127] The Hutus were dominant in the Rwanda republic which became independent in 1962. Over the next 30 years, the Hutu ruling elite of Rwanda, under President Grégoire Kayibanda, did everything possible to demonise and marginalise the Tutsis, turning them into ethnic scapegoats.[128]

Kayibanda's rule was increasingly autocratic and despotic.[129] He was deposed in 1973 by a Hutu major-general, Juvénal Habyarimana, whose regime was, at first, relatively tolerant, and some – but not many – of the restrictions on Tutsis were relaxed.[130] It, too, however, was increasingly despotic, even totalitarian. The Rwandan economy was relatively satisfactory, but declined considerably with a sharp drop in coffee prices in 1990. From the late 1980s, too, exiled Tutsis (with some support from Hutu dissidents) created an army in exile in Uganda and in 1990 invaded the country.[131] This invasion failed, due in part to Belgian intervention on the side of the Hutu government. The early 1990s were a period when some progress was made at negotiations aimed at ethnic reconciliation, leading to the Arusha Accords of August 1993 which promised evolution to a multi-party democracy.[132] Side-by-side with this, however, ultra-nationalist and hardline elements within the Hutu-dominated power structure increasingly enunciated an ideology of Hutu supremacy and hatred towards the Tutsis, whom they viewed as the embodiment of all the evils which beset the country, using an ultra-nationalist radio station and extremist newspapers.[133] The Rwandan military, an enormously powerful element there as elsewhere in Africa, was armed to the teeth, thanks to generous French military aid, growing in size from only 5,000 to 40,000 in 1993–4; the regular army also trained thousands of paramilitary and military forces, imbued with hatred towards the Tutsis.[134] Owing to the invasion of the country by Tutsi forces in 1990, the Hutu nationalists viewed themselves as national patriots engaged in repelling the threat of invasion.

By 1994, in the context of a declining Rwandan economy, the country was a tinderbox set to explode, although few could have foreseen the magnitude of the catastrophe which was about to unfold. On 6 April 1994 Rwandan president Habyarimana and the president of neighbouring Burundi, Cyprien Ntariyamira, were killed in a plane crash. The cause of the crash is unknown, but it seems likely their plane was shot down by extremist Hutu military forces.[135] Almost immediately, a wave of killings of Tutsis in Rwanda began, a slaughter almost without parallel in modern history in peacetime. From the moment of the plane crash, militia road-blocks appeared on the streets of Kigali, the national capital, and the mass shootings began of 'enemies' of the regime. The woman prime minister of Rwanda, Agathe Uwilingiymana, a moderate, was assassinated, as was the country's chief justice.[136] Between early April and late May a continuing slaughter of Tutsis and liberal Hutus by extremist forces in the Rwandan army and paramilitary forces went on without respite. While many of the victims were shot, very large numbers were killed by slashing machetes ('*panga*' in Swahili), normally a common agricultural tool. Vast numbers of *pangas* had been sold to the militias in February 1994.[137] The killings appear to have been centrally directed by Rwanda's military and central government and obeyed almost without question.[138] Tens of thousands, perhaps hundreds of thousands of Hutus took part in the slaughter, many ordinary peasants who had been armed to 'kill the enemy Tutsi'.[139] No one was spared: women, children, the elderly, those seeking refuge in churches or embassies. Rwanda became, literally, a bloodbath: 40,000 bodies were recovered from Lake Victoria, which became seriously polluted as a result.[140] By mid-May, 60,000 bodies had been picked up by refuse lorries in Kigali and summarily buried.[141] Many victims of the *pangas* died slowly; there were innumerable rapes, mutilations and enormities of every kind.[142]

It seems likely – as extraordinary as this may sound – that 800,000–850,000 persons were killed in Rwanda in less than two months.[143] This estimate, by Gérard Prunier, is based in detailed demographic evidence. About 800,000 Tutsis were killed: only 130,000 survived, inside Rwanda or in Burundi.[144] In addition, between 10,000 and 30,000 moderate Hutus were killed.[145] Rwanda produced many superlatives among genocides. The rate of killing in Rwanda, over 100,000 *per week*, was probably higher than that attained by the Nazis at the peak of the Holocaust. About 86 per cent of all Tutsis, at least those living in central Africa, appear to have perished in the Rwandan genocide. Again, this apparently represents a higher percentage of deaths among a victimised group than possibly in any previous 'ethnic' genocide: about 40 per cent of Europe's Jews (including those in the Soviet Union) survived the Nazi Holocaust. About 11 per cent of the Rwandan population perished, a higher percentage than any national total apart from Pol Pot's Cambodia, where the slaughter lasted for more than three years. As a result, Rwanda's population, estimated at 7.8 million in April 1994, totalled only 7.4 million in 2002, eight years later, despite an annual population growth rate of 1.2 per cent.[146]

The response of the outside world to these horrors has rightly been criticised as appallingly inadequate, with virtually no international effort made for weeks to halt the carnage. As Samantha Power notes in her book *A Problem From Hell*, the Western powers' response was to withdraw their embassy staff and to decline to authorise more than minimal UN military involvement, whereas a few thousand men might well have been able to halt the killings.[147] This attitude had several causes. The United States had intervened in nearby Somalia in 1993–4 in a mission to re-establish order which had plainly failed, with American troops withdrawn only a few weeks before the Rwanda genocide began. Virtually no one in the American government knew anything about Rwanda, an utterly remote francophone country where the United States had no interests of any kind.[148] The Congressional Black Caucus, one of the few established interest groups which might have taken a public stand, was silent for many weeks.[149] The eyes of the world were focused on South Africa, where the peaceful end of Apartheid took place in May 1994. In contrast, virtually no Western reporters covered Rwanda.[150] President Bill Clinton and his advisers, normally sensitive to human rights issues, were anxious to avoid an unlimited military involvement or ever-mounting expense in central Africa. After Somalia, the feeling was, naturally, that America could not throw good money after bad with another ham-fisted African intervention, although the two situations were entirely different and a Western military presence in Rwanda would almost certainly have saved innumerable lives. The role of France, too, was very questionable, its aim being to preserve its influence in a francophone country by arming and supporting the regime in power, however despicable.

While overt racism certainly played no part in the attitude of the Western world towards the Rwandan genocide, it is difficult to believe that many people in the West really cared whether 100,000, or 500,000, or 800,000 perceived as illiterate savages who had contributed nothing to the world's stock of achievement and culture lived or died. An interesting experiment in fact suggests itself. If two collectors had been stationed in any shopping mall in the Western world at the time of the genocide, one raising money to stop 100,000 Tutsi children from being murdered by Hutus, the other raising money to stop 100 elephants from being slaughtered by poachers, which would collect more? If you had bet on the elephants, it is safe to say you would have put some change in your pocket.

As a result of these causes, the United States was careful not to use the term 'genocide' to describe the Rwandan situation, using all sorts of excuses to avoid employing what became known as the 'g-word'.[151] This was because genocide was recognised as a crime against humanity requiring international intervention. During the three months of the Rwandan slaughter, President Clinton never even assembled his senior advisers to discuss the situation.[152] It now seems clear that this was one of the greatest foreign policy failures of the Clinton administration, a fact that President Clinton himself admitted in 1998.[153]

The slaughter in Rwanda in 1994 was probably the closest approach to a genocide, in the commonly held meaning of the term, in the post-war era, a genocide in the strict and narrow sense in which a whole people were marked for extermination. Given its roots in an ideology of ethnic hatred widely expostulated throughout Rwandan society, it also arguably bears a closer resemblance to genocides of the era of totalitarianism, especially to Nazism, than virtually any similar event in the past half-century. Yet it also remains *sui generis* and poorly understood: for instance, many African societies are riddled with tribal hatreds, have powerful, often vicious military forces – and so on – but none has experienced a genocide on a similar scale. The Rwandan horrors deserve continuing study for what they reveal about the potentiality for murderous violence in the contemporary world.

The aftermath of the Rwandan genocide was also unexpected. Extraordinarily, the Tutsi-dominated Rwandan Patriotic Front was able to launch a successful attack on Rwanda, seizing power after a 14-week campaign in July 1994. This led to the flight of 2 million Hutus to Zaire, where they remained until 1996. Despite continuing violence, especially conflicts with neighbouring Zaire, a measure of calm returned to Rwanda and in 2000 Paul Kagame was elected the first Tutsi President of the country. In September 1998 Jean Kambanda, Prime Minister of Rwanda in the period of the genocide, was sentenced to life imprisonment for his part in these events by a UN Tribunal. He was the first person convicted under the United Nations' 1948 Convention on Genocide. In April 1998, 22 persons were executed in Rwanda for their role in the genocide, but few of the thousands of others who took part in the slaughter have been brought to justice. Rather remarkably, in June 2001 a Belgian court convicted two Rwandan Roman Catholic nuns and two other Rwandans for their role in the 1994 genocide, but there appears to be little will or determination, either in Rwanda or elsewhere, to pursue many other murderers involved in Rwanda's atrocities.

The Indians of the Amazon Basin

A different kind of genocide has been alleged about the Indians of the Amazon Basin in Brazil. Most examples of alleged genocide or mass murder have occurred during wartime, or occasionally in the midst of a civil war. In contrast, the decimation of the Indians of the Amazon Basin, according to civil rights advocates, has taken place in the course of the economic development of the area.[154] Beginning around 1973, in order to facilitate economic development, the Brazilian government systematically destroyed the traditional forest environment of Indian tribes such as the Yanomamos. A gold rush, and the possibility of jobs for the impoverished inhabitants of Brazil's slums, triggered an invasion by outsiders virtually uncontrolled by the government. As a result of deliberate massacre, the usual psychological effects of the impact of the West on preliterate peoples, and, above all, the introduction of previously unknown diseases, the population of Indians in the north-west rain forests of Brazil apparently declined drastically. On one estimate, the number of Yanomamos declined from 15,000 in 1985 to less than 8,000 in 1995.[155] A massacre of 23 Indians by settlers allegedly occurred in September 1993.[156] The Indian population of the Rondônia area of Brazil declined from an estimated 30,000 in 1950 to 5,000 by 1990.[157] International protests in the 1980s led to an official change in Brazilian government policy in 1988 in the interests of halting development in the rain forest areas and recognising the rights of the Indians; in the same year, charges of genocide were brought against five men who allegedly 'intended ... to exterminate' the Xarcariba Indians of Minas Gerais.[158] As the fate of Yanomamos shows, however, these protective measures have not necessarily been effective. The Yanomamos (according to a highly sympathetic account) are said to be among 'the most primitive, culturally intact people in existence in the world. They are literally a stone age tribe ... Their numbering one, two, and more than two.'[159] Few such tribes remain intact anywhere in the world today, and one might readily imagine the enormous pressures to disregard them and their societies in the interests of economic development. What sets their fate apart from that of millions of other 'primitive' peoples over the past 500 years is that they unquestionably enjoy the sympathy of the outside world, with many advocacy groups around the world protesting at what one critic described as 'the last days of Eden'.[160]

Conclusion

Although the twentieth century has been described as an 'age of genocide', this description seems accurate only in a limited sense. When the ideologically motivated slaughters of the post-1945 period discussed in the previous chapter – all of which were Marxist massacres under Stalin or Asian Communist leaders – are put to one side, what remains is a ragbag of ethnic cleansing, mass killings in wartime (often in a civil war) and Third World slaughters. Contrary to what one might suppose in advance, these genocides and democides appear to have no real or predictable pattern, and were certainly occasioned by no single source. Virtually every tropical African country is an artificial, post-1880 creation, its boundaries determined from Europe and coinciding with no real tribal divisions. Yet brutal post-independence tribal wars or slaughters have not been as common as one might suppose, and arguably only in Rwanda did real genocide occur. Murderous dictators, many clearly psychopathic, have emerged nearly everywhere in the Third World, and the military has played a key role almost everywhere, yet only among a select number of regimes has anything like genocide occurred. In 1900 there were fewer than 50 sovereign countries in the world, nearly 20 in Latin America. There were only eight independent countries in all of Africa and Asia. In 2003 the United Nations had 191 member states, many impoverished, many virtually unknown in the Western world. It is safe to say that a majority of people in the English-speaking West have never heard of such countries as Belize, Burkina Faso, Djibouti, Equatorial Guinea, Guinea-Bissau, Kyrgyzstan, Micronesia, Palau, Sao Tomé and Principe, or Vanuatu, all of which are member states of the UN, and could not find them on a map.

There is more than ample room, in a world with a multiplicity of sovereign entities, many ruled by dictators or one-party regimes, many wracked by deep ethnic or religious hatreds, for genocides and mass murders on an ever-recurring scale. Yet the point needs to be made that these have occurred only with surprising infrequency. There may well be a constant 'background noise' of mass violence in many of these states, but the inarguable cases of mass slaughter or genocide are, when one considers the matter, notable for their infrequency rather than the reverse.

Within the developed world, there has been since the end of the Cold War a clear trend to greater democracy and a categorically greater sensitivity to human rights – so much so that the pendulum may arguably have swung too far, in areas such as the control of economic migrants posing as 'asylum-seekers', in the other direction. The institutionalisation of democracy throughout the developed world, possible only since the fall of Communism, is arguably the greatest single step which can be taken towards a peaceful world, for it is a striking fact that no democracies have ever gone to war against one another.[161] While war is not invariably the cause of genocide, in the modern world genocides have often been the product, direct or indirect, of wars, while democratic government, with its emphasis on human rights, is not often the breeding ground of mass slaughter. The past quarter century has also seen a marked increase throughout the West in the sensitivity of intellectuals and opinion-makers to genocide or any hint of genocide. The fundamental shift, for example, in perceptions of 'ethnic cleansing', seen as recently as the late 1940s (or later) as a relatively humane approach to ethnic hostilities created by border changes or the fortunes of war, is an example of this, as are the network of international courts to try cases of genocide, the interest by the major powers in bringing (arguably only some) genocidal leaders and perpetrators to justice, and the enormous, perhaps excessive, interest in the Jewish Holocaust and other modern slaughters.

If an accurate view of the post-1945 situation is that both instances of genocide and the conditions in which they are engendered have diminished rather than increased, there is obviously little room for complacency that the world has truly reformed. The possible causes of mass slaughter are only too evident, especially from the deadly combination of religious fundamentalism and terrorism. Yet there are also, quite surprisingly, many grounds for believing that the world has learned a lesson.

Notes and references

1   Mark Kramer, 'Introduction', in Philip Ther and Ana Siljak, eds., *Redrawing Nations: Ethnic Cleansing in East-Central Europe 1944–1948* (Lanham, Maryland, 2001), p.1. See also Andrew Bell-Fialkoff, *Ethnic Cleansing* (New York, 1996).

2   *Ibid.*

3   *Ibid.*, p.3. Obviously there were examples of distinctive ethnic/religious minorities forced to leave their homeland earlier than this, for instance the numerous medieval expulsions of Jews (eg from England in 1290 and Spain in 1492) and Huguenots from France in 1685, but the application of 'ethnic cleansing' in the context of the modern nation-state only came later.

4   These figures, probably the most accurate of several estimates, are derived from the map 'Ethnic Cleansing in Europe, 1944–1948', facing p.1 in Ther and Siljak, *op.cit.* See also 'The Expulsion of Germans from Poland and Czechoslovakia', in Norman M. Naimark, *Fires of Hatred: Ethnic Cleansing in Twentieth-Century Europe* (Cambridge, Mass., 2001), pp.108–38; Alfred M. De Zayas, *Nemesis at Potsdam: The Anglo-Americans and the Expulsion of the Germans: Background, Execution, Consequences* (London, 1977), and *idem*, *A Terrible Revenge: The Ethnic Cleansing of the East European Germans, 1944–1950* (New York, 1994); and Radomir Luza, *The Transfer of the Sudeten Germans: A Study of Czech-German Relations, 1933–1962* (London, 1964),

5   For instance, Israel W. Charny, ed., *Encyclopedia of Genocide* (two volumes, Santa Barbara, Cal., 1999), mentions the expulsion of the Sudeten Germans

in less than half a page (p.297, based on 'Press Reports' rather than in an article written by an authority) and makes no mention whatever of other German expellees, Poles, Ukrainians or Belorussians among the ethnically cleansed. Frank Chalk and Kurt Jonassohn, eds., *The History and Sociology of Genocide: Analysis and Case Studies* (New Haven, Conn., 1990) omits any mention of these expulsions.

6 De Zayas, *op.cit.*, pp.38–9.

7 *Ibid.*, p.40.

8 *Ibid.*, pp.238–9.

9 Cited in *ibid.*, p.11.

10 *Ibid.*

11 Cited in *ibid.*, p.16.

12 *Ibid.*, esp. pp.80–4, and Krystyna Kersten, 'Forced Migration and the Transformation of Polish Society in the Post-war Period', in Ther and Siljak, *op.cit.*, pp.75–86. See also the other essays in this collection on this subject, *ibid.*, pp.75–86.

13 Naimark, *op.cit.*, p.114.

14 *Ibid.*, p.120. About 200,000 Sudeten Germans remained.

15 *Ibid.* See also the relevant essays in Ther and Siljak, *op.cit.*, pp.197–260; and Luza, *Transfer*, pp.267–316.

16 Luza, *op.cit.*, pp.293–300.

17 Orest Subtelny, 'Expulsion, Resettlement, Civil Strife: The Fate of Poland's Ukrainians, 1944–1957', in Ther and Siljak, *op.cit.*, p.155. See also Jerzy Kochanowski, 'Gathering Poles into Poland: Forced Migration from Poland's Former Eastern Territories', and Marek Jasiak, 'Overcoming Ukrainian Resistance: The Deportation of Ukrainians within Poland in 1947', in *ibid.*

18 Subtelny, *op.cit.*, p.164.

19 For a cogent defence of the Sudeten German position, however, see De Zayas, *op.cit.*, pp.17–37. De Zayas points out that incorporating several million Germans into the Czechoslovak state ran contrary to the spirit of national self-determination espoused by Woodrow Wilson, and that the Sudeten minority had been subject to considerable discrimination even in democratic Czechoslovakia.

20 See the essays on this subject in Ther and Siljak, *op.cit.*, pp.263–325.

21 Ana Siljak, Conclusion, in *ibid.*, p.327.

22 There are innumerable accounts of the birth of Israel, only a handful of which can be cited here. These include Howard M. Sachar, *A History of*

Israel (Oxford, 1976), pp.330–8; Ahron Bregman, *Israel's Wars, 1947–93* (London, 2000), pp.1–26; and Mark Tessler, *A History of the Israeli-Palestinian Conflict* (Bloomington, Ind., 1994), pp.273–83. On the Partition and its aftermath, see Benny Morris, *Righteous Victims: A History of the Zionist-Arab Conflict, 1881–2001* (New York, 2001), pp.180–9.

23 Bregman, *op.cit.*, p.9.

24 Gerald Fleming, *Hitler and the Final Solution* (Berkeley, Cal., 1994), pp.102, 104.

25 Benny Morris, *op.cit.*, p.166; Zvi Elpeleg, *The Grand Mufti: Haj Amin Al-Hussani, Founder of the Palestinian National Movement* (London, 1993), pp.64–73.

26 Bregman, *op.cit.*, p.7.

27 Henry Cattan, *The Palestine Question* (London, 2000), pp.78–9.

28 Benny Morris, *The Birth of the Palestinian Refugee Problem, 1947–1949* (Cambridge, 1989), pp.10–15.

29 *Ibid.*

30 Morris, *Birth*, pp.41–57.

31 *Ibid.*, p.58.

32 *Ibid.*, p.287.

33 Tessler, pp.282–3, citing Ann Moseley Lesch's report, 'Closed Borders, Disabled Lives: Palestinian Writings'.

34 Efraim Karsh, *Fabricating Israeli History: The 'New Historians'* (London, 1997), pp.37–68. For the view of Zionist design, see Norman G. Finkelstein, *Image and Reality of the Israel-Palestine Conflict* (London, 1995), esp. pp.51–87.

35 Morris, *Birth*, pp.297–8.

36 *Ibid.*, p.297.

37 *Ibid.*, pp.275–85.

38 *Ibid.*, p.259.

39 The 'right of return' of the refugees still remains a very visible demand among hardline Palestinian writers. See, for instance, Naseer Aruri, ed., *Palestinian Refugees: The Right of Return* (London, 2001). Many pro-Zionists regard the emigration of the Palestinians as, in effect, part of an exchange of population in which perhaps 1 million Sephardi Jews from the Afro-Asian world left their homes for Israel during the period 1948–57. Many of these, especially Jews from Egypt and Iraq, were driven out by nationalist Arab governments in conflict with Israel.

40 Larry Collins and Dominique Lapierre, *Freedom at Midnight* (London, 1975), p.101. This remains the most vivid and best-known account of Indian independence and the turmoil which accompanied it. See also Ian Talbot and Gurhapal Singh, eds., *Region and Partition: Bengal, Punjab and the Partition of the Subcontinent* (Oxford, 1999); Gopa Dashkola, *Stern Reckoning: The Survey of the Partition of India* (Delhi, 1992); Sukeshi Kamra, *Bearing Witness: Partition, India, and the End of the Raj* (Calgary, 2002); and Paul R. Brass, 'The Partition of India and Retributive Genocide in the Punjab, 1946–47: Means, Methods, and Purposes', in *Journal of Genocide Research*, Vol.5, No.1 (March 2003).

41 Collins and Lapierre, *op.cit.*, p.102. Like many other ultra-nationalists, Jinnah was thus highly marginal to the group he championed.

42 C.N. Vakil, *Economic Consequences of Divided India: A Study of the Economy of India and Pakistan* (Bombay, 1950), p.71. Population figures are for 1941.

43 The idea of 'Pakistan' formally originated at a dinner at London's Waldorf Hotel, on the Strand, in 1933. It grew out of a typed proposal by a Muslim Indian graduate at Cambridge, Rahmat Ali, written earlier in 1933, in which he named the proposed state 'Pakistan' from the names of the Punjab, Kashmir, Sind, the North-West Frontier and Baluchistan, areas of high Muslim population in British India.

44 Collins and Lapierre, *op.cit.*, p.102.

45 Vakil, *op.cit.*, p.71.

46 Collins and Lapierre, *op.cit.*, pp.25–6.

47 *Ibid.*, p.29.

48 Vakil, *op.cit.*, p.71.

49 Collins and Lapierre, *op.cit.*, p.319.

50 Vakil, *op.cit.*, p.71.

51 Satya M. Rai, *Partition of the Punjab: A Study of its Effects on the Politics and Administration of the Punjab (I), 1947–56* (London, 1965), pp.72–3.

52 Collins and Lapierre, *op.cit.*, pp.298–9.

53 *Ibid.*, p.301.

54 *Ibid.*, p.286.

55 Vakil, *op.cit.*, pp.406–7.

56 Collins and Lapierre, *op.cit.*, p.170.

57 Ian Talbot, 'Literature and the Human Drama of the 1947 Partition', in Talbot and Singh, *op.cit.*, p.238.

58 On which see Gurdit Singh and Carol C. Fair, 'The Partition of Punjab: Its Impact upon Sikh Social and Cultural Space', in *ibid.*, pp.253–68.

59 John P. Thorp, 'Bangladesh in Genocide', in Charny, *op.cit.*, pp.115–16; Wardatul Akmam, 'Atrocities Against Humanity During the Liberation War in Bangladesh: A Case of Genocide', *Journal of Genocide Research*, Volume 4 (December 2002), pp.543–60.

60 David Martin, *General Amin* (London, 1974), p.14. On Amin, see also Jan Jelmert Jorgensen, *Uganda: A Modern History* (London, 1981), pp.267–330; T.V. Sathyamurthy, *The Political Development of Uganda: 1900–1986* (Aldershot, 1986), pp.609–57; Steven L. Jacobs, 'Idi Amin', in Charny, *op.cit.*, p.349; and Daniel Chirot, *Modern Tyrants: The Power and Prevalence of Evil in Our Age* (New York, 1994), pp.373–93.

61 Jorgensen, *Uganda*, p.320. Other accounts deny that Amin served in the Second World War (eg Martin, *op.cit.*, p.15).

62 Martin, *ibid.*, pp.16–23. Amin had four wives (*ibid.*, p.17).

63 Jorgensen, *op.cit.*, pp.213–66.

64 Martin, *op.cit.*, pp.11–13.

65 *Ibid.*, p.12.

66 Jorgensen, *op.cit.*, p.288. Other East African states had also expelled their Asian mercantile class.

67 See the list in *ibid.*, pp.310–12.

68 Jacobs, in Charny, *op.cit.*, p.349, places the figure of Amin's victims at 'more than 300,000'. This is echoed by Chirot, who states that 'by late 1978, at least 300,000 had been killed. Hundreds of thousands more had fled.'

69 On Saddam, see Geoff Simons, *Iraq: From Sumer to Saddam* (Houndmills, 1996), pp.271–381, and Samantha Power, *A Problem from Hell: America and the Age of Genocide* (New York, 2002), pp.171–246.

70 *Ibid.*, pp.305–17. Simons, *op.cit.*, (p.317) estimates that 300,000 Iraqis and between 420,000 and 580,000 Iranians died. 15,000–20,000 Shi'ite Muslims were expelled from Iraq (*ibid.*, p.309).

71 Steven L. Jacobs, 'Saddam Hussain', in Charny, *op.cit.*, p.515; Samantha Power, *A Problem from Hell*, *op.cit.*

72 Chirot, *op.cit.*, p.304.

73 John F. Burns, 'How Many People Has Hussain Killed?', *New York Times*, 26 January 2003, cited by Professor R.J. Rummel on the H-Genocide website. Rummel estimates that Saddam probably murdered 350,000–400,000 Iraqis.

74 Another appalling situation which should be mentioned here is the fate of

Christians in the Sudan. See the Review Article by Paul Bartrop, 'Focus on Sudan' (*Journal of Genocide Research*, Volume 3 (June 2001, pp.285–91)) for a recent discussion of the literature.

75 On the Biafran conflict, see Frederick Forsyth, *The Biafra Story* (Harmondsworth, 1969); Ntieyong U. Akpan, *The Struggle for Secession, 1966–1970: A Personal Account of the Nigerian Civil War* (London, 1972); Zdenek Cervenka, *The Nigerian War, 1967–1970* (Frankfurt-am-Main, 1971); and A.H.M. Kirk-Greene, *Crisis and Conflict in Nigeria: A Documentary Sourcebook, 1966–1970* (two volumes, Oxford, 1971).

76 Forsyth, *op.cit.*, p.112.

77 *Ibid.*

78 Torben Jorgensen and Eric Markusen, 'Ibos, Genocide of (1966–1969)', in Charny, *op.cit.*, p.347.

79 For instance, in R. Ernest Dupuy and Trevor N. Dupuy, *The Collins Encyclopedia of Military History* (London, 1998), p.1447.

80 Jorgensen and Markussen, *op.cit.*

81 Quoted in Forsyth, *op.cit.*, p.217. Of course, in a sense he was quite correct: the Allies, especially Britain, deliberately blockaded Germany and its associated powers during both world wars with the aim of bringing about mass starvation if possible. No one questioned this at the time, and this policy certainly contributed to the Allied victory in 1918.

82 *Ibid.*, p.209.

83 *Ibid.*, p.210.

84 See the examples alleged by a Nigerian government spokesman (a physician), cited in Kirk-Greene, *Crisis and Conflict*, Volume 2, pp.300–1.

85 Cited in Forsyth, *op.cit.*, p.221.

86 On the Bangladesh war, see Richard Sisson and Leo E. Rose, *War and Secession: Pakistan, India, and the Creation of Bangladesh* (Berkeley, Cal., 1990); Chalk and Jonassohn, *History and Sociology of Genocide*, pp.394–7; John P. Thorp, 'Bangladesh, Genocide in', in Charny, *op.cit.*, pp.115–16; Wardatul Akmam, 'Atrocities Against Humanity During the Liberation War in Bangladesh: A Case of Genocide', *Journal of Genocide Research*, Volume 4 (December 2002), pp.543–60.

87 Thorp, *op.cit.*, p.116.

88 Chalk and Jonassohn, *op.cit.*, p.396. The figure of 1–3 million dead is repeated in Akman, *op.cit.*, p.549.

89 Thorp, *op.cit.*, p.115. Akman, *op.cit.*, claims that 200,000 women were raped.

90 On these events, see J.D. Legge, *Sukarno: A Political Biography* (London, 1972), esp. pp.395–409; John Hughes, *The End of Sukarno: A Coup that Misfired: A Purge that Ran Wild* (London, 1968), esp. pp.184–96; Arnold C. Brackman, *The Communist Collapse in Indonesia* (New York, 1969); Chalk and Jonassohn, *Genocide*, pp.378–83; Robert Cribb, 'Indonesia, Genocide in', Charny, *op.cit.*, pp.354–6; and *idem*, 'Genocide in Indonesia, 1965–1966', *Journal of Genocide Research* (Volume 3, June 2001), pp.219–40.

91 Sukarno's name at birth was Kusno Sosro Sukarno; his mother was a Balinese Hindu (Legge, *Sukarno*, pp.16–17).

92 Hughes, *End of Sukarno*, pp.180–1.

93 *Ibid.*, p.89; Chalk and Jonassohn, *op.cit.*, pp.381–2, citing Harold Crouch, *The Army and Politics in Indonesia* (Ithaca, New York, 1978).

94 *Ibid.*

95 Hughes, *op.cit.*, p.188.

96 *Ibid.*, pp.189–91.

97 Chalk and Jonassohn, *op.cit.*, pp.380–3.

98 See the interesting discussion in Brackman, *Communist Collapse*, pp.175–203.

99 John G. Taylor, *East Timor: The Price of Freedom* (London, 1999), pp.1–13. See also 'East Timor' in 'East Timor, Genocide and Denial in', in Charny, *op.cit.*, p.191–4.

100 Taylor, *op.cit.*, p.210.

101 *Ibid.*, pp.106–10; Charny, *op.cit.*, p.193.

102 On the history of Yugoslavia and conflict and ethnic cleansing in the former Yugoslavia, see Norman M. Naimark, 'The Wars of Yugoslav Succession', in *idem*, *op.cit.*, pp.138–84; R.J. Crampton, *The Balkans Since the Second World War* (London, 2002), esp. pp.11–37, 113–15, and 239–92; Sabrina P. Ramet, *Balkan Babel: The Disintegration of Yugoslavia from the Death of Tito to the War for Kosovo* (Boulder, Col., 1999); Tim Judah, *Kosovo: War and Revenge* (New Haven, Conn., 2002); and Power, *op.cit.*, pp.247–328, 391–474.

103 Map, 'Regions of the Former Yugoslavia', in Eric Markusen, 'Ethnic Cleansing and Genocide in Bosnia and Croatia, 1991–1995', in Israel W. Charny, *op.cit.*, p.636.

104 Judah, *op.cit.*, pp.50–2.

105 Markussen, *op.cit.*, p.642.

106 Judah, *op.cit.*, esp. pp.61–98.

107 Crampton, *op.cit.*, p.274.

108 Although these massacres occurred just a few years ago, in Europe, and just before a cease-fire, the casualty figures in Kosovo appear to be subject to even greater margins of error than are normal. As of November 1999, the Hague Tribunal investigating Kosovo atrocities had found only 2,108 bodies (Naimark, *op.cit.*, p.182). The estimate of '10,000 to more than 100,000' is found in Israel Charny and Steven L. Jacobs, 'Ethnic Cleansing and Genocide in Kosovo and a Controversial Major International Response by NATO, 1999', in Charny, *op.cit.*, p.644, and is consistent with other estimates reported in Naimark, *ibid.*, pp.181–2.

109 Naimark, *ibid.*, p.183. Naimark is careful to note, however (n.172, p.239), that 'it is very hard to know exactly how many have died' in Yugoslavia, and stresses that 'journalists tend to exaggerate the numbers killed'.

110 *Ibid.*, pp.167–70.

111 *Ibid.*, p.168.

112 *Ibid.*, pp.167–72. Estimates of Bosnian women raped range from 20,000–50,000 (*ibid.*, p.169).

113 *Ibid.*, p.174.

114 Philip Johnston, Peter Day and Sean O'Neill, 'Secret Plans for the New Partition of Ireland' (London), *Daily Telegraph*, 2 January 2003, p.6. This report was based on previously confidential British Cabinet papers which were released under the 'Thirty Year Rule', wherein most confidential British government documents are made available to researchers after 30 years. In the mid-1950s Eamon De Valera, Ireland's formidably nationalistic leader, stated that he 'was optimistic about a united Ireland because "even exchanges of population were not impossible these days",' apparently having in mind that the Protestants of Northern Ireland could be removed to Great Britain! (Tim Pat Coogan, *De Valera: Long Fellow, Long Shadow* (London, 1995), p.644).

115 *Ibid.*

116 Markussen, *op.cit.*, p.643.

117 For a balanced but rather critical account of NATO's activities, see Power, *op.cit.*, pp.391–473.

118 *Ibid.*, p.472.

119 An excellent introduction to this subject is Gérard Prunier, *The Rwanda Crisis: History of a Genocide* (London, 1995). See also Alain Destexhe, *Rwanda and Genocide in the Twentieth Century* (London, 1995); Linda Mervyn, *A People Betrayed: The Role of the West in Rwanda's Genocide* (London, 2000); Arthur Jay Klinghoffer, ed., *The International Dimension*

of Genocide in Rwanda (Houndmills, 1998); and Power, *op.cit.*, pp.329–89.

120 Prunier, *op.cit.*, p.4.

121 Destexhe, *op.cit.*, p.37.

122 *Ibid.*

123 Prunier, *op.cit.*, pp.5–9.

124 Destexhe, *op.cit.*, p.40.

125 Thus, attempts to blame the Germans and Belgians for the origins of the Rwanda genocide (as in Destexhe, *op.cit.*, pp.40–1) seem misdirected.

126 *Ibid.*, pp.41–4.

127 Prunier, *op.cit.*, pp.41–5.

128 Destexhe, *op.cit.*, pp.44–7.

129 Prunier, *op.cit.*, pp.57–61.

130 *Ibid.*, pp.74–6.

131 *Ibid.*, pp.90–120.

132 Destexhe, *op.cit.*, p.46.

133 *Ibid.*, pp.29–30. There were very few independent sources of information in Rwanda.

134 *Ibid.*, p.29.

135 Prunier, *op.cit.*, pp.220–8. In 1972 in Burundi, an estimated 100,000–300,000 Hutus were killed by Tutsis, in retaliation for a Hutu-led rebellion in which several thousand were killed (René Lemarchand, 'Rwanda and Burundi, Genocide in', in Charny, *op.cit.*, pp.508–9). This was obviously one of the contributory factors in the 1994 Rwandan genocide.

136 *Ibid.*, pp.229–30.

137 *Ibid.*, p.243.

138 *Ibid.*, pp.245–6.

139 *Ibid.*, p.247. The Rwandan army and militia probably numbered 90,000 (*ibid.*, p.243).

140 *Ibid.*, p.255.

141 *Ibid.*

142 *Ibid.*, p.256.

143 *Ibid.*, p.265. Some credible estimates are even higher, in the range of 950,000–1 million.

144 *Ibid.*, pp.264–5.

145 *Ibid.*

146 Statistics from the *Time Almanac 2003* (Boston, Mass., 2002), p.848.

147 Powers, *op.cit.*

148 Powers (*ibid.*, p.330) cites staff officers at the Joint Chiefs of Staff in the Pentagon who, on learning of the 6 April 1994 plane crash, asked 'Is it Hutu and Tutsi or Tutu and Hutsi?'.

149 *Ibid.*, p.376.

150 *Ibid.*, p.375.

151 Power, *op.cit.*, pp.358–64; Klinghoffer, *op.cit.*, pp.91–100.

152 Power, *op.cit.*, p.370.

153 *Ibid.*, p.386.

154 See Chalk and Jonassohn, *op.cit.*, pp.412–14; 'Hands Across the World: Yanomamo Indians' (website as Indian-cultures.com/Cultures/yanomamo. html), which contains references to numerous other advocacy groups and relevant works.

155 'Hands Across the World', *ibid.*

156 *Ibid.*

157 Chalk and Jonassohn, *op.cit.*, p.414.

158 *Ibid.*

159 'Hands Across the World', *op.cit.*

160 Cited in Chalk and Jonassohn, *op.cit.*, p.414. The website on the Yanomamos cited here lists advocacy groups concerned with their fate in Brazil, London, Massachusetts and California. It is also necessary to make the point that the Edenesque depiction of such tribes might well be highly problematical. The Yanomamos, for instance, 'cremate their dead, then crush and drink their bones in a final ceremony intended to keep their loved ones with them forever'. Young boys 'begin at an early age to practice archery skills, often with a lizard tied to a string' (Hands Across the World', *op.cit.*).

161 This proposition has received a good deal of discussion in some political science circles in recent years. For a full examination of the issues, see Spencer R. Weart, *Never at War: Why Democracies Will Not Fight One Another* (New Haven, Conn., 1998).

CHAPTER 6

• • • • • • • • • • • • • • •

Outlawing genocide and the lessons of history

If the period since the Second World War has been – as some observers maintain – an age of genocide, it must be realised that it is also an age in which, for the first time in history, genocide has been outlawed and penalised by the international community. During the past 10 or 15 years, these efforts at outlawing genocide appear to be increasingly successful, and are certainly taken more seriously than ever before. However, many barbaric lapses have tragically occurred.

It almost goes without saying that serious efforts to define and penalise genocide began with, and as a result of, the Holocaust. Following the Armenian genocide of 1915, there were serious but largely unsuccessful efforts to bring its perpetrators to justice, but no successful moves were ever made by any international body to outlaw genocide, and nor did the great powers ever attempt to do so. In part this was because, except for the Armenian case, no clear-cut examples of genocide occurred in the Western world prior to the Second World War, and in part because, with the arguable exception of a brief period of international cooperation and conciliation in the latter 1920s, the major powers always reserved to themselves the right to behave as necessity and *realpolitik* dictated, if these powers were not indeed overtly totalitarian. It is, however, perfectly true that international conventions and treaties from 1899 onwards attempted to outlaw war as well as 'crimes against humanity', a term which was used by the Allies in international discussion and treaties about the Armenian genocide and alleged war crimes carried out by Germany during the First World War.[1]

Nevertheless, the experience of the Jewish Holocaust changed everything and, it is likely, will for ever determine and delimit all discussion of genocide and all attempts to define and penalise the crime. The singularity of the Holocaust was probably apparent to highly intelligent observers while it was occurring, for instance to Winston Churchill, who famously commented in July 1944 (in a marginal note, written to Anthony Eden) that 'there is no doubt that this is probably the greatest and most horrible single crime in the whole history of the world'. The liberation of the German concentration camps by the Allied armies in the spring of 1945, with the resultant photographs and newsreels of piles of corpses and of the living skeletons who survived, for ever changed Western man's perceptions of the limits of human evil. As noted in a previous chapter, the Nuremberg Tribunal of leading Nazis was, initially, in large measure a trial of Nazi Germany's surviving top leaders for starting the Second World War by unprovoked aggression. For this reason, Hermann Goering, who had virtually no direct role in the Holocaust, was the chief defendant at Nuremberg, while the first article of indictment against the Nuremberg defendants was that they had engaged in the 'preparations, initiation, [and] waging' of 'a war of aggression ... in violation of international treaties'. The graphic evidence of Nazi genocide and other atrocities carried out by the Hitler regime at Nuremberg was, however, so traumatic that Nuremberg *became* a trial about the Holocaust: indeed, it became the archetypal trial of the perpetrators of genocide, despite the fact that the defendants included only a minority of men who had taken any direct part in the Holocaust, and failed to include (apart from Hitler, Himmler and Heydrich, all dead, or the missing Eichmann) any commandants of the extermination camps or senior leaders of the SS death machine. Some of the most appalling of these were tried and condemned at subsequent trials, but Nuremberg itself did not begin primarily as a trial about genocide, although it quickly became one.

The effects of the Holocaust were so shocking and disturbing, that it was possible, soon after the war, for the United Nations to outlaw genocide. This did not, however, happen by accident, but through the efforts of dedicated activists. Among these, one man stands out. This man coined the word 'genocide', and was perhaps more responsible than anyone else for bringing the concept of genocide into the mainstream, especially in the realm of international law. He was Raphael Lemkin (1900–59). Lemkin was a Polish-born Jewish lawyer whose life was a rather sad one.[2] Prior to the Second World War, he worked for the Polish government and, as early as 1933, attempted to convince the League of Nations to adopt a ban on mass slaughter, without success. Lemkin fled to America in 1941. In 1944, in his book *Axis Ruler in Occupied Europe*, Lemkin coined the term 'genocide' to describe Nazi policy towards the Jews and other minorities (Lemkin's family in Poland perished). He was significant, if not instrumental, in conceiving the idea of the post-war Nuremberg Tribunal of Nazi war criminals. In 1948, with the help of United Nations General Assembly President H.V. Evatt of Australia, he was chiefly responsible for the adoption of the 'Convention for the Prevention and Punishment of Genocide', the first and most important international law outlawing genocide. (Extracts of this are reprinted below in an Appendix.) Lemkin's record represents a truly incredible set of achievements for an immigrant to America with no resources or organisational assistance, and Lemkin was nominated at least four times for the Nobel Peace Prize. Yet no rewards came his way. He died, penniless and unmarried, in a shabby one-room apartment in Manhattan's Upper West Side at the age of only 58, 'saddened unbearably by the failure of his adopted country to ratify the "Genocide Convention" '.[3]

During the 1950s Lemkin worked tirelessly, single-handedly and at his own expense, to further the anti-genocide cause, yet remained virtually unknown and without influence. Amazingly, and disturbingly, he could not find a publisher for his three-volume *History of Genocide*, which exists (still unpublished) only in typescript, as do many of his other manuscripts.[4] If anyone ever died just too soon, it was Raphael Lemkin. A year or two after his death the Eichmann Trial occurred, which brought the Holocaust into a world-wide spotlight and initiated the growing tidal wave of works on the Holocaust and other genocides. Had he lived longer, it seems highly likely that Lemkin would have become internationally renowned (and, in all likelihood, a recipient of the Nobel Peace Prize and many other honours) with, doubtless, publishers falling over themselves to produce his works and give him a platform. The concept of 'genocide', the world of genocide research, and international sanctions against genocide, all arguably owe more to

Raphael Lemkin than to any other person: if ever there was a 'prophet without honour', Lemkin was this man.

Despite the tragic failures of Lemkin's career, in 1948 the United Nations voted to outlaw genocide, which it did in the Convention on the Prevention and Punishment of the Crime of Genocide. The UN General Assembly initially passed a resolution, in 1946, proclaiming that 'genocide was the deprivation of the right to existence of a group in the same fashion that homicide was the denial of the right to exist of an individual'.[5] There was considerable debate among the UN member states on the desirability of a more sweeping resolution, especially from the United States and the Soviet Union, both of which feared – for different reasons – that it would be used invidiously against them.[6] The final resolution, approved by the UN General Assembly in December 1948, was surprisingly broad. For instance, although the 'intent to destroy, in whole or in part' a definable group, became the touchstone of genocide, no definition of 'motive' was included in the final draft for fear that a listing of specific motives would allow any future defendant at a genocide trial to claim that he acted out of a different motive from that enumerated, and hence be acquitted.[7]

The debate over the treaty was also surprisingly wide-ranging, with many of the queries brought up recently in academic debate about the meaning of genocide being raised at the time. Despite Stalinism, the Soviet and Eastern bloc delegates did not act in a notably negative or tendentious way concerning the adoption of that kind of a treaty as such, although the Soviet Union wished the definition of genocide 'to be exclusively related to Nazi crimes' (they did not get their way), while 'political groups' were deliberately excluded from the final resolution.[8] Many other aspects of the 1948 Convention (which came into force in January 1951) have been repeatedly criticised, for instance the fact that signatory nations themselves are responsible for enforcing the provisions of the Convention, the lack of an international penal tribunal to try genocide cases, and the lack of any distinction between gradations of seriousness in the Convention's definition of genocide.[9]

It is no exaggeration, moreover, to say that the 1948 UN Resolution was forgotten, if it did not actually become a dead letter, for at least the next 30 years, and almost never figured in any aspect of public debate on the committing of atrocities, past or present. There is, for instance, no evidence that any aspect of the Eichmann trial of 1960–2 proceeded with the 1948 UN resolution in mind in any more than a tangential and background sense, his kidnapping, arrest, trial and execution being justified by the Israeli government (with the approval of most of the world) in the name of the Jewish people, as just retribution for his role in the Holocaust. An international trial for Eichmann would have been out of the question and automatically rejected by the Israeli government: the *point* of the trial was that while the Jews of wartime Europe had been powerless, by 1960, the Jewish people had been empowered, with the ability to punish their mortal enemies, by the creation of the State of Israel. Many reasons can be given for the fact that the UN Convention was forgotten. Broadly speaking, there were no well-recognised or infamous examples of what would now be termed 'genocide' anywhere in the world between about 1950 and the 1970s, the obvious exception to this being the mass political killings in the Communist bloc. However, so long as the Cold War remained the central political fact of the world, a seemingly permanent division of the world, and so long as the Soviet Union, armed with nuclear weapons, and Communist China were great powers, nothing could be done effectively to penalise political killings in the Communist bloc. On the contrary, after Stalin's death in 1953, it appeared that the Soviet Union was slowly but surely moving out of a regime based on terrorism and mass killings into one where the Gulags were gradually reduced if not emptied. While the West certainly based its foreign policy, broadly speaking, around the strengthening and augmentation of human rights, this mainly took the form of hostility to Communist totalitarianism.

With the 1970s, and more emphatically from the 1980s, however, this began to change, and the concept of a genocide began to enter the Western world's mainstream discourse for the first time since the late 1940s. Among the causes of this change were the growing centrality to Western consciousness of the Holocaust, now universally internalised as the essence of evil, the Civil Rights movement in the United States and the effects of anti-colonialism in international affairs, and the example of the Pol Pot massacres of 1975–9, slaughters which appeared to rival the Holocaust in awfulness, that occurred with little or no effective international protest. The turning point, however, was probably the end of the Cold War in the 1985–91 period, and the replacement of the Soviet Union and its satellites by democratic regimes. Once this occurred, the central aim of American foreign policy may be seen as having altered, in a perceptible fashion, from the containment of Communism to the protection of human rights by opposing those smaller totalitarian regimes which were, for whatever reason, regarded by the United States as inimical to its interests. In 1986 (under Ronald Reagan) the United States finally ratified the UN Genocide Convention, something it had pointedly refused to do during the previous 36 years.[10]

American ratification was hedged with reservations, for instance one forbidding the submission of any case to the International Court of Justice without specific American consent. These reservations were necessary to placate conservative (and some liberal) opinion in the United States which feared, for instance, that an American president could theoretically be extradited to another country and tried there for ordering a military invasion (such as has occurred in Kuwait, Somalia, Iraq and other places in recent years) in which many deaths occurred, or in which the American government could be successfully sued for some event of the distant past which might be construed as 'genocidal', such as slavery, policy towards American Indians, or the dropping of two atomic bombs on Japan in 1945. It is self-evident that the overwhelming majority of Americans would react with fury if international genocide legislation were used for any such purpose, and any such legislation would quickly become a dead letter in the Untied States.

During the 1990s, the new awareness of genocide became something of a staple as an underlying motivating force in American, and to a lesser extent, European foreign policy. This emerged most strongly in the response to 'ethnic cleansing' in former Yugoslavia after 1991, as well as in aspects of Western policy in Iraq (especially *vis-à-vis* the Kurds) and Somalia. As noted in Chapter 5, this awareness manifestly was absent during the appalling genocide in Rwanda in 1994, but has nevertheless become a recognised, even central, component of American foreign policy, such that the failure of the United States to intervene to stop genocide (as in Rwanda) is now widely and severely criticised, even by sources which would normally be hostile to American intervention in the internal affairs of other countries.[11] As well, in 1998 the United Nations established a Permanent International Criminal Court to try individuals for genocide, war crimes and crimes against humanity, which has successfully tried and convicted those guilty of genocidal crimes in Yugoslavia and Rwanda. How effective or wide-ranging any such court, or any such legal process, is likely to be is a matter of dispute. For instance, not one single person has ever been tried or convicted by any court in any country of any 'crime against humanity' carried out by the Communist government of the Soviet Union, although the Gulags were in operation until the mid-1980s, or by the Franco regime in Spain, which ended only with Franco's death in 1975. Willingness to arraign and convict such persons reflects the commitment of today's governments, and it is obvious that only occasionally, and in special circumstances, will those accused of carrying out 'genocide' be brought to justice.

There are, additionally, innumerable legitimate and far-reaching questions about the very nature and definition of 'genocide' which remain unanswered and hotly disputed. Most Roman Catholics (and adherents of many other religions) would, for instance, regard abortion as a form of genocide, yet virtually all Western liberals (and feminists) would reject any such suggestion with horror: abortion seldom or never figures in any recent Western work on genocide, although, to its opponents, millions of human beings are legally 'murdered' every year.[12] In this case, the gap between anti- and pro-abortion opinion is, literally, philosophically unbridgeable, but there are many other cases: for example, virtually the whole of Islam as it exists in much of the Muslim world appears radically inconsistent with Western liberalism by sanctioning violence and murderous acts in *jihads* against 'infidels' which would strike many in the West as genocidal in extreme cases. It is thus certainly not the case that anything like a consensus exists on what constitutes genocide or how to penalise it, however much Western, chiefly American, notions of genocide have moved from the periphery possibly to the centre of international discourse in the past two decades.

What does this study of the history of genocide show? A number of things, perhaps rather surprising, are apparent. Genocides and mass killings are almost certainly more common in pre-literate societies than in more 'advanced' ones: far from being the idyllic paradise of 'noble savages', pre-literate societies were repellent in their continuing barbarism and penchant for mass killing. This long-term decline in constant mass murder occurred in part because of the effects of the higher religions and the spread of ethical considerations; in part because institutions like slavery substitute for actual mass killing. This process of the gradual but perceptible diminution in actual instances of genocide – notwithstanding the mislabelling of Western slavery and colonialism as 'genocide' – continued, however, in a hit-or-miss basis, until 1914. The terrible effects of the First World War were to create an 'era of totalitarianism' which brought to power, in Communist Russia and in Nazi Germany, and later in Communist Asia, regimes committed to mass killing as a deliberate and central aspect of policy (although the scale of killings under Communism has often been exaggerated).

The genocidal aspects of the 'era of totalitarianism' obviously reached its apogee in the attempt by Nazi Germany to exterminate European Jews. To the vexed question, 'was the Holocaust unique?' one must answer that in many ways it was, especially its deliberate creation of a continent-wide killing machine and the single-minded pursuit of extermination as policy, although it is also readily identifiable as a product of its time and place, without real precedent or any likelihood of repetition. In a real sense, the 'era of totalitarianism' was an aberration in the evolution of Western history. The unexpected overthrow of Communism in the 1990s has led to the hegemony of the English-speaking democracies, and centrally the United States, whose agenda has increasingly included the prevention of genocide and the suppression of genocidal regimes. Genocide in the contemporary period has not been commonplace – we do *not* live in an 'age of genocide' – but has occurred rather unpredictably and haphazardly, although the horrors of such genocides as that in Rwanda in 1994 are obviously real.

It may seem naive and unrealistic to conclude on such an optimistic note, but such seems plainly to be the most accurate reading of the facts of history. Are there realistic dangers of genocide today? Obviously there are, especially from an armed and dangerous fanatical Islamic fundamentalism committed to hatred and terror against the West in general, and Americans, Britons, Israelis and a handful of other *bête-noire* nationalities in particular. Not coincidentally, Islam is arguably the only socio-cultural system in the world to have successfully avoided being crucially influenced and moulded by the European West, with its traditions of toleration and pluralism. The threat posed by militant Islam must be met and defeated: as almost always in the modern world, this depends crucially upon the steadfastness and resolution of the Western world, especially the English-speaking democracies, who carry the torch of Western civilisation and who, in this struggle, must and shall be victorious.

Notes and references

1 Uwe Makino, 'Final Solutions, Crimes Against Mankind: On the Genesis and Criticism of the Concept of Genocide', *Journal of Genocide Research,* Vol.III (1), March 2001, pp.52–4. On the 1948 Convention, see 'United Nations Convention on Genocide', in Charny, *op.cit.,* Volume I, pp.575–7; Leo Kuper, *Genocide: Its Political Use in the Twentieth Century* (London, 1982).

2 On Lemkin, see Steven L. Jacobs, 'The Papers of Raphael Lemkin: A First Look', in *Journal of Genocide Research,* Vol.I (1), 1999, pp.105–14; and *idem,* 'Raphael Lemkin, in Charny, *op.cit.,* Volume II, pp.402–4.

3 Jacobs, 'Lemkin', in Charny, *op.cit.,* p.403. The United States failed to ratify the UN Convention on Genocide until the 1980s.

4 Jacobs, 'The Papers of Raphael Lemkin', *op.cit.,* p.109. One publisher (in August 1958) informed Lemkin that 'it would not be possible for us to find a large enough audience of buyers for a book of this nature' (*ibid*).

5 Matthew Lippman, 'A Road Map to the 1948 Convention on the Prevention and Punishment of the Crime of Genocide', *Journal of Genocide Research,* Vol.IV (2), June 2002, p.177. This summarises the drafting of the 1948 resolution.

6 *Ibid.,* p.179.

7 *Ibid.,* p.181.

8 Makino, *op.cit.,* p.56.

9 Balint, *op.cit.,* pp.576–7.

10 Herbert Hirsch, 'United States Ratification of the UN Genocide Convention, in Charny, *op.cit.,* pp.596–8; Lawrence J. LeBlanc, *United States and the Genocide Convention* (Durham, N.C., 1991).

11 On the development of this policy see Power, *op.cit., passim.*

12 For instance, abortion is literally not mentioned in the two volumes of Israel W. Charny, ed., *Encyclopedia of Genocide* (Santa Barbara, Cal., 1999).

The United Nations Convention on the Prevention and Punishment of the Crime of Genocide (Adopted 9 December 1948)

[Extracts]

The Contracting Parties,

Having Considered the declaration made by the General Assembly of the United Nations in its resolution 96 (I) dated 11 December 1946 that genocide is a crime under international law, contrary to the spirit and aims of the United Nations and condemned by the civilized world;

Recognizing that at all periods of history genocide has inflicted great losses on humanity; and

Being convinced that, in order to liberate mankind from such an odious scourge, international co-operation is required,

Hereby agree as hereinafter provided:

ARTICLE I

The Contracting Parties confirm that genocide, whether committed in time of peace or in time of war, is a crime under international law which they undertake to prevent and to punish.

ARTICLE II

In the present Convention, genocide means any of the following acts committed with intent to destroy, in whole or in part, a national, ethnical, racial or religious group, as such:

(a) Killing members of the group;
(b) Causing serious bodily or mental harm to members of the group;
(c) Deliberately inflicting on the group conditions of life calculated to bring about its physical destruction in whole or in part;
(d) Imposing measures intended to prevent births within the group;
(e) Forcibly transferring children of the group to another group.

ARTICLE III

The following acts shall be punishable:

(a) Genocide;
(b) Conspiracy to commit genocide;
(c) Direct and public incitement to commit genocide;
(d) Attempt to commit genocide;
(e) Complicity in genocide.

ARTICLE IV

Persons committing genocide or any of the other acts enumerated in article III shall be punished, whether they are constitutionally responsible rulers, public officials or private individuals.

ARTICLE V

The Contracting Parties undertake to enact, in accordance with their respective Constitutions, the necessary legislation to give effect to the provisions of the present Convention and, in particular, to provide effective penalties for persons guilty of genocide or of any of the other acts enumerated in article III.

ARTICLE VI

Persons charged with genocide or any of the other acts enumerated in article III shall be tried by a competent tribunal of the State in the territory of which the act was committed, or by such international penal tribunal as may have jurisdiction with respect to those Contracting Parties which shall have accepted its jurisdiction.

ARTICLE VII

Genocide and the other acts enumerated in article III shall not be considered as political crimes for the purpose of extradition.

The Contracting Parties pledge themselves in such cases to grant extradition in accordance with their laws and treaties in force.

ARTICLE VIII

Any Contracting Party may call upon the competent organs of the United Nations to take such action under the Charter of the United Nations as they consider appropriate for the prevention and suppression of acts of genocide or any of the other acts enumerated in article III. . . . .

Index